# DEATH AND REDEMPTION

# DEATH AND REDEMPTION

## The Gulag and the Shaping of Soviet Society

*STEVEN A. BARNES*

PRINCETON UNIVERSITY PRESS

PRINCETON AND OXFORD

Copyright © 2011 by Princeton University Press

Published by Princeton University Press, 41 William Street, Princeton, New Jersey 08540
In the United Kingdom: Princeton University Press, 6 Oxford Street,
Woodstock, Oxfordshire OX20 1TW

press.princeton.edu

Library of Congress Cataloging-in-Publication Data

Barnes, Steven Anthony.
Death and redemption : the Gulag and the shaping of Soviet society / Steven A. Barnes.
    p.  cm.
Includes bibliographical references and index.
ISBN 978-0-691-15108-3 (hardcover : acid-free paper) —
ISBN 978-0-691-15112-0 (pbk. : acid-free paper)
1.  Glavnoe upravlenie ispravitel'no-trudovykh lagerei OGPU—History.
2.  GULag NKVD—History. 3.  Concentration camps—Soviet Union—History.
4.  Concentration camps—Social aspects—Soviet Union—History. 5.  Prisons—Soviet
Union—History. 6.  Prisons—Social aspects—Soviet Union—History. 7.  Political
prisoners—Soviet Union—Social conditions. 8.  Prisoners—Soviet Union—Social
conditions. 9.  Forced labor—Social aspects—Soviet Union—History. 10.  Soviet
Union—Social conditions.  I. Title.
HV9712.B27 2011
365'.4509470904—dc22      2010047824

British Library Cataloging-in-Publication Data is available

This book has been composed in Sabon

Printed on acid-free paper. ∞

Printed in the United States of America

10 9 8 7 6 5 4 3 2 1

TO ERIKA

# CONTENTS

# ACKNOWLEDGMENTS

A book can never be completed without support and assistance from many sources. I would especially like to thank my doctoral adviser and friend, Amir Weiner, for his patience, valuable advice, and critique at every stage of the project. The final revisions would have never been finished without the expertise and advice of my mentor, colleague, and best friend at George Mason University, Rex Wade. Finally, special thanks goes to my graduate school colleague and longtime friend Andrew Jenks, who has challenged and sharpened my thinking over many years.

My research and writing was generously supported by Stanford University's Department of History, George Mason University's Department of History, the Anatole Mazour fund, the International Research Exchanges Board, the Giles Whiting Foundation, the Social Science Research Council, the MacArthur Consortium in International Peace and Cooperation coordinated by the Center for International Security and Cooperation at Stanford University, the Davis Center for Russian and Eurasian Studies at Harvard University, the Kennan Institute at the Woodrow Wilson International Center for Scholars, the Virginia E. Hazel Research Leave fund at George Mason University, and the Allen and Gwen Nelson Junior Faculty Research fund at George Mason University. Thanks also to the National Endowment for the Humanities for its support of the http:// gulaghistory.org Web site, which now houses many documents used in this study.

Alma Sultangalieva, Kaidar Aldazhumanov, Zhambyl Artykbaev, and Diusetai Shaimukhanov were absolutely critical in generously smoothing the path to archival access in Kazakhstan. I am especially grateful to the underpaid and overworked staff of all the Russian and Kazakhstani archives used in the present study. Thanks also to the library and archives at the Hoover Institution on War, Revolution, and Peace—a resource without parallel.

Stephen Kotkin graciously offered valuable advice at the project's earliest stages. Numerous other colleagues have provided intellectual critique and emotional support. My thanks to Norman Naimark, Terrence Emmons, Robert Crews, Katherine Jolluck, Lynne Viola, Claudia Verhoeven, Steven Harris, Matthew Romaniello, Charles Lipp, Cynthia Hooper, Miriam Dobson, Margaret Paxson, Yuri Slezkine, Elizabeth Wood, Jehanne Gheith, Pamela Kachurin, Golfo Alexopoulos, Ron Suny, Alexandru Lesanu, Eric Lohr, Richard Stites, Michael David-Fox, David Nordlander, Paula Michaels, Liz Tarlow, Penny Skalnik, Elizabeth Wood, Vladimir Brovkin, Stuart Finkel, Paul Stronski, and Ann Livschiz. The anonymous readers for Princeton University Press offered challenging and helpful critique.

Special appreciation to all those who got me involved in the public and digital history of the Gulag, and helped me learn how to present the topic to a general audience. I hope this has found its way into my book. Thanks to Louis Hutchins, Marty Blatt, Viktor Shmyrov, Tatiana Kursina, Oleg Trushnikov, Roy Rosenzweig, Dan Cohen, Tom Scheinfeldt, Elena Razlogova, Stephanie Hurter, Gwen White, Anastasia Mikheeva, Sheila Brennan, Jeremy Boggs, Mikhail Vinokur, and David Hosford.

Participants in Stanford's Russian and East European history workshop read drafts of several chapters and offered valuable advice. Various parts of the text benefited from the participants in the Washington, DC, Russian history workshop as well as from workshops and conferences at the University of Maryland, the University of Chicago, the School of Slavic and East European Studies at University College London, Duke University, the University of North Carolina at Chapel Hill, the University of California at Berkeley, Miami University in Ohio, the University of Toronto, Harvard University, and the University of Hawaii.

From the first day to the final printing, the assistance of the staff of the history departments at Stanford and George Mason was crucial. Special thanks goes to Monica Wheeler, Gertrud Pacheco, and Lynn Kaiser at Stanford, and Laura McCloskey, Sharon Bloomquist, Susie LeBlanc, and Carrie Grabo at George Mason.

The responsibility for the content is, of course, entirely my own.

Finally, thanks to my parents and my wife, Erika, for their personal support; to my two daughters, Julia and Emma; to the Don, the Doc, and the Bird for laughter unending; to Ron Shults for fostering in me a love of books; and to Vitalii and Iuliia Kapinos for the special friendship that made my time in Karaganda better than bearable.

DEATH AND REDEMPTION

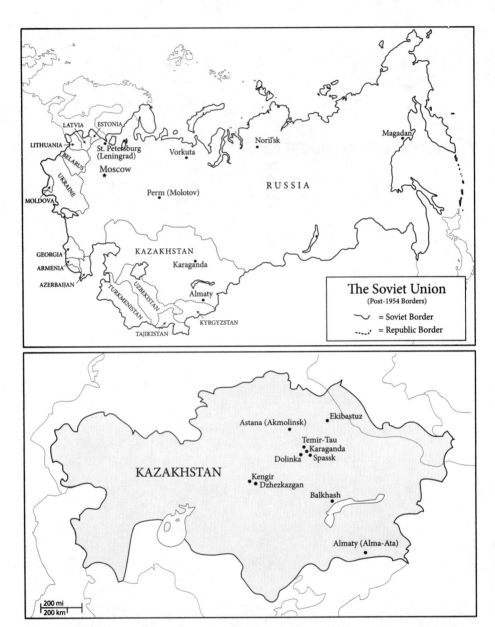

**Maps of** Kazakhstan (above) and the Soviet Union (top). City names given according to post-Soviet usage and with Russian spelling (earlier historical names provided in parentheses). Maps drawn by Stephanie Hurter.

# INTRODUCTION

IN ONE OF THE TELLING EPISODES of his history of the Gulag, Aleksandr Solzhenitsyn relates the tale of a prisoner ship convoy headed for the Dalstroi goldfields of the notorious Kolyma. As the convoy approached Magadan, the ships got stuck in the icy waters of the Kolyma River. The prisoners were forced to disembark and walk across the frozen river to the shore. Solzhenitsyn continues:

> Nonetheless, continuing to play out the farce of correction, in other words, pretending they had brought not simply bones with which to pave the gold-bearing Kolyma but temporarily isolated Soviet citizens who would yet return to creative life, they were greeted by the Dalstroi orchestra. The orchestra played marches and waltzes.[1]

What could possibly seem more out of place than an orchestra trumpeting the arrival of a prisoner convoy into the depths of the Gulag?

In 1950, the American Alexander Dolgun sat outside the gates of the Steplag labor camp in the Karaganda region of Kazakhstan. His welcome to the camp was almost surreal.

> I began to feel as though I was hallucinating again because I could hear music, a band, playing some kind of bravura march. It sounded weak and the instruments were not well tuned, but the rhythm was fast and I was sure it was coming from inside the gate. I had a sense of deep cosmic horror that made me dizzy. In the distance I could see the silhouette of the corpses on the wagon. The band seemed to be playing some kind of grotesque farewell. Then it got worse. Out of the gate came, in lines of five abreast, a column of *walking* corpses in black cotton jackets with white number patches.... The music ... came from a pitiful little band of prisoners lined up near the ... guardhouse.... Faces of death playing a lively march.[2]

The Gulag was a massive phenomenon. Understood here in its broadest sense as the entire Soviet forced labor detention system, the Gulag destroyed the lives of a large portion of the Soviet population.[3] The overall detained population in the camps, colonies, prisons, and internal exile reached a maximum in the early 1950s well in excess of 5 million people. Throughout the Stalin era, some 18 million people passed through the prisons and camps of the Gulag, and another 6 or 7 million were subject to internal exile. From 1921 to 1953, according to official figures, some 800,000 people were sentenced to death by the Soviet secret police organs alone. Furthermore, no fewer than 1.6 million died in the appalling conditions of the Gulag camps. We will never know for certain how many died during the process of exile, but that number also likely exceeds 1 million people. While these numbers are smaller than we once thought, they still bespeak an enormous institution that touched the lives of a tremendous portion of the Soviet population, whether as prisoners themselves, or as their relatives, coworkers, or friends. Even those who survived had their lives destroyed by this brutal institution.[4]

Yet conceptualizing the role played by the Gulag in the Soviet polity is fraught with apparent contradictions. Exploitation, oppression, and mass death coexisted with reeducation, redemption, and mass release. Solzhenitsyn copes with the contradiction by relegating correction to the category of farce—one more sadistic, cruel joke perpetrated by an unjust, immoral, and atheistic regime. Nevertheless, one cannot avoid asking why the Soviet authorities went to such lengths to maintain the "farce of correction." Why were these new arrivals to the "Arctic death camps" of Kolyma or those in the Kazakh steppe greeted not by a show of force but rather by an orchestra playing marches and waltzes?[5] Why did Soviet authorities expend such tremendous energy to replicate the Soviet social and cultural system within the Gulag via an extensive indoctrination network—a continuous process extending from the prisoner's arrival until their departure (dead or alive)? Soviet authorities had the know-how, experience, facilities, and will to violence to exterminate every one of the millions who passed through the Gulag, but they chose not to create a truly genocidal institution.

This book will explore the Gulag through these contradictions. It provides a close study of the camps and exiles in the Karaganda region of Kazakhstan along with a general reconsideration of the scope, meaning, and function of the Gulag in Joseph Stalin's Soviet Union. Focusing on Karaganda offers a number of benefits to an examination of the history of the Gulag. First, a concentrated look at a single locality allows for a study of the massive phenomenon of the Gulag without giving up the chronological breadth that is important to understanding shifts in its operations through the period (approximately 1930–57) when it was at its height. Second, exploring the Gulag at the local level reveals the operation of the system at the very point of contact between Soviet authority and its detained subjects. If one limited their study of the Gulag to the directives emanating from Moscow, a key part of the story would be lost, as these directives were frequently altered, ignored, or undermined at the local level. Moscow's directives were often contradictory or at least competitive with one another. The Gulag served many different functions—economic and penal—and the demands of one function usually interfered with another. At the local level, camp authorities were forced to work through these contradictory demands to decide what held priority. Third, Karaganda is a particularly advantageous location to carry out a local study. It housed one of the largest and longest lasting of the Gulag's corrective labor camps—the agricultural camp Karlag. Simultaneously, the Karaganda region was a destination for significant populations of internally exiled peoples—the special settlers—allowing for the study of the relationship between exile and camps in the Gulag universe. Furthermore, Karaganda included four of the limited number of special camps (*osobye lageri*) created after 1948, and one of those, Steplag, was the sight of one of the three major prisoner uprisings in the immediate post-Stalin era. Karaganda was one of few locales to experience most of the major institutions and events of the Gulag's history. As such, it is not necessarily representative of all other Gulag institutions. Only two other locales also experienced every one of these phenomena (Vorkuta and Noril'sk). Still, it does allow for a close examination of a wide array of the events and institutions in the Gulag, and facilitates an overall evaluation of the system's operation.

It is not wise, however, to limit one's consideration to a particular locale when exploring the Gulag's role in the Soviet Union. While a fixed locality gives a certain manageability and entry point to a study of the Gulag, and each Gulag camp had certain particularities, an important general story must be told in order to conceptualize the full role that the system played in the Soviet Union. The Gulag consisted of all its institutions operating together. Different types of institutions and different institutions of the same type operated together in a systematic hierarchy that allowed for the placement of prisoners in accord with their perceived level of danger. Moreover, the circulation throughout the system of prisoners, central directives, and reports on major events in specific camps created a certain amount of uniformity and shared culture across the Gulag. The entire institution must be understood with reference to its myriad parts. Consequently, this study attempts to understand both the particularities of one local Gulag experience, while also exploring the general story of the Gulag system. As such, when necessary to this more general story, I will draw on materials from other Gulag camps.

This book is based on a number of important sources. First, the central Gulag administration archives along with other materials from the central secret police apparatus provide a global view of the system along with its rules and priorities. Second, local administrative documents and individual prisoner files from the Karlag and Steplag archives in Karaganda reveal the interaction between Karaganda and Moscow as well as the attempt of local authorities to wade through competing demands from Moscow. While these administrative documents are crucial to understanding the purpose and structure of the Gulag system, they are not sufficient in themselves to reveal how Gulag inmates subjectively experienced the camps.[6] Individual prisoner memoirs show the reality of the

Gulag experience and allow an extensive consideration of social identity in the Gulag.

Given the veritable mountain of source material now available, it is critical that the scholar make difficult choices to keep the topic manageable while not giving up the breadth of source types that provide a fuller picture of life in the Gulag.[7] Unfortunately, some scholars have argued for the elimination of memoir sources from our repertoire due to their problematic nature.[8] Memoir sources, of course, must be subject to the same level of critical analysis as any other type of source. They are not without their problems, though as we will see throughout this study, official documents can also give a skewed picture of reality on the ground. Gulag memoirs, rarely written contemporaneous with the events that they describe, raise the difficult question of the accuracy of memory. The necessarily selective nature of the memories that their authors choose to reveal can often reflect the author's political, philosophical, or religious concerns along with a concern to "testify," thereby preserving the memory of their experience.[9] Furthermore, memoirs are frequently impacted by other entries into the genre, as their authors are usually influenced consciously or unconsciously by the things they have read.[10] By their very existence as Gulag memoirists, authors were "victims" of the Soviet regime and hence prone to an especially negative outlook on the Soviet system, yet as we will see, not all of them were or became opponents of that regime. Thus, memoirs can seem an inextricable mix of partial, unreliable, individual and/or collective memory combined with the current concerns of authors at the time they write.[11]

This, however, focuses only on the problems with memoirs. They reveal the subjective experience of the camps as understood at a given moment in time. They must be used to supplement the understanding of the camps that one gets from official documents. Things from above often look quite different than things on the ground. The subjective experience of memoirs is also critical to getting some sense of how Gulag prisoners lived in (and in the case of memoirists, survived) the camps. Their point of view certainly must be scrutinized, as I do especially in chapters 3–6 when discussing Gulag "identities." Still, no memoir is a priori unusable. In fact, as we will see, historians like Solzhenitsyn accomplished a great deal with the use of memoir and oral testimony alone.[12]

The first three chapters of the book focus on the 1930s' Gulag, looking at the institutions, practices, and identities that emerged in the Soviet penal system. The following three chapters explore the evolution of those institutions, practices, and identities through the cataclysmic events of total war, postwar reconstruction, and the emergence of new leadership after the death of Stalin. Chapter 1 offers a general reconsideration of the Gulag's origins and the role it played in Stalin's Soviet Union, and an extended look at the variety of institutions that together made up this penal universe. The Gulag must be understood through a consideration of all its major institutions, showing how they worked together as an entire penal system and how they evolved over time. Chapter 2 looks at the Gulag and the Karaganda camps in the foundational era—the 1930s— and the practices of the camp system as they were shaped in that important decade. Only by exploring the wide array of Gulag practices can we understand the variety of functions of the Gulag and how the local camp authorities waded through the often-competing demands from the center. Chapter 3 offers a conceptualization of the identities of Gulag inmates as foisted on them by Soviet authorities and as understood by the prisoners themselves. The chapter reveals how these identities significantly shaped the means and capacity for survival in the Gulag system, as a complex matrix of identities emerged that ordered prisoners hierarchically from the most to the least redeemable.

Going beyond the late 1930s, which is too often treated as an end point in the history of Stalinism, chapter 4 concentrates on the Gulag during the Armageddon of the Great Patriotic War. It shows how the institutions, practices, and identities of the Gulag shifted in accord with the demands of total war. The war was an era of mass release on an unprecedented scale side by side with the highest mortality rates in the history of the Gulag system. Chapter 5 takes the Gulag into the postwar era when authorities used the institution in an attempt to reassert social control. At the same time, arrivals from the newly annexed western territories and former Red Army soldiers dramatically altered the social world of the Gulag prisoner. With the creation of the special camps for an exclusive portion of the political prisoner population, Gulag authorities unwittingly set the stage for violent resistance from their prisoners in the post-Stalin era. Finally, chapter 6 looks at the explosive uprisings in the Gulag after Stalin's death with a particular focus on the forty-day revolt at the Kengir division of Steplag. It also examines the new leadership's policy that largely emptied the camp and exile systems of all those charged with either petty or political offenses, dramatically altering the Soviet penal system for good.

The Gulag had its roots in the immediate aftermath of the October Revolution. The growth and development of the Gulag can be tied directly to the broader events in Soviet history.[13] The Gulag gave birth to a society that mirrored in so many ways Soviet society at large: hierarchies of class and nationality, sharp distinctions between political and nonpolitical inmates, veteran prestige after the war, and reconstruction of gender identities. So, too, the Gulag experienced and participated in the campaigns of Stalin's revolution, including such things as cultural transformation, political education, industrialization, shock work, and

Stakhanovism. Prisoners suffered from food shortages, usually at a more severe level, when the same occurred in Soviet society at large. The Great Patriotic War rocked and reshaped the Gulag, while surveillance permeated its spaces much as in Soviet society itself. No less was the Gulag shaken by the death of Stalin. The mass camp strikes after Stalin's death paraded a strikingly Sovietized population. On the one hand, Stalin's death was cause for joyous celebration among the prisoners. On the other hand, prison uprisings were formulated as workers' strikes. What were the demands of these prisoners? Unconditional release? No, they wanted to receive treatment equal to other workers. They sought to be included in the Soviet working class and Soviet society.

These are the outlines of the story to be told, the contradictions to be explored, to reconceptualize the operation of the Gulag—one of the most brutal institutions of a lethal twentieth century.

# Chapter 1

# THE ORIGINS, FUNCTIONS, AND INSTITUTIONS OF THE GULAG

W HILE EARLY STUDENTS of Soviet history certainly identified terror as perhaps the definitive characteristic of the Soviet polity, their abiding conviction that a sentence in the Gulag represented *death* inhibited serious study of *life* within the Gulag. Even for those few scholars who sought methodically to understand life in the Gulag, the camp was little more than a site of exploitation and inevitable death. While terror, and the Gulag as an integral part of that terror, found itself at the center of early conceptualizations of the Soviet experience, the prisoner was thoroughly marginalized from understandings of the revolutionary transformation of society.[1]

Scholars of the Gulag have understood its emergence and role in the Soviet Union primarily in three distinct yet overlapping ways, emphasizing in turn the economic, the political, and the moral. While no scholar offers a monocausal explanation of the Gulag, they have typically placed particular stress on one of these factors. The economic understanding posits the Gulag as essentially a slave labor system emerging as a result of Stalin's crash industrialization policies.[2] Even proponents of this approach understand its limitations. The camp system was far from economically efficient, even in the world of inefficient Soviet industry.[3] Arrests occurred chaotically and inefficiently, catching camp administrators unaware and unprepared. Arrests were not limited to healthy young men who could withstand work in the Gulag's harsh climates but also included women, children, the elderly, and invalids. Anne Applebaum, for instance, notes that the economic "illogic" of the mass arrests have led "many to conclude that arrests were carried out primarily to eliminate Stalin's perceived enemies, and only secondarily to fill Stalin's camps." Like many others before her, Applebaum argues that the explanations are not "entirely mutually exclusive either. Stalin might well have intended his arrests both to eliminate enemies and to create slave laborers."[4] Nonetheless, she generally adopts the economic motive for understanding the Gulag. This book, a careful study of life inside the Gulag's institutions, will show the limitations of the economic understanding of the Soviet penal system. Many aspects of Gulag administration on the day-to-day level belie any economic rationality, and point to the camps as penal institutions concerned with differentiating and evaluating their prisoners, with important secondary concerns about the economy.

The political understanding of the Gulag sees the system, in Robert Conquest's classic formulation, as not primarily a means of economic exploitation but rather "*politically* efficient. They effectively isolated masses of potential troublemakers, and were a great disincentive to any sort of anti-Stalinist activity, or even talk."[5] Conquest's portrayal of life in the camps amounts to a slow, steady march toward death. Prisoners were worked as hard as possible and given a precisely measured amount of food to guarantee that they would not survive. On this regimen they inevitably reached "the last stage in the camps," when "debilitated to the degree that no serious work could any longer be got out of them, prisoners were put on sub-starvation rations and allowed to hang around the camp doing odd jobs until they died."[6] The labor camps, in this political understanding, were really "death" camps. Few made it out alive. As Conquest writes, "Releases were very rare, and survival until the post-Stalin amnesties rarer still. The length of sentence . . . made little difference. . . . Upon the expiration of a sentence, it was usual for prisoners to be called before a Special Section officer and given a few more years."[7] No doubt the camps were intended to remove those deemed unfit or dangerous from Soviet society, but with the benefit of archival access that was denied to scholars of Conquest's generation, we know that substantial percentages of the Gulag population were released to return to Soviet society. What are we to make of these people? This book will carefully evaluate that question.

Finally, we come to the moral interpretation, which lies at the heart of the work that forms the foundation of Gulag studies: Solzhenitsyn's multivolume "experiment in literary investigation," *The Gulag Archipelago*. Solzhenitsyn's work remains the most comprehensive available study of everyday life in the Gulag. The achievements of *The Gulag Archipelago* are perhaps more amazing today than when it was first published. Solzhenitsyn completed extensive research through oral history, circulated underground (*samizdat*) manuscripts, and prepared his lengthy texts despite the significant personal danger of doing so. Notwithstanding these limitations on Solzhenitsyn's ability to work freely, his work remains unparalleled in the attempt to integrate an understanding of Gulag daily life into the broader context of Soviet and world history. No other work comes near the depth of his psychological probing of the Gulag experience.[8] Even Applebaum's more approachable catalog of Gulag suffering, though modeled on *The Gulag Archipelago*, pales in comparison to Solzhenitsyn's multifaceted work.

Throughout the present study, I call on Solzhenitsyn's insights extensively but cautiously. His work is problematic in some ways, particularly because it does not fall strictly in the genre of the historical monograph; rather, it is a combination of genres—documentary history, memoir, oral history, literature, and political-moral polemic. His sources and personal experience are especially valuable for their presentation of the prisoner's view of life inside the corrective labor camps. Alternative sources confirm most of his conclusions about the living conditions in the camps.[9] Nonetheless, his sources were less accurate in their speculations about the number and socioethnic makeup of the camp population.

*The Gulag Archipelago*, however, must be approached not just as a primary source but also as a work of history that stakes out a strong position on the moral significance of the Gulag. In Solzhenitsyn's analysis, the spread of the Gulag represents the triumph of immorality cloaked in the justification of ideology.

> Ideology—that is what gives evildoing its long-sought justification and gives the evildoer the necessary steadfastness and determination. That is the social theory which helps to make his acts seem good instead of bad . . . so that he won't hear reproaches and curses but will receive praise and honors. . . . Thanks to *ideology*, the twentieth century was fated to experience evildoing on a scale calculated in the millions.[10]

Ideology in *The Gulag Archipelago* is devoid of all constructive content. It lacks all relationship to ideas and worldviews, and is reduced to an empty "justification" for evildoing. For Solzhenitsyn, human nature contains an evil, dark side. Ideology effaces any checks on that evil, and the Gulag is the direct consequence.

In terms of reconciling the economic, political, and moral interpretations, the opening of the former Soviet archives has yielded mixed results to date. Much of the first decade of archival access was spent chasing the headline-gathering issue of the total number of victims, with little consideration for the role played by this system of victimization in the first place. Otherwise, scholars have often focused on extremely narrow questions, avoiding broad conceptual issues. The tide is fortunately beginning to turn.[11] Of particular significance is Oleg Khlevniuk's *The History of the Gulag: From Collectivization to the Great Terror*.[12] Simultaneously a monograph and a publication of documents, the book benefits from Khlevniuk's careful and studied hand at working through the documents. Unfortunately the book limits itself to the 1930s, and because of its documentary nature does not seek to integrate memoirs into the story of the Gulag. Still, it makes a number of important contributions to our understanding of the camp system and its relationship to the highest levels of Soviet power. Lynne Viola's recent *The Unknown Gulag: The Lost World of Stalin's Special Settlements* is the definitive study of the Gulag exile system in the 1930s.[13] In particular, she reveals the critical role of collectivization and de-kulakization in the initial mass growth of the Gulag. A wide variety of local studies have appeared in recent years. While each is a significant study in its own right, none seek a full conceptualization of the entire Gulag system.[14] Finally, a group of young scholars working under the leadership of the economist Paul Gregory has been poring over the Gulag archives in an effort to understand the economic operation of the camp system. This group's insights, published in *The Economics of Forced Labor in the Soviet Union* and elsewhere, have shed light on the inefficiencies and economic idiocy of the camp system.[15] But the exclusive focus on economics is frequently too limited a framework to understand all the workings of the Gulag, as will be apparent throughout the present work.

To this day, the most important archival-based revelation remains a preliminary study by J. Arch Getty, Gábor Tamás Rittersporn, and Viktor N. Zemskov. Their study showed, among other things, that the Gulag had a revolving door with approximately 20 percent of inmates released every year.[16] The Gulag was not a death chamber, as at least some Gulag inmates were deemed fit for release. The ramifications of this discovery needed to be pursued. If some inmates were going to be released back into Soviet society, how was it decided who would be released and who would not, and what, if anything, were Soviet penal authorities doing to make their inmates ready for release?

The present study seeks to understand the role played by the Gulag in the construction of a socialist society and the new Soviet person. In this respect, I examine the ever-evolving relationship among Bolshevik ideology, historical circumstances, and the institutions, practices, and identities of the Gulag. Ideology in this case reflects Hannah Arendt's understanding of the phenomenon. It refers to an idea (or a worldview) *and* the logic of its application to understanding and transforming the course of history.[17] Ideology in this sense is neither pejorative nor artificial. It is not a false consciousness foisted on an exploited class by their exploiters to hide the very fact of their exploitation. It is not, as Solzhenitsyn would have it, an empty vessel that "gives evildoing its long-sought justification." And it is not an ex post facto justification for institutions created and maintained for more utilitarian reasons.[18] Ideology as used here is a vision of what a society should become and the nature of the methods to realize that vision. Ideology is not a road map, and it is not some genetic code that can be deciphered as the key to understand a regime's every action. Ideology does not operate in a vacuum. It is more than some ethereal theory worked out by intellectuals and divorced from real life. Ideology operates in real historical circumstances. It shapes and is shaped by the responses to those circumstances. Ideology makes certain responses to historical circumstances more likely and other responses less likely.

While ideology played a significant role in the development of the Soviet Gulag, this book does not seek to reduce its explanatory framework to the "primacy of ideology" but rather attempts to take up Michael David-Fox's call for "multi-dimensional conceptual frameworks" in the field of Soviet history.[19] The Gulag, after all, cannot be understood and explained merely by reference to the tenets of Marxism or Bolshevism. The Gulag emerged as the concrete historical response to a number of contingent factors, including the tsarist experience with forced labor, the late nineteenth-century invention of the concentration camp, the crime and chaos of a period of revolution and civil war, and the attempt to industrialize rapidly a backward peasant economy to prepare it for an anticipated war with capitalist powers. Furthermore, Bolshevik ideology was not constant and unchanging. It changed over time. It was interpreted and expressed in different ways by different historical actors. Yet Bolshevik ideology performed a meaningful part in the Gulag's development. Bolshevik visions—of creating a perfect society, struggle as the motive force of history, enemies blocking the path to and contaminating utopia, labor as the defining feature of humanity, and criminality as created by social conditions—all combined with historical circumstances to make the creation and mass expansion of the Gulag possible. Here in the Gulag, in this secretive and lethal corner of the Soviet enterprise, ideology mattered, and if it mattered here, it mattered everywhere.

In this book I refer frequently to *Belomor*, the celebratory volume on the early 1930s' construction of the White Sea–Baltic Sea Canal by Soviet concentration camp prisoners.[20] *Belomor* was without question a work of propaganda, and it has been rightly condemned for whitewashing the brutality and death that accompanied the canal's construction. The volume offers a series of anecdotes about the alleged "reforging" and reclamation of Belomor prisoners through Soviet forced labor.[21] Nonetheless, the least interesting thing we can learn about the *Belomor* is that it is a work of propaganda. This is too obvious. Much can still be gleaned from exploring the type of whitewashing that it represents. Soviet authorities could have withheld forced labor from public view entirely. Certainly by the later 1930s, Soviet authorities simply refused to speak publicly about the Gulag. In the early 1930s, however, they not only spoke about it but also celebrated it. The book was immediately translated into English and offers up Soviet forced labor as the very forefront of world penal practice.

The volume is something of an ideal-type presentation of early Stalinist penal ideology. In many ways, it set the terms of ideological discussion about penal labor in the Soviet Union. Despite the fact that Soviet authorities would shut down public discussion of forced labor, the present book reveals how works like *Belomor* continued to appear throughout the Gulag's history inside the camps whether in camp newspapers, like Karlag's

*Bolshevik's ideology* [margin annotation]

*Putevka,* or in special publications stamped "for use inside camps only." While the Gulag was increasingly hidden from public view, such that open publication of works like *Belomor* at home and abroad, or national subscriptions to camp newspapers like that of the Solovetsky labor camp in the 1920s, ended by the mid-1930s, these types of materials were not the product of a single moment, a temporary belief in the malleability of the criminal. The continued appearance of these materials within the camps reveals a much more complex relationship with the subject of individual redeemability. Throughout this book, then, I compare the presentation in *Belomor* and these other volumes of propaganda to the real institutions, practices, and identities developed in the Gulag and Karaganda's Gulag in particular, thereby facilitating the evaluation of ideology's impact on the development of the Gulag and the Soviet polity at large. Gulag history was marked by a series of crises, competing demands from central and local Soviet authorities, and frequent cynicism about the institution's reeducation mandate. The present book shows how ideology interacted with these elements to produce an especially Soviet penal institution that played an integral role in the construction of a Soviet civilization.[22]

Even though I will show the complexity surrounding the possibility of prisoner rehabilitation in *Belomor* and other works in this redemption genre, these were far from the final words on Soviet ideology related to its prisoner population. Also important was the constant propaganda barrage aimed at Gulag camp guards and employees emphasizing the dangerous as well as treasonous nature of their prisoner population. These sometimes-conflicting messages—of prisoner reformability and prisoner danger—animated Gulag activity. As I will demonstrate, the death of prisoners was always accepted as part and parcel of the work of the camp system. This presented yet another challenge to the notion of the prisoner as redeemable. Thus, *Belomor,* with only a single prisoner death recorded in its pages, is only a partial account of the ideological frameworks shaping the Gulag along with the relations of its authorities and prisoners. Yet given the constant release of a significant portion of the Gulag population throughout the institution's history, it is quite clear that redeemability, at least for some segment of the prisoner population, was never totally abandoned.

A term in the Gulag would appear to epitomize the prisoner's total marginalization from Soviet society. After all, the Gulag was quite literally in the margins. While Gulag institutions existed throughout the Soviet Union, its largest and most notorious outposts populated extreme geographic regions of the Soviet Union; Solovki, Vorkuta, Noril'sk, and Kolyma from west to east delineated the Soviet northern border, while other Gulag facilities—including those in Karaganda, the locus of the present study—filled Soviet Central Asia. The Gulag held those who were declared harmful to or unfit for the society being built. Some Gulag inmates would be defined as criminals in most societies, and some would not—the de-kulakized peasant, for example.[23] Prisoner correspondence was extremely limited and censored. The prisoner of the Gulag virtually disappeared for the duration of their stay in the Gulag, and millions of the Gulag's inmates would never return, dying somewhere on the vast stretches of the Siberian taiga or in the Central Asian steppe.

Yet it would be an error to see the Gulag and its inmate as marginal to Soviet society. The Gulag and its inmates were an integral part of the Soviet project—the revolutionary creation of a polity without margins. Neither the Gulag nor the prisoner was marginal in the Soviet polity. Rather, the Gulag and the prisoner, standing at the crossroads of inclusion in and exclusion from the Soviet social body, were essential components of a particular Soviet modernity.

Solzhenitsyn quite accurately states that "the Archipelago was born with the shots of the cruiser *Aurora*"—that is, with the onset of the Bolshevik revolution itself, for the Gulag's existence depended on the revolution, and the revolutionary reshaping of society depended on the Gulag.[24] The Gulag, like the revolution, was a product of a new modern political ethos that extended throughout the Euro-American world, saw society as a subject to be sculpted, and rejected limitations on the application of state power to this goal. This new political ethos of modernity can be construed broadly as an epistemic transformation, although its importance to the current study in revolution and penal policy can be simplified to a few characteristics. First, and from this perspective foremost, modernity is characterized by a politics of rational and scientific transformation of humanity. With roots in the Enlightenment and the scientific revolution, this new political rationality envisioned a human being no longer entrenched in a preestablished order but instead as a subject who can and must redefine that order.[25] Important in this respect was the "birth of the social." The emergent practices of quantification led to a notion of society as something that could be "known." Statistical representations of society facilitated the application of bodily images and hygienic practices to the social body. In accord with the transformative nature of modern politics, once society could be known, it could also be controlled, transformed, and healed. This new outlook had substantial effects on penal practice. Statistics revealed the ever-present nature of criminality, which in representations of the new social body took on the role of illness or infection. The disease of the social body could not be ignored, and thus the social body had to be protected from the criminal. In some cases, the isolation of the criminal (exile) could serve the purposes of social prophylaxis, but with society envisioned as a unified body, no individual, not even the exiled or imprisoned, was totally outside the social body.

Isolation alone could not make the social body totally safe. Consequently, penal practice moved beyond isolation to the reformation (healing) of the criminal soul.[26]

From its earliest days, the Bolsheviks' revolution was driven by this modern desire to transform society, to engineer a new socialist soul. While the new politics of social engineering was by no means an exclusively Bolshevik phenomenon, the Bolsheviks brought their own particularities to this transformative vision. The Bolshevik worldview could not envision social transformation through mere legislative action. Rather, the Bolsheviks expected—and even sought—struggle, merciless class struggle. The Soviet ethos assumed the existence of internal enemies—a contamination of the body politic.[27] Instead of negotiation, accommodation, and bargaining with societal filth, violent purification of the body politic was the appropriate mode of operation.[28] Furthermore, the Bolsheviks felt themselves in a race with time. In the often-quoted phrase from his 1931 speech, Stalin declared, "We have fallen behind the advanced countries by fifty to a hundred years. We must close that gap in ten years. Either we do this or we'll be crushed."[29] The Gulag was an imprecise, crude tool for the transformation. During this chopping of wood, Soviet authorities accepted, chips were going to fly, but the forest would be refashioned. In the harsh conditions of the Gulag, the social body's filth would either be purified (and returned to the body politic) or cast out (through death).[30]

A sense of the radical importance that the Bolsheviks accorded their project and the measures appropriate for completing it can be gathered from the metaphors they used to describe their work. First, criminality was an illness to be cured by the socialist government. In the words of the authors of *Belomor*, "The Government . . . takes a slice of this reality, a part of the Socialist plan—the Belomorstroy—measures a tiny dose for you and it will cure you, the criminal, with the truth of Socialism."[31] *Belomor* further referred to the "diseased and dangerous people" who in this book "themselves tell of their cure."[32] Yet the Bolsheviks were not merely physicians scientifically curing their patient. They viewed themselves as engineers reforging human raw material.[33] The choice of an industrial metaphor in Stalin's Soviet Union was unsurprising, and the conscious use of the term reforging carried with it all the connotations of the steel industry—the passage of materials through extreme heat and pressure to transform them into utterly new products.[34] Finally, the Bolsheviks viewed criminality in relation to class war. Crime was a remnant of class exploitation. It was not the working-class criminal but rather the bourgeois class enemy who was responsible for crime. The battle against criminality thus became intimately tied to the one against the class and later the people's enemy. The enemy, the Bolsheviks believed, must not be allowed to spread its harmful influence to society at large, and therefore had to be isolated from society until such time as it was reformed or destroyed.[35]

In this light, Solzhenitsyn's tale of the prisoner ship greeted by the Dalstroi orchestra is not a contradiction requiring explanation. Rather in the Soviet ethos, the coexistence of violence and transformation—creation and destruction—was no contradiction at all. In fact, one was unimaginable without the other.[36] Vyshinskii, the chief prosecutor of the notorious Great Terror trials, himself said as much: "All Soviet penal policy is based on a dialectical combination of the principle of repression and compulsion with the principle of persuasion and re-education.... The two-in-one task is suppression plus re-education of anyone who can be re-educated."[37] Thus, the great construction project at Magnitogorsk could be simultaneously the "most potent symbol of the heroic building of socialism," and "a place of exile" without contradiction and without need for further explanation.[38]

In the Bolshevik struggle to transform the social body, no action, not even inaction, was apolitical. This Manichaean ethos recognized only "for us" and "against us" without neutral ground. Every individual had to be judged and placed in one of these fields. The Bolsheviks sought to create by force a polity without margins, a polity in which *all* would participate. The construction of Soviet socialism was fundamentally and forcibly about inclusion; nobody could sit out this revolution, not even the prisoner. The engineers at Belomor failed to prove their redemption, because they "felt that they were not active participants in a grandiose construction, but merely accidental lookers on."[39] The margins were re-centered; nobody, not even the prisoner, remained marginal.[40]

The Gulag played a key role in the realization of this Soviet revolutionary project. Threat of punishment in the Gulag was one of many means used to compel compliance with newly emerging societal norms. In this respect, the Gulag served a substantially similar function to all modern penal institutions. Compliance with societal norms in the Soviet case, however, involved substantial active participation in the ongoing revolution. A virtual cult of action operated in the Soviet Union, and the Gulag itself made the prisoner an active part of the revolutionary transformation. In 1936, the Karlag newspaper *Putevka*, popularizing the Stakhanovite movement among prisoners, noted that the Stakhanovite movement was "Marxism in action," complete with a set of two line drawings. The first illustration showed an individual sitting at a desk reading in front of a series of books by Karl Marx, Friedrich Engels, Vladimir Lenin, and Stalin with the caption "Reading a chapter from Marx." Below that was another drawing of a man in a hard hat in front of overflowing train cars of coal with the caption "Writing a chapter from Marx."[41] As a slogan posted at the Solovetskii camp at the end of the 1920s declared, "A prisoner is an active participant in socialist construction!"[42] Even Solzhenitsyn himself recognized the Soviet polity as a society in which there was "no place for forced idleness."[43]

Bolshevik penal policy viewed labor as the key to reforging the prisoner and making them fit for a place in the new Soviet society. A poster at Kolyma in the late 1930s proclaimed that "our selfless labor will restore us to the family of the workers."[44] In the Bolshevik vision, to overcome the bourgeois devaluation of labor that led the proletarian to become criminal, penal institutions had to teach the criminal the value of labor—echoing the long-held Marxist view that labor was the activity that differentiated the human from the animal.[45] In their labor, it was believed, prisoners would see and take pride in their contribution to the construction of socialism. When the Gosudarstvennoe Politicheskoe Upravlenie (GPU, or State Political Directorate) official Semen Firin was sent to Belomor, he was reminded that his task was "not only to increase production but also, above all, to organise educational work. . . . [T]here are no incurable criminals."[46] Labor was not only the means but also the measure of an inmate's reform, and corrective labor was among the first innovations in Soviet penal practice.

The Soviet penal system was composed of a diverse range of institutions, prisoners, and practices. Yet through all its diversity, the Gulag was integrated at every point into the broader Soviet enterprise. Not only do the turning points of Soviet history express their influence in the Gulag compound; the Gulag was subject to every Soviet campaign from Stakhanovism to the politicization of everyday life. Social identities in the Gulag were even reconfigured on the basis of social hierarchies emergent in broader Soviet society. These institutions, social hierarchies, and practices brought the revolution to every individual daily. Each day, the individual prisoner had to prove their capacity for redemption. The Gulag was a total institution. From the organization of labor to officially sponsored cultural activities, from life in the barracks to the extensive surveillance system, every inch of the Gulag was filled with a new "socialist" content. Whether one explores the institutions, identities, or practices of the Gulag, it emerges as a transformative space—a site where society and the individual were remade for entry, or denied entry, into the imagined socialist future.

## The Hierarchy of Detention: The Institutions of the Gulag

One way to understand the constantly shifting line between those Gulag inmates considered redeemable and those to be permanently excluded from Soviet society is to explore the diverse range of Gulag institutions. The term Gulag calls to mind the notorious forced labor camps in the extremes of Siberia such as those found along the Kolyma River. These corrective labor camps, however, of which Karlag was one, comprised only one of a number of distinctive Gulag penal institutions.[47] Prisons, special prisons, special camps, corrective labor camps, special settlements, corrective labor colonies, and noncustodial forced labor (essentially a system of fines), not to mention special-purpose institutions like the scientific prison institutes (the *sharashki* of Solzhenitsyn's *The First Circle*), filtration camps, and prisoner of war (POW) camps, afforded the authorities at different times a panoply of destinations for their detained populations. The array of institutions offered a gradation of detention, allowing the sorting of prisoners into different levels of isolation according to their perceived level of danger for Soviet society and their perceived chances for release.

The large category of corrective labor camps was also comprised of a diverse hierarchy of institutions. The entire collection of corrective labor camps was arranged in a rough geographic hierarchy, in which camps located in particularly remote regions of Siberia, the Far North, and Kazakhstan were categorized as "distant" camps, and were reserved for the most dangerous inmates. Even among the distant camps a further subhierarchy emerged in which Kolyma occupied a special place as the Gulag's worst possible destination. Prisoners in other camps were often threatened with transfer to Kolyma for violations of camp order. Even within individual camps, a hierarchy of subinstitutions allowed an even finer sorting of inmates into camp divisions with different levels of regime ranging from light, general, and strict to *katorga* (the strictest of all) subdivisions. Furthermore, one could officially be a prisoner of a camp but be allowed to live outside the camp zone altogether.

As will be seen in detail in the chapters below, Gulag history was marked by a constant expansion of the hierarchy of institutions. New forms of detention were established at both the lighter and harsher ends of the spectrum, and finer gradations of institutions were inserted into the middle of the hierarchy, as Gulag authorities sought to sort their population into ever-finer subgroups based on a hierarchy of presumed redeemability. While that hierarchy was not static, the institutions are introduced briefly here in approximate order from those with the populations deemed least to most redeemable.

## Execution

Execution was the ultimate punishment meted out by the Soviet penal system, and until the postwar period, it was also the only punishment, at least theoretically, with irreversible consequences (postmortem rehabilitation notwithstanding). Soviet authorities did not fear getting blood on their hands in this battle with alleged enemies of Soviet power. According to figures gathered by V. P. Popov, during the period from 1921 to 1953, Soviet secret police organs alone sentenced some eight hundred thousand people to death.[48]

On the one hand, Soviet propagandists and ideological thinkers constantly emphasized the reformability of criminals and denounced, quite vociferously, biological understandings of the regime's enemies. On the other hand, it was always understood that no enemy could be allowed to interfere with the construction of the coming communist utopia. The Soviet leadership and its secret police organs had no inhibitions about taking the lives of their enemies, and considering the stakes—the creation of utopia, a virtual heaven on earth—mistakes were only seen as permissible in the direction of killing too many rather than too few. During the mass campaigns of the Great Terror in 1937–38, execution quotas were handed out region by region (and to Gulag camps). While the terror was undoubtedly directed from the center, local authorities immediately set out to "fulfill and overfulfill" their plan, and thus it did not take long for a frenzy to start of regional leaders writing to Moscow for permission to exceed those quotas.[49]

All convicted persons in the Soviet Union who escaped the sentence of execution and entered the gates of a Gulag camp had survived the first great break point between life and death, between reincorporation into Soviet society and total fatal expulsion from it. This study begins at that moment, when an inmate entered the Gulag proper. It was, however, far from the last time that a prisoner would teeter on the brink between life and death. As we will see, many Gulag practices—if not specifically designed to cause prisoner deaths—were at least designed with little concern for the maintenance of prisoner lives. Moreover, prisoners could be and were executed while in the Gulag.

## Prisons

Prisons occupied two spaces within the Gulag system. First, in the guise of interrogation prisons, they held nearly all inmates subject to individual arrest. They stood at the gates of the Gulag, housing individuals until judgment and sentencing determined the future site of the prisoner's detention. The interrogation prisons and their notorious torture regimes are well known from Solzhenitsyn's chilling descriptions. Interrogation prisons served as the locus of selection, where a prisoner was evaluated according to the prospects for redeemability. While an inmate was in the interrogation prison, the first life-or-death decision between execution and detention was made. It was in the interrogation prison that prisoners awaited their fate—their sentence and future destination within the Gulag system.

The interrogation prison was an institution quite different from all others in the Gulag. Located chronologically in the presentence phase of the Gulag experience, the interrogation prison was not designed to deal with who a prisoner would become but rather to determine who a prisoner was. As such, the interrogation prison did not seek to integrate its prisoners into the life of the society and instead isolated them throughout the course of interrogation.[50]

Prisons were also located in the range of postsentence punishments. For those condemned individuals who avoided a death penalty, the prison was reserved for the least redeemable. Prisons were places of total isolation, reserved for those deemed too dangerous and corrupting to come into contact with the Gulag population at large. They also held well-known foreigners, famous people, or purged secret police operatives in total isolation from other prisoners.[51] For example, the orders for mass operation 00447 of the Great Terror against "former kulaks, criminals and other anti-Soviet elements" declared that "the more inveterate and socially dangerous" of those who were not condemned to death should be given eight to ten years in prisons, while the rest would be sent to camps.[52] Convicts could receive a specific sentence to prison from judicial or police organs. Labor camps also had the authority to transfer inmates to prisons. The latter was reserved for those who proved themselves especially incorrigible in the camps. As the declaration accompanying their transfer went: "All measures of correction exhausted, corrupts other prisoners, not suitable for labor camp." Lists of those transferred to prisons were then posted in the camps as a means of deterring others.[53] A different type of prison—the internal camp prison (usually called a "penalty isolator")—occupied the space between the camp and prison. Camp authorities created these internal camp prisons to punish their inmates for short periods for violations of camp discipline and refusal to work. Penalty isolators were among the most hellish places in the Gulag—usually dark, cold, and damp, without sheets or blankets, and often with the prisoner stripped to their undergarments. Only repeated or especially severe violations resulted in transfer out of camps and into separate prisons.

As a place for those deemed unfit even for camps, the prison occupied the lowest rung on the institutional ladder of redeemability. In accord with this position, the inmates of the prisons were forcibly excluded from collective life, the basis of official Soviet efforts at creating a new person. In contrast to the labor camp inmates who were housed in barracks, and relatively free in their nonworking hours to move about the camp compound and mingle with fellow inmates, prison inmates were kept in solitary confinement cells, until the sheer volume of arrests forced the authorities to put multiple inmates in a single cell.[54] No collective cultural activities or reeducation efforts were found in the prisons. Talking, singing, tapping on cell walls, and going near cell windows were all officially prohibited, although they occurred. The only activities officially allowed to the prisoners were all solitary—reading library books, say, and solitary exercise in the prison yard. So little did the authorities care about the reeducation of these prisoners that they did not even maintain the most modest control over access to reading material; the content of the prison library was so poorly controlled that many of the books made available to prisoners had been long since withdrawn from public libraries.[55]

The comparative exclusion of the prisoners vis-à-vis the camp inmates becomes even clearer when examining Eugenia Ginzburg's transfer to camp life. In 1939, Ginzburg's sentence (along with many others in her solitary confinement prison) was revised to a term in a corrective labor camp, and she immediately noticed the transition from solitary to collective life. Prisoners were no longer hidden from one another but instead were formed up into groups. Ginzburg recognized that the solitary prisons had been

> inconsistent with the tempo of the age and with its economy. . . . Everything that had hitherto been strictly forbidden was suddenly enjoined with the same severity. For instance, at Yaroslavl [her prison] there was no greater crime than to try to enter into relations with the other prisoners. . . . But from the day in July 1939 on which we crossed the threshold of our cells for the last time, we were obliged to do everything together—whether it was working, sleeping, eating, bathing, or going to the lavatory.[56]

Once branded the most incorrigible, the prisoners were unable to completely erase the distrust aimed at them. Even in the corrective labor camp, they were stamped as "people from the prisons," who were "the worst criminals, the worst off, the worst everything."[57] Nonetheless, they were now included in the grand crusade, and Ginzburg herself would be released from Kolyma at the conclusion of her ten-year sentence.

## Katorga Camp Divisions and Special Camps

Although they will be discussed at greater length in chapters 4 and 5, a brief note should be made here of the katorga camp divisions and the special camps. The tsarist state had utilized a form of forced labor detention, which it labeled katorga. The Soviet government initially cast the term aside, as it considered katorga to be a reactionary element of the unjust tsarist penal system. In 1943, the term returned, as the Gulag created katorga divisions within regular corrective labor camps to hold a select portion of inmates deemed to be the most dangerous. The katorga divisions were especially strict, located in the Gulag's harshest places, and performed the most dangerous labor tasks. In 1948, the practice was extended to an entire new group of independent camps dubbed special camps.

Both katorga divisions and special camps introduced a number of camp practices previously unknown in the Gulag, including the use of handcuffs, numbers on inmate clothing, locked barracks, and perhaps most significant, the isolation of a select portion of political prisoners from the criminals. The conditions in katorga divisions and special camps were more brutal, and the death rates were much higher, than in their regular camp cousins. Release from the special camps was a much less common affair, as their inmates typically had long sentences corresponding to the perceived level of dangerousness of their crimes. Furthermore, the creation of the special camps was accompanied by the application of permanent exile to all those released from such institutions—the first ever sentence other than execution that precluded a priori at least a theoretical end to punishment. While attention to prisoner rehabilitation was not completely abandoned, it took a much less prominent role in these places, as they held those inmates who were the least likely to make a full return to Soviet society.

## Corrective Labor Camps

The corrective labor camps are those most typically associated with images of the Gulag. They were the most direct descendant of the secret police camp system of the 1920s and early 1930s. These camps were initially reserved for prisoners who either had been sentenced to more than three years or had been sentenced by organs of the Ob'edinennoe Gosudarstvennoe Politicheskoe Upravlenie (OGPU, or Joint State Political Directorate) itself. After the merger of detention institutions in 1934, the corrective labor camps were reserved for prisoners sentenced to more than three years, while the corrective labor colonies held those with shorter sentences.[58] This provision alone strongly affected the composition of the camps' population. Few "political" prisoners arrested for so-called counterrevolutionary crimes were sentenced to less than three years, so most of them found their way into the corrective labor camps. Of the hordes of common criminals who filled the Soviet penal system, only those convicted for the crimes perceived by the Soviet government to be the most serious were imprisoned in the camps.

The corrective labor camps were generally located at the most extreme edges of the Gulag. Their number included the notorious Kolyma,

Vorkuta, Noril'sk, and Karaganda camps. Gulag camp death rates, though quite variable over its history, were always high. Depending on the year and reliability of official statistics, somewhere from 1 to 25 percent of the Gulag camp population died per annum from a wide array of causes including illnesses related to starvation, accidents at a work site, and violence from both guards and other prisoners. Thus for many, a sentence in the corrective labor camps was actually a death sentence. Nonetheless, no matter how harsh the conditions, the prisoners of the corrective labor camp were not necessarily considered irredeemable. Some former prison inmates in fact thought of the labor camp as a definite step up, at least initially. As a Communist true believer named Tanya exclaimed to Ginzburg on their transfer from prisons to corrective labor camps, "Even now, things are better than in Yezhov's time: he kept us two years in solitary, but now we're getting a chance to work and develop the Far North, which shows they know we're good workers."[59] Ginzburg herself was not quite such a believer, but even she recognized that the camps were a step closer to the "tempo of the age."[60]

## Special Settlements

The *spetspereselentsy*, or the residents of the "special settlements," were the exiles of the Soviet penal system.[61] In many ways, the special settlers were a group quite distinct from the other residents of the Gulag. Yet they were emphatically part of the Gulag system.[62] Special settlement entailed far more than mere exile. Like their relatives in the corrective labor camps, the special settlers were subjected to exile combined with labor and other measures of forced rehabilitation.[63] Nevertheless, the special settler lived with the free population and in many ways lived like them. The special settlers occupied a space halfway between freedom and the concentration camp. Their next step could lead them in either direction.

The special settlers fell into two main groups: the former kulaks exiled during the collectivization campaign of the early 1930s, and the nationalities exiled in whole or part starting in the latter half of the 1930s and continuing to the postwar period. In general, exile occurred in groups, while arrest and sentence to labor camps took place individually. The special settlements were located throughout the Central Asian republics and Siberia. Nearly half of the special settlers in 1944 were spread through the republic of Kazakhstan, while the Uzbek Republic, Kirghiz Republic, Novosibirsk Oblast, Omsk Oblast, and Krasnoiarsk Krai each lodged over a hundred thousand special settlers.[64]

A quick overview of life in special settlements can be gained from the experience of Rachel and Israel Rachlin, deported in 1941 from Lithuania.

While their experience is not universal, it reveals the main contours of life as an internal exile in the Soviet Union. The Rachlins, like most exiles, whether among the kulaks of the early 1930s, or the "punished peoples" of the latter 1930s and the war years, were not arrested, interrogated, or charged with any particular violation of the criminal code. They were sent to their place of exile as a family (although in some cases the men were arrested, separated from their family, and sent to labor camps, while the rest of the family was exiled as special settlers) and remained together as a family throughout their period in special settlement.[65] The presence of families among the special settlements added a generational facet to this particular institution of the Gulag. For example, October 1932 saw approximately fifteen thousand children under the age of fourteen among the forty-two thousand special settlers at Magnitogorsk.[66] The children of the special settlement were not themselves suspect but rather were considered to be in serious danger of contamination by their suspect elders. Soviet authorities constantly feared the "pernicious influence of the kulak ideology" on the settlement youths, and inadequate educational facilities for the youths were cause for special reprimand.[67] At the same time, the children were the first to regain passports and the right to move away from the settlements.

Still, the life of the special settler was similar to that of the free worker living in the same region. Along the Rachlins' transport route, representatives of local enterprises frequently came and chose from among the deportees to fill the needs of their industry. The Rachlins lived not behind barbed wire but instead on a state farm (sovkhoz), where they were paid as free workers.[68] In general, the special settlers were required to provide for themselves, just as the free population had to do. They held jobs, and tended private plots or other individual gardens. Once the basics of life had been established, arriving exiles were supposed to be placed on salary. From that point, they had to take care of themselves, even though 25 percent of their income went to the administration of the special settlements. Invalids and the elderly among the exiles who were unable to work and had no relatives with them were to be placed in a special section of the special settlements, and would be given supplies for free. Women with babies and no head of household were also to be provided with supplies temporarily until they could gain paid work.[69] Of course, reality often differed from what official documents prescribed, on occasion leading to cruel mass death.[70]

Deportees with education and talent were not necessarily barred from politically sensitive positions. Israel Rachlin became a teacher at a local school in Iakutsk. (He taught the German language, of all things, during the war—a rather surprisingly sensitive position for an unreliable element.)[71] Later, when working for an experimental agriculture facility, he served as the facility's representative in all legal matters. The Rachlins were allowed to vote, and their children grew up as their free peers did, joining the Young Pioneers and later the Communist Youth Leagues (Komsomol).[72]

Despite the similarities between the Rachlins' life and that of the free workers, the involuntary detention—the severe restrictions on freedom of movement—of the special settler was ever present. The Rachlins may have worked in a sovkhoz with free workers, but they were required to appear twice monthly at the local People's Commissariat of Internal Affairs (NKVD) office.[73] Gulag authorities were constantly preoccupied with preventing the escape of special settlers from their place of exile. In all periods of special settlement, the deportees were uniformly considered unreliable elements by the Soviet authorities. Throughout their frequent transfers from location to location, their substantial files traveled from one local NKVD chief to another. Relocation happened many times, continously tearing asunder the life that the deportees had built in their latest locale. The Rachlins also describe a perpetual fear of arrest and transfer to a labor camp. Further, while deportees like the Rachlins constantly sought survival through less physical work, their uncertain position always left them subject to the whims of a politically conscious manager or NKVD chief, who could take away their position and force them into physical labor.[74]

Special settlers were spread throughout the hinterlands of the Soviet Union, including Magnitogorsk. Stephen Kotkin contrasts life in the special labor settlement to the local corrective labor colony. The special labor settlement, created in 1931 to house recently de-kulakized peasants, was initially treated much more severely than the corrective labor colony, which held the "socially friendly" criminals. The "class enemy" special settlers were immediately enclosed by barbed wire, but this soon came down. Considered incorrigible by virtue of their class background, they were subject to less intense propaganda than the colony inhabitants. Unlike common criminals, most peasants remained in the area even after their rights were restored by the constitution of 1936. In this case the de-kulakized peasants were allowed to join the "grand crusade," and they did so, many staying on at Magnitogorsk even after their passports were restored to them.[75]

One other group of exiles should be mentioned, although they will be discussed further below. Most prisoners were subjected to some form of exile on their release from corrective labor camps. Some were refused permission to live only in certain special regions of the Soviet Union (usually near borders or military resources), while others were denied the right to live in the country's largest cities. Many who were released from corrective labor camps after the completion of a sentence were subjected to a form of exile that was similar to that of the special settlers—that is, they were specifically required to live within the boundaries of a particular region.

The world of the deportee was an integral part of the Gulag, and ties between exile and camps were always tight. On the one hand, the exiled person was always particularly vulnerable to arrest and incarceration in the camps. For example, in July 1931, OGPU authorities in Kazakhstan were ordered to arrest all priests, monks, and former officers in exile without families. The arrestees were then transferred to the Kazakhstan Corrective Labor Camp (Kazitlag), the short-lived forerunner of the Karaganda region's main camp, Karlag.[76] At the same time, exiles and camps often populated the same regions. This was certainly the case in Karaganda, where the camp largely provided agricultural labor and the exiles largely provided workers for the mines.

Camp prisoners who had committed crimes while in exile were returned to their place of exile on completion of their sentence. Prisoners whose families had been sent into exile were also deported to join their families on completion of their camp term, although truly exceptional prisoner–shock workers could earn not only their own early release but the release of their families from exile as well.[77] For kulaks arrested and given sentences of punishment in the camps, the presence of a family in exile could be a positive development. Gulag authorities were quite concerned with the capacity of families to survive in the head of household's absence. Consequently, in July 1931, Gulag chief Lazar Kogan ordered that kulaks who had been arrested and given sentences of under three years could be released to join their families in exile. Even prisoners with sentences longer than three years were often released to join their family with the assent of central Gulag authorities. Kulaks without families, however, were required to complete their camp sentence. The same order created bureaus in special settlements with the task of locating and reuniting family members sent to exile in different regions.[78]

In the early 1930s, some OGPU camps were also given jurisdiction over the exiles in their region. Exiled kulaks in and around Akmolinsk were initially the responsibility of Kazitlag authorities. In late May 1931, an OGPU department was created to administer special settlements in Kazakhstan, and shortly after Kazitlag was ordered to transfer all exiled kulaks and the administrative staff responsible for them to the new administration's authority.[79]

## Corrective Labor Colonies

The corrective labor colonies are perhaps the forgotten component of the Gulag. Little about them appears in the published documentation, and they still await a full-length study in their own right. Their inmates are not included in the pantheon of well-known Gulag memoirists. Perhaps, more than anything else, this reflects the nature of the colonies' inmates. Corrective labor colonies were set up in a fashion quite similar to the corrective labor camps, but the inmates of the colonies were subject to shorter sentences, usually less than three years. Consequently, few of the political criminals found their way into the colonies, which were filled largely with common criminals, few of whom left memoirs of their experiences. Unfortunately, they are largely beyond the scope of the present study as well. The Karaganda region was dominated by its major corrective labor camp and extensive system of internal exiles, and it barely had a corrective labor colony presence. On January 1, 1940, only 8,000 corrective labor colony prisoners were housed throughout the Kazakh Republic at a time when the entire Soviet Union saw 316,000 such prisoners. The vast majority, some 241,000 colony prisoners, were kept inside the Russian Republic, but even the Ukrainian and Uzbek republics held more colony prisoners at this time than did the Kazakh.[80]

Corrective labor colonies differed from corrective labor camps in three main ways: they were typically less remote geographically, held prisoners with sentences under three years, and were much smaller. Corrective labor colonies were quite literally found in every part of the Soviet Union, and many were no larger than the smallest subdivision of the larger labor camps. Often, the labor colonies were established in a particular location only to provide labor for one enterprise.

Kotkin, in portions of his work on Magnitogorsk, has provided enough material to render a few impressions of the labor colony. Due to the short sentences, new arrivals and releases were frequent in the corrective labor colony.[81] These inmates were most clearly considered redeemable. In fact, they were expected to make a return to society. As such, they were typically hit with a barrage of cultural and educational propaganda. A corrective labor colony was established in Magnitogorsk in 1932. The colony, in Kotkin's words, "tried to create a version of the revolutionary crusade and impart its values to the convicts." Inmates thus were expected to learn a profession. The colony had its own newspaper, library, shock workers (who held their own conference, complete with orchestra), Stakhanovites, plays, films, political circles, and all the accompaniments of a typical 1930s' work collective. Contrary to the practice at Magnitogorsk's special settlement, the inmates at Magnitogorsk's corrective labor colony were initially unconfined. The inmates were, after all, from among the ranks of those considered class allies and the socially friendly. Soon, however, a rash of escapes and "mayhem" brought barbed wire to the colony, along with practices becoming common in the corrective labor camps deeper in the heart of Siberia: the division of the colony into sectors, the creation of punishment/isolation areas, and a "special regime" barracks. Armed guards began to escort the inmates to work, and the inmates were fitted with distinct clothing and haircuts, which prevented them from disappearing among the local population. Ultimately, most of the efforts at reforging these criminals proved unsuccessful, and most of those released from the colony left Magnitogorsk.[82]

Finally, brief mention should be made of a judicial sentence reserved for particularly minor crimes. People could be sentenced to "corrective labor without deprivation of freedom" for relatively minor crimes. These sentences typically took the form of a fine, as a portion of the convict's wages was garnisheed for the period of the punishment, though the convict would remain unconfined and at their former place of work.

· · · · ·

I began with an intriguing contradiction: Solzhenitsyn's tale of an orchestra greeting prisoners at Kolyma. Yet the story does not represent a real contradiction. The Gulag was simultaneously, and for Soviet authorities unproblematically, a site of both violence and reform—death and redemption. From a prisoner's first day in the Gulag, they were confronted by a social space permeated by Soviet-style socialism. Bands played; posters announced the duty to remake oneself; collective life dominated both barracks and labor; and people died in unspeakably brutal conditions—all in the name of engineering a total human transformation. In some measure, the authorities succeeded. Prisoners learned to negotiate that social space, and in so doing learned to live on Soviet terms. Prisoners related to one another and their conditions through categories fostered by the Gulag authorities. When prisoners rose in the 1950s to challenge Soviet authority, they characteristically mounted that challenge in the form of a workers' strike—that is, in the terms available in their social space, which were the terms of Soviet socialism, the terms of the Gulag.

The Gulag, then, comes to appear as a last chance for its prisoners. In the Gulag, people would either die, or be transformed and returned to Soviet society (even if the transformation was never exactly what Soviet authorities envisioned). The story of the Gulag is the story of prisoners attempting to negotiate that last chance—to survive—amid an ever-changing set of institutions, practices, and social identities that shaped their lives.

# Chapter 2

# RECLAIMING THE MARGINS AND THE MARGINAL: GULAG PRACTICES IN KARAGANDA, 1930s

Every ravine, every gully, every stream presented itself as a kind of fortress that was stormed in battle by the hero-organizers of Karlag agriculture. Yesterday's wreckers, bandits, thieves, and prostitutes, gathered from the various ends of the Soviet country, under the able and experienced Chekist leadership, accomplished great things. Burning with the flame of constructive enthusiasm, valuing highly and proud of that faith placed in them, the former lawbreakers stormed the semideserts of Kazakhstan.

—Karlag's "official" history, sent to central Gulag authorities in 1934

IN SPRING 1938, at the age of twenty-two, Militsa Stefanskaia arrived at Karlag, the large agricultural corrective labor camp centered in the steppe of Kazakhstan's Karaganda region. Stefanskaia was born to a Smolensk intelligentsia family. Her father leaned politically toward the Bolsheviks and joined the Red Army shortly after the October Revolution. In the early 1920s, her family moved to Moscow, where her father and grandfather worked in the young Soviet government. On the night of November 1, 1937, Stefanskaia, an employee of a medical institute library, was arrested. She spent seven months in prison, and after a few interrogations was sentenced to three years for alleged counterrevolutionary activity and sent to Karaganda. Though this was quite a light sentence in these years of the Great Terror, the term in the Gulag would tear Stefanskaia's life apart. In her memoirs, Stefanskaia vividly recalls her trip to Karaganda: "The train went through the steppe. The naked Kazakh steppe, steppe and more steppe—I do not remember anything else.... We went and went. The steppe flashed past the windows—we had gone to Kazakhstan.... And we kept going and going. Where to? Nobody knew."[1]

Sixty-eight years later, in March 2006, I visited a Karaganda camp graveyard holding thousands of former Soviet Gulag and World War II POW graves. The cemetery was in the empty steppe near Spassk, just south of the city of Karaganda. At various times, Spassk was a division of Karlag, a POW camp, and a division of the postwar special camp Steplag and the graveyard held victims of all these institutions. Long unmarked, the cemetery today includes numerous monuments placed by visiting foreign delegations in honor of their compatriots who found their final resting place in the Kazakh steppe. On this day, the temperature hovered right around freezing—significantly warmer than the forty below of just a few months earlier—but the winds swept across the flat open steppe, piercing through my thick winter coat and several layers of clothing. As I ran from monument to monument snapping photographs of this cemetery, with quick breaks in a car to warm up, I was forced to try to imagine just how brutal life as a camp inmate in the Karaganda region would have been, working out in the steppe with inadequate clothing in temperatures much lower than I faced. After all, Galina Aleksandrovna Semenova, one Karlag prisoner in the late 1930s, recalled temperatures reaching as low as negative sixty-four degrees Celsius (such that when it improved to negative fifty degrees, they said it was "warming up"), extreme winds, and snow so deep that the barracks were totally buried and darkened, and prisoners had to dig their way out.[2] Winter must have seemed endless in this steppe, and looking at the untrammeled view in every direction, escape must have seemed impossible without trees or even hills as cover. Many never escaped and never left this steppe alive, with most ending up in graveyards that remain unmarked to this day.

## Founding Karaganda's Gulag

In September 1934, Karlag officials proudly sent a history of their concentration camp's first four years in Karaganda to the central Gulag authorities in Moscow. The first section, "Four Years of the Struggle for Reclamation of the Semi-Desert and for Reforging," placed the camp's creation in the political context of the Great Break.

> [Karlag] did not emerge accidentally, just as nothing appears accidentally in the great proletarian country in the epoch of the dictatorship of the proletariat under the leadership of the party of Lenin with the genius leader of the world proletariat com[rade] Stalin at its head. At the XVI Congress of the VKP/b/ com[rade] Stalin put before the party, before the working class and all the laborers of the countries of the Soviets, one of the most important problems— THE PROBLEM OF THE RECLAMATION OF THE MARGINS, the problem of its economic flowering on the basis of the newest techniques and socialist forms of the organization of economic activity. The margins liberated by the Great October Revolution from the rampant exploitation and oppression

of the capitalists—the former subcolonies of the tsar—by the historic decisions of the XVI Congress of the Communist Party were included in the plan of socialist construction as powerful bases of raw materials, as centers of heavy industry, born in the margins by the will of the Bolsheviks.[3]

Rich as it was in natural resources, especially coal, the Karaganda region was certainly ripe for development. The region's resources, while known in the tsarist era, remained underdeveloped until the 1930s. Lenin signed a decree in May 1918 nationalizing the Karaganda coal mines, Spassk brass works, and Uspenskii copper mines from the Russian and foreign investors who had begun their development in the nineteenth century. In 1920, he ordered the study of the region's subsoil to prepare for the development of its natural wealth.[4] Massive development of the region, however, awaited the era of the First Five-Year Plan as well as the explosive growth of the Gulag's exile and prisoner populations in the area. In fact, development of the Karaganda region's natural resources proceeded hand in hand with the growth of Karaganda's Gulag.

As early as 1925, Soviet authorities had identified the Kazakh steppe as a likely destination for their labor camp inmates.[5] Yet the history of corrective labor camps in the Karaganda region really began with the arrival in late 1930 of a handful of Chekists and their prisoners to establish a subdivision of an OGPU camp called the Kazakhstan Corrective Labor Camp (Kazitlag, or Kazlag). Headquartered in Almaty, Kazitlag included far-flung divisions engaged in labor at the brickyards of the Turksib construction project and paving the streets of Almaty. In Karaganda, Kazitlag operated the state farm (sovkhoz) Gigant. In July 1931, some 1 million hectares of land (just under 2.5 million acres, or 3,900 square miles) were transferred to Kazitlag for agricultural use.[6]

The first winter at Kazitlag's Gigant division was quite difficult. Prisoners faced living conditions that are only hinted at in the official history: "The winter of 1930 passed in unbelievably harsh conditions: there were no living quarters. The camp population was accommodated willy-nilly [koe-kak]."[7] The Karaganda region was sparsely populated and lacked building materials. Prisoners lived in tents, mud huts, and even under the open sky, as the construction of living space lagged behind the expansion of the prisoner population throughout Karlag's history. Inmates built their own prison camps. Barely able to provide for themselves, the prisoners were also required to provide food and construct living space for the rapidly expanding peasant exile population.[8] The official history, unsurprisingly, contains no information on prisoner deaths, but given the shortage of housing, extreme climatic conditions of the Karaganda region, and famine that struck Kazakhstan in the early 1930s, they were substantial.[9]

Kazitlag was disbanded within a year. All of its subdivisions were liquidated with the exception of Gigant, whose agricultural territory became the basis for a new independent camp: Karlag.[10] Karlag was one of the largest (geographically and in terms of prisoner population) and longest-lasting camps in the Gulag system. Its administrative center was ultimately placed in the village of Dolinka, located approximately forty-five kilometers outside the city of Karaganda. The former Karlag administration building still stands in Dolinka today. The hulking two-story neoclassic building stands abandoned—a bizarre site with its columns rising out of a little village of dilapidated one-story shacks.

Karlag was the central institution of the Karaganda region, even though one finds nary a mention of it in Soviet-era histories and encyclopedias of the region. Karaganda would become the second-largest city in Kazakhstan, but representative of the true order of the region, it would only officially achieve the status of "city" in 1934, fully three years after the founding of the concentration camp that bore its name. The camp was ordered hierarchically, with a varying number of camp subdivisions administratively subordinate to the central camp authorities. These camp subdivisions administered a large number of camp points, and the actual locales housed varying numbers of prisoners. The camp's core territory spread some 300 kilometers from north to south and 200 kilometers from east to west, but it also encompassed independent divisions in and around Akmolinsk and Balkhash (350 and 650 kilometers, respectively, from the camp's administration). It would later spread even farther with the addition of a camp division around the city of Dzhezkazgan in Kazakhstan.[11]

Karlag was primarily, though not exclusively, an agricultural camp established to transform the semidesert of the steppe into a productive agricultural base for the provision of livestock and crops to the region's growing population engaged in the extraction of natural resources. The formation of Karlag as an independent camp followed almost immediately on the heels of a Central Committee resolution in August 1931 on the development of the Karaganda basin as the Soviet Union's number three provider of coal. While the late Soviet history of Karaganda emphasizes the city as "an offspring of October," and carefully enumerates the fifteen hundred Communists, three thousand Komsomols, and twelve thousand miners and builders sent to Karaganda in 1931–32 to construct the coal basin, Karaganda was perhaps more accurately an offspring of the Gulag, particularly of Karlag's prisoner population and the region's population of internal exiles, starting with kulaks and later an array of deported nationalities.[12]

The agricultural task before Karlag was daunting. They camp was asked to develop a semidesert that exceeded in size many European countries.[13] With what must have been a tremendous understatement, the 1934 Karlag history noted that more than a few "skeptics, opportunists, and pessimists" disseminated their doubts about the possibility of accomplishing such a major task given the climatic and soil conditions of the region. Yet many were also, no doubt, caught up in the atmosphere of "revolutionary times . . . of socialist construction [when t]here are no fortresses that the Bolsheviks cannot storm."[14]

Nonetheless, in these conditions Karlag somehow established a semblance of mechanized agriculture in the steppe. Its authorities brought combines, tractors, and automobiles to what they thought of as an "empty" steppe.[15] Prisoners built massive irrigation works, damming up regional rivers, and they turned Dolinka into a small city with electric stations, radio stations, repair shops, and the like. They also constructed the roads and railroads that connected "the periphery with the center."[16] Exiled special settlers to the region built railroad lines connecting Gigant with the city of Karaganda and the Uspenskii mines. At Gigant, they planted wheat, corn, oats, and other grains, and raised cattle and sheep. Labor camp prisoners also directly participated in the initial construction of coal mines in the region, although they would mostly give way to the special settlers for the mining work.[17] By 1933, Gulag officials envisioned prisoners and special settlers extracting over 70 percent of all mined coal in the Karaganda coal basin.[18]

Primarily, though, the prisoners of Karlag were involved in agricultural work—and in massive proportions. In 1934, Karlag covered 1.7 million hectares, on which the prisoners operated eight state farms (sovkhozov) for livestock, and planted over 32,000 hectares of land in grains, producing over 22,500 tons, or 143 percent of their annual plan, with another 20,000 hectares opened and ready for the following year. Another 210,000 hectares were cultivated for hay. Plans were under way to prepare 45,000 hectares with irrigation from dam works. In addition, Karlag had at that time over 37,000 head of cattle, 60,000 head of sheep, and 700 sows. The work was completed, much of it without the benefit of tractors, with a total prisoner population of just over twenty-five thousand by the end of 1934.[19] In that year, Gulag agricultural facilities, of which Karlag was the most important, reportedly provided all meat and dairy products to the entire camp system, along with 70 percent of its potatoes and vegetables.[20]

Karlag and central Soviet authorities indeed acted as if the lands of Karlag were empty. But the population on the territory at the time of the camp's founding is estimated at eighty thousand Kazakhs along with another twelve hundred households of Germans, Russians, and Ukrainians. Portions of these populations were forcibly resettled in 1930–31 out of the camp's territory, but within the Karaganda region. The resettlements occurred as part of the collectivization and de-kulakization campaigns in the region. Prisoners were then dispatched around the camp's lands to build barracks, railroads, and other infrastructure. The land was definitively claimed from the native population for the camp, even to the point of destroying the graves of Kazakh notables to use the stones in camp construction.[21]

The formation of Karlag and the establishment of agriculture in the steppe were of added significance in the midst of the collectivization drive. Karlag was supposed to be a shining example of the possibilities of socialist agriculture. Despite the difficulties, bragged the authorities in their self-history, Karlag was able to overfulfill its agricultural plan for 1931, and considering the nature of the officials' criminal human resources, they provided a strong example for local collective farms.

The propagandistic declarations in Karlag's official history were in great part hyperbole and self-promotion, yet they also contained something of the tenor of the age. For as the official history noted repeatedly, and as camp practices showed time and time again, Karlag's work was not just about its economic role. As Karlag officials wrote in 1934, their task was not only to introduce a huge territory "into the stock of socialist agriculture but also to return tens of thousands of former lawbreakers reforged in the hearth of collective labor into the ranks of the genuine shock workers of socialist construction."[22]

Karlag was an integral part of the approach to this problem, where local camp authorities "battled" for the "reclamation of the semidesert and the reforging" of criminals into honest Soviet citizens. Karlag's primary tasks, as described in the official history, were twofold: the development of agriculture in the vast desert-steppe of central Kazakhstan to support the emerging industrial centers of the region, and in coordination with these "economic-political tasks to solve the social-political task of the reeducation of tens of thousands of former lawbreakers" through instruction in collective agricultural labor.[23]

## The Practices of the Gulag

These two primary tasks, the economic and the penal, drove the history of Karlag and the Gulag itself. While the economic and the penal often worked in complementary ways, especially with regard to the practice of corrective labor, the tasks usually competed for attention and caused conflict. Individuals with authority at all levels of the Gulag and individual camp administrations wrestled with the competing tasks, fearing the consequences of failing in either sphere. Exploring the practices of the Gulag, as they emerged and were reshaped throughout the 1930s, allows

TABLE 1.1
1930s Karlag and Soviet Corrective Labor Camp Populations

| Date | Karlag Population[1] | Population of all corrective labor camps[2] | Population of corrective labor camps and colonies[3] |
|---|---|---|---|
| 1930 | | 179,000 | |
| 1931 | | 212,000 | |
| 1932 | 10,400[4] | 268,700 | |
| 1933 | | 334,300 | |
| January 1, 1934 | 24,148 | 510,307 | |
| January 1, 1935 | 25,110 | 725,483 | 990,554 |
| January 1, 1936 | 38,194 | 839,406 | 1,296,494 |
| January 1, 1937 | 27,504 | 820,881 | 1,196,369 |
| January 1, 1938 | 31,548[5] | 996,367 | 1,881,570 |
| October 1, 1938 | 40,109 | | |
| January 1, 1939 | 35,072 | 1,317,195 | 1,672,438 |

1. Karlag's population compiled from GARF, f. 9414, op. 1, d. 1155, l. 20; *Sistema ispravitel'no-trudovykh lagerei v SSSR 1923–1960: Spravochnik* (Moscow, 1998), 285. Diusetai Aimagambetovich Shaimukhanov and Saule Diusetaevna Shaimukhanova *Karlag* (Karaganda: Poligrafiia, 1997), 19, offer figures without exact dates or archival citation that are generally close to those figures, with the exception of a population in 1931 of 21,329 that seems unlikely given the population in December 1932 found in official documentation.
2. Gulag labor camp populations are from GARF, f. 9414, op. 1, d. 1155, l. 1a; they do not include exiles or inmates of prisons or corrective labor colonies.
3. Iurii Nikolaevich Afanas'ev, et al., eds., *Istoriia stalinskogo Gulaga: Konets 1920-kh–pervaia polovina 1950-kh godov: Sobranie dokumentov v semi tomakh* (Moscow: Rosspen, 2004), 4:129–30.
4. Karlag population in December 1932.
5. Of this number, seventy-three hundred (or 23 percent) were sentenced for counter-revolutionary crimes. Ibid., 4:70.

us insight into these tasks placed before individual camp employees and shows us how prisoners negotiated the demands from those authorities in an attempt to survive until release from the Soviet penal system.

## Corrective Labor and the Gulag's Economy

The dramatic growth of the Gulag, including its Karaganda outposts, into a mass social institution was sparked by collectivization and the concomitant attempt to "liquidate the kulaks as a class." The secret police *troiki* (committees of three with the administrative power to sentence individuals to punishment) saw, in official Soviet terms, a "colossal growth in the number of accused" appearing before them. In 1929, they had handled 5,885 cases, while in 1930 the number grew 7550 percent to 179,620.[24] Furthermore, by October 1931, nearly 1.2 million people had been exiled during the process of collectivization, which along with de-kulakization drove the exiling and frequent arrest of these so-called kulaks.[25] No evidence points to collectivization and de-kulakization as a process primarily motivated by the need for labor power either in camps or the locales of special settlement. Rather, these policies were decided on for political purposes related to Soviet power in the villages—collectivization as a way to modernize and create a purportedly socialist agriculture that enabled the state to reliably extract grain from peasants, and de-kulakization as a manifestation of the expected class war in the village as well as to remove those who opposed the collectivization process. Only once this political decision was made did Soviet authorities approach the question of what to do with these individuals, or how best to make use of them.[26]

Gulag authorities were not demanding more prisoner laborers. They were instead always running behind the curve, trying to find ways to make productive economic use of their burgeoning prisoner population.[27] As Oleg Khlevniuk has put it, "In the early 1930s . . . mass arrests were not really dictated by economic needs. On the contrary, the OGPU leadership frantically tried, and often failed, to find occupations for the tens of thousands of prisoners."[28] The key events in the growth of the Gulag's prisoner population were external to the Gulag itself. Although most kulaks were sent into internal exile during the "liquidation of the kulaks as a class," they also constituted the first major infusion of prisoners into forced labor camps in the Stalin era. Their arrival made the camp system a major social and economic institution for the first time. The camp population quickly reached some 180,000 by the beginning of 1930—a population several times the limit on labor camp populations envisioned only six months earlier. Similarly, Gulag authorities did not request or even foresee the explosive growth of the prisoner population resulting from the law of August 7, 1932 on the theft of socialist property, the introduction of the passport system and its demand to cleanse the cities of socially dangerous elements, the Great Terror of 1937–38, the labor discipline laws of 1940, the waves of mass deportation of nationalities during the war, or the law of 1947 on property theft.[29] If arrests and terror were driven primarily by the desire to fill the camps with laborers, one also questions why so many potential prisoner-workers were executed? All of these massive campaigns of repression dramatically increased the size of the Gulag, and each of them can be explained with reference to political events external to the Gulag itself and its "need" for labor. The introduction and intensification of terror and mass arrest in the Soviet era simply cannot be understood according to an economic, slave-labor logic, when real (if false) fears of enemies populated the public and private rhetoric of those involved in the terror apparatus. Finally, the notion that the Gulag and arrests were primarily driven by the need to gain slave laborers is challenged by the presence of numerous arrestees—the elderly and the invalid—who were not fit to labor in these extreme conditions.[30]

If economic demands did not propel the growth of the Gulag, what role did they play? Economic production was one, but only one, of several tasks assigned to the Gulag. Aside from isolating, indoctrinating, and punishing inmates, the camp system was expected to use forced laborers (arrested for other reasons) to complete economic tasks of significance to the Soviet state. The most fundamental rule of the Gulag labor camp was that "every prisoner must work as appointed by the administration of the camp."[31] Labor was the defining feature of the Soviet Gulag, and it occupied an overwhelming portion of a prisoner's daily life. Prisoners often spent up to twelve hours per day at work, not including travel to and from the workplace. Not uncommonly, prisoners got less than four hours of sleep.[32] The Gulag made a substantial, if costly, contribution to the Soviet economy from the 1930s through the 1950s. Gulag laborers completed such massive construction projects as the White Sea to Baltic Sea and Volga River to Moscow River canals, opened up gold mines along the far east's Kolyma River, built rail lines throughout the Soviet Union, felled timber in Siberia, produced oil and coal in places like Vorkuta, Noril'sk, and Karaganda, and operated large agricultural enterprises in Siberia and Karaganda.

The compound term corrective labor, so prominent that it appeared in the names of two of the Gulag's most important institutions—the corrective labor camp and the corrective labor colony—must be understood with reference to both halves of the phrase. In scholarly studies, the corrective aspects of this Soviet practice are often eradicated in favor of an understanding of labor as exclusively a practice of deriving economic benefit from slave labor. Yet in the Soviet Union, corrective labor involved a great deal more than mere economic output, much as Leon Trotsky envisioned compulsory labor not just as a means of economic output but as the main force for building socialism too.[33] Corrective labor entailed a combination of economic output with human transformation. Whether in a corrective labor camp or a special settlement, all able-bodied inmates of the Gulag were required to work, as a measure of punishment and a means of rehabilitation.

Similar to labor in the Soviet Union at large, labor in the camps was intensely politicized. Labor, in the Bolshevik worldview, was the defining feature of human existence. It had been devalued and denigrated by the capitalists, but as *Belomor* declared, "Work in the U.S.S.R. has in reality become a matter of honour, a matter of glory, a matter of valour and of heroism. . . . Labour is no longer a hateful means of existence, but the rational expression of a happy life."[34] Production meetings were frequently called to address problems of "slackening morale," and "how to increase output quickly so we won't be ashamed of our failure to provide our country with the quantity of coal needed to build up our industrial potential, increase the wealth of our citizens, and strengthen the position of the Soviet Union in the world."[35] Or as Solzhenitsyn writes, "Every prisoner had to be informed about the production plans! And every prisoner had to be informed about the entire political life of the country! Therefore at morning line-up . . . there was a 'five-minute production session,' and after returning to camp . . . there was a 'five-minute political session.'"[36] Corrective labor was supposedly "not that kind of work which dries out the mind and the heart of the human being [but rather] the miracle work . . . , which transforms people from nonexistence and insignificance into heroes," in the words of Stalin's prosecutor, Andrey Vyshinsky.[37] At the seventh All-Union Congress of Soviets, the people's commissar of justice explained that "labor is the best means of paralyzing the disintegrating influence . . . of the endless conversations of prisoners among themselves in the course of which the more experienced instruct the newcomers. . . . It is essential to teach [the prisoners] to become accustomed to Communist, collective labor."[38]

Thus, prisoners in the Gulag not only had to work; they also had to "realise the significance of the great task which has been entrusted to the G.P.U. by the Party and the Government."[39] The labor of Sing Sing in which the prisoner spent an entire day moving a pile of stones only to spend the next day moving them back again was supposedly not the model for Gulag labor.[40] Corrective labor comprised an integral part of the greater Soviet project, and the camps' educational apparatus taught the inmates the details of the plan and the place of Gulag labor within that plan. Through participation in the projects of Soviet society, it was thought, prisoners could successfully return to that society.

Historians of the Gulag have rarely given much credence to the ideological elements of its rise, and understandably so. Given the incredible brutality of life in the Gulag, the high mortality rates, and the lack of concern for individual human life, how are we to think of all this as anything but a propaganda fig leaf? Scholars therefore reduced the corrective element of the Gulag to the work of the camp system's Cultural-Educational Sections (KVChs), and labor itself is understood only in economic terms.[41] Such observations miss the tie between correction and death in the Gulag. Brutality was itself part and parcel of the ideology of labor in the Gulag. Labor was not only the means but also the measure of rehabilitation—and failure in the reeducation process was meant to be fatal. As we will see, several other Gulag practices ensured that labor, reeducation, and death were tightly connected. Reeducation and redemption were not just window dressing but rather life-or-death issues for Gulag prisoners. The task of reeducation was never intended to be an easy process. Given this, camp cultural activities coexisted with the harsh nature of corrective labor, with the two working together to forge a new person and destroy those incapable of reformation.

Political indoctrination was ubiquitous in the Soviet Union both in and out of the Gulag. In free Soviet society, workers were often required to spend their lunch hours discussing the international situation or the building of socialism. Similarly, exiles were constantly called on to exhibit a proper political attitude toward their work. Ultimately, the politicization of labor signifies a radical difference in the Bolshevik attitude toward labor. Industrialization was not only about the construction of factories but also about the construction of a new person and civilization.[42]

The debate about the Gulag's economy has been a long one. Arendt was among the early skeptics about the profitability of Soviet forced labor. She suggests that although mass arrests were quite possibly the Soviet method of "solving its unemployment problem, it is also generally known that the output in those camps is infinitely lower than that of ordinary Soviet labor and hardly suffices to pay the expenses of the police apparatus."[43] One of the more important conclusions of the best recent scholarship on the Gulag has been putting to rest once and for all the illusion that forced labor was free, or even cheap. As the editors of *Istoriia stalinskogo Gulaga* conclude, "The Gulag was a drain on the economic resources of the country. The productivity of Gulag labor was low and a matter of constant concern to Gulag authorities."[44] Forced labor was ineffective, almost exclusively physical, and unqualified, and its productivity remained low. Even as early as the Solovetskii camp's operation in the 1920s, Soviet authorities recognized that their penal institutions were failing in the mission to be self-supporting.[45] During the 1930s, they may have convinced themselves that the camps were profitable, as the Gulag participated in the great construction projects of building socialism, and began the extraction of rich deposits of natural resources in places like Vorkuta, Kolyma, and Karaganda. Even if the Gulag was profitable during this time—something that has not been demonstrated yet in the literature—it still would not indicate that it was more efficient than other means of getting labor power to these projects. Regardless, as early as World War II, the Gulag chief recognized that the average daily output of the Gulag laborer was 50 percent lower than the output of a free laborer.[46] Yet even in wartime, when the Soviet state needed to make efficient use of all its resources just to survive, dismantling the Gulag was never even considered.

Although Gulag authorities attempted almost perpetually to improve the Gulag's productivity, the Gulag as an economically profitable institution was always undercut by the Gulag as a highly secretive detention institution for those considered dangerous to Soviet society. The Gulag was a financial catastrophe for the Soviet state. Why, then, did the system prosper? On the one hand, we can certainly understand how Soviet authorities may have deceived themselves for years about the profitability of the operation. Or perhaps they continually believed that they could tinker with the system to make it profitable. Above all, the Soviet secret police organs had a significant self-serving institutional interest in fostering a belief in the profitability of Gulag labor, which would lead to further increases in their own budget and staffing.

Ultimately, though, the focus on profitability is mistaken. One must consider that the Gulag was in fact a penal institution first, and a productive institution second. In the Gulag, it often even seemed that the process of labor was more important than its output, its productivity. Why was it necessary for prisoners to manually dig a trench in minus-thirty-degree weather? It certainly was neither productive nor economically rational, but the key statistic for the Gulag bureaucracy was "labor utilization" (*trudovoe ispol'zovanie*). Every prisoner had to work. The prisoner's actual production was generally secondary. Furthermore, the Gulag's role in the battle with alleged class enemies and enemies of the people was far more critical to Soviet authorities than its profitability. In all the efforts of Gulag bureaucrats to increase productivity and decrease costs, one cost-cutting tactic was never even considered: reducing the size of the militarized guard. In actuality, the militarized guard as a percentage of the detained population grew significantly through the history of the Gulag.[47]

Labor was, of course, always an immensely important part of the Gulag's activities. A number of historians have focused on the documents related to the establishment of a large number of new OGPU camps in the early 1930s aimed at "colonization" (*kolonizatsiia*) and exploiting the material wealth of the geographically distant parts of the Soviet Union.[48] These writers draw the conclusion that the expansion of the Gulag in the period of the First Five-Year Plan was thus primarily economically determined.[49] Yet central OGPU orders for the recruitment of staff into these new camps reveal that colonization was to be cultural as well as economic. The enthusiasm and energy of the Chekists was praised for making the Solovetskii camps a success in the "industrial and cultural development" of the far north. Recruiting staff for the new camps was therefore a priority. As Karlag administrative documents reveal, "The new camps under Chekist leadership, just like at Solovetskii, must play a transformative role in the economy and culture of the distant margins."[50] The colonization of the periphery was part and parcel of the Stalinist revolution from above that sought to bring the fruits of socialist civilization to every corner of the Soviet Union. Applebaum herself notes that "in Kolyma, as in Komi, the Gulag was slowly bringing 'civilization'— if that is what it can be called—to the remote wilderness. Roads were being built where there had only been forest; houses were appearing in the swamps."[51]

Moreover, these officials were meeting to determine what to do with the already-arrested prisoners who were overcrowding the existing prisons. They were not planning or even asking for further arrests to fulfill economic goals. Faced with a Soviet economy that was demanding labor and the well-established practice of labor as a method for reeducation, it is no surprise that they would decide that prisoners must work. Prisoners sitting idly in isolation would have been contrary to the tenor of the age. Further, removing prisoners and exiles to remote locations served the task of isolating individuals deemed dangerous to state and society. If the conditions of the Gulag's remote locations killed many, so be it. Punishment was also part of the mandate.[52] If it increased the power and influence of the secret police apparatus, all the better in the officials' eyes.

None of this is to say that labor productivity was not a factor in the Gulag. Throughout the Gulag's history, Gulag authorities sought ways to make their prisoners more productive while also cutting costs. As just one example, in 1934, following the emphasis on economizing and cost accounting in the Soviet's Second Five-Year Plan, Gulag authorities sought to make their camps self-funding by pushing responsibility for economizing down to the prisoners themselves. In this case, they decreed the creation of a system of "labor columns." Each labor column was given the responsibility for operating without financial losses. Unlike previous experiences, which focused the prisoner laborers on output without regard to the costs involved, they would now need knowledge of input as well. Labor columns were required to learn and stay within the plans for expenditures of such camp resources as the workforce, auto transport, the amortization of instruments, and the repair and provision of new tools. In addition to receiving financial premiums for high labor output, labor columns and prisoners could earn bonuses for savings on the expenditure side of the ledger. The labor column was given collective responsibility for its production figures and behavior. Yet even in this practice, the work was far from "just" economic. Information and education were seen as key to raising prisoner productivity and lowering resource expenditure. All members of a labor column lived together, and they were to police themselves, "reforging the negative element and studying the personality of every inmate." The labor column was responsible for ensuring the cultural education of all its members, especially for the eradication of illiteracy in its ranks. Prisoners systematically failing to fulfill their labor norms, refusing to work, and violating camp rules were removed to special labor columns under strict guard.[53]

In spite of these efforts, and many others throughout the history of the Gulag system, the penal institutions would never be made profitable or self-funding. Nonetheless, they not only continued to operate, they expanded.

## Survival of the Fittest: Food and Labor in the Gulag

[Fellow prisoner and brigade leader Gromov] poked his finger into my chest. "You work, you eat. You stop working, you die. I take care of my people if they produce, but loafers don't stand a chance."[54]
—Janusz Bardach, *Man Is Wolf to Man*

The close tie between death and correction in the Gulag cannot be fully understood without reference to the provision of food in the camps. Correction was never guaranteed to all prisoners, and food operated in such a manner that those determined to be irredeemable were placed on a downward spiral toward death. The provision of food served the system of both punishment and reward in the Gulag. The main practice related to food was the "differentiation" of rations—a practice that like so many others in the Gulag, echoed practices in Soviet society at large.[55] According to official regulations, and usually in practice, prisoners received different amounts of food corresponding to different levels of labor productivity. This was a high-priority Gulag activity. In 1934, Karlag's director wrote to his subdivision heads that the completion of the production program was dependent on the differentiation of food provisions. The practice was the primary means for dealing with "idlers and simulators." The director also noted that the constant failure to provide adequate and quality food to prisoners who were working well completely undermined the system.[56]

While this system certainly served to cajole prison laborers to increase output, it also functioned within the system to tie the measure of redemption to the fulfillment of work norms. The failure to fulfill norms evidenced a failed commitment to self-rehabilitation. Nobody was understood as "unable" to fulfill norms. Rather, the failure to fulfill norms was treated as a willful activity, as an indication that a prisoner was still an enemy and actively resisting participation in the grand crusade of Soviet socialism. Reduced rations were the main cudgel to destroy that resistance. Reduced rations, so the theory went, would break down a prisoners' resistance, compel them to improve their labor performance, and thus lead to their reeducation, or if the prisoners continued to "resist" reeducation by failing to fulfill norms, their rations would lead to starvation and death, removing them from Soviet society once and for all.

Soviet authorities were constantly adjusting rations in an attempt to find that precise point between survival and death. Similar to the ever-growing differentiation of institutions that aimed at an ever-finer categorization of prisoners according to their perceived level of danger and capacity for reeducation, Gulag authorities eventually developed a highly differentiated set of official rations. At times, there were as many as nine different levels of official rations.[57] A differentiated approach to the prisoner population was always an important part of Gulag practice and reveals that economic considerations were never the only priority. As early as 1930, central OGPU authorities authorized the creation of work teams for weakened prisoners to work light duty three to four hours per day for four to six weeks in order to improve their health and allow them to return to full labor capacity. Yet, this provision specifically included in the light-duty work teams only those who had already shown "good behavior and a conscientious attitude toward labor."[58] Not all prisoners were eligible for this potentially life-saving (and labor-saving) practice. The Gulag never tried to save all of its prisoner laborers, only those who had shown some measure of reconstruction into honest citizens.

Of course, even the productive prisoner was often short of food in the Gulag. When the Soviet Union went through particularly hungry times, the Gulag prisoner, the lowest priority in Soviet society, suffered severely. Food, especially the lack of adequate food, was a constant preoccupation of the Gulag prisoner. Even though official regulations prohibited the reduction of prisoner rations "below an established calorie minimum," rarely was even the most productive prisoner laborer guaranteed enough rations to survive.[59]

When official channels failed to provide adequate food for survival, and when many prisoners were quite deliberately placed on starvation rations as a means of punishment, a secondary market in food arose.[60] Prisoners jockeyed for the privileged positions in the camp that provided access to food. Many of those who survived did so thanks to getting jobs in camp kitchens or tending to vegetable gardens and crop fields. As we will see below, access to food was a driving factor in the creation and maintenance of a prisoner society. Nationality, friendship, and membership in criminal gangs—the categories of a prisoner's existence—were important elements in determining who gained access to food outside the official ration system and with whom well-placed prisoners shared their privileged access to food.

Often survival in the face of the cycle toward death caused by the tie between food rations and labor output was only possible with the help of someone else—help that generally came at a price. Bardach recalled his work in the Gulag timber industry.

> As Pike [his work partner] and I grew weaker, we fulfilled less and less of our norm and received less and less to eat. One afternoon [brigade leader] Kovalov took me aside and said, "Let me have your boots. Then I'll put you back on full rations. I'll also give you an extra *paika* [ration], or even two." My boots were my only treasure. But the sucking in my intestines nearly drove me to eat boiled shoe leather or the bark from a tree, and in the evening I gave Kovalov my boots.[61]

Frequently, contacts with people outside the camps—whether relatives who might send a food parcel or locals who might provide food products through black market transactions—were crucial to survival beyond the official rationing system. Gulag authorities attempted to maintain control over these external sources, either by treating the receipt of packages as a privilege that could be taken away or by engaging in a constant battle against black market transactions. Nonetheless, the repeated focus on these practices in Gulag documentation reveals that the officials were never able to gain control over them. Particularly problematic in this regard was the way that the external provision of food undermined the system of differentiating food rations—a key aspect of official control over who would survive and who would not in the Gulag system.

## Diverse Gulag Living Conditions

After the time spent at work, prisoners spent most of their time in their living quarters. Often, but not always, labor camp prisoner living space accorded with typical visions of concentration camp life. Walls of stone, wood, or even just barbed wire topped with watchtowers surrounded camp zones of barracks and communal buildings like cafeterias, medical clinics, baths, and the like. Each camp zone differed in certain details. Some had no walls, just barbed wire; some had no medical clinic or no bath. Sometimes communal facilities were shared among neighboring camp zones. Nonetheless, the typical camp zone involved some type of guarded exterior boundary, usually surrounded by a free-fire forbidden zone, and an interior within which prisoners were relatively free to move during their nonworking hours.

Yet a great diversity marked living conditions in the Soviet corrective labor camps. Different prisoners in different camp divisions enjoyed different levels of free movement. At its most basic level, the freedom of movement within the camp zone signaled the fundamental difference between the concentration camp and the cellular prison. Prisoners usually noted the difference immediately on arrival, and at least until the more brutal realities of camp life set in, they could even find the atmosphere of the concentration camp a refreshing change from the prison. Thus, Stefanskaia recalls her first impressions on her spring arrival at Karlag. Sun, grass, wildflowers, and fresh air were all an improvement over crowded, dark prisoner cells saturated with the smell of the cheap prisoner "tobacco" *makhorka*. Her attitude changed quickly, however, as she completed the seventy-kilometer march to the transit camp. "Sand, coal and scorching heat! . . . The steppe with its grasses ended. Here was Karaganda's transit camp. Barracks. They led us behind the barbed wire, counted and turned us over to the camp's directors. Many barracks. Many prisoners."[62] Quickly, the labor camps earned a harsh reputation in the prisoner world. As former Kolyma prisoner Vladimir Petrov recalled hearing from one transit camp prisoner, "Everybody who wants to survive must do all he can to avoid being sent to a camp, since even the best camp is many times worse than the worst prison."[63]

Stefanskaia's story itself, though, reveals a Gulag world that is less familiar but surprisingly common. She soon made her way from the transit point to the camp division at Dolinka, where prisoners were divided according to their alleged crime and the length of their sentence. Karlag was a large camp geographically. As an expansive state farm with migratory grazing livestock and crops spread around the steppe, Karlag was even more diffuse and sparsely populated than most Gulag camps. Many of Karlag's prisoners moved about with their herds, living in far-flung corners of the camp's steppe, without zones, barbed wire, or barracks, and frequently without guard. As much as possible, Karlag authorities sought to allow free movement only to the most trusted prisoners, which meant those who had proven their capacity for rehabilitation through their labor performance, behavior in camps, class background, alleged crime, or sentence—all the categories according to which prisoners were constantly evaluated. But the extremely mobile nature of Karlag's work often forced them to allow even so-called counterrevolutionaries and hardened recidivists to live outside of camp zones.

Keeping prisoners outside of camp zones and sending them to work without an accompanying armed guard were practices by no means unique to Karlag. Every camp used these strategies to cope with the persistent shortages of camp zones and armed guard staff. Central Gulag authorities rather grudgingly tolerated such practices, seeking to ensure that only the most trusted of prisoners were allowed out without guard. Thus, they strictly forbade counterrevolutionary and other prisoners deemed particularly dangerous, especially those known to be inclined toward escape, from being kept outside zones and working in unguarded brigades. Even these rules were broken a lot, however, as local camp authorities attempted to balance their assigned economic tasks, the profile of their prisoner population, and their available facilities. The particularities of Karlag's economic tasks made such conditions more common, and the related problems of meeting the competing demands of economic production and maintaining strict isolation and guard of especially dangerous prisoners caused constant difficulties for camp authorities.

Stefanskaia was fortunate not to be one of those kept under perpetual surveillance, always living behind barbed wire and under armed guard even at work. Even though she had been convicted of a counterrevolutionary crime, she was placed in a general unguarded camp zone and was free to work in any part of Karlag's agricultural zone without an armed guard accompanying her to work. Stefanskaia soon became acquainted with a veterinary medic who had earned the right to move freely about the camp's territory. Along with Liusia, a female prisoner friend, she began to work as the veterinary medic's assistant. At first they continued to live in the camp zone at Dolinka, but as part of their work, they traveled rather freely around the steppe caring for ill sheep. Days among the flowers and grasses were a sharp contrast with the filth and criminal "exotica" of the camp zone. As she described it, "My God, it was such beauty! It was as if we had fallen into another world."[64]

Soon, Stefanskaia and Liusia began to live full time near the veterinary station with the medic and another female prisoner. They lived "like one family." Her life had certainly changed from the prison, train, and camp zone.

> We forgot that we were prisoners that before us was a long term. This was all the particularity of grand Karlag. It is very big. Its territory is huge. In the middle of Karlag is the convoyed zone. Strict regime. Everyone is under strict supervision and convoy. But the rest of the prisoners, those under the "general" regime, live without convoy. The camp is agricultural and the unconvoyed mass of prisoners was occupied in agriculture, animal husbandry and sheep herding.[65]

As Stefanskaia was quick to point out, her good fortune was only a relative phenomenon. In losing her freedom, she had lost much. Her contemporaries at home "received higher education, their chosen profession, established their personal lives, started families and participated in the life of our country. But we were prisoners and our life did not belong to us." Yet she really *lived* in the Gulag. Her story reflects the great diversity of the Gulag experience. Some concentration camp prisoners lived behind barbed wire, under constant armed guard, and with relatively little personal space or time. Some lived, as did Stefanskaia, in conditions almost indistinguishable from the internal exile population. Stefanskaia's freedom, of course, was significantly curtailed. She could not return to her old life. Still, she was held neither behind barbed wire nor under armed guard. As we will see, she even fell in love.[66]

Karlag's particularities as an agricultural camp exerted a strong influence on daily life inside and outside its porous borders. With so many prisoners living outside of camp zones without guard in the steppe, Karlag's capabilities of preventing the mixing of camp and noncamp populations were quite limited. This manifested itself in many ways. First, Karlag authorities blamed contact between the prisoner and free populations of Karaganda for crimes and disorders committed in the camp. In February 1938, they noted that such contacts facilitated the theft of camp property, speculation, and other criminal activities on the part of both prisoners and voluntary camp employees. Camp employees sent letters for prisoners outside the camp censorship system, distributed the best food and living conditions to their prisoner acquaintances, and provided vodka for them. Prisoners even engaged in drinking and dancing parties at the apartments of camp employees. All of these events prompted Karlag's leadership to remind its employees that the camp "was not a sovkhoz and was not a recreation spot but was a place of concentration for elements opposed to the Soviet system and dangerous for society."[67]

In April 1934, central Karlag authorities complained bitterly of prisoners' ever-more-frequent drinking of alcohol. Drunken prisoners, they claimed, had led to a growth in criminal activities in the camp, including murders. Two of the numerous sources of the alcohol were identified: free citizens living in settlements near the camp's borders, and prisoners working in transport who had contacts with the world outside the camp.[68]

Karlag authorities issued a regular stream of decrees, the very existence of which testified to their powerlessness in fully isolating the camp from the surrounding free populations. Given that a great many Karlag prisoners lived outside confined camp zones and moved about the steppe in their agricultural labors, this inability to keep prisoners isolated from the free population is unsurprising. Nonetheless, it was a constant source of concern for Karlag officials, who feared not only the negative consequences for their control of the prisoner population but also the possible physical danger and potentially contaminating effects of prisoners on free Soviet society. Reports include drunken prisoners descending on the city of Karaganda, getting ahold of a weapon, and shooting a local resident, or prisoners spreading communicable diseases to the free and exile populations.[69] Yet they also feared intellectual contact between the prisoner and free populations. A memo from August 1937 reminded local camp subdivisions that their cultural brigades and theatrical groups were forbidden from performing in front of audiences from among the free population.[70]

Gulag authorities used the diversity of living conditions in the camps as a way to reward and punish their prisoners. Those who had proved themselves reliable were transferred to an easier camp regime with fewer restrictions on movement, lighter work duties, and enhanced access to the necessities of survival. Exactly the opposite occurred for those prisoners deemed particularly dangerous and inveterate in their enemy activity. These prisoners were sent to harsh camp divisions where survival was more difficult due to heavy labor and poor access to supplementary food provisions.

## Guarding "Enemies"

The Gulag employed a large staff of administrators and armed guards both centrally and at each individual outpost. The "voluntary" staff of the Gulag was an enormous expense that served to undermine considerably any chance that prisoner laborers would be profitable. By January 1, 1945, the Gulag counted over 273,000 employees (of whom 104,000 worked as guards)—a number not including prisons, children's colonies, and the administration of road construction, which all also belonged to the penal system. By March 1953, this number grew to 445,000 (of whom 234,000 worked as guards). Yet according to official accounts, the Gulag was always understaffed.[71] As a result of understaffing, the line between prisoners and voluntary Gulag workers was often fuzzy. Prisoners were employed in camp administration and even the camp guard itself. Furthermore, Gulag employees knew all too well how quickly they could be arrested and become prisoners themselves. Even camp chiefs could swiftly make the trip from commander to prisoner. O. G. Linin was the chief of Karlag through much of the 1930s. In February 1937, he was awarded a medal for "grand accomplishments in agriculture and for showing initiative and energy." On December 29 of that same year, Linin was removed from his post, and arrested for "disorder" in the work of the camp and for "wrecking."[72] I have been unable to determine his fate. His permanent replacement, V. P. Zhuravlev, did not arrive from his post as chief of the Upravlenie Narodnogo Komissariata Vnutrennykh Del (UNKVD, or Directorate of the People's Commissariat of Internal Affairs) of the Moscow region until June 22, 1939.[73]

The gap between prisoners and camp employees was rather clear, though. Camp guards and staff often operated in the camps with a great deal of independence and impunity. Consequently, the attitude of Gulag staff toward their work and prisoners could make a tremendous difference in the quality of daily life. It was not uncommon for camp guards and staff to beat prisoners. Camp employees sometimes ordered the arrest and incarceration of prisoners in penalty units, even when they did not have the authority to do so. Sometimes the central camp administration learned of these official violations of camp rules and regulations, and sometimes they lodged complaints and even threatened or punished the perpetrators.[74] Official documents nevertheless fail to record much of the brutality in the camp relationship between Gulag employees and prisoners, which is detailed at great length in memoirs.

Camp employees fulfilled a wide range of tasks. They were cultural educators, camp division directors, medical officials, and record keepers. The camp employee, however, with whom the prisoner had the most frequent and direct contact, was the member of the militarized guard (*voennizirovanie okhrany*). The number of camp guards grew throughout the Gulag's history in both absolute terms and proportion to the prisoner population. But camp authorities were always calling for more guards and complaining about their inability to fill all the available positions. The militarized guards were employees of the Gulag, but according to central Gulag authorities in 1940, the guards primarily came from the ranks of demobilized Red Army soldiers and young commanders from the troops of the NKVD.[75] Gulag guards were the least educated segment of Gulag employees. In 1946, for example, 87 percent of the guard had less than a middle school education.[76] In 1940, some 107,000 guards were tasked with the isolation of prisoners, convoy of prisoners to and from work sites, guarding of prisoners at the work site, transferring prisoners from one camp to another, and search for escapees.[77]

Recruiting employees for the militarized guard was difficult, much as it was for recruiting employees for any Soviet enterprises located in the Soviet Union's extreme geographic locations. Many of the camps were in virtually uninhabitable parts of the Soviet Union. Nonetheless, from the early 1930s central camp authorities continually stressed the need to recruit qualified employees into the camp system—"firm Chekists, voluntarily choosing to work [in the camps.]" A number of incentives were given to recruits, including bonus pay of up to 50 percent depending on the location of their camp work, two months of yearly vacation, and the possibility after a three-year period of working in the camps to transfer to "operative" work in the location of their choice.[78] Petrov reported a conversation with a camp guard about recruitment techniques:

> During their service in the Red Army all soldiers were constantly under observation. . . . Toward the end of their army tenure the most [politically] reliable of the men were transferred to the N.K.V.D. troops of internal defence. Here they were offered higher pay and numerous privileges to make them sign up with the N.K.V.D. on a voluntary basis for a period of from three to five years, or for permanent duty. Many soldiers were tempted by these offers. . . . Those

who volunteered for this service were usually men not well adapted to normal working life because they were not too bright, lacked professional skills, or preferred an easy life. As guards in our camps they really did have a pretty easy time of it. They were not bothered with drill, their duty hours were usually short—on the average not more than four or five per day—and they were excellently fed. They had little to complain about.[79]

Petrov's description of the incentives conforms with official documents, but his portrait of the Kolyma camp guard's duty as easy seems unlikely to say the least. Even working short hours would have been little comfort given the extreme climatic conditions of Kolyma. Granted, Kolyma guards were immeasurably better off than their prisoner wards. Still, moving about in Kolyma weather with prisoners was no light matter, especially considering the harsh punishment that could result from a single prisoner escape. The same can be said of Karlag (and many other Gulag camps), where harsh winter winds, extreme blizzards, soaring summer temperatures, and the existence of many prisoners outside the camp zones made their work particularly difficult. Without question, the brutalities of life as a guard contributed to the brutalities carried out by guards on prisoners.

As with the prisoners themselves, and as was common at any job in the Soviet 1930s, Gulag authorities implemented a comprehensive program of political education and morale building among their employees. Every camp had its own political department (*politotdel*) composed primarily of Communist Party and Komsomol members who oversaw educational work among camp staff and guards. Such educational work took several directions. First, political education sought to raise feelings of pride at being Chekists. Each year's December 20 anniversary of the Cheka's 1917 formation (the first Soviet secret police agency) was widely celebrated in the Gulag. Speeches and events reminded camp employees and guards of the glorious history of the VChK-OGPU-NKVD, "the weapon of the proletarian dictatorship."[80] The October Revolution, camp employees were reminded, was not—and could not be—the final and decisive blow in the battle with the ruling classes. The role of the Chekist was in armed defense of the proletarian dictatorship from the forces of internal and international counterrevolution. The camp system's political department took this opportunity to emphasize repeatedly that the OGPU was a fighting organ, engaged in pitched battle with the remaining elements of capitalism that resisted the final construction of a classless society.[81]

Educational activities among camp staff and guard always focused on their role in the Soviet battle with its enemies. Gulag employees were on the front lines of this particular fight and were reminded repeatedly of the danger to Soviet society that their prisoners presented. Gulag authorities tried repeatedly to raise fear, suspicion, and hatred of the prisoners. Whenever incidents of prisoner resistance occurred, especially incidents involving the killing or wounding of guards or staff, central Gulag authorities made sure to send out a description of the events to all Gulag camps, with instructions that all Gulag employees be made aware of the incident.[82]

This type of propaganda could be quite effective. Petrov recalls the guards in Kolyma:

> A considerable percentage of these guards were members of the Young Communist League, wholly convinced that their happy life was possible only because of the Soviet government. They were therefore most ready to defend that government from the disarmed and helpless "enemies of the people" who were held in concentration camps. In fact, they were systematically indoctrinated with the idea that camp inhabitants were all dangerous criminals whom one could treat like the scum of the earth with complete impunity. . . . Instances of guards using their fists on the slightest provocation were becoming more and more frequent.[83]

Even more intriguing is a letter sent on March 4, 1964, from an anonymous correspondent to the Central Committee about Solzhenitsyn's *One Day in the Life of Ivan Denisovich*. The author, a fifteen-year employee of a postwar labor camp and a party member, took considerable exception with a number of elements in Solzhenitsyn's portrait of camp life. While the author's comments in some ways relate to particularities of the postwar Gulag, they offer here testimony to the power of official propaganda on many Gulag employees. Although the Gulag employee for the most part believed that Solzhenitsyn was correct in his presentations of daily life in the camps, he was especially displeased with the notion that the novella's katorga camp division was filled with "innocent and very good people." If only innocent people were imprisoned there, he asked, "then where did they send the genuine enemies of Soviet power like the Vlasovites, the Banderites, the police and the Bandits of the [Baltic] military-fascist organizations," and so on. Not a word of Solzhenitsyn's tale, he complained, revealed the "frightful crimes" committed by these enemies.[84]

As to daily life, the anonymous correspondent objected to Solzhenitsyn's characterizations of the camp's internal surveillance system, especially his references to informants as "stoolies" (*stukachi*) and "bitches" (*suki*). Surveillance work in camps for the especially dangerous prisoners "had an especially important significance—the eyes and ears of the camp leadership. It was assigned to the timely discovery and prevention of all criminal activities in the camp . . . [with] special attention paid to preventing escapes, criminal-bandit activities, murders, bribery, beatings of prisoners and so forth." The camp leadership recruited prisoners into service as informers as part of the attempt to make them into good Soviet citizens to "influence them to turn their back on their criminal past and honestly complete their sentence in the camp. (Those who declared that they were wrongly convicted, as is right, were not recruited.)" The absence of informants, he concluded, would have brought the camp to a state of "anarchy."[85]

Although Gulag propaganda constantly focused on the redeemability of its prisoner population, a counternarrative accompanied this message. It spoke of a highly dangerous prisoner population composed of enemies bent on the destruction of the socialism that the entire Soviet Union was engaged in constructing. Local camp authorities, and especially the guards most directly in contact with the prisoners and with this counternarrative, dealt with these mixed messages, and consequently often treated their prisoners with the complete disregard of the subhuman.

In spite of all the propaganda and punishments aimed at discouraging close contact between guards and prisoners, both memoirs and official documents attest to the inability of Gulag authorities to prevent these relationships. Camp employees drank with prisoners, engaged in surreptitious transactions with prisoners, took on female prisoners as lovers and domestic servants, and otherwise took part in illicit activities from the point of view of central Gulag officials. Despite frequent attempts to end these practices, they continued throughout the history of the camp system, not least because many of the guards and administrators in the camps were prisoners and former prisoners.[86] Furthermore, on their own volition, Gulag authorities often chose to behave with kindness toward their prisoners, without regard to material gain. The guard-prisoner relationship was nonetheless typically one of barbarous cruelty. Camp officials were more likely to reward than to punish a guard for shooting a prisoner "attempting to escape."[87] Lengthy reports detail incidents in which guards shot prisoners, usually with the short conclusion to each that "weapons were used properly."[88]

Due to the difficulties in recruiting staff and guards, former prisoners usually filled many of the voluntary positions in camps. Of course, for many former prisoners, the level of voluntariness in staying on as employees of the camp was questionable at best. Many released prisoners were refused permission to return to their homes, generally with notations of a certain number of cities in which they could not live. This dramatically reduced their freedom of movement and left them the option of taking work in the camp system, which they knew, or moving to a location where they had no contacts whatsoever. The developing camp system took advantage of this precarious position. Thus, in December 1930 Arkadii Vasil'evich Orlov-Rumiantsev was dispatched to the concentration camp centered in Akmolinsk (presently Astana, the capital of independent Kazakhstan) to work in the accounting department. Orlov-Rumiantsev had spent 1926–28 as a prisoner in the Solovetskii camp for illegally crossing a border. He was released early for a positive attitude toward labor and discipline, but due to his conviction was denied permission to live in Moscow, Leningrad, Khar'kov, Kiev, Odessa, Rostov on the Don, or near any borders. Consequently, he had agreed to work for the OGPU's camp system.[89]

It was not just former prisoners, though, who held positions in the camp administration. Throughout the history of the Gulag, certain prisoners themselves worked in various administrative, supervisory, and even security roles in the camps. The chief of the OGPU camp system Kogan noted in a letter from April 1931 to all OGPU camp chiefs that difficulties in filling staff positions had led them to employ "prisoners not sentenced for counterrevolutionary crimes" as lower camp administrative staff and armed camp guards. He was concerned, however, about providing the proper "stimulus for correction and excellent work" of these prisoners who had been removed from general work. As a result, then deputy OGPU chief Genrikh Iagoda ordered that for "absolutely faultless behavior and outstanding work," prisoners in these positions could earn a reduction of their sentences by one-third. Prisoners qualifying for this sentence reduction could petition the central Gulag authorities for early release.[90] Subsequent correspondence between central Gulag authorities and Kazitlag reveal that counterrevolutionary prisoners were also being employed in such positions, but they were ineligible for early release.[91]

The issue of counterrevolutionary prisoners working in the camp administration or guard was a long saga. The camps were driven by the competing demands of filling the posts necessary to complete their work and preventing enemies from working in sensitive positions. The task was all the more difficult, because often it was precisely the counterrevolutionary prisoners who had the necessary education, training, or skills to complete certain camp tasks. Counterrevolutionary prisoners served their camps as bookkeepers, engineers, draftspeople, and doctors. Yet it was their employment in the camp guard that caused officials the greatest consternation. In November 1930, Kazitlag authorities complained of guards employed from among prisoners "politically alien to the contemporary order . . . kulaks and those sentenced for banditism and under counterrevolutionary articles." The decree demanded an immediate purge of the guard staff to remove such people.[92] In 1931, Kazitlag authorities ordered that a prisoner with an improper class background be removed from the guard at Dolinka.[93] The problem of cleansing the administration and guard of certain types of prisoners was never solved, nor did the necessity of employing some prisoners in sensitive positions ever come to an end. On January 1, 1939, fully twenty-five thousand "well-recommended prisoners" continued to be employed as camp guards.[94]

## Surveillance and Escapes in the Gulag

In the camps, prisoners were quickly made to understand that they would be strictly monitored throughout their stay in the Gulag. From their arrival into the Gulag system, prisoners were subject to intentional humiliation, the destruction of all private space, and the assertion of total state control over their lives. Not even the body was a private domain. As Margarete Buber-Neumann, a prisoner at Karlag, recalled of her time in prison prior to arriving in the camps: "A bodily search at the Lubianka is the thing to let you know to the full what being a prisoner means; not even the most intimate parts of your body are any longer decently your own; you are no longer a human being; you are a thing, an object to be mauled unceremoniously."[95]

Modern prison systems were built based on the ideal of the panopticon. That is, they were specifically constructed in such a way that all prisoner cells were visible to guards and prison authorities at all times.[96] The concentration camp was something quite different, built on the model of a military encampment. Watchtowers on the corners of a concentration camp facility offered a clear sight line of a camp's perimeter and some visibility of the interior of a camp's zone. The typical zone, though, had barracks and other buildings within its walls that provided interior spaces invisible to the prying eyes of the state. In the historical development of the concentration camp, such a system made sense. The camps of the South African Anglo-Boer War were not designed as a penal system but instead were holding pens for the rural populations that were supporting the irregular Boer resistance. British colonial authorities did not care much about what happened inside these camps, so long as their prisoners stayed there. So the concentration camp setup, with its capacity to prevent escape, worked for these needs.

The Gulag was something different. It was both a concentration camp and penal system, and Soviet authorities cared deeply about what was going on inside the barbed wire and the minds of the prisoners themselves. Consequently, the camp system developed an extensive system of internal surveillance primarily operating through prisoner informants in order to keep track of things inside the camp. The system of surveillance is perhaps one of the most interesting and telling practices of the Gulag. Why was it necessary to fund a broad system of surveillance in the deepest reaches of the Gulag, where escape was rare and surviving escape was nearly impossible? Surveillance was ubiquitous in the Gulag. From their interrogation cell to their prisoner transports, and ultimately to their labor camp or special settlements, Gulag inmates were subject to constant and intense surveillance. While informants were especially important for revealing escape plans and attempts, they also reported on outbreaks of disease and supplied the material for reports on the camp population's mood.[97]

A large surveillance apparatus operated inside the Gulag. Officially referred to as the Operative-Chekist Department or Third Department, we know much about surveillance and informants from the memoir literature. The Gulag's surveillance system, however, remains the primary off-limits topic in terms of access to archival documentation.[98] Nonetheless, a great deal can be learned about surveillance from the hints in publicly available documents. First, the top priority in the Third Department's work was the prevention of escape. Second, it is quite clear that the Third Department, the surveillance section, was responsible for monitoring both camp inmates and employees. The main interest of the Third Department as related to camp employees was the maintenance of vigilance against escape, and the prevention of ties between prisoners and guards or other staff that might lead to escapes, theft of camp property, or other violations of camp rules. Thus, the Third Department of the Samarskoe subdivision was criticized severely in May 1934 by Karlag's Third Division director for its failure to prevent multiple escapes or recover the escaping inmates. Its battle against escape, alleged the director, was fake and existed "only on paper." Where, he asked, was its claimed "strong" network of informants or "multi-member" action group for liquidating escapes that had singularly failed to prevent "a colossal number of escapes"—one-quarter of all escapes in Karlag?[99]

Gulag guards knew that they could be quite severely punished if escapes occurred. In the Stalinist Soviet Union, everything was treated as political. Machines did not just break; industrial accidents were no accident. Every negative occurrence could potentially be treated as an instance of criminal sabotage, and many Gulag inmates arrived in just such a way. Bardach, for example, was a Red Army tank driver during the war. He accidentally rolled the tank during a river crossing and found himself soon in Kolyma on charges of "wartime treason." In such an atmosphere, the escape of an enemy from the clutches of the Gulag was always treated as potentially treasonous, and could lead to criminal punishment for the guards and camp authorities responsible for preventing escape. Nobody in Soviet society was inherently trustworthy.[100] An escape could mean that the guards and administrators were part of, or sympathetic to, the anti-Soviet activities and conspiracies that were imagined to be everywhere. For this reason and because of the constant barrage of propaganda that taught Gulag employees that they were guarding extremely dangerous anti-Soviet people, guards often reacted quite brutally to escape attempts. Bardach recalled the guards' words after recapturing him from an attempted escape from a prisoner train during the war.

> "I think we need to teach the *ze-ka* [prisoner] a lesson so no one else tries to escape. Let's bloody him up and parade him in front of the prisoners."
> . . . "You don't need to kill him. Just make it so he'll never want to fuck again."
> "You fucking slime!" A belt buckle smashed across my stomach.
> "Give me the belt! I'll castrate him for life."
> "Smash his balls."
> "Beat his face to a pulp!"
> . . . The buckle smashed across my ribs and abdomen again and again.

After the guards beat Bardach severely, the commander ordered them to show his beaten and bleeding body to the other prisoners as a warning of what might happen to future escapees.[101]

Weak surveillance work and a failure to recruit enough prisoner informants were frequently offered as the main cause of excessive escapes.[102] Preventing escape was objectively one of the Gulag's greatest success stories, even if camp authorities were never satisfied. While significant numbers of prisoners managed to escape in each year of the 1930s, once the Gulag system had passed through its initial growth phase, escape began a steady decline. From an all-time high of over 83,000 escapes in 1934, escape totals decreased, even as the prisoner population continued to grow. By 1939, escapes were a relatively rare occurrence, never again exceeding 12,500 in any particular year, even as the population of the Gulag swelled in the postwar period to its highest levels. In fact, through the years 1944–53, escapes never exceeded 4,500—a minuscule portion of the Gulag population.[103] For camp authorities, though, these escape totals were still much too high. Central Gulag officials clearly expected that escapes should reach zero. Even one escape was evidence of a failure on the part of camp staff, guards, and surveillance personnel. Consequently, the decrease in escapes entailed no reduction in surveillance or camp guards.[104]

Punishment for escapes, like so much else in Gulag practice, was a differentiated affair. Certain types of prisoners were understood as the most dangerous, and their attempts to escape would be punished most severely. While all escapes were treated as "the most malicious form of sabotage and disorganization of camp life and production," and all escapees after 1939 were subject to criminal penalties, for a select group of prisoners, the penalty was to be death. This included the usual contingent of the "most dangerous" inmates: "counterrevolutionaries, bandits, robbers and other especially dangerous criminals along with prisoners of other categories, who have escaped repeatedly."[105]

Karlag officials relied on their camp's particularities as an agricultural enterprise as an excuse for their escape figures. With the dispersed nature of the camp population, it was simply impossible, they argued, to string enough barbed wire to reduce escape numbers to zero. Yet no matter how often Karlag authorities complained to central Gulag about the specificities of their camp, severe criticism continued, and the primary blame for escape was placed on a lack of vigilance, discipline, and appropriate education for the responsible parties from the camp chief down to the individual members of the militarized guard.[106]

The surveillance system was tasked with providing that discipline among camp employees. Their operatives monitored, policed, and punished the camp administration and guards. Violations of discipline were rife among camp staff. Drinking, sleeping on duty, and cavorting with prisoners—the violations were many and varied. Occasionally, the brutal actions of camp staff and guards were actually brought to light by prisoners. A Karlag report from October 1933 related the investigation of "criminal violations of corrective labor policies" in Koturskoe subdivision's camp point Sasykul'. Prisoner witnesses and a Third Department investigation revealed several instances of brutal treatment of prisoners refusing to work. One time, a cord was used to tie several of these prisoners' hands behind their back and bind them to one another. They were displayed to other prisoners as an example and only released when they asked to go to work. In another situation, three prisoners had their hands and feet bound with cord, and were tossed out into the cold weather, where they were left for three hours until the pain became so great that they agreed to go to work in exchange for being untied. Other camp subdivisions were warned not to repeat such actions.[107] It is unclear whether such practices actually stopped after the Third Department's intervention. But even if this particular brutality was ended, no doubt it was simply replaced by the many other cruelties of Gulag life. Still, on this one occasion, the surveillance apparatus operated in favor of the prisoners.

Unsurprisingly, the surveillance apparatus was much more likely to cause trouble for prisoners than to help them. The authorities had eyes seemingly everywhere, reading prisoner correspondence, listening to prisoner conversations, and watching prisoner activities. The labor camp inmate did not know who was an informant, so everybody was suspect—a factor creating great rifts and distrust in Gulag society. In spite of the overwhelming presence of surveillance in the Gulag, however, the layout of a concentration camp differed markedly from the prison panopticon. On the one hand, the system of anonymous informants left substantially less private space for the prisoner. No matter how close a prisoner became with one of their fellow unfortunates, they could never be absolutely certain that they were not in the presence of an informer. The Gulag represented, par excellence, what Arendt termed a "system of ubiquitous spying, where everybody may be a police agent and each individual feels himself under constant surveillance."[108] At the same time, not every prisoner was an informer. Every personal interaction inside a concentration camp was potentially under the watchful eyes of the surveillance apparatus, but not every personal interaction was under actual surveillance. The concentration camp itself—the massing of large numbers of prisoners who were relatively free to move about within the camp zone during non-working hours—left great potential for unwatched spaces. The existence of these uncontrolled spaces was a source of enormous discomfort for camp authorities, and explains to a large extent the constant growth of the surveillance apparatus in regions where escapes were unlikely and the capacity of prisoners to harm Soviet society was extremely limited.

## Reforging: The Meaning of Reeducation in the Gulag

> Socialism is creeping in everywhere around you, and even within you.
> —*Belomor*, describing the feeling to be engendered in the wayward prisoner by the Cultural-Educational Section's permeation of the entire camp space with socialism

Hand in hand with the corrective elements of labor came the didactic work of the KVCh. All camps and colonies operated a KVCh subordinate to both their individual camp leadership and the central Gulag Cultural-Educational Department. In 1931, Gulag chief Kogan wrote to Kazitlag about the cultural-educational and political work of the camps. These tasks, he noted, have two goals: "a) to achieve full class stratification of the prisoners and with the help of the strata socially close to us to carry out the necessary measures, and b) to correct and politically educate the socially close element."[109] From the Gulag's early days, then, Kogan laid out the fundamentals of "reeducation" Gulag style. Reeducation would be a high-priority activity for the camps, but it would be carried out in a differentiated fashion. Not all were redeemable. Educational work, furthermore, would "achieve full class stratification of the prisoners"—that is, it would play an integral role in the very definition of who was redeemable and who was not.

The primary job of the Gulag's educational workers, as described by Karlag authorities in 1935, was "the reforging of former lawbreakers in the matter of returning to socialist society former socially dangerous people as enthusiasts for socialist construction."[110] Regardless of the exact terminology used, the matter was always the same. Fundamentally, educational workers were responsible for reeducating those Gulag prisoners who could be made fit for a return to Soviet society. Two particularly important elements arise from this basic premise. First, prisoners could be made to return to Soviet society by using the same political drives launched in Soviet society itself. Thus, both consciously and unconsciously, the educational workers of the Gulag were re-creating Soviet society inside the labor camps. Second, educational workers spent much more effort on those prisoners deemed of high potential to earn their way back to Soviet society and repeatedly took actions limiting the access of the most suspect prisoners to educational activities. Educational activities in the Gulag were never uniform. They always served to further distinguish prisoners from one another.

Economic production was itself always a high concern of cultural-educational work. Many students of the Gulag have naturally focused on this to argue that the educational apparatus was merely a propaganda show designed to exhort prisoners to work harder. Without question, KVCh documents reveal repeatedly the institution's responsibility for labor productivity, but this was always tied to the task of reforging criminals. The two activities were understood as inseparable, because the improvement of economic production, like every other qualitative issue of Soviet life, was understood in an incredibly political and ideological manner. In some respect, the call to improve labor production was an integral part of the Gulag's mandate to create honest Soviet citizens of its criminal inmates. After all, what was a better indication of full involvement in Soviet society than being a productive laborer?

The camp system spent a lot of resources on educational activities. Nonetheless, great cynicism frequently surrounded the project, which is unsurprising given the brutal conditions in the Gulag that reduced prisoners to subhuman conditions and the constant calls for vigilance in watching over allegedly highly dangerous populations. Individual chiefs of camps and camp subdivisions were usually reluctant to commit the resources necessary for cultural-educational activity. They perceived the rather-vague activities of remaking prisoners to be a waste of resources, time, and staff in the face of more concrete economic targets. Cultural-educational activities required the provision of such frequently scarce items as paper, ink, and prisoner laborers. As with nearly every other demand placed on them by central Gulag authorities, Karlag officials relied on the camp's agricultural particularities to explain the difficulty in carrying out educational work with their prisoners. The dispersed, unconcentrated character of Karlag's prisoner population made the provision of classes and cultural activities a difficult question of logistics and personnel. Only during the winter period did a substantial number of prisoners attend literacy classes.[111] Despite their recurrent and justified protests, Karlag's authorities were never released from their duty to complete these crucial Gulag tasks.

The failure to pay adequate attention to educational work itself could result in severe criticism from higher levels. In fact, failure in the economic sphere was laid primarily at the doorstep of poor cultural-educational work. Central camp authorities often complained of the "great divide" between cultural education and production, when they should be closely coordinated with one another.[112] Such complaints persisted throughout the Gulag's life span. Much as the repetitive documentary warnings about shortcomings in living conditions in the camps failed to lead to significant improvements, little evidence indicates that the constant barrage of directives on educational activities had much impact, except to the extent that they prevented the abandonment of educational activity in its entirety. Educational work was uneven in the camps. The memoir literature reveals the wide range in cultural and educational activities in the camps. Some places at some times took the whole operation quite seriously, but it was just as often ignored or at least shunted off to the margins of camp activity.

One should certainly be careful not to make too much of the "educational" apparatus of the Gulag. It was, at most, a rather marginal activity, pushed on to the few nonworking hours of the day. Yet the KVCh did operate throughout the history of the camps.[113] To focus solely on the indoctrination apparatus itself, though, fails to appreciate the role in Bolshevik ideology accorded to labor itself. Furthermore, one must understand the tie between reeducation and release in the camps—a feature discussed in more detail below. Without understanding educational activities, labor, and release/death all in conjunction with one another, the system can never be explained.[114]

A great deal can be learned about the ongoing redefinition of "honest Soviet citizens" from the particular methods and content chosen in this effort to educate criminals into that very ideal. The KVCh's activities along with the Soviet vision of its ideal citizen were both tied first and foremost to labor. The work of the KVCh appeared everywhere in the camps driving prisoners toward a new version of themselves. KVCh posters at the Solovetskii camp declared, "Through work we shall return to society" and "Work redeems guilt." And in the theater, signs stated, "Work without art is barbarity."[115] The slogan above the camp gate at Vorkuta read, "Welcome! We greet you with bread and salt. By honest work we will give coal to our country."[116] Labor was frequently tied to the international context. Thus in 1930, the Solovetskii camp newspaper declared that events on the Chinese Oriental Railway "evoked the

just indignation of the Solovetskii inmates. . . . [H]undreds of convicts .
. . signed a collective appeal for permission to organize a Shock-Labour
Day."[117]

Most important, the KVCh proclaimed, "A prisoner is an active participant in socialist construction!"[118] To prepare the prisoner adequately
for reintegration into the Soviet polity, the Gulag participated fully in the
broad range of labor productivity programs during the period of socialist
construction. In the early 1930s, Gulag camps actively engaged in socialist competition and the shock worker movement.[119] Karlag attributed its
own early successes to the personal visit of Gulag chief Matvei Berman in
1931 and his urging of prisoners to work as "shock workers," and as such
"to start decisively on the path of reforging and to try with all their force
to make right their guilt before Soviet power."[120] The corrective labor
colony of Magnitogorsk held a number of shock worker conferences,
complete with orchestra and group renditions of the "Internationale."[121]

The title shock worker entailed far more than mere labor productivity.
Solzhenitsyn recalled the rhetoric on the Belomor Canal: "In order to get
the title of shock worker it was not enough merely to have production
successes! It was necessary, in addition: (a) to read the newspapers; (b) *to
love your canal*; (c) to be able to talk about its significance." The shock
worker had to be politically educated, understand the importance of their
work, and carry the appropriate attitude toward their labor.[122] *Belomor*
depicted the unredeemed convict as typified by a lack of interest in and
pessimism about the canal. Consequently, the prisoner was unable and
unwilling to fulfill the norms. Only the inculcation of a spirit of optimism
and interest in the canal allowed the individual to undergo the requisite
transformation allowing them to perform in excess of the norm, form a
brigade, and teach the brigade to overfulfill the norm. Consider the story
of Engineer V. N. Maslov, who "had no faith whatsoever in the possibility
of creating an immense canal. . . . He was willing to place at the disposal
of these people his knowledge and his brains, but no more. Not a single
emotion. Not a single smile." But ultimately, Maslov solved unsolvable
engineering problems and became "convinced of the advantages of Socialist organisation of labour." He was released early, but continued to
work on the project, earning the Order of the Red Banner. Such stories
are repeated endlessly in *Belomor* and became the motif for all redemption tales told in the Gulag.[123]

After Aleksei Stakhanov kicked off the movement that would bear his
name by producing record levels of coal in the Donbass on August 31,
1935, the Stakhanovite quest for production records predictably made its
way to the Gulag.[124] In November 1935, the Magnitogorsk labor colony
held its own Stakhanovite conference.[125] As in Soviet society, however, the
Stakhanovite movement often prompted resistance from officials, who

recognized the false nature of Stakhanovite records. Often, an entire enterprise saw its work interrupted to prepare the conditions for a single worker to break a record. Local officials and managers also recognized that Stakhanovite records usually merely paved the way for an overall increase in production targets, merely making it more difficult for an enterprise to meet its production plans. Local Soviet economic enterprises understood the Stakhanovite movement as more about putting on a political show than increasing overall economic productivity. The same ambivalence toward Stakhanovism was evident in local Gulag outposts as well—perhaps even more so. Enthusiasm for prisoner production achievements and reeducation was particularly difficult to maintain in the face of the barrage of propaganda reminding camp staff that they were guarding dangerous enemies of the Soviet state. Thus, it was unsurprising to find Karlag officials complain in March 1936 about the "absence of necessary care and attention for STAKHANOVITES and SHOCK WORKERS, not to mention rank-and-file inmates" in the establishment of normal living conditions—problems that were undermining camp productivity and increasing the number of prisoners refusing to work.[126]

Issues of the newspaper *Putevka* (*Path*), a production of Karlag's KVCh, were filled with articles on labor heroism among the prisoners, shock workers, and Stakhanovite movement. These articles frequently represented the close tie between prisoner attitudes and production. One article on how to bring the Stakhanovite movement into animal husbandry in the camp was titled "Mainly—This Is to Love Your Work."[127] In another issue, the record-setting prisoner miner Senkul Kurmanbaev succeeded in part because "he loved the mine and his work." So when he learned of the Stakhanovite movement, he immediately agreed to work by these methods and completed 677 percent of his daily quota on his big day. The article came complete with a line drawing of Kurmanbaev.[128] Other articles covering the Stakhanovite movement called for an "exchange of experience," explained the operation of the "Stakhanovite cafeteria," a special facility providing enhanced food rations to the Stakhanovite prisoner, and included prisoner-written pieces such as "How I Became a Stakhanovite."[129]

The work of the KVCh was not limited to labor campaigns alone. The KVCh led the types of cultural activities common throughout Soviet society. They supervised the Gulag's participation in the nationwide campaign to stamp out illiteracy.[130] Radio loudspeakers filled every barrack with the sounds and educational messages of Radio Moscow.[131] The KVChs sponsored political lectures, professional and technical training courses, and oral readings of newspapers.[132] Barracks and camp workplaces were festooned with slogans, photographs, and illustrations, similar to what one would find in Soviet society at large.[133]

Camps usually published their own newspapers.[134] As early as the 1920s, the Solovetskii camp published its own newspaper and journal, and made subscriptions available to the general public.[135] By the 1930s, camp newspapers were marked for camp use only, but they continued to occupy significant camp resources.[136] In March 1937, Karlag's administration celebrated the fifth anniversary of the general camp newspaper, *Putevka*. The paper's circulation had grown to 6,500, and it oversaw the production of 202 wall newspapers as well as the distribution of camp bulletins and flyers. The tasks of the paper over that period included "the cultivation of the new man, reforging of his consciousness, familiarizing with labor the hundreds of delinquents who had never known what labor meant and who had lost the proper path in life.... Together with the masses and at their head, *Putevka* stormed the half-wild Kazakh steppe, transforming this region of the fearless bird into a blossoming oasis of Kazakhstan's socialist agriculture."[137] The title of the newspaper, *Putevka*, evoked the famous Soviet film *Putevka v zhizn* (*The Path to Life*, sometimes in English as *The Road to Life*), which depicted the reeducation of juvenile delinquents.

Although they happily celebrated the newspaper's anniversaries, Karlag authorities were at best ambivalent about bringing camp newspapers to their prisoners. With the expansive nature of Karlag, merely getting newspapers to the prisoners could prove to be such a hassle that camp staff resisted assigning resources to distribution. This was equally as true of papers from outside the camps like *Pravda* and *Izvestiia*, which were supposed to be made available to prisoners, as it was for papers produced in the camps. In some cases, prisoners working in the KVCh were hoarding the newspapers to trade or sell for such uses as cigarette wrappers.[138] Yet it should be emphasized that Karlag did not abandon the production and distribution of newspapers entirely, despite its drain on scarce material and human resources.

The issues of *Putevka* covered a wide variety of production topics and carefully prepared stories about life in the camp. Many articles in *Putevka* could sit just as easily in the pages of *Belomor*. For example, on December 24, 1936, *Putevka* printed an article on its front page titled "My Thanks to the Chekists." Presumably written by a prisoner named Krasil'shchinov, the article told the story of the author's trip from a hardened thief who continuously refused to work in the camps and spent all his time in penalty isolators, to a model prisoner who was trusted to work without convoy guards and was appointed a brigade leader. Ultimately, wrote Krasil'shchinov, he enrolled in specialist training in Karlag to become a technician in sheep breeding. Although the course work was difficult, and in frustration he began showing up late for classes or skipping them, plus returning to his old ways, because of the "attention and care" of the teachers, Krasil'shchinov corrected himself and started to learn well. As a result, he was working in the camp in sheep breeding and emoted, "I love my work and I love labor." He wrote to thank the camp administration and teachers for helping him become a man, and declared that he would never return to the thieving life.[139] Of course, just as with the stories in *Belomor*, it is impossible to evaluate the truthfulness of this one, but it is important for the picture it reveals of the ideal reeducated inmate.

Not all articles in *Putevka* emphasized positive outcomes. The newspaper was filled with criticisms of prisoners and the camp administration. Sometimes, *Putevka* included caricatures of prisoners who failed in their work. One drawing was based on the reporting of a *lagkor* (a camp correspondent—essentially prisoners who wrote from their local subdivisions to the camp newspaper with critiques of problems in the camp). The lagkor portrayed a prisoner who completely ignored his fifty-nine head of sheep, failing to feed or water them for over a day. The drawing showed a prisoner walking away from bleating sheep, sticking his tongue out at them. A short poem underneath furthered the criticism.[140] Lagkory could also criticize camp authorities themselves. One wrote about the refusal of the camp subdivision director to take them to the baths for over three months. Another complained that prisoners were freezing, because the barracks were unheated, while in other barracks prisoners completely lacked bunks and had to sleep on the floor.[141] At times, the lagkory signed their letters to the newspaper, but others came from "a witness" or with just a single letter for a name.

*Putevka* also included articles on topics related to events happening outside the camp, whether locally or internationally. Thus, one issue that had numerous articles on the Stakhanovite movement in Karlag also included articles on the opening of a highway between Karaganda and Balkash—a development that would allow Karaganda's coal to be used in a much wider sphere. Further, articles appeared on the opening to the public of an apartment in which Lenin lived in Pskov and the Italian-Abyssinian War.[142] Through these articles, frequently republished from other organs of the Soviet press, the camps sought to include their prisoners in the general political atmosphere of Soviet society.

The KVChs also prepared wall newspapers throughout the Gulag to publicize the exploits of a camp's most productive prisoners and cast shame on its worst. In fact, the KVChs made wide use of shame in their attempts to transform prisoners. The KVCh loudspeakers would wake the prisoners to the disdainful sounds of "Shame on the loafers!" followed by a listing of the lagging workers.[143] Along with the portraits of shock workers and the reforged, the KVCh would hang caricatures of the slackers on wall newspapers, with one such image depicting "a disheveled man with angrily bared teeth; next to him is a bourgeois, with a gold chain across his waistcoat. Under the disheveled man is an inscription: 'Fyodor Zhigalov is a traitor to the workers.'" Zhigalov wrote a letter to the camp newspaper declaring, "And when I saw myself this morning drawn arm-in-arm with a capitalist, and it was written underneath that we both work together with the class enemy, then I understood that I was really a class enemy. . . . I'm ashamed that I wanted to stop the construction, and that I'm a class enemy of the Soviet Government."[144]

Many labor camps, again starting with the Solovetskii camp, also operated their own theater groups, orchestras, and folk music ensembles. Many of the so-called cultural brigades offered a wide range of performances. Access to camp entertainment from the 1920s' Solovetskii camp was reserved for camp officials and those prisoners holding privileged positions—the same prisoners who by cooperating with camp authorities or other powerful prisoners garnered better access to food, clothing, living space, and other commodities of camp life.[145] Ginzburg described the cultural brigade as "a serf theater that staged shows for the camp officials who were bored in those provincial backwaters." Only a few prisoners "selected from the trusties and shock workers were allowed into the back rows."[146]

While prisoners were typically subjected to every educational and political campaign that occurred in Soviet society as a whole, a few propaganda practices were deemed too risky in camps. For example, a November 28, 1931, OGPU Gulag circular sent to Karlag ordered "comrade courts" in concentration camps dissolved. Comrade courts had been created by a Russian Soviet Federative Socialist Republic (RSFSR) state decree of February 20, 1931. By November, they had only made an appearance in a few camps, and then without the express sanction of central camp authorities. Clearly, practice had already revealed to these local camps that a propaganda campaign outside the camps should be immediately introduced in the camps. In this case, they were wrong, and they were warned that the introduction of new practices in the future should be preauthorized. No specific reason for the decision was given, but one suspects that Gulag authorities were cautious about handing prisoners the type of authority that came with punishing their fellow inmates. Still, they were concerned with "the organization of the social opinion of the socially close strata against the violators [of camp discipline]." They felt that the appropriate means included the more easily controlled media of the camp press, wall newspapers, brigade meetings, reading, and explaining camp decrees at roll calls as well as through other forms of cultural-educational work.[147]

The distinctions between camp propaganda work and the general Soviet experience comes into particularly sharp relief during major state holidays. In the camps, holidays like the anniversary of the October Revolution were a cause of great uneasiness. It was on such days that camp authorities most feared their prisoners. Consequently, restrictions on prisoners were typically ramped up around holidays. For example, in late October 1937, Karlag's chief issued an order on preparations for the coming celebration of the revolution's twentieth anniversary. From November 5 to 9, all movement of prisoners inside and between camp subdivisions was forbidden. Camp supply chiefs and subdivision chiefs were ordered to ensure proper food and fuel supplies so that no trips beyond the camp's boundaries would be necessary during the holiday period. From November 6 to 8, in several of the camp's subdivisions located in greater proximity to free populations, no prisoner was allowed to go beyond the barbed wire at all, with only a few exceptions for those required to run the camp's priority facilities like its electric station. Any prisoner found during this period on the streets of Dolinka without a special pass (all regular passes were void during the holiday period) was immediately placed in a prison cell. Finally, all prisoner visits with relatives were suspended from November 1 to 10.[148]

Prisoners also recall the uneasiness around holidays. Petrov remembers preparations in Kolyma for the first elections to the USSR Supreme Soviet in 1937. On the one hand, prisoners were allowed or even required to participate. "The free employees held meetings, organized election districts, painted placards and slogans. Incidentally, the entire technical work of these preparations was done by prisoners—carpenters, joiners, painters, artists, etc." Election day itself was another matter. "On special instructions directly from the new N.K.V.D. head, Yezhov, a reinforced military guard was thrown around all the camps, ostensibly in order to prevent anti-Soviet demonstrations. I remained free along with several workers, since it was necessary to set up a festive illumination on the roof of every village house.... [T]he official government candidate received twelve more votes than there were voters in Kolyma."[149]

Did the prisoners buy into all of this educational activity? Were they in fact reformed? These questions are not so easily answered. On the one hand, living through an extreme experience like the Soviet concentration camp changed everybody. That change, however, did not necessarily correspond to the theories behind the KVChs' work. Prisoners did quickly learn to at least mouth the language of redemption. Perhaps this was all that was required. In Kotkin's memorable formulation, it was not necessary that Soviet citizens believed, only that they acted as if they did so. Labor colony inmates at Magnitogorsk repeatedly professed their own transformations "in language strikingly reminiscent of what could be heard from accomplished workers outside the colony: they were laboring, studying, making sacrifices, and trying to better themselves." Yet at the same time they continued to express openly their sentiment against the Soviet regime, and in spite of shock worker conferences and the Stakhanovite movement, absences, disorganization, drunkenness, and feigned illnesses remained rampant among Magnitogorsk's labor colony population.[150]

It would be quite an understatement to say that many prisoners were skeptical of the Soviet government's seriousness about reeducation in the harsh environs of the Gulag. Petrov recounts his arrival off a ship at Kolyma:

> Standing at the broadside I saw a small open space on the shore being quickly cleared of boxed-up merchandise and filled with a crowd of guards who had just arrived in automobiles. Some of them held dogs on leashes—big, well-fed sheep dogs.
>
> A gangway was laid directly to the shore and an empty barrel was set at its upper end by the gate. Up on this barrel climbed a camp official who addressed us in words something like this:
>
> "Comrades! You have all committed various crimes against our just worker-peasant laws. Our great government has granted you the right to live, and a great opportunity—to work for the good of our socialist country and the international proletariat. You all know that in the Soviet Union work is a matter of honour, a matter of glory, a matter of valour and heroism, as was said by our great leader and teacher, Comrade Josef Vissarionovich Stalin. Our worker-peasant government and our own Communist party do not inflict punishment. We recognize no penal policy. You have been brought here to enable you to reform yourselves—to realize your crimes, and to prove by honest, self-sacrificing work that you are loyal to socialism and to our beloved Stalin. Hurrah, Comrades!"[151]

Did Petrov's prisoner comrades answer the official's hurrah? Most responded with silence, while one prisoner toward the back let off a string of obscenities. In this case, then, the prisoners did not even mouth the words.

On the other hand, we have seen articles in *Putevka* in which prisoners write of their reeducation. We'll never be certain that prisoners really wrote these articles, of course, or if they did so, that they were sincere. Yet below, we will meet prisoners who speak not with words but rather actions. Released prisoners fought valiantly at the front in World War II. Some of these prisoners would even send letters back to their camp KVCh thanking it for turning them into honest Soviet citizens and fighting heroes. Prisoners measured themselves by their labor performance, just as Gulag authorities did. Furthermore, we will find prisoners resisting Gulag power in Soviet terms.

Whether or not the prisoners took the work of the KVChs seriously, central Gulag authorities certainly did so. Consonant with the tenor of the age, every problem in the Soviet Union was understood in political terms—either as the result of enemy activity, or the failure of leading Soviet workers to inculcate the proper attitude and education level among the Soviet population. This was as true inside the camps as it was outside. Typically, the first place that central Gulag authorities looked when they discovered shortcomings in a camp was at the work of educational officials—both those responsible for educating prisoners and those responsible for educating other camp employees. Consequently, throughout the history of the Gulag, the camp system never seriously contemplated the disbandment of the KVChs. Even as it became clearer that the camp system was a financial drain on the state budget, that the promise of cheap prisoner labor never came to fruition, the response of central authorities was never to eliminate the costly cultural-educational activities.

Despite the repeated emphasis on remaking prisoners, Gulag authorities never imagined that they would reforge all of their inmates, nor did they hope to do so. Granted, the Solovetskii magazine tried to convince its readers that "even the most die-hard criminal could be reformed. . . . [T]he Soviet prison was capable of changing man."[152] And Ginzburg was not wrong to note that the KVCh itself was "based on the premise that even out-and-out enemies of the people might respond to benevolent re-education efforts."[153] Nevertheless, throughout the Gulag's history, a great deal of confusion and contradiction reigned in the question of other prisoners, especially the counterrevolutionary prisoners, and their relationship to cultural-educational work. Was the counterrevolutionary prisoner fit for attention from an apparatus designed first and foremost for the reeducation of prisoners into honest Soviet citizens?

In August 1937, Karlag issued an order for the removal of all counterrevolutionary prisoners from posts running camp clubs as well as leaders of drama circles and agitation brigades. Counterrevolutionary prisoners could only be used in "technical" work in the KVChs. Moreover, "the more dangerous k-r [counterrevolutionary] element: spies, terrorists, Trotskyites and others," could not be used in any forms of "club-mass work."[154] Of course, the necessity for such a decree only highlights the fact that such prisoners were active participants in the KVCh. As we know, many of the counterrevolutionary prisoners were educated and talented cultural figures—exactly the kind of person needed to operate camp theaters, newspapers, musical productions, and so on. It therefore should be of little surprise that official documents repeatedly return to proposed prohibitions on the use of certain categories of counterrevolutionary prisoners in cultural-educational work.

The constant invocations of a ban on cultural-educational activities with certain subsections of the prisoner population again contradict the notion that the KVChs' work was simply and exclusively a matter of propagandizing for better prisoner labor productivity. If cultural-educational work was solely aimed at increasing labor output, why would Soviet authorities exclude, even just in principle, any part of their prisoner population from these activities? Would they not want to induce every prisoner to work harder regardless of the crime they had committed? The KVChs were deeply enmeshed in the Gulag's project of defining the line between reintegration into and permanent exclusion from Soviet society. Camp authorities had limited resources to complete their educational work, and as we have seen, it could be a costly project inside Gulag camps. So they focused their reeducation activities on those they believed most likely to be reeducated, and in so doing further defined the line between those who could and could not be reeducated. Being defined as unworthy of reeducation greatly increased the chance of dying in the camps. The question of different prisoner groups' worthiness for inclusion in cultural and educational activities played an important part in the maintenance of a hierarchical categorization of inmates, as pursued further in the next chapter.

## Punishment

Controlling and limiting access to food was not the only means of punishment available to Gulag officials. To maintain order in the camps, good prisoner behavior, and high labor output, Gulag officials devised an extensive penalty regime. Prisoners could be placed on a penalty regime for organizing or on suspicion of being inclined to organize an escape, or systematic violations of camp discipline.[155] Karlag officials had the authority to sentence prisoners to various penalty regimes for a wide variety of offenses, including a chronic refusal to work or chronic failure to fulfill work norms. Often, punishment involved the removal of the undisciplined prisoner from the regular camp zone and barracks in order to prevent the "influence of the negative element on other prisoners."[156] Camp chiefs, and even the heads of camp subdivisions and camp points, had the authority to place prisoners in penalty barracks, penalty isolators, or penalty camp zones for limited periods of time.

Penalty facilities varied in all camps, including Karlag. They included solitary confinement cells, group cells, and locked barracks. Conditions in punishment facilities were notorious among prisoners throughout the Gulag. Cells were generally unheated and damp, and prisoners were typically deprived of bedding while under punishment. Prisoners in punishment facilities were often required to continue work in their regular brigade while spending all nonworking hours in their camp prisons. Sometimes punished prisoners were transferred for work at especially physical and dangerous projects. At other times, the punished prisoner was locked up twenty-four hours a day without working. All punished prisoners received a reduction in their food ration, but those who were prohibited from working saw their food supply cut even more severely. Those who did continue to work were transported to and from the work site under an enhanced armed guard. They were also subject to more intense searches before reentering the camp. Penalized prisoners were denied all manner of prisoner privileges, including correspondence, the receipt of packages, smoking, singing, and visitation with relatives.[157]

Gulag authorities placed the highest priority on the guarding of punished prisoners. Central camp authorities demanded that every Karlag camp subdivision allocate "the very best workers" of their division for the administration of the internal prisons. They were supposed to subject camp inmates in the penalty institutions to intensive educational work in order to return them as soon as possible to the general camp population. Until that time, they were to be strictly isolated from their fellow prisoners.[158]

When the penalty facilities of individual camp subdivisions failed to eliminate camp disorders, central authorities ordered the construction of special penalty camp divisions. In August 1937, the deputy people's commissar of internal affairs issued an order on improving discipline in the camps and strengthening the battle with "the especially negative elements who are systematically violating camp order." In response, Karlag ordered the construction of a central penalty camp point at the Dubovka mine. Prisoners could be transferred to the penalty division for up to six months on the order of Karlag's chief and up to a year with the assent of central Gulag's director. During that period, punished prisoners were placed on the camp's penalty ration, denied the right to earn time off their sentence for good work performance, refused visits and correspondence with family, and only allowed to work under armed guard. A six- or twelve-month sentence in the penalty division on the penalty ration could well be a death sentence. Prisoner rations were always barely enough to survive, and any substantial reduction of those rations could easily be fatal, especially over any extended period. An internal prison was built to house for up to thirty days those prisoners who continued to violate the camp rules while in the camp's central penalty division. At the same time, prisoners who exhibited exemplary behavior and conscientious attitudes toward their work could be released from the penalty institutions early.[159]

Transfer to a penalty camp division often was a much less formal process than that identified above. Every camp rather naturally had certain subdivisions where the work was harder, the climatic conditions were more severe, and the general atmosphere was more brutal. Camp memoirists frequently wrote about transfer from one camp subdivision to another as a means of punishment without being certain whether such camp divisions were formally considered penalty divisions. Thus, Ginzburg recalls her transfer to Izvestkovaia, the reputed "last circle" of Kolyma's version of Dante's *Inferno*. "I was the first political to find herself in that lepers' colony. . . . Presumably [the warden's] idea was that I should be made to realize that my unprecedented action had put me on a level with common criminals. Not until a year later did I learn that she had banished me to Izvestkovaya for *no more than* one month, for—of course—a purely reeducative purpose."[160] At other times, the punishment of prisoners merely took the form of removal from privileged positions. Petrov remembers his disagreement with a camp employee during his Kolyma period as a prisoner living outside the camp zone. As punishment, he was immediately sent from Magadan to the goldfields.[161]

Gulag authorities thus utilized the vast array of camps and subcamps to maintain discipline plus compel reeducation, but they also used frequent transfer from institution to institution (within an individual camp and between camps) to tear asunder the prisoner's important networks of assistance, which often made survival possible.[162] In this way, Gulag authorities sought to undermine patronage networks, criminal organizations, and nationalist groups. Not only were such organizations perceived as a potential threat through organized resistance; the mere existence of alternative means of survival outside official Gulag channels threatened official control of the entire system. Yet the constant upheaval had unintended consequences. Rather than tearing apart prisoner society, it actually contributed to the creation of a broad community of Gulag residents. Transferred prisoners carried their experiences from institution to institution, contributing to the uniformity of prisoner society across the Gulag. While the authorities sought to minimize these problems by performing transfers at night and without forewarning, they could only prevent prisoners from carrying material belongings to their next institution. Memories of experiences were not left behind.[163] The recurrent transfer of prisoners as punishment would return to haunt the Gulag in the early post-Stalin era, when transferred prisoners carried Gulag rebellion from one camp to another.

When all penalty measures had been used and a prisoner continued to disobey camp rules, labor camp authorities were authorized to transfer them to a prison. An NKVD regulation from 1935 mandated the transfer to prisons of camp inmates "carrying out active counterrevolutionary activity and receiving an additional sentence in the camp for this." Transfer also applied to "malicious bandits who had escaped multiple times, who tried to continue these activities in the camps, and who had been convicted for this." Finally, camp authorities were to transfer to prisons "the malicious uncorrected element who disorganizes camp life." Transfer to prisons was an extraordinary measure only to be used when all other measures had been exhausted. Such transfers required the consent of central Gulag authorities. Transfers were initiated by a camp's Third Department, which gathered all compromising material on the prisoner for review by the camp director. If the camp chief agreed with the proposal to transfer the inmate to a prison, the materials were sent to central Gulag for review.[164]

## Reward, Release, and Death

A system of reward existed alongside the system of punishment. Rewards offered a stimulus to higher labor productivity and maintenance of camp discipline. These rewards could take the form of monetary bonuses, an improvement in living conditions, transfer to lighter camp regimes, visitations with relatives, the receipt of packages and correspondence, and an early release. Prisoners were even given a wage at various times and places in Gulag history. Typically, the form of payment was little more than a notation in a prisoner's account, which they may or may not have been able to cash in at the end of their sentence. Sometimes, as an additional reward, a prisoner would be allowed to use a small amount of their account to purchase items at a camp commissary, or send some or all of the money to their family.[165]

Visits with relatives were, according to Karlag's 1935 chief Linin, "one of the highest forms of rewarding the inmate for his work and behavior in the camp . . . not only in production but also in daily life." Any prisoner who requested a visit underwent a thorough evaluation to determine their worthiness for such a reward. The entire reward process formed a significant element in the ongoing individualized evaluation of the Gulag prisoner. In this, wrote Linin, the camp's subdivisions were failing seriously. In the evaluations, they had written comments such as "relationship to labor is good, a shock worker, disciplined, actively participates in societal work, etc." Yet, he complained, they wrote this way about prisoners who had been in the camp for quite a long time and about prisoners who had been there "ONE month and even less." They had even written the same remarks about prisoners who had been convicted of committing crimes while in the camp, had received a new sentence, and were sitting in one of the camp's internal prisons. Linin sternly warned that the continuation of this system of "rubber-stamping evaluations" would lead to criminal charges "FOR CONSCIOUS TIES WITH AND SUPPORT OF PRISONERS."[166]

Far and away the most important reward that a prisoner could ever receive was release. In any given year during the period 1934–53, 20 to 40 percent of the Gulag population was released. No year saw the release of fewer than 115,000 inmates, and the number of released could reach one-half million and more.[167] Like other practices, release was tied to the redemptive tasks of the Gulag. Numerous decrees of the Gulag authorities authorized early release to prisoners who distinguished themselves through their work record. Galina Aleksandrovna Semenova was arrested on November 29, 1937, as a result of her husband's arrest on March 15 of the same year. Writing years later about her experience in Karlag, she asked, "You might raise the question of how I was freed early on March 22, 1944—two years before the end of my term? They freed me for successful engineering work and behavior."[168]

Such practices were typical in the Gulag. For example, at Belomor, an order dated March 8, 1932, authorized rewards (including early release) for "inventions and rationalisation measures." For evaluation, the nature of the invention or measure was to be recorded, along with the inventor's name, his qualification, the position he held, and "a report on his general efficiency and behaviours."[169] This measure again illuminates the dual purpose of labor: productivity and reform. The criteria for early release included increases in productivity, but also the individual's personal qualities and attitude. *Belomor* tells us that 12,484 prisoners were freed on completion of the canal "as people who were entirely reformed" and that 59,516 people had their sentences reduced as "active workers on the construction."[170]

Most releases occurred as a routine part of the expiration of a prison term. The bureaucratic detail involved in keeping track of the sentences and expiration dates of sentences for large prisoner populations was certainly no small matter. For instance, in 1939 alone, releases for the expiration of a sentence or other reasons totaled 223,600 from corrective labor camps and 103,800 from corrective labor colonies.[171]

Regulations required camp authorities to provide their subdivisions with lists of prisoners subject to release for the completion of their sentence at least two months prior to their scheduled release date. The subdivision was then required to check the list against its own records and report any discrepancies. At the time of their release, most Karlag prisoners were sent back to the "liberation point" at the Dolinka camp division. There, their files were thoroughly reviewed again, personal belongings were returned (if they still existed), and the prisoners' individual financial accounts were settled (what portion, if any, of prisoners actually received wages on their release and how much is still unclear). The Soviet Union had a number of "regime points"—that is, areas that required special permission in order to live in them. Comprised of the largest Soviet cities and border regions, former prisoners were typically forbidden from living in or even passing through such areas. No list of these areas was to be published, however.

Prisoners could only be informed verbally of the location of these forbidden zones. Consequently, one of the last orders of business prior to prisoners' release was to ask where they planned to live, at which time they were informed whether they were allowed to live in their place of choice. Prisoners were provided with a brief document attesting to their release, given travel documents, and allowed to take documents with them attesting to their completion of training in industrial specialties. Otherwise, prisoners were not allowed to take any documents with them on their release. Those of military age were informed of their obligation to register with the military commissariat in their new place of residence. Prisoners subject to exile were informed of their return to exile.[172]

We learn from Ginzburg and other memoirists that those released were often refused permits to return to their native region. Frequently, the released prisoners were forced to remain in the area of their former camp, usually working in the same industries they had as prisoners. Ginzburg was even forced to carry with her "Form A," which detailed her criminal past, her camp term, and that she had been released subject to deprivation of civil rights for five additional years.[173] Nonetheless, she was also hired to teach in a local preschool, where she was "required to cultivate not only the feeling of love for the Soviet homeland but also the feeling of *hatred* for its enemies."[174]

Many camp subdivision directors, intentionally or not, often held prisoners past the completion of their sentence. Karlag authorities complained about the problem on many occasions.[175] It remains unclear whether camp authorities were trying to keep the extra working hands around longer, or whether they simply did not want to devote the resources necessary to keeping track of the end of prisoner sentences, especially with the complicated system of earning credit toward early release.

Other than serving out their term in full, many prisoners throughout the Gulag's history earned early release. The primary method for gaining an early release was through a system known as "accounted working days."[176] Under this system, each day in which a prisoner completed 100 percent or more of the daily labor norm counted as more than one day toward the completion of their sentence. The exact regulations governing early release constantly changed. In November 1931, for example, Gulag director Kogan ordered that sentence reductions for "prisoner–shock workers" should be increased. First-category prisoner–shock workers would henceforth earn three days toward the completion of their sentence for every two days of labor, instead of the previous four days for three days of labor. Second-category prisoners saw their credits increase from five for four to four for three.[177]

Significantly, to earn the highest rate of return on accounted working days, prisoners not only had to perform extraordinarily in labor production but also had to show themselves as active participants in the "social-cultural work of the camp."[178] Prisoners could build up a substantial credit toward early release under the accounted working day system, but the balance was always tenuous, and any or all of it could be taken away as punishment for violations of camp discipline. Accounting extra days toward early release was suspended during any period that a prisoner spent in a penalty division, even if the prisoner continued to perform productive labor during that period.[179] Furthermore, as with all Gulag practices, accounted working days were introduced in a differentiated fashion. For prisoners sentenced to imprisonment for espionage, terror, sabotage, and treason against the motherland, and also for former members of counterrevolutionary parties and groupings, prisoners of foreign birth, and those sentenced for counterrevolutionary offenses, the practice of accounted working days could only be used with explicit permission from central Gulag authorities and in no cases prior to the end of their first year of imprisonment. Even if they were granted accounted working days, the credits were given at the lowest rate of all prisoners. First-category prisoners from working-class and other acceptable Soviet backgrounds earned a higher rate of return on their accounted working days than second-category prisoners who had been from faulty class or political backgrounds, and had previously been denied voting rights (lishentsy).[180] Prisoners could earn even higher rates for being prisoner–shock workers or Stakhanovites.[181] The system of accounted working days was a major paperwork operation, as each prisoner's file would be filled during each quarter with evaluations and tallies of the days they had earned toward the completion of their sentence.[182]

Early release could also be earned by petition, sometimes in response to particular decrees from central camp authorities issued to ease camp overcrowding. Sometimes the type of outstanding prisoner who received early release was granted more complete reentry into Soviet society than would a prisoner who had completed their entire camp term. Hence, in 1933, the OGPU decreed that "in exceptional circumstances and in relation only to especially outstanding shock workers, who had proven through actions their rejection of their criminal past, who had actively participated in the cultural and social life of the camp, and who had overfulfilled their production targets," application for early release could include a request for a certificate giving them the right to receive a passport to live in restricted areas of the Soviet Union requiring a passport. Every truly outstanding prisoner–shock worker, regardless of their crime, was eligible for this privilege, although only those convicted of everyday and official crimes could apply to live in border regions.[183] Even more important for prisoners whose families lived in exile while they were in camps, those who earned release under these conditions earned the release of their families from internal exile as well.[184]

Early release was always used for propaganda inside the camps. Group releases were announced at roll calls, in production meetings, and during educational sessions. On January 28, 1935, fourteen Karlag prisoners were released early and one prisoner had his sentence reduced after the camp leadership petitioned to central Soviet authorities on their behalf. In the directive read aloud to the rest of Karlag's prisoners, the authorities noted that the commutation of the sentences for these reforged prisoners showed "that only collective shock work, active participation in social-mass work, and exemplary behavior in daily life will lead to early release." Additionally, they continued, "in relation to those who have not yet recognized their shameful past, who have not yet started on the path of correction, and continue in their persistent obduracy to interfere with the socialist state as it constructs the great foundation of socialism, they will be subjected to the strictest measures."[185]

Finally, early release occurred as a result of mass amnesties. These will be discussed in greater detail in the chapters that follow, as the major Gulag amnesties took place during the war, immediately after the war, and after Stalin's death.

The exact opposite, of course, could always be true. Prisoners were frequently sentenced to additional camp terms or even execution for consistent failure to complete work norms, refusal to work, self-mutilation as a means of avoiding work, and other violations of camp discipline. The tie between labor performance and behavior in the camps was thus directly related to the question of survival, release, or retention in the camps for longer periods of time.[186]

The practice of conditional early release, in all its manifestations, created certain economic problems for the camps. While on the one hand, it served as a stimulus toward an increase in labor productivity, it also resulted in the release of the most productive inmates. As the war grew ever closer, this seemed to be ever more of a problem. In 1938, Stalin had personally stepped in to end the practice of earning accounted working days toward early release, arguing, "We are acting poorly, we are disturbing the work of the camp. Freeing these people is, of course, necessary, but from the point of view of the national economy, this is bad. . . . [W]e will free the best people, and leave the worst."[187] Stalin's intervention was a clear violation of a long-established Gulag practice that had tied redemption and therefore release with high labor productivity. Several high authorities including Chief Prosecutor Vyshinsky opposed the move, although in vain. While this move was clearly based primarily on economic considerations, it was not the only factor, as attested by a decree that quickly followed, ending early release for invalids as well.[188] Even from the economic point of view, the end of accounted working days was a mixed bag, and Gulag authorities would move for a limited reinstatement of the system after the war as a way to increase labor output.[189] After the end of conditional early release and the system of accounted working days in 1939, stimulus to increase labor output was to be limited to the provision of extra food and supplies, monetary bonuses, and transfer to an easier camp regime for good performance. The failure to fulfill norms or active interference in the completion of labor norms, it was ordered, had to be dealt with strictly, and the punishments run from worsened material conditions of life in the camps all the way to the imposition of the death penalty.[190] As such, the provisions of the decree ending early release continued to tie access to the means of survival in the camps to labor performance.

Survival until release was a difficult matter indeed. The significant portion of releases over the life of the Gulag should not obscure the tremendous death rates. Looking at just the years 1930 to 1939 in relation to the numbers of prisoners and deaths in labor camps alone, the figures are striking in several ways. First, no clear trend can be discerned in prisoner deaths, in either absolute or relative terms. In the prewar era, the most lethal year was 1933 (the year of the great famine that wreaked such incredible destruction throughout the Soviet Union), when better than 15 percent of the camp population died (over sixty-seven thousand prisoner deaths). While 1934 saw the death of just over 5 percent of the camp prisoner population, and about 4.3 percent of the combined camp and colony population, the number dropped to fewer than 4 percent in the camps (2.75 percent in the combined camps and colonies) in 1935 and less than 2.5 percent in the camps (2.1 percent in the combined camps and colonies) in 1936. In 1937, deaths began to increase again, just topping 3 percent in the camps (and 2.2 percent in the camps and colonies combined) and jumping almost threefold during the terror year of 1938 to over 9 percent in the camps (and 5.4 percent in the camps and colonies combined). The next year saw the death rate plunge again to under 4 percent and it would go even lower in 1940 before the outbreak of war brought the deadliest years in Gulag history.[191]

The numbers are striking, if not surprising, in many ways. First, prisoners clearly died at significantly higher percentages in the camps than in the colonies. This is not startling, given that the camps were in the more remote geographic locations, had prisoners with longer sentences, and thus had more prisoners who were excluded from privileged positions and practices like early release. Given that this was the prisoner contingent considered most dangerous and least redeemable, the higher death rates among labor camp prisoners is consonant with the general operation of the system. Second, the figures show that death rates in the Gulag followed the larger events inside the Soviet Union. As such, the highest death rates of the 1930s are unsurprisingly found during the years of famine and the Great Terror. World War II will lead to a further shock in the system, with death rates unheard of in other years while the war was going against the Soviet Union, and these death rates would turn around along with the fortunes of the war. Further, the figures are striking for the different trend found with prisoner escapes. Throughout the 1934–39 period, escapes declined in both absolute and relative figures. The jump in the death rate in 1938 could be explained in part by the chaos of a rapidly growing camp population and the raging of the Great Terror, yet that chaos did not cause a corresponding rise in the number of escapes. Rather, the different trajectories of death and escape during this period provide additional evidence that Gulag authorities cared far more about the elimination of escapes than the elimination of death.[192]

One major objection to the volume *Belomor* is its complete refusal to discuss the death of prisoner laborers working on the canal. Only once does a death creep into the narrative, and then only briefly and as a result of a freak accident.[193] Yet inside the camps, death was understood as part and parcel of the operation of the system. One photograph in the International Memorial Society's collection reveals a great deal. In the photograph, we see a propaganda graveyard created by one camp's cultural-educational apparatus. This pretend grave site, marked "the graves of the lazy," shows the presumed fates of prisoners Mavlanov, Gaziev, and Pazorenyi. Each prisoner's grave is marked with his name and a percentage: "Mavlanov 22%," "Gaziev 30%," and "Pazorenyi 48%." The implication was clear. For those who failed to fulfill their work norms, the graveyard was their inevitable fate.[194] Gulag authorities were unembarrassed about the tie between the failure to fulfill labor norms and death. In fact, they announced as much publicly to their prisoners. Such an attitude allowed Gulag authorities and local camp officials to exploit their prisoners mercilessly, constantly pushing for prisoners to be forced into the heaviest forms of labor regardless of their state of health. It was apparent that excessive deaths among the prisoner population were never to be judged too harshly.[195]

It is not coincidental that the memoirists who have made us all so familiar with life in the Gulag were all able in one fashion or another to avoid the hardest of physical labor. Moreover, we find that a substantial portion of the memoirists spent their time in the postwar Gulag, where they would ultimately be released in the broad amnesties of the mid-1950s. Edward Buca survived by selling goods and using the profits to bribe useful officials. Joseph Scholmer was able to parlay a camp job as a doctor into additional money to purchase food. Solzhenitsyn spent a portion of his sentence in the first circle, a *sharaga* or *sharashka* where scientific knowledge brought improved conditions and easier work. The need to avoid general-assignment work was pressed on Solzhenitsyn by a fellow inmate at a transit prison and has been acknowledged by one memoirist after another as the key element in their survival. Yet survival was also strongly a function of a prisoner's allies in the camp—alliances built along the matrices of prisoner identity.

•   •   •   •   •

The Gulag's practices had largely been established by the end of the 1930s. Practices had been set up and even codified in a detailed set of regulations in 1939 for constructing and running Gulag institutions. They defined the line between survival and death in the Gulag system, tying prisoner survival to measures of reeducation. Even the population of the camps seemed to undergo a certain stabilization with the decline of the Great Terror and end of the practice of early release. No longer could prisoners earn extra credit toward an early release for fulfilling their work norms. Rather, all prisoners were required to serve their entire sentence. But the combination of detailed regulations governing the camps and a stabilized workforce only appeared to stabilize the camps. The extremely close connection between life in the Gulag and life outside the Gulag guaranteed that this stabilization would be short-lived, lasting only until the next shock wave of Soviet history.

A prisoner culture and society emerged in the 1930s as each prisoner sought to negotiate these practices in an effort to survive. Although this culture and society would also undergo significant changes with the onset of total war, many of the categories that defined prisoner society had been established during the 1930s, bearing striking resemblances to social identities in the Soviet Union at large.

*Chapter 3*

# CATEGORIZING PRISONERS: THE IDENTITIES OF THE GULAG

I thought about how my file had traveled all the way across the Soviet Union on a parallel journey, how it had followed me without getting lost among the thousands and thousands of other files. My fate was in that file.... On the front page was a large stamp—"KOLYMA-TFT." The last three letters stood for ... "hard physical labor."
   —Janusz Bardach on seeing his prisoner file

In corrective-labor places of imprisonment, *it is very important* who [a prisoner is] and for what [a prisoner] finds himself [in the place of imprisonment].
   —A prisoner of the Dolinka division of Kazitlag objecting to the wall newspaper article "Down with Chauvinism," October 4, 1931, in which the author stated, "It is not important, who [a prisoner is], for what and how [a prisoner] finds himself here, but it is very important who [a prisoner is] and how he holds himself here."

THE SOVIET REGIME EXPENDED tremendous energy in its effort to learn who its prisoners were. While it herded millions of people into the Gulag, often as members of mass collectives, it created a separate personal file on each prisoner held in camps, colonies, and prisons, and frequently kept individual files on exiles as well. In their attempt to "know" their prisoners, Gulag authorities gathered several types of information that could be used for individual evaluation along with the generalization and categorization of the inmate population. Each individual file typically contained an identity questionnaire, a copy of the prisoner's conviction (usually a summary of the case, if a court convicted the prisoner, and a brief statement of the crime and sentence, if a secret police organ did the deed), and a number of prisoner evaluations (*kharakteristiki*). Often, the file contained copies of appeals of conviction and action taken, information on disciplinary violations while in the camp, receipts for personal property brought to the camp, and release papers or death certificates. Out of this information, Gulag officials at the central and local level created statistical generalizations about their prisoner population—gender, nationality (ethnicity), education level, category of crime, length of sentence, health, labor utilization, norm fulfillment, escapes, disciplinary violations, and so forth. The individualization of prisoners coexisted at times easily and at other times uneasily with the generalization and categorization of prisoners.[1] These files accompanied prisoners throughout their Gulag experience, and authorities reviewed the files repeatedly—during amnesties, general release, appeals, and so on—as the primary way of determining if a prisoner deserved to be released under this or that legal provision.[2]

In the individual evaluations evident through prisoner files, the most important documents were the evaluations, which summed up in brief the prisoner's current camp identity and served to determine the prisoner's station in camp life. As a rule, the evaluation included, among other items, the prisoner's age, article of conviction, by whom convicted, term, beginning and ending of sentence, date of arrival to the labor camp, category of labor capacity, specialty, quality of work, norm fulfillment percentage, attitude toward labor, illnesses and their length, rewards and punishments, and an educational evaluation, including the prisoner's attitude toward the camp administration and other prisoners, their participation in cultural work, and their behavior.[3] Many of these files still exist in the archives of local Gulag camps. Working in the archives of Karaganda, I was given wide access to these files on former prisoners, while the archivists spent their time using the files to provide information on former prisoners to the survivors themselves or their descendants. The files almost without exception showed significant care in completing these evaluations.

In many ways, then, the evaluation of prisoners was specifically individualized, but this practice of individualized evaluation coexisted uneasily with the use of collective responsibility (*krugovaia poruka*). Through much of Gulag history, prisoners lived, worked, and ate as part of a labor brigade. The responsibility for meeting labor norms was placed on the entire brigade, and escape attempts could lead to punishment for everyone. Assigning individual credit for labor quota fulfillment fell to the brigadier, typically a fellow prisoner, thus placing an important element of the prisoner evaluation in the hands of prisoners themselves. The upside, for authorities, was that collective responsibility extended social control beyond where Soviet authority could reach, giving every member of a brigade incentive to keep their fellow prisoners in line. It did remove some control over the individualization of evaluation, punishment, and ultimately survival, however. It could be difficult for a prisoner to survive a bad brigade or even a bad brigade leader.[4]

One of the common features of the modern polity is the obsession with categorizing its members. This categorization arises from and is integral to the modern political need to know the social body in order to transform it, and is evident in the emergence of the census, ethnographic expeditions, public health, surveillance, and other practices designed to provide information to the state about its population. The practice of categorization allows the modern state to simplify and represent a population too large to know on an individual basis. It combines the seemingly contradictory elements of individualization and generalization. Knowing every detail of every individual citizen's life supplies more data than even the modern state can use. Consequently, the state simplifies and generalizes certain elements of individual identity that it deems particularly critical. The explicit and implicit assumptions derived from an individual polity's ideological assumptions shape the selection of the defining categories of generalization. At times—for example, in the case of Jewish identity in the Nazi polity—a single category of identity can virtually trump and render moot all others. In other cases, states operate based on a complicated matrix of identities not easily reduced to the one or two most significant categories. This process is both individualizing and de-individualizing. On the one hand, it leads to a certain leveling of individual differences among a state's population. On the other hand, the constant drive to subject every single citizen to this process of categorization forces the modern state to engage with each citizen individually.

In the Soviet Union, the practice of categorization took on an especially political form. Whatever the specific criteria of categorization, and as we will see, they changed frequently, categories related directly to the individual's perceived political reliability. The practice of population cataloging existed in a particularly intense form in the Gulag. In camps and exile, an elaborate and ever-shifting hierarchy of identities emerged from this incessant categorization, bearing tremendous similarities to the social hierarchies found in Soviet society at large. Not only were prisoners defined in opposition to the camp authorities but they also were themselves divided at different times by class background, national origin, gender, article of conviction, military status, and so on, all of which bore a direct relationship to a prisoner's perceived redeemability. Categorization in the Gulag served as a source of power, both in the relationship between authorities and prisoners, and among the prisoners themselves. As Ginzburg noted, "There was no equality in this new circle of Dante's Inferno. The camp population was divided by the devilish ingenuity of our torturers into numerous 'classes.'"[5] Categorization also served as a means of social prophylaxis, allowing camp authorities to define dangerous prisoners and take measures to prevent them from contaminating the less dangerous prisoner population.

Identity in the Gulag operated primarily along two axes: who the prisoner was prior to their arrival in the Gulag, and who the prisoner had become while in the Gulag. When a prisoner arrived in the Gulag, they stepped right into a matrix of identity in which they held a specific place defined by the type of crime committed, or their gender, class, or national identity. Nonetheless, the prisoner was not completely precluded from improving their position in the eyes of Soviet authorities.

From at least the promulgation of the corrective labor code in 1924, penal policy in the Soviet Union was engaged in this sort of relentless categorization of prisoners. The code envisioned a complex classification of prisoners based first on the class identity of the individual prisoner and the category of crime committed, and second on the prisoner's behavior while in the place of imprisonment. Thus, prisoners were initially divided into three categories: category one for prisoners requiring "strict isolation"; category two for those not belonging to the laboring classes who committed crimes owing to their class habits, views, or interests, and category three for all prisoners not belonging to the first two categories. These three categories were then assigned to three ranks: beginning, intermediate, and higher. All prisoners from categories one and two began their imprisonment in the beginning rank, while prisoners from category three could begin in any of the three ranks according to the penal authorities' decision. Based on their success in work and study, or their violations of the rules of penal institutions, prisoners could be transferred to higher or lower ranks, although prisoners from the first category were not allowed to advance beyond the beginning rank before completing half of their sentence and prisoners of the second category not before completing a quarter of their sentence. All prisoners were required to spend a third of their sentence in the intermediate rank before becoming eligible for further advancement. The three ranks were associated with a progressive system of privileges and relaxation of the level of detention in their penal institution.[6] As we will see, the system of categories and ranks envisioned by these rules laid out the basic principles on which the system of prisoner categorization operated throughout the Gulag's history.

While the gap between camp authorities and individual prisoners was overwhelming, identity in the Gulag was to some extent a two-way street. As we have seen, camp authorities were never able to monitor every minute or inch occupied by the prisoners. In their free movement around the camp zone after working hours, work in labor brigades, functioning as camp administrators, doctors, cooks, and guards, the prisoners had time and space to claim as their own. In all these moments and inches, prisoners shaped their own society, often using the same categories of identity favored by camp authorities themselves. While the Gulag authorities foisted distinct identities on the camp population, the prisoners also played an important role in taking on and giving form to the emerging categories of identity. Typical is the experience of Danylo Shumuk in his first cell of a Gulag prison, where he was immediately asked, "When and where were you arrested, and on what charges?" Only after hearing his response did the other prisoners treat him to white bread and sour cream.[7] Scholmer faced the same questions: How many years? What paragraph were you sentenced under? Were you really a spy?[8] As Gustav Herling explains it, "Those who guarded closely the secret of their sentence and imprisonment were considered either too proud to be admitted to the solidarity of the prisoners, or else as potential spies and informers."[9] One's past, sentence, and nationality—in short, the categories of one's identity—were the admission tickets to the "solidarity of the prisoners" as surely as they conditioned the authorities' treatment of the prisoner. The effectiveness of official categorization is only emphasized further by its utilization in prisoner relationships.

The remainder of this chapter will assess the main axes on which Gulag identity was formed, revealing both the way that identities were defined by Gulag authorities but also the way that individual prisoners utilized these identities in organizing their own life and their own Gulag society. With small distinctions, these forms of identity operated across the Gulag, in all its range of institutions and locales.

## Political Prisoners and Common Criminals

In accord with the fundamental tenets of Marxist ideology, class was from the revolution a primary category of identity in the Soviet Union. This was no less true inside the Gulag, where discrimination according to class was a near-constant feature of daily life. While the ways in which class was understood in the Gulag and the Soviet Union changed over the course of the 1930s, particularly with the promulgation of the new Soviet constitution in 1936 and the concomitant declaration of the obliteration of enemy classes in the Soviet Union, class never entirely surrendered its role in the Soviet matrix of identity.[10] In the Soviet Union, class was always understood in a rather Manichaean fashion. Classes were either friendly or the enemy. In the Gulag, class was represented by the political prisoner/common criminal axis. The common criminal represented the proletariat of the Gulag—the friendly class—while the political prisoner—in official Gulag parlance, the counterrevolutionary criminal—stood in for the bourgeoisie, the class enemy.

The Russian revolutionary movement looked proudly on the history of political prisoners in pre–Soviet Russia.[11] These prisoners attained a certain notoriety and popularity among segments of tsarist society. In prisons and exile, they held dear their moral code of behavior, privileges vis-à-vis criminals, and self-government. Identification as a political prisoner was crucial to obtain these privileges. In the periodic tsarist amnesties, only political prisoners were released.

In the first years of the Soviet period, the term political prisoner was reserved for those individuals who were members of leftist political parties. In the 1920s' Solovetskii camp, only the 450 or so members of the leftist political parties were given the rights of political prisoners. They were quartered separately, free to move within their territory of the camp, lived with their families, received rations from the political Red Cross, and "*were spared re-education.*"[12] Over time, Soviet authorities limited the use of the term political prisoner, with its connotation of the innocent martyr suffering for the cause. First, the term was refused to the "White guardists" of the "counterrevolutionary" parties—that is, all parties that were not expressly socialist. The socialists themselves then were excluded from the ranks of the political prisoner until only a Communist could be a political prisoner. With the promulgation of the criminal code and introduction of Article 58 in 1926, the political prisoner in the Soviet Union officially disappeared.[13] While the prisoners themselves generally referred to all those arrested under Article 58 as politicals, Soviet authorities referred to these individuals as counterrevolutionaries.[14]

Being tagged a counterrevolutionary had real and sometimes lethal consequences for the Gulag prisoner. Nonetheless, Soviet justice used the term in a malleable fashion. The provisions of Article 58 were so broad and vague that a crime prosecuted under other articles of the code today could be reinterpreted as Article 58 offenses tomorrow (and vice versa).[15] As Solzhenitsyn quite properly noted, "In all truth, there is no step, thought, action, or lack of action under the heavens which could not be punished by the heavy hand of Article 58."[16] Furthermore, Soviet authorities frequently treated groups of prisoners sentenced under other articles of the criminal code as the virtual equivalents of counterrevolutionaries. One need not necessarily be branded with Article 58 to be treated as the worst enemy of the Soviet state.[17] Of course, individuals in the Soviet Union could easily find themselves arrested and charged as a counterrevolutionary for having committed no crime at all. The prevalence of arrests under Article 58 should not necessarily be taken as evidence of widespread counterrevolutionary activity or even opposition to Soviet rule.

Even the 58s were subject to a further subcategorization. For example, when building the Moscow-Volga Canal, some 58s were taken into the labor collectives, but only those with sentences under five years. When the new special regime camps were created after the war, only a select portion of the "most dangerous" 58s was transferred into its institutions. The transfers were based on the particular sections of Article 58 under which the prisoner was sentenced.[18]

No matter how malleable the application of Article 58, those branded with the number were subjected to a much harsher Gulag regime. No matter the number of prisoners sentenced under Article 58, official documents and memoirs attest time and again to the importance of the category in the construction of Gulag identity. In general, the authorities treated the so-called counterrevolutionary prisoners with great suspicion. The redeemability of this group was questionable at best. They received the longest sentences. They were often excluded from early release. They were most likely to serve their sentences in the Gulag's most extreme geographic locales, and were usually excluded from working in their specialties. As early as 1930, their redeemability was placed in question when they were denied the opportunity to join the new work communes at the Solovetskii camps. The members of this new shock worker movement were placed in their own barracks, where they got softer beds, warmer clothes, and better food. Although these communes were short-lived, the principle of excluding the 58s from many of the most progressive forms of correction survived.[19] Time and again, being a counterrevolutionary in the Gulag meant that it would be much more difficult to survive the Gulag.[20]

Of course, the exclusion of the 58s in practice never quite reached that imagined in theory. Regulations officially prohibited 58s from holding privileged positions in the camps, but the predominance of engineers and other specialists among the political prisoner population ultimately overran this official proclamation.[21] Although the 58s were supposed to have only limited exposure to the cultural activities of the camp, Solzhenitsyn himself participated in amateur theatricals in the camps.[22] In addition, while their capacity for redemption was questionable, the counterrevolutionary criminal who had survived to reach the Gulag was not considered hopelessly irredeemable. If they were, they would have been executed, as so many others were. At the final conference of the GPU construction of Belomor, Firin propagandistically declared:

> When we sentenced them, we did not consider them—either the political or the criminal law-breakers—to be hopeless material for the coming classless State. . . . We tried to re-educate our class enemy as well. We did a great deal of work with them. . . . And now the Soviet workers must receive them well, in a friendly fashion, with no reservations or doubts.[23]

Karlag loudly and proudly trumpeted the heroic activities of many Article 58 prisoners in the history prepared and submitted to central Gulag officials in 1934. In a section enumerating the active organizers and builders of Karlag agriculture, a host of current and former Article 58 prisoners were celebrated for their contributions. For instance, the prisoner Trautman, sentenced under Article 58 for wrecking, was "from the first days" an active participant in the organization of work in the camp. Together with several other engineers, he prepared the technical foundations for Karlag's work.[24] Then the prisoner Gureev, an agronomist sentenced under Article 58, arrived at Karlag in 1931. He organized and completed the sowing campaign of 1931, was subsequently released, and then became the director of a Karlag production division.[25] The list continues with zoologists working in livestock breeding, agronomists involved in scientific crop research, professors, veterinarians, engineers, and economists. In all, over thirty Article 58 prisoners are trumpeted as examples of the successes of Karlag, in both its productive pursuits and remaking of the individual. Many of these prisoners, it was noted, had already been released or had seen their sentences reduced substantially for their good works, and all of those released had chosen to stay on at Karlag and work as free individuals.[26]

In 1936, a crossroads was reached, where the definition of the Gulag's enemies was sharply altered. The adoption of the Stalin constitution in December of that year was accompanied by the announcement that socialism had been achieved, and that the Soviet Union was now officially a socialist state of workers and peasants.[27] The capitalist past could no longer excuse crime. Consequently, achieving redemption in the near term became much more difficult. As the Great Terror ensued, massive numbers of enemies were executed in and out of the Gulag. Order 00447, the mass operation of the Great Terror against "former kulaks, criminals and other anti-Soviet elements" included a quota of 10,000 to be sentenced to death among the prisoners of NKVD camps.[28] Outside the Gulag, the NKVD executed at least some 680,000 people in 1937–38—more than twenty times the execution total for any other two-year period.[29] In Karlag, long lists of executed prisoners appear frequently in the records. Those unable to prove their capacity for rehabilitation during the preceding transition period were now annihilated. The threshold of redeemability was drawn significantly higher during the terror. Central Gulag authorities, in the midst of the terror, undertook a review of individual prisoner files, including surveillance reports, in a search for compromising materials on all counterrevolutionary criminals whose camp terms had recently expired or were about to expire. Although it is not spelled out specifically, the implication was clear that some portion of these prisoners were not going to be released.[30] They may have been fit for rehabilitation and release in an earlier era, but times had changed, and the criteria for release had stiffened.

After 1936, a significant rhetorical shift accompanied the rigidified definition of the counterrevolutionary. Class enemies were transformed into enemies of the people, anti-Soviet elements, and fascists, in accord with the declining importance of class and rising importance of ethnicity that accompanied the "victory" of socialism.[31] Not coincidentally, the term enemy of the people appears in two articles of the Soviet constitution of 1936 itself.[32] Galina Ivanova uncovered further changes in terminology during this period. While the early 1930s saw Gulag prisoners called shock workers and Stakhanovites, a decree in September 1937 declared that it was "a political mistake" to apply the term Stakhanovite to a prisoner. From that point forward, such positive terminology was to be replaced with more neutral terms like camp population, labor fund, or simply *zeki*, an abbreviated form of *zakliuchennye* or prisoners.[33] All these terms continued to refer to the same prisoners, yet a reconfiguration of the crucial categories ordering Soviet society was reflected in the shift in the Gulag's terminology. During the terror years of 1937 and 1938, the transformation was lethal for many Gulag prisoners.

The opposite side of the authorities' innate (but not inflexible) distrust of the socially harmful 58s was their fundamental belief in the reformability of the socially friendly common criminal. This vision of criminal reformability derived directly from the Bolshevik worldview. As Maksim Gorky once stated to a group of convicted thieves: "After all, any capitalist steals more than all of you combined!"[34] The Bolsheviks held to certain truths: "there are no inveterate criminals, no inveterate rascals, but there were once abominable and odious circumstances, which manufactured criminals and rascals [but] our country is magnanimous, beautiful and strong.... [W]e must love and beautify our country."[35] Common criminals, it was reasoned, arose only in response to the devaluation of labor under repressive capitalist control. As a result and part of the beautification (socialization) of the social body, the criminal would come to recognize the value of work and would be redeemed. In accordance with the Bolshevik preference for the "proletarian" common criminal, an order was issued at Belomor declaring, "All criminals coming under Article 35 of the Code, all social miscreants and women, were to receive the best and most humane treatment."[36] At Karlag, the deputy chief wrote in 1932 that one of the camp's main tasks was the cultural and political education of the prisoners, "in the first order the layers socially close to the working class."[37]

The construction of a boundary between the 58s and common criminals served to focus the self-representation of the socially friendly on the negative portrait of the socially harmful. By revealing a picture of the less redeemable to the thieves, their own redeemability was affirmed. The link was made explicit. Speaking to the convicts at Belomor, a GPU officer pointed out that the working person who had committed some criminal act or other had to be punished. "But," he proceeded, "we must prevent this worker who has got into trouble from falling under the influence of the counter-revolutionaries, who have been sent here for entirely different things." Nonetheless, the counterrevolutionaries were not cast off, nor were they isolated totally from the common criminal to whom they posed a threat. In fact, as part of their own rehabilitation, common criminals must actively aid the rehabilitation of counterrevolutionaries. As the GPU officer concluded, "The road for your return to your factory or kolkhoz [collective farm] before your terms expire is not closed, provided you show us here that you work loyally and honestly and will help us take care of and re-educate the counter-revolutionaries."[38] In accord with this level of trust, camp authorities were authorized to take prisoners sentenced for noncounterrevolutionary crimes and exhibiting exemplary behavior in camp into a wide array of positions within the camp, including administrative positions and armed camp guards.[39]

In some limited sense, the authorities were able to fix the representation of the socially friendly/socially harmful boundary. A former thief proclaimed in a letter to *Literaturnaia Gazeta* in 1962: "I was even proud that although a thief I was not a traitor and betrayer. On every convenient occasion they tried to teach us thieves that we were not lost to our Motherland, that even if we were profligate sons, we were nevertheless sons. But there was no place for the 'Fascists' on this earth."[40] Frequently, the 58s became the verbal target of the common criminals' own declaration of importance. Gustav Herling recalls the insults tossed about by the "children" in the prisons after a lesson from the education officer: "Accusations of 'Trotskyism,' 'nationalism,' and 'counterrevolution' were constantly flung out at us from their corner, then assurances that 'Comrade Stalin did well to lock you up,' . . . all this repeated again and again with . . . cruel, sadistic persistence."[41]

While the authorities ascribed a negative but malleable connotation to the term counterrevolutionary, the educated prisoners—largely from among the ranks of the political prisoners—who left us memoir evidence reverse the signs, drawing an even sharper distinction between politicals and thieves. These prisoners carried with them a social memory of the privileged position of politicals in prerevolutionary prisons and places of exile. Even as late as the 1940s, when Solzhenitsyn first passed through the Gulag's gates, this identity was directly descended from the glorious tsarist history of political prisoners. In Solzhenitsyn's first cell at Lubianka, he met an "old fellow," Anatolii Fastenko, a sixty-something social democrat, who proved to be an important "keeper of the old Russian prison traditions."[42] The prisoners often discussed "how it used to be in prison," and listened to Fastenko's firsthand stories about the former "honor" of being a political prisoner and the traditional generosity extended to them even by those with whom they were not acquainted.[43] In this living tie to the past, and through those acquainted with him and others like him, the tales of the "triumphant ethics of the political prisoners," the long-established privileges, and the self-government for political prisoners were passed on to new generations of inmates.[44] As a result of this reverence for the glorious past of the political prisoners, individuals with lengthy experience in the camps came to serve as the de facto leaders of the prisoners in times of crisis and uprising. The bonds to the world of the political prisoner were further strengthened after the annexations of territory and their accompanying arrests in 1939. By that time, more than twenty years after the October Revolution, direct veterans of the prerevolutionary prisons like Solzhenitsyn's Fastenko must have become relatively rare. The annexations created a whole new generation of prisoners, many with experience as political prisoners in Polish or German detention. They would bring their prison traditions and utterly different ideologies to the Soviet Gulag.

The self-styled politicals counterposed their identity to that of the common criminal, uniformly claiming consistent and continuous victimization of the politicals by the criminals. Furthermore, they asserted that this victimization was carried out at the behest of—or at least with the acquiescence of—the camp authorities themselves. Of all the tales of torture and privation that fill Solzhenitsyn's multivolume opus, he seems most offended by the loss of the privileged position of the political prisoner and the perceived coddling of the thieves. More than any other memoirist, Solzhenitsyn draws the picture of these two groups in garish terms. Politicals were "guilty of nothing" and "unprepared to put up any resistance." They were "submissive sheep" at the mercy of the "wolf." On the other hand, "the tattooed chests [the common criminals] were merely the rear ends of the bluecaps [Gulag officials]." "You'll not get fruit from a stone, nor good from a thief."[45] He accuses these "parasites" of an unwillingness to work, entering the war only to pillage the occupied territories, and illiteracy or indifference to written literature. Solzhenitsyn denies a distinction between the "honest thieves" and the "bitches."[46] (Typically the former are identified as those refusing to cooperate with the camp authorities, while the latter were those who did.) Nor was Solzhenitsyn in any sense alone in his extreme characterizations of the criminal element. Ginzburg declared that *the professional criminals are beyond the bounds of humanity.*[47]

Even memoirists who did not go to such extremes often expressed shock after contact with the criminal world. Stefanskaia recalls her arrival at Karlag. "First I saw the criminals, 'the *blatnye*' as they were called here. . . . Seeing us coming on *etap* [a prisoner transport] dressed decently with suitcases, they shouted: 'Counterrevolutionaries, they are bringing the counterrevolutionaries . . . now we will smoke!'" Unfortunately for the blatnye, however, the new camp arrivals were immediately placed in quarantine and strictly isolated. Among the many pleasures for

Stefanskaia, when she went to work in the veterinary service outside the camp zone, was the escape from the filth of the criminal world—their tattooed bodies, vulgar language and songs, and "criminal exotica."[48]

Other prisoners had a different perspective. Petrov remembers "two sharply different groups" of nonpolitical criminals, surprisingly characterizing prisoners convicted of more serious crimes as less threatening in the camps.

> The smaller group . . . consisted of well-seasoned bandits and murderers, largely with a death sentence commuted to ten years in a concentration camp. On the whole they were quite decent fellows who realized their own worth, feared no person or thing, were able to crack anybody's head without a moment's hesitation, and knew how to make others respect them. . . .
>
> The other nonpolitical group, made up of petty crooks and pickpockets, was a constant source of trouble. . . . These creatures in the image of man sang prison songs incessantly. . . . Most of their songs were utterly obscene, and their perpetual swearing was done with variations of the most elaborate kind. One had to be constantly on the alert in order not to have something stolen by them. . . . [They] stole from the "devils," the name applied mostly to peasants sentenced for counter-revolution. These devils, who included all helpless prisoners, mainly of the political category, had a miserable time of it. Downtrodden and frightened to death . . . they did not have the courage to offer resistance to the "socially elect" dregs of society.[49]

Still other memoirists attribute their successful survival at various points to their capacity to come to some accommodation with the camps' criminal elements. Bardach frequently befriended criminal elements by serving as their storyteller. He entertained them with tales that he derived from books he had read and stories he knew. Moreover, he exhibited a mastery of the crudities of the criminal language, the use of which distinguished him from the "mama's boys" in the eyes of his criminal companions. Through his friendships with criminal elements, Bardach earned their protection from attacks by other criminals, and gained access to additional (often stolen) food, space, clothing, and other material items, which allowed him to maintain his bodily strength.[50] Buber-Neumann was advised by acquaintances to tell other prisoners during transport that she was a prostitute or thief, not a political. Criminal prisoners were willing to make space in the train cars for a prostitute as opposed to a political.[51]

Professional criminals—that is, those who formally or informally associated themselves with criminal gangs in the Gulag—marked their identities in a number of specific ways. First, they famously tattooed their bodies, offering immediate visual evidence of their identity. Yet the professional criminals also identified themselves through participation in an elaborate Gulag criminal subculture—a subculture that Soviet officials battled unsuccessfully to destroy. The professional criminals played cards, sang, listened to stories, and swore. Their language was notorious for its vulgarity. Bardach recalled his initial encounter with them in his first prison cell:

> I stayed near the latrine barrel. . . . One of the young hoodlums jerked my head toward him. His hand was filthy, and his outstretched arm was blackened with tattoos. "Bet you'd like one like this." He pulled his penis out of his pants and held it in both hands, pointing it toward me. "Take a good look. You're gonna suck a lot of 'em." . . . He squatted and peered at my face. "You look at me when I piss, but don't open your mouth or I'll piss in it."[52]

No wonder, then, that the writers of *Belomor* focused on the need for beautification in the criminal's life. While *Belomor* often praised the work of the KVCh, progress in creating a cultured society was less successful. "The liquidation of illiteracy is spreading? True enough, but the shock-workers of the fourth division complained of the vulgar language used at the club. The wall newspapers still sang vulgar songs. The string orchestras amused themselves with public-house ditties."[53] The theater groups at the Solovetskii camp were defended on the grounds that "a criminal joining the group drops such deplorable habits as gambling, using foul language, etc., not to mention the benefit of his or her own involvement in cultural pursuits."[54] The Gulag officially aimed to instill new habits of cleanliness, both of body and language, in order to make the professional criminal prisoner suitable for a return to society. Of course, this aspect of Gulag ideology was particularly ironic, given that one would never describe anything about the Gulag with the term cleanliness, and the Gulag itself served the maintenance, development, and spread of the vulgar criminal language.

The politicals were in a lot of ways a more diffuse group. They did not even agree among themselves, at least in memoirs, about who the legitimate political prisoners were. Solzhenitsyn refuses to grant that all the 58s were politicals, or that all politicals necessarily 58s. He writes, "If not struggle with the regime, then moral or energetic resistance to it—that is the chief criterion [in determining who was a political]. And the manner of which 'article' was pasted on didn't mean a thing. (Many sons of the liquidated 'kulaks' were given thieves' articles, but in camp showed themselves to be genuine politicals.)"[55] In a way, Solzhenitsyn is quite right. The question of who was a political and who was a thief was a complex one. True professional criminals, those who were members of criminal gangs with all the accompanying rituals and tattoos, could just as easily find themselves arrested and convicted for a crime placed under Article 58. The provisions of Article 58 were so broad that *any* criminal act could be interpreted also as a counterrevolutionary crime. At the same time, vast numbers of Soviet citizens were arrested for offenses that were not political in nature but instead were so minor that it would be quite difficult to understand them as criminal—the peasant arrested for taking a few potatoes from a field during a famine, say, or the worker who came afoul of harsh labor laws that threatened criminal punishment for tardiness to work. In some ways, all of these prisoners really made up a third category, sometimes referred to in the Gulag as *bytoviki*, or those who committed *byt* or "everyday life" crimes. Many of these prisoners no doubt worked too well in the camps for Solzhenitsyn to consider them truly political, though. Stefanskaia saw the work of some of these prisoners at a Karlag dairy farm. There, the petty criminal prisoners (she specifically uses the term bytoviki) worked "seriously and conscientiously" even without a convoy guard on duty.[56]

Meanwhile, Solzhenitsyn was pointedly trying to cleanse the ranks of the politicals from Trotskyites, Communists, and other pro-Soviet prisoners.[57] The question of both Communists and pro-Soviet political prisoners in the Gulag was indeed an interesting one. As Buber-Neumann described it:

> Gradually I got to know the Russian prisoners. We were all supposed to be political offenders, but they were strange political prisoners. . . . I never heard a word of criticism of the Soviet regime from a Russian prisoner the whole time I was in the Butirka [prison in Moscow]. If they had kept quiet for fear of denunciation, it would have been understandable, but there were one or two cliques in our cell who vied with each other in proclaiming their devotion to the Soviet regime and their loyalty to the Party.[58]

These political prisoners widely believed that their own arrest was a mistake or the result of enemy activity, but they thought that their fellow prisoners were guilty of their crimes. Buber-Neumann recalls a conversation with one such prisoner named Katia:

> "What on earth are you here for?" I asked.
> "I'm the victim of a Trotskyite slander," she declared, sticking out her chest virtuously. "But you just wait: I'll pay them back for it, the scoundrels."
> "Oh, so you're innocent, like everyone else here," I said.
> "I don't know about that," she replied. "I only know my own case and that of one or two of my friends. You must remember that I come from a family in which there are nine Stakhanovites and in my factory I was known as the non-Party Bolshevist."
> "But, Katia," I continued, "you've talked with the others here just as I have; haven't you got the impression that they're really all innocent; that they really haven't done anything against the Soviet government?"

She looked at me with fanatical hatred in her eyes. She didn't want them to be innocent. "They haven't arrested half enough yet," she spat. "We must protect ourselves from the traitors."[59]

Ginzburg, herself a former party member, recalls similar attitudes among Communists in the Gulag. Anna, a fellow prisoner, confided in Ginzburg "as one Party member to another." Anna often expressed her concern that another prisoner, a Socialists Revolutionary, might overhear her. "You realize, Genia, she really is *the* class enemy. Mensheviks and SR's, you remember."[60]

If their fellow prisoners were not necessarily taken for innocent, many Communists in the Gulag were reluctant also to cast blame on Stalin or the Soviet system as a whole. As Ginzburg noted, "I met many people in the camp who managed to combine a shrewd sense of what was going on in the country at large with a religious cult of Stalin."[61] Yet even if she were one of the "shrewd" ones, adding this up to a thorough critique of the Soviet system was near impossible. She wondered if

even now—we asked ourselves—after all that has happened to us, would we vote for any other than the Soviet system, which seemed as much a part of us as our hearts and as natural to us as breathing? Everything I had in the world— the thousands of books I had read, memories of my youth, and the very endurance which was now keeping me from going under—all this had been given me by the Soviet system, and the revolution which had transformed my world while I was still a child. How exciting life had been and how gloriously everything had begun! What in God's name had happened to us all?[62]

The political prisoner/common criminal axis of identity was only one of many that operated in the Gulag. Nonetheless, it was accorded tremendous importance by both prisoners and authorities. It shifted in the war and postwar eras, especially as it was more and more displaced by the significance of national identity in the camps with the annexation of the western borderlands in the Stalin-Hitler pact of 1939. Nonetheless, national identity was already assuming prominence prior to 1939.

## The Gulag's Nationalities

Overlapping the boundaries of the political prisoner/common criminal categorization was the broad hierarchy of nationalities. Official Soviet policy and practice on the issue of nationality—a Russian term almost but not quite coterminous with ethnicity—have been discussed in great detail in recent historical works.[63] Despite its official Marxist presumption that nationalities would disappear, Soviet authorities accepted nationality as a really existing phenomenon and even took significant measures toward the development of national identity among the peoples of the Soviet Union. As with the issue of social class, official Soviet policy and practices outside the Gulag strongly affected the authorities' attitude toward national identity inside it. This impact, again similar to that of class identity, extended to the prisoners themselves, though the results were not what Soviet authorities expected.

In the early 1930s, precisely during the period in which Soviet authority was fostering the development of national identity, especially among the smallest ethnic groups (the so-called national minorities, or *natsmeny*) of the Soviet Union, and denouncing great power chauvinism, especially among the Russian population, the same policies found their way into the Gulag. Gulag officials treated national minorities—essentially the non-European prisoners in the Gulag—(along with women) as a group of prisoners requiring remedial training to raise them to a cultural level appropriate for Soviet society. Prisoners among these groups were deemed unfit for Soviet society merely by the presumed cultural level of their nationality. Yet unlike later Soviet peoples repressed on account of their nationality, these prisoners were by no means treated as unredeemable. Their nationality was not genetically incapable of achieving the appropriate cultural level for socialism. Rather, their cultural growth, in the minds of Soviet authorities, had been stunted by the repressive Russian chauvinism of the tsarist empire. Their time in camp, then, was officially aimed at overcoming these historical handicaps.

At Belomor, many spent their time as members of a "national minority division."[64] Although membership in a particular nationality did not foreclose the possibility of rehabilitation, the redeemability, especially of the non-European nationalities, was by no means assured. On the one hand, we find in Belomor that "it is hard to guess, looking at these people, dressed in Bokhara robes, turbans, long mountaineer's coats, jackets, and long shirts, which of them are the future record-breaking brigadiers and which the intractable obstructors." That is, you could not tell merely by their national and cultural origins which would become fit Soviet citizens, and which would not. On the other hand, we read that "it was dark and dirty in the national minority barracks. On the beds sat Uzbeks, Bashkirs, Tadzhiks, Yakuts—the most backward people on the construction, branded as idlers in the camp paper *Reforging*."[65] The official view of national identity in the Soviet 1930s, even when it offered the promise of lifting up (civilizing, in the favored imperialist term) these oppressed peoples, continued to operate within an essentializing script toward nationality—in short, all members of a nationality were viewed as alike. It is but a short step from that view to one in which an entire national group is irredeemable.

Much as particular organizations were being created for Soviet nationalities around the Soviet Union, Karlag created special national minority divisions and brigades in the early 1930s, with particular attention to the creation of separate divisions for Kazakh prisoners. In these divisions, Kazakhs were brigade leaders, and production meetings were held in the native language. Karlag published an edition of the camp newspaper in the Kazakh language. Furthermore, Karlag authorities demanded that translators be provided to these Kazakh divisions so that prisoners could gain access to services in the camp as well as the camp administration. Though officials expended many words calling for attention to the Kazakh divisions, the reality was quite different. Life in one of the Kazakh divisions, even in official documentation, was difficult. Karlag authorities frequently complained that the European prisoner populations and even Karlag employees themselves treated the national minorities poorly, consigning them to the worst living spaces, providing them the worst food, and even engaging in beatings of Kazakh prisoners. These activities were all taken as signs of continuing national chauvinism that must be defeated, but little indicates that real changes occurred.[66]

The national divisions in the early 1930s differed from those created in the 1940s and 1950s at Karlag for Chechens. These later divisions were primarily focused on keeping Chechens separated from Russians to prevent ethnic violence, while the national divisions for Kazakhs were ostensibly created to assist these prisoners in developing national consciousness and to raise their cultural level. Yet Karlag officials always cast a wary eye on the Kazakh prisoner population. Since most of the Kazakh prisoners lived in much closer proximity to the camp prior to their arrest than most other prisoners, Karlag authorities particularly feared their capacity to escape and quickly mix in with local populations. This was especially possible given their ability to speak a language indecipherable to most Karlag authorities. Karlag always worried contact between its large mobile and unguarded prisoner population and the local free populations, but these fears were enhanced in the case of the Kazakh prisoners. By the late 1930s, Kazakh prisoners in Karlag would become a rarity, as most Kazakhs were sent to Gulag locales outside the republic.

By the mid-1930s, concerns with national minorities and great power chauvinism disappeared from the Karlag administrative records. This did not indicate, however, that national identity had become less important in the Gulag. Rather, the focus of concern had changed. The national minorities were no longer assumed to be "backward" in the Soviet Union but instead on the level of everybody else.[67] This increased anxiety as opposed to reducing it. In fact, from the mid-1930s to the 1950s, one finds a mountain of evidence pointing toward a certain "ethnicization" of official conceptions of the enemy and in the Gulag. While this ethnicization process gained momentum in the war and postwar years, it began in the 1930s, especially after the adoption of the constitution. With the class enemy "officially" destroyed, the Soviet Union, it was declared, had become "a unified brotherly family of the working peoples of all nations."[68] Henceforth, individuals—and enemies—were defined less in class and more in national terms. Of course, class as a category was never abandoned, but nationality became more important than ever. As class enemies became enemies of the people or anti-Soviet elements, they became defined as enemies of the Soviet nation—that is, they came to be understood in the language of nation.[69]

The process of ethnicizing the enemy is most obvious in the case of the population of internal exiles. In the early 1930s, the process of internal exile that created the populations of the special settlements was almost entirely a result of the drive to collectivize agriculture and destroy the kulaks "as a class." By the end of 1932, the number of deported kulaks reached 3.2 million. Exile in the early 1930s was thus a matter of class identities and class enemies. Granted, the first deportations of ethnic minorities commenced as early as 1930 with the deportation of Poles from the Vinnytsia and Kiev regions, but these were rather exceptional cases.

Since kulak was a category of class, defined in Marxist terms by one's relationship to the means of production, it was something that could be changed and was not inherent in a person from birth. Class and class attitudes came from one's social surroundings. Soviet authorities showed particular concern that kulak parents not be allowed to influence negatively their children's development. The children were especially innocent—not born kulaks, but potentially susceptible to the wrong kind of influence. They were the most redeemable. Consequently, serious attention was paid to educating the younger generation in the special settlements in order to counteract any negative influence from their social surroundings.[70] Even the parents, though, were considered potentially open to reeducation in the right social surroundings. Soviet policy toward these kulaks therefore would undergo numerous changes. As the Soviet Union officially approached socialism and the official destruction of enemy classes, which would no longer exist under socialism, restrictions on the kulak exiles were eased. As early as 1931, a decree promised to restore voting rights to exiled kulaks after five years if during the interim they proved themselves to be honest Soviet working citizens.[71] Broad amnesties in 1935 and 1938 removed many former kulaks from the status of special settlers. Nikolai Bugai estimates that their number had dropped to just over 970,000 by 1939.[72] Furthermore, conventional terminology quickly named these people "former kulaks," placing the focus on putting their kulak identities into their past and providing a strong indication of the perceived malleability of class identities. In fact, one finds variations on the term "former" throughout official Gulag and Soviet documentation—former lawbreakers, former kulaks, former criminals, former people, and so forth, all indicating a belief in individual human malleability. In the suspicious Stalinist Soviet Union, however, nothing was ever really former. It was never truly possible to prove that you had put your old life and ways behind you. You might, after all, simply be clever, mouthing the words and doing the right things as a way to hide your enemy activity. Soviet authorities were never comfortable that they could really see into the individual's soul and be certain of where they stood. Given such a mind-set, it is unsurprising that one of the mass operations of the Great Terror of 1937–38 was aimed in part precisely at those former kulaks who had allegedly continued their enemy activities, including many who were still in the Gulag itself, whether in exile or camps.[73]

The trajectory of these former kulaks from dangerous to (semi)rehabilitated is strikingly reversed in the case of nationalities, and by the time of the war, exile by nationality became the predominant form of internal deportations. Starting with the early 1930s, one can follow a trajectory that saw exile by nationality take on an ever more undifferentiated form. At first, Soviet authorities exiled small national populations from border regions, and even then the border area was not completely cleansed of a particular nationality.[74] The first big turning point occurred in August 1937, when all Soviet Koreans living in the Far Eastern regions of the USSR, no fewer than 175,000 people, were deported to the Central Asian republics. While this was not the first Soviet ethnic deportation—not even the first deportation of Soviet Koreans—the Korean deportation in 1937 was a watershed moment. This was the first time that an entire nationality was removed from a particular region.[75] The deportation of the Koreans was undifferentiated. Neither class position nor even Communist Party membership could exempt one from deportation.

Nevertheless, the deportation of the Far Eastern Koreans still differed from the wartime deportations, when every last member of particular nationalities living anywhere in the Soviet Union were subject to exile. In 1937, only the Far Eastern Koreans—those Soviet Koreans living in prescribed geographic areas of the Soviet Union—were subject to deportation. Soviet Koreans living outside these regions were initially subject to no official discrimination. While their conationals in exile were not allowed to serve in the Soviet military, a few dozen of the small number of Soviet Koreans not subject to exile and its restrictions served in the army, and three received the title "Hero of the Soviet Union."[76] Only in 1945–46 was internal exile extended to all Soviet Koreans.[77] Wartime exile operated in a much more undifferentiated fashion, as entire nationalities, regardless of their location in the Soviet Union, were deported. Additionally, the war saw the transition from national enemies from

among the Soviet nationalities with external homelands to Soviet nationalities collectively punished for the alleged treasonous activities of the
entire nationality.

Gulag labor camp authorities of the 1930s were also concerned about
nationalities with external homelands, and these concerns directly affected practices in the camps. For example, an order in 1935 for one
Karlag division to provide forty of its prisoners for transfer to a camp
near the Soviet Union's eastern border (the exact location is not revealed)
included an explicit provision forbidding the inclusion of prisoners of
Chinese, Korean, or Japanese nationality, regardless of the crime for
which they were imprisoned.[78] The Great Terror included a significant
national orientation as well, although it continued to seek out enemies
from among the former kulaks.

While the story of the reeducation of these Gulag inmates and deportees defined by national "contingent" is a complicated one that will be
explored in future chapters, a few words are necessary now. Kate Brown,
in her study on the peoples of the Ukrainian-Polish borderlands, argues
that "deportees were transformed into mostly willing colonizers of the
Kazakh steppe as they took up a stake in the Soviet modernizing project." Drawing this conclusion largely from interviews conducted with the
Ukrainian and Polish exiles who remained in northern Kazakhstan in the
late 1990s, and NKVD reports of conversations among deportees in the
1930s, she shows how these people focused on "the accomplishments of
resettlement." For example, she relates one story of Edward Vinglinskii,
who "speaks with a pride of how he and others covered the naked steppe
with a mantle of crops and built with their own hands European-style
farm communities." Further, she notes that "even former deportees still
bitter about the Soviet state spoke with pride about its accomplishments."
And she indicates a certain colonizing impulse in their stories of their
past as they wrote of bring civilization to the steppe and "teach[ing] the
Kazakhs how to live."[79] While this by no means signals that these people
had been thoroughly reeducated, it is suggestive of the way in which a
certain Soviet ethos operated that focused on labor accomplishments as
the measure of a person.[80]

So the Gulag had already experienced a certain ethnicization by the
end of the 1930s. Nonetheless, the war was a watershed in the development of this axis of identity for both authorities and prisoners.

## Gender and Sex in the Gulag

Although Soviet authorities sought from the earliest days of the revolution to create equality between the genders, by no means did they ever try

to eliminate gender difference and separate gender identities.[81] Women had their own special place in the Gulag's identity universe. They were treated as remedial subjects, officially required to work on par with men, but nonetheless subjected to cruelty specifically due to their gender. In the early 1930s, women appeared in a position similar to the national minorities. That is, they were considered to be a group in need of reme-dial instruction, although their cultural level was generally low due to their oppression in the tsarist era; special attention was required to raise the cultural level of women so they could take their rightful place in Soviet society. Gulag authorities continued to operate based on notions that women were best suited for certain labor tasks. Thus, the women of Karlag were more likely than the men to be involved in the production of textiles and less likely to work in the mines. Yet the actual content of educational activities with women was typically similar to that used with the national minorities.

While women were supposedly separated from men in the Gulag, com-plete physical separation of the sexes would never occur. From the early 1930s right through the late 1950s, Gulag authorities repeatedly called for the separation of men and women into independent camp divisions. This happened in some corners of the Gulag, but in most places at least some contact between the genders continued to take place. Women often would be located just across the barbed wire from men in separate divi-sions of the same camp. Thus, few women lived their Gulag experience in the complete absence of men. Given that men made up an overwhelming portion of the camp population, however, many Gulag divisions did exist that were completely male with no women in sight.

The separation of men and women had profound effects on the lives of Gulag inmates, who frequently spent many years in the camps. Far beyond the issue of sexual relations, gender separation disrupted many aspects of individuals' social life. Prisoners often struggled to maintain their normal lives. Consider, for example, Catholics in the camps. Since the church only allowed men to serve in the priesthood, the separation of Catholic women from Catholic men denied these women access to the sacraments. While men could find many corners in the camps invisible to the prying eyes of the state to practice their beliefs, women could not. Mass was celebrated in the barracks, mine shafts, and forests whenever the guards had been drawn away. But women did find their own methods to practice their religion. In some camps, where men were nearby, "Cath-olic women would write down their sins on a piece of paper or tree bark with a number, which would be smuggled to the priests on the men's side. The priests would go along the fence and silently dispense absolution to the women, who held up their fingers to identify themselves, and smuggle penances back to them." Similarly, Catholic camp marriages also took place, with the bride and groom standing on opposite sides of the barbed wire fence while the priest witnessed their vows.[82]

While all Gulag prisoners were vulnerable to the arbitrariness and brutality of Gulag staff, leadership, and guards, women faced a particular vulnerability. Euphemistically termed "compulsion [of women] to cohabitation" in Gulag communiqués, administrative staff took advantage of their access to the means of survival to force female prisoners into sexual relationships with them. As one complaint of the Karlag leadership reveals, these women were typically "called out for night work" or were "selected" to work as domestic servants. Women usually were not only beholden to camp staff but also to prisoner specialists or other privileged prisoners who had been allowed to employ female prisoners as domestic workers as well. Repeated orders to end these practices were never successful.[83]

The exact level of coercion involved in sexual relationships between prisoners and camp employees is not always clear. To a certain extent, the prisoners and camp employees were part of the same social circle. Prisoners often worked in the camp guard and the camp's administrative offices. Camp employees were frequently themselves former prisoners. The ties between camp employees and prisoners, as repeatedly condemned in official documents, were generally quite close. Yet the relationship was inherently an unequal one.

One Karlag directive from 1938 revealed not only sexual relations between prisoner women and the camp's male employees that amounted to "the violent compulsion of female prisoners to cohabitation" but also sexual relationships between male prisoners and female camp employees or female members of a camp employee's family.[84] Conflicts over women could at times turn violent. In April 1934, one Karlag employee named Egorov decided he wanted to "cohabit" with a female prisoner who was already involved with a male prisoner working in the camp administration. Egorov sent his male competitor off on business and "entered into ties" with the female prisoner. On his competitor's return and discovery of the duplicity, the male prisoner killed Egorov.[85]

Pregnancies and the spread of venereal diseases provided a constant reminder to Karlag authorities that the "problem" of sex in the camp had not dissipated. Venereal disease, in particular, was thought to arise from newly arriving prisoners already having the disease, sexual contact between prisoners or between prisoners and those who came to visit them, and sexual contact between the free population surrounding the camp and Karlag's militarized guard (many of whom were also prisoners). Karlag authorities ordered that "all decisive measures" be used to stop sexual promiscuity in the camp, including the "concentration of women in separate camp subdivisions from men" along with the elimination of all possible contact between free and prisoner populations except that occurring in official matters. The spread of venereal diseases in the camp had become so common in 1937 that two camp points were specifically set up to serve as "venereal isolators"—one for female prisoner patients, and the other for males—while the camp's chief ordered a universal medical exam of the prisoner population to uncover all hidden venereal cases. Prisoners were not excused from work during their recovery period, though.[86]

Karlag authorities complained a lot, as they did in June 1936, about "camp disorders" such as "the open cohabitation of male and female inmates" with the full knowledge of local camp administrators. Promiscuity and prostitution, it was noted, led to other violations of camp and labor discipline. The contact between male and female prisoners had become so open that on many occasions, a released prisoner would stay in the area "for several months" awaiting the release of their "husband" or "wife." Prisoners would refuse to work in protest of decisions to relocate them or their camp spouse to other camp subdivisions, and even had the temerity to make what they thought were "legal demands" to live together with their spouse in the camp. These things happen, it was explained, because the camp's leading workers and division chiefs "have forgotten that we work in a camp, where the camp regime for prisoners is a mandatory and integral part of the measures for carrying out corrective-labor policy." Karlag central authorities under these circumstances ordered that cohabiting prisoners be sent to separate camp divisions, promiscuity and especially prostitution be punished by the deprivation of accounted working days earned toward a reduced sentence, and all prisoners working in administrative, specialist, or leadership posts who used these positions to manipulate women into sexual relationships be threatened with punishment.[87]

In October 1941, the cohabitation of guards with female prisoners (along with guards drunk on duty) was criticized at the Gulag's central level. Some guards were found to have provided material assistance to women in exchange for sexual relations. In one case, the guard Novikov committed suicide after his cohabitation with four different female prisoners was uncovered. Even worse, from the point of view of Moscow, many of the outrages were happening with the acquiescence and even participation of the camp subdivision commanders as well as the guard command staff themselves. Furthermore, 50 percent of all disciplinary charges had been brought against either Communist Party or Komsomol members.[88]

Gender identity was a complex affair in the Gulag. Both male and female prisoners have described a certain loss of "womanhood" among female Gulag prisoners—an erasure of the difference between the sexes. As Petrov put it,

> The fate of a woman fallen into the hands of the N.K.V.D. is a terrible one, particularly if she is young. A man can sometimes go through all his prison years and not lose his human image. This is difficult to accomplish, especially on a long term, but it *is* possible. A woman can never do it. Once cast into a prison or a concentration camp, she is lost forever, both to her family and to society as a whole.[89]

Ginzburg felt similarly. She recounted the wailing of a certain peasant woman. "Saints above . . . they must think we're not human, making us walk past the men with nothing on like this. Are they out of their minds or something?" To which came the response, "Didn't your interrogators teach you in '37 that there are no differences of sex where spies, saboteurs, terrorists, and traitors are concerned?" The erasure of differences between the sexes seemed even starker when Ginzburg saw a group of prisoner women: "With their shaven heads, they all looked alike, as though mass-produced in a horror factory."[90]

Reclaiming some semblance of a normal life and their gender identity was, for some, a celebrated triumph for a Gulag prisoner. For Stefanskaia, new clothes and true love allowed her to reclaim her womanhood. She recalled the indignities of wearing camp clothing and related happily the day that she received packages from her parents filled with her clothes—dresses, skirts, and boots. She was allowed to wear these clothes in Karlag. Dressed like a free woman, she felt that her life in the camp improved remarkably. Stefanskaia was soon working on one of the camp's dairy farms when she met and fell in love with a fellow prisoner, Igor Frolov, a twenty-six-year-old veterinary assistant from Leningrad with seven years of experience as a Gulag prisoner.[91] While Stefanskaia found love in Karlag, she thought of her experience as unique: "Love in a camp is a difficult thing! A camp was not made for love." Sure, she observed, in an agricultural camp where men and women worked side by side deep in the steppe without an armed guard, things happened. "But this was not love, and it was not marriage." The camp was a place of fleeting acquaintances, she remarked, where people could never count on being together for long, so "love died."[92] Yet she did fall in love, and given the nature of life in Karlag, was even able to live with her true love in the camp almost freely. Frolov had earned a position with a great amount of freedom to move around the camp, and he used that freedom to set him and Stefanskaia up in their own residence near one of Karlag's remote lakes. The two managed to live together for some time, dodging authorities who, given the conditions of Karlag, thought little about seeing a male and female prisoner moving about freely through the camp territory. Eventually

Stefanskaia even became pregnant, gave birth to a son, and was released from the camp.

Semenova recalled a female prisoner who became involved with a prisoner who was a former high NKVD official. They had a daughter while in the camp and also got an official marriage after they were both released. Semenova helped the woman get a job in the mine construction trust in Karaganda, where the woman awaited the release of her husband.[93] Orlando Figes recounts the story of Ketevan Orakhelashvili, who was arrested after her husband had been shot in 1937. Orakhelashvili married a Karaganda camp administrator on her release in 1942. They continued to live in Karaganda, and her new husband continued to work for the Gulag system.[94]

Love was not always, however, an uplifting story in the Gulag. Although the exact facts of their relationship (that is, whether it was one of love or coercion) and their demise cannot be determined, one report tells of a camp guard, Fedor Bondar', who killed the prisoner Aleksandra Medvedeva before turning the gun on himself. On examination, authorities found a note in his pocket declaring that the prisoners were cohabiting and had decided to commit suicide together.[95] Semenova recalled one female prisoner who "had ties" with a prisoner tractor driver, a bytovik. From jealousy, the bytovik bit off her nose. According to Semenova, she wanted to kill herself, until one surgeon managed to fashion something of a nose for her.[96]

During the years of the Great Terror, Karlag became home for a famous subdivision dubbed Alzhir. This Russian acronym, with the same Russian name as Algeria, stood for the Akmolinsk Lager' ZHen Izmennikov Rodiny (Akmolinsk Camp for Wives of Traitors to the Motherland). It held many women who had been charged under NKVD order no. 00486 as ChSIR—Chlen Semei Izmennikov Rodiny (Member of the Family of Traitors to the Motherland)—for their marriage to those charged and often executed during the Great Terror.[97] Their sentences were not to be less than five to eight years. The initial order required that all "wives" be sent to a special division of Temlag, but that camp soon became overcrowded, necessitating Alzhir's creation at Karlag. Alzhir, the largest of the camps for wives, held many notable individuals from the Soviet Union's cultural and political elite.

The order forbade the arrest of wives who were pregnant or had nursing children, but in practice this was frequently violated.[98] Their children were also to be investigated if they were older than fifteen. If determined to be socially dangerous, then depending on their age, the level of danger they presented, and the possibility of their correction, these children were to be sent to camps, colonies, or "special-regime" orphanages. Other younger children were to be placed in orphanages, unless nonrepressed family members could take them.[99] Many women would never find their children again or would only be reunited with them after many years.[100]

The women of Alzhir performed a wide variety of economic tasks. Semenova, a prisoner at Alzhir, recounted her initial work:

> My first responsibility in the Akmolinsk camp in the winter (when our *etap* arrived) was to take the frozen horse feces out of the zone, where I passed the reins to the next criminal in line, and he took it on to the fields. The feces were frozen in clumps; its loading and unloading was not my responsibility, as I was suffering with the attacks of a femoral hernia.[101]

Other women participated in heavy outdoor work. According to Semenova, the hardest work was the manual creation and transfer of adobe bricks, each weighing twenty kilograms. She explained that the work was too heavy for many of the women prisoners, and as if to emphasize the "de-womanizing" nature of the work, she wrote that several ended up with a prolapsed uterus. Further, nearly all women at Karlag "stopped their female functions (that is, their monthly)."[102]

Although it took some time for a correct diagnosis of her hernia, Semenova was transferred to light physical labor afterward. Soon, though, Karlag officials came looking for specialists, and Semenova went to work as a construction engineer in the camp. She was the chief engineer on Alzhir's main project: the construction and operation of a major textile factory that mostly produced clothing for the Red Army. The textile factory, she wrote, saved many women from heavy outdoor labor in the extreme conditions in Karlag. Semenova worked on other projects in Karlag, including the construction of a mechanized butter factory (which she proudly noted won an award for the highest-quality butter production in Kazakhstan) and a vegetable-drying enterprise. The vegetable-drying enterprise was nearly destroyed in a fire near the end of Semenova's time in Karlag. She earned an early release for her productive work, but chose to stay and work on the reconstruction of the vegetable-drying enterprise. After its completion, Semenova remained in Karaganda, where she worked in the mine construction trust in the region and for other enterprises in construction.[103]

Semenova earned great trust from Karlag's authorities. She was ultimately allowed to travel freely around the territory as part of her work. When on business, she was dressed in civilian clothing so that nobody would know she was a prisoner. Usually, she wrote, those who accompanied her on these trips "were unarmed and got drunk," so she was freed from their escort. Her work was not without significant dangers, though, as traveling around the territory of Karaganda was quite difficult, especially in the winter months. She recalled one trip to the city of Karaganda to visit the camp's meat combine in early 1941. The four travelers returned on a dark, moonless night on two young stallions. With the danger of unseen wolves in the steppe, it took them twenty-two hours to make their way through the negative-forty-eight-degree weather, and the party was reprimanded for returning late.[104] She was also subject to denunciation, including once during the early days of the war when a "stoolie" informed on her for "praising German technology." Luckily for her, camp authorities brushed aside most of the complaints against her, given her successful work for Karlag.[105]

The special divisions of the corrective labor camps for wives, including Alzhir, were dismantled on May 21, 1939, and their inmates were reintegrated into the general camp population unless they were deemed socially dangerous, in which case they were sent to Kolyma or the camps of the far north.[106] After this point, Alzhir's inmates were integrated into the general camp population of Karlag, although at least some effort was made to keep them in separate female-only divisions.

Though much less commonly discussed in official documentation and memoirs, women were not the only victims of sexual assault in the Gulag. Similar to other prison systems that practiced gender segregation, some men—especially those who were young or of small stature—were frequently raped and sexually subjugated. Bardach, one of the least reticent memoirists about describing the brutality of the Gulag in stark detail, wrote about one incident:

> An excited group of prisoners gathered around a bench next to the wall. Those in the back row were jumping up, trying to see over the heads and shoulders of those in front, who were shouting obscenities and holding their penises. . . . A young man lay on his stomach [in the baths], and another man lay on top of him, embracing him around the chest and moving his hips back and forth. His back was tattooed with shackles, chains, and the popular Soviet slogan "Work is an act of honor, courage, and heroism." On both sides were trumpeting angels. He breathed heavily, while the young man underneath moaned and cried out. The spectators shouted. I caught sight of the young man's grimacing face.[107]

Nonetheless, even Bardach was unwilling to specifically say whether he had personally been a victim of rape in the Gulag. The existence of homosexuality in the Gulag and its manifestations as well as the issue of sexual assault on men, thus have been understudied to date.[108]

● ● ● ● ●

The institutions, practices, and identities of the Gulag were shaped by official Soviet understanding of its enemies along with the line between redemption and death. As prisoners attempted to negotiate survival in the Gulag, and as local Gulag authorities wrestled with the sometimes-conflicting demands placed on them by central Gulag authorities, a Gulag society emerged that in many ways mirrored Soviet society at large. The line between redemption and death, however, was in constant flux. As such, the institutions, practices, and identities were also in flux. Events external to the Gulag itself would reshape Soviet society and hence also life inside the camps.

# Chapter 4

# ARMAGEDDON AND
# THE GULAG, 1939–1945

I N APRIL 1943 a tremendous flood hit the Dzhartass dam, a key
element in Karlag's irrigation system.[1] As the Sherubai-Nura River
pounded the dam with rising water and icy floodplain runoff, the
left floodgate became clogged with ice, endangering the dam's integrity.
Its collapse would strip Karlag's vast agricultural area of irrigation, and
threaten the vegetable supply to the city of Karaganda and the surrounding areas. The assistant director of the Karlag administration, Katerinenko, called in explosives experts from Karaganda to break up the ice
from under the floodgate. They refused, stating, "We will not go under the
flood gate to explode the ice; you are sending us to death." Katerinenko
looked around and saw Vissarion Nikolaevich Pilishchuk. Pilishchuk
had been arrested in 1938 and charged as a counterrevolutionary criminal under Article 58. A Red Army veteran, he arrived at Karlag in 1940
and spent the winter nights of 1942–43 exploding the frozen ground to
loosen it for daytime removal by other prisoners in building irrigation
canals. Katerinenko told Pilishchuk, "We need to explode the ice under
the left flood gate." As Pilishchuk recounts, "Weighing the situation as it
was in the country and at Stalingrad, I said, 'I will go and explode the ice
under the flood gate.'" Attaching twenty-five-kilogram bags of explosives
around his body, Pilishchuk spent two hours in and out of the water
under the floodgate. He became gravely ill and temporarily paralyzed,
but the dam was saved.[2]

Pilishchuk's tale, told in a letter written some forty-five years after the
events, reads almost as if it comes directly from *Belomor* or other ideological tracts expounding the theory and practice of Soviet penal policy.
Here, a prisoner not only performed heroic feats of labor but understood
and directly related these feats to the current political situation in the
country as well. While Pilishchuk's protestations of innocence would not
find their way into such ideological works, the manner in which he pro-
claims his innocence itself attests to the power of the Gulag's indoctrination system. Pilishchuk described his decision to accept the nighttime
explosive work at Karlag during the winter of 1942–43: "I already had
a pass and could move about without convoy. My goal was to establish
the grain base for the front, and then to request Stalin to review my case

and, if I was not guilty, to send me to the front."[3] The chronology that Pilishchuk sets up is striking. First he would perform his feats of labor and then request that his case be reviewed. Implicitly, Pilishchuk accepted the notion that his labor would be in part the measure of his innocence. As we will see, labor as a means and measure of rehabilitation continued throughout the wartime Gulag. Pilishchuk's feat also was more than matched by prisoners dispatched to the front, further tying the fate of the Gulag's inmates to the rest of the Soviet Union.

## The Gulag and the War

By mid-1939, the Gulag seemed to reach a moment of stability following the upheavals of the 1930s. As a truly mass Soviet social institution housing millions of prisoners, the Gulag had existed for nearly a decade. The Soviet Union had passed through its Great Break, built socialism, and survived the near self-immolation of the 1937–38 terror. The instructions in 1939 on the operation of Soviet corrective labor camps codified the Gulag's policies developed over that tumultuous decade. The abolishment of conditional early release for prisoners even seemed to offer a certain stabilization of the camp contingent.[4] Yet two events of world historic proportion upset this normalcy. As so many times before, external events echoed inside the Gulag as the practices, institutions, and social hierarchies shifted in accord with changes in the Soviet Union and world at large.[5]

First, the 1939–40 annexations of portions of the former Polish state and the independent Baltic countries along with their reannexation in the wake of the Nazi retreat brought new populations to Soviet and Gulag society, with significant long-term impacts for both. As the new regions were integrated into the Soviet Union, their populations were subjected to Soviet social engineering, which had been refined throughout the interwar period. Deportations and arrests greeted the new Soviet peoples. These "Westerners" impacted Soviet society and the Gulag in myriad ways. Unlike the entire generation that came of age solely under Soviet conditions, the Westerners carried with them experiences and social memories outside the Soviet system.[6] Many were even members of nationalist movements that offered fierce resistance to Soviet rule. The effects of these peoples on the Gulag and Soviet Union were evident throughout the war, postwar, and post-Stalin eras, especially during the latter, when they took a leading role in the wave of strikes and uprisings in the post-Stalin Gulag.

The second event that sent shock waves through Soviet society and the Gulag was the onset of total war on June 22, 1941. Like every other combatant, the Soviets were forced to launch a total mobilization of their human and economic resources in the face of an unprecedented conflict in which the boundaries between the military and civilian spheres were consciously erased. The war was truly a Soviet Armageddon, as the Nazi war of extermination could only be met with an equally ferocious Soviet war effort. Having passed through the crucible of war, Soviet society would never be the same. The Soviet rear faced three interconnected campaigns during the war: the demand for increased labor output with less material input, intensified political exhortations to heroic labor, and a wide-scale battle to cleanse the home front of actual and imagined enemies. The Gulag was a cornerstone in all three drives; it was both a microcosm of the Soviet home front and an integral participant in the mobilization of Soviet society.

The Soviet battle with its perceived internal enemies continued throughout the war, and the Gulag continued to play an important role in this fight. Yet like before the war, Soviet authorities went to tremendous lengths to re-create Soviet society within the Gulag, and an examination of this internal Gulag world highlights significant elements of the wartime mobilization of Soviet society. The stifling atmosphere of Armageddon inside the wartime Gulag was evident in five primary elements that reflected its relationship with the outside Soviet world: changes in the Gulag's population and daily life in the wartime camps, economic production, political education, the battle with the especially dangerous inmates, and the ethnicization of the Gulag. While the Gulag's specific production tasks were reoriented toward military industry, its raison d'être of the prewar years—the definition and enforcement of the boundaries between reintegration into and final excision from the Soviet social body, and as such the definition and enforcement of the proper characteristics of the Soviet citizen—was altered but never dropped. Although in economic and administrative terms the Gulag emerged as a burden to the Soviet state during the war, the Soviet leadership never entertained the notion of dismantling the system. The Gulag was a pillar of the Soviet system, as crucial for its role in the battle to cleanse and shape the Soviet home front as for its role in military production.

## New Inmates, New Culture

In 1940–41, the professional criminals in the Gulag's northern camps "strutted around like dandies" in tight-fitting jackets and the other latest fashions arriving on the backs of the Westerners, those prisoners coming from the newly annexed territories of western Ukraine, western Belorussia, Bessarabia, and the Baltic states. The new styles of vests, coats, hats, and silk scarves—mostly stolen from their original owners—symbolized the arrival of new and distinctly non-Soviet populations into the Gulag.[7] By the signing of the Nazi-Soviet pact in 1939, revolution, civil war, famine, collectivization, industrialization, constructing socialism, and terror had created a new Soviet civilization—one utterly different from that found in the newly annexed territories, where new nation-states, national majorities and minorities, ethnonationalism, failed liberalism, economic depression, right-wing rule, and multiple competing political parties and movements were the dominant motifs of interwar life.

The annexations disrupted Gulag society as it had developed by 1939. The population of the Gulag had also changed in the first twenty years of Soviet rule. Gone were most of the prisoners with experiences and memories of tsarist prisons and exile, when the political prisoner was accorded a privileged status. Gone too were most of the Mensheviks, Socialists Revolutionaries, monarchists and others with opposition political programs and experience. After 1939, a new generation of prisoners arrived, and they were of a different sort. Many new prisoners had experienced Polish prisons, where political prisoners were still given status and privileges. These peoples, many of them Communists, shared with their new comrades in detention the tales of their struggles for special status as political prisoners in Poland. They spoke of hunger strikes, demonstrations, escapes, and clandestine ties with their party comrades outside prison. They talked about their continuation of political activity, discussion, and education within the Polish prison system. They also told tales of life outside the Soviet Union. Sometimes, even interrogators showed great curiosity about such matters.[8] Many other new prisoners were members of nationalist organizations, and some even had experience in the violent resistance of nationalist partisan armies. Not only were the ideologies of these nationalist organizations and armies explicitly anti-Soviet but their penchant for violent resistance even in the face of overwhelming odds also brought a radically new element to Gulag society that would have a major long-term impact.[9]

In some ways, the Gulag barely took notice of the different backgrounds of these Westerners. They were integrated into the populations of already-existing and newly emerging Gulag camps. They were subjected to the same endless process of education and forced corrective labor. As Yehoshua Gilboa wrote:

> The educator's task was to give us pep talks to complete the quotas, work harder for the good of the country, and do penance for our sins. It was not enough that our square and cubic meters of work determined the size of our bread ration, impelling us to greater effort for the sake of one or two hundred grams. It also seemed necessary to try to transform sinners and

jailbirds into partners in the grand pretentions of the fatherland, partners of a mighty people sweeping along in an access of love toward the brilliance of Communism.[10]

Perhaps the most intriguing aspect of Gilboa's recollections is that Soviet authorities made no distinctions among these newly Soviet peoples when it came to proselytizing for the "fatherland."

Yet these prisoners and exiles from these formerly non-Soviet territories were different, and they were recognized as such by their fellow prisoners and Gulag authorities. Gulag memoirs and official documentation consistently refer to them collectively as Westerners, identified as a specific group defined primarily in opposition to those who had long been Soviet citizens.[11] While the effects of these people on Gulag culture are only vaguely evident during the war, their arrival was a crucial event in Gulag history.

World events played a particularly important role in the upheavals faced by these new Gulag arrivals, especially among the arrivals from Poland. Mass arrests and deportations followed hard on the heels of Soviet power in the region. From January through October 1939, NKVD arrests throughout the Soviet Union ranged between 1,500 and 3,000 per month. In November and December, NKVD arrests jumped to 14,000 and 10,000, respectively—a surge attributable entirely to the new waves of arrests in the annexed territories. Throughout late 1939 and 1940, NKVD arrests in the newly occupied territories accounted for an absolute majority of such arrests in the entire Soviet Union. From 1939 to 1941, 110,000 to 130,000 people were arrested in these territories, and between 309,000 and 327,000 were exiled from the former Polish lands.[12]

After the Nazi invasion of the Soviet Union, Poland's status changed to an official ally of the Soviet Union. Consequently, an agreement was worked out for the release of Polish citizens incarcerated from 1939 to 1941 for the purpose of forming Polish military units to fight against the Nazis. During the war, over forty-three thousand Polish and ten thousand Czechoslovakian citizens were released from camps and colonies in accord with these nations' new status as allies.[13] But release from camps did not immediately mean release from the Soviet Union altogether. In November 1941, over thirty-six thousand Polish citizens released from labor camps were resettled in various regions of Kazakhstan.[14] Almost all of the Polish citizens in internal exile, camps, or prisons in the Soviet Union in August 1941 were amnestied by September 1942, with the significant exception of some twenty-one thousand Polish army officers murdered by the Soviets at Katyn.[15] At Karlag, releases of Polish prisoners began on August 27, 1941, and proceeded at a rate of two to three hundred per day, for a total of approximately three thousand.[16]

Yet it should be emphasized that not all Poles were released. Those excluded were Poles sentenced after July 30, 1941 for desertion from the Red Army, those found guilty of being agent provocateurs in the Polish Communist Party, Komsomol, or Comintern, and those convicted of serious criminal offenses.[17] Even for those who were released, the trip out of the Soviet Union was often a long and winding one, and not infrequently took them back into the Gulag's clutches. At times, it was Polish conceptions of nationality that kept former Polish citizens in the Soviet Union, as was the case with Gilboa, a former Polish citizen of Jewish origin. After his release from a Gulag camp, Gilboa attempted to enlist in the Polish military being formed in Soviet Central Asia, but he was kept out for his Jewishness. As he put it, a "black mark had been discovered by the Polish nobles, lieutenants, and majors which could not be erased—circumcision." Failing to gain entry into the Polish Army, Gilboa traveled around Central Asia looking for a place to fit in and hoping for a way out of the Soviet Union. On December 7, 1942, he was rearrested in Kazakhstan and given a new sentence of five years in the Gulag.[18] Another Polish citizen, Jerzy Kmiecik, was released from Karlag in September 1941, and roamed around Soviet Central Asia for five months and by his estimation fifty-five hundred miles in search of a recruitment center for the Polish Army. He was finally able to join the Polish Army and escaped the Soviet Union on March 24, 1942.[19]

The effect of a world historical event like the Nazi-Soviet pact and the related dismantling of Poland was not confined to the new prisoners that the Gulag received from the new territories. The pact called forth two long-established facets of Gulag life—the spread of rumors among prisoners, and an intense interest in international affairs—to raise hopes among some prisoners for a change in their situation.[20] The focus of these rumors on international affairs to an extent was driven by Soviet authorities themselves, who constantly urged prisoners to understand the international significance of everything that they did. Thus, prisoners sought signs in international affairs that their own situation would change either by amnesty or an amelioration of camp conditions. In Karlag, a group of prisoners was investigated in late 1939 and early 1940 for systematically refusing to work in the camp based on their religious convictions as members of the Genuine Orthodox Church (Istinnaia Pravoslavnaia Tserkov'). These prisoners had been arrested at various times for their opposition to collectivization and refusal to interact in any way with Soviet authorities, whom they reportedly referred to as a "satanic force."[21] The prisoners steadfastly refused to sign any documents of their investigation, and one, Vasilii Petrovich Selivanov, refused to have his fingerprints or photograph taken until physical force was applied.[22] One witness noted that the church members constantly made statements against

Soviet power, such as declaring that it was "godless and it should fall in 1940. . . . Germany is destroying Poland and then . . . the Soviet Union." Another witness described their assertions that biblical prophecy taught that Soviet power would fall in 1940.[23] Soviet authorities took the spread of negative rumors quite seriously during the war, and on July 6, 1941, the Presidium of the Supreme Soviet applied criminal penalties to the spread of "false rumors."[24] Among these adherents of the Genuine Orthodox Church, two were sentenced to death, and two were given additional sentences in camps.[25] While the Soviet Union would not fall in 1940, the German invasion and the incursions deep into Soviet territory by early 1942 fueled many such rumors. Kmiecik recalled the rumors spread around Karlag with the German invasion, especially about the release of all nonpolitical prisoners. According to Kmiecik, many of his fellow prisoners expressed their desire to join the Red Army in hopes of deserting to the German side.[26]

## Surviving Armageddon: Gulag War-Time Demographics

On January 1, 1939, the camps, colonies, and prisons of the Gulag officially held nearly 1,990,000 prisoners. Of the 1,290,000 corrective labor camp prisoners, 107,000 were women. The contingent of counterrevolutionary camp prisoners numbered 440,000.[27] In just two years, the total camp, colony, and prisoner population had risen by almost 1 million to nearly 2.9 million persons in January 1941. Another 930,000 individuals were detained in exile.[28] While the arrival of the Westerners was a significant contribution, the Gulag's population growth was largely attributable to strict new labor discipline laws passed in 1940.

The Gulag population changed rapidly after the Nazi invasion. Most important, the camp and colony population dropped by half through 1944—the first substantial population decline in Gulag history. Mass release and mass death reduced the overall camp and colony population from 2.3 million at the start of the war to 1.2 million on July 1, 1944.[29] For individual camps, however, populations increased, as they tried to integrate prisoners evacuated from the camps and colonies located near the front. Although the Gulag opened forty new camps and twenty new regions of colonies during the war, it closed sixty-nine camps and sixteen regions of colonies (with over a hundred individual industrial and agricultural colonies).[30] For Karlag, the integration of these evacuated prisoners was one of its greatest challenges of the early war years. Karlag's population grew from 29,000 prisoners (18,000 men and 11,000 women) on March 1, 1939, to 34,000 (equally divided between men and women) on January 1, 1941, and then to 44,000 (23,000 men and 21,000 women) on

February 1, 1943.[31] The main influx was prisoners evacuated from other camps, so that the Karlag population grew significantly during the war even as it experienced large-scale releases and frightful mortality rates. At the same time, the special settlement population grew rapidly due to the wartime deportations of national populations. New camps were created for POWs as well as repatriated civilian and military populations.

While the term Gulag typically raises visions of Siberia and Kazakhstan, it must not be forgotten that the Gulag also had a significant number of camps, prisons, and colonies in the western part of the Soviet Union. In his 1944 report on activities during the war, Gulag chief Viktor Nasedkin noted that the Gulag had been forced to evacuate 27 camps and 210 colonies with one-third of the entire camp and colony population (750,000 prisoners) from areas overrun by the Nazis.[32] The evacuations were hasty, inefficient, and a tremendous burden on the Soviet infrastructure already straining to evacuate Soviet economic enterprises from the same regions. In July 1941, Nasedkin wrote to NKVD Chief Lavrenty Beria and his deputy Vasilii Chernyshov describing the difficulties faced in the evacuation process, especially the unavailability of railway cars, forcing some 40,000 prisoners in Ukraine and 20,000 prisoners in western Belorussia to evacuate on foot.[33] Often these evacuations occurred under Nazi fire, leading Gulag guards to be even crueler than usual toward their wards. Bardach recalled a hasty march from a prison near the front to a train station.

> A lanky dark-haired boy about sixteen years old remained next to one of the fallen prisoners. "It's my father! He's dying! Help him!'" . . . A Mongolian guard struck the boy in the head with the butt of his pistol. "Get up and get back in the column!" The bleeding youngster lay next to his father, hugging him tightly. The guard kicked the boy repeatedly, but he didn't move. As the guard leaned over them, the boy turned and spat in his face. Two shots rang out, and the two bodies were dragged to the side of the road.[34]

Bardach was fortunate enough to be evacuated by train rather than by foot, but it was no easy ride on what one fellow prisoner called a "filthy, stinking, motherfucking cattle car." Prisoners were the lowest priority for access to all the necessities of life throughout the war, and train travel would be no exception. Even Bardach's cattle car "did not move very quickly . . . often diverted to a siding, sometimes for two or three days, because the stations were overwhelmed with other trains carrying soldiers, tanks, and cannons." The prisoners "only got water to drink twice a day, and all had to drink from a single cup chained to the wall. With no water for washing and no toilet paper, everything we touched caused diarrhea."[35]

Considering these difficulties, Nasedkin proposed that some of these prisoners be released rather than evacuated. He contended in his July

1941 letter that many of the evacuees were sentenced under the labor discipline laws of June 26 and August 10, 1940, "for ordinary, unimportant
crimes." Many others were pregnant women, women with young children, and juvenile offenders. Nasedkin argued that it was not in the interests of state safety to expend the same effort on isolating them as on the
isolation of state criminals—"counterrevolutionaries, bandits, recidivists
and other especially-dangerous criminals." He proposed the release of
all prisoners being evacuated who were sentenced under the 1940 labor
discipline laws, except those classified as malicious hooligans (zlostnykh
khuliganov) or recidivists; sentenced for ordinary, unimportant crimes
with a sentence of less than a year; pregnant women or mothers of young
children, and not sentenced for counterrevolutionary crimes, banditism,
or recidivism; all juvenile criminals, except recidivists; and chronic invalids, except counterrevolutionary and especially dangerous criminals.
He also proposed that they order all those who were released during the
evacuations and of fighting age to report to military commissariats for
induction into the army. The total freed under his proposal, he estimated,
would be around one hundred thousand.[36]

Nasedkin's proposal was not only adopted but also greatly expanded
to include even those prisoners in camps not subject to evacuation.
On July 21, 1941, Karlag received orders from the union-level NKVD
and procurator to release all prisoners meeting the criteria proposed in
Nasedkin's letter. Camp officials were also ordered to explain clearly to
the released prisoners that they would be dealt with especially harshly if
they committed new crimes in the future.[37] Throughout the Gulag, over
1 million camp and colony prisoners sentenced for crimes perceived as
insignificant were released to join the Red Army on the basis of two decrees of the Presidium of the Supreme Soviet from July 12 and November
24, 1941.[38] By August 1, 1944, nearly 6,700 former Karlag prisoners
had joined the Red Army—4,900 of whom had been released before the
scheduled end of their camp term.[39] Those sentenced for "counterrevolutionary and other especially dangerous crimes" were specifically excluded
from the releases.[40] In all, some 550,000 elderly, invalids, and pregnant
women were released early.[41]

In some measure, releases to join the Red Army were also extended to
the exile population, where just over 60,000 exiled former kulaks were
released. Exile continued to operate largely as a family operation, such
that the release of a head of household from exile into the Red Army entitled the entire family to release from their special settler status. The total
number of exiled former kulaks dropped from 910,000 on January 1,
1942, to 670,000 on January 1, 1944, and 600,000 on January 1, 1946.[42]

For those left behind, the wartime Gulag saw an unparalleled battle for
survival. As in the Soviet Union at large, the wartime Gulag experienced

death at rates unrivaled at any other point in its existence. Even according to the Soviets' own figures, likely understated, frightful mortality rates
struck the Gulag, much higher than in the prewar years. The steep rise
in mortality rates is largely attributable to the disastrous food situation
in the Gulag and Soviet Union as a whole in 1942–43, the disorganized
evacuations of camps near the front, and a general tightening of the isolation of the especially dangerous prisoners excluded from the wartime
releases.[43] As hunger struck Soviet society, it hit the Gulag population—
the lowest priority for the Soviet state and the least capable of organizing an informal system of food supply outside the state—particularly
hard. Food rations for the Gulag were decreased significantly during the
war.[44] Not even productive labor could guarantee sufficient food during
the hungry war years, when the average prisoner calorie intake dropped
by no less than 30 percent.[45] Reports from all over the Gulag flooded
into the central administration, complaining of the decreased health of
the camp inmates due to the decline in food provisions. In 1943, Chernyshov declared that a failure to improve the food situation would be
"catastrophic."[46] While Gulag prisoners had typically supplemented their
rations as much as possible through informal contacts within the camp
as well as with relatives and the local population outside the camp, the
tightened isolation of prisoners during the war cut off these valuable survival supply lines. Furthermore, at the point when the prisoners reached
their most desperate level of starvation, Gulag authorities prohibited the
receipt of packages from relatives.[47] One of every four inmates in Soviet
corrective labor camps and colonies died in 1942. Just over one of every
five died in 1943. During the worst months in mid-1942, the death rate
approached 3 percent each month. From January 1, 1941 through January 1, 1945, Gulag authorities documented 822,000 deaths in the camps
and colonies.[48] A scholarly compilation of statistics from central Gulag
materials reveals the total deaths in the Gulag system from January 1,
1941 through January 1, 1946, as 932,000, or over 56 percent of all
documented Gulag deaths between 1930 and 1956.[49]

   The situation in Karlag mirrored that in the Gulag at large. Deaths at
Karlag reached 591 in October 1942, 771 in November, 1,381 in December, 1,447 in January 1943 (3.2 percent of the camp population),
1,404 in February (3.3 percent of the camp population), and 1,063 in
March. Karlag was one of the deadliest locales in the Gulag in 1943,
with total mortality rate for the year of approximately 29 percent (2.42
percent each month) of the average camp population, or a total loss of
over 13,500 prisoners in Karlag for the year. This compares to an overall
Gulag death rate for 1943 of approximately 22.4 percent, and a death
rate in Kolyma—that most notorious of Gulag locales—of approximately
12.6 percent. Although it is mere speculation, the particularly high death

rates in Karaganda likely arise from its lack of involvement in the direct production of war matériel, or the production of the Kolyma gold that was used to generate hard currency and support lend-lease. Thus, even though Karlag was an agricultural camp, it was low in the pecking order for supply of the necessities of survival, including food, in which area the camp never became self-sufficient.

Most of the deaths were related, at least officially, to specific illnesses (scurvy, tuberculosis, etc.), although the lack of sufficient food was certainly the key factor, especially since Karlag chief Zhuravlev himself noted that the camp was free of an "epidemic." Between October 1942 and February 1943, the number of hospitalized prisoners at Karlag doubled to over 4,000, while the camp only had the capacity for 2,025 hospitalized prisoners.[50] Semenova recalled many prisoners getting pellagra at the beginning of the war, and that two barracks in her camp zone were freed up for pellagra sufferers.[51] Some camp divisions were significantly worse than the camp average. Hence, in the newly acquired Dzhezkazgan camp division, 7 percent of all prisoners died during June 1943 alone.[52] Dzhezkazgan would quickly gain the reputation of being the "harshest division of Karlag."[53] The prospect of surviving for even one year in a camp with such a high death rate was disturbingly low. At Karlag, the greatest number of deaths apparently occurred among those prisoners arriving from evacuated camps near the front. Nearly 65 percent of the deaths noted above happened within the first six months of a prisoner's arrival at Karlag (and 44 percent in the first three months).[54] The high death rates among new arrivals recall Gilboa's description of the commonest expression in the camps: "You'll get used to it. . . . If you don't get used to it, you'll croak."[55]

A series of local and central directives illustrates the conditions faced by these prisoners, and the knowledge of these problems by all responsible officials. Whereas central Gulag authorities mouthed their concern without providing any real assistance in ameliorating conditions, Karlag officials continually sought excuses to deflect blame. On November 19, 1941, central Gulag authorities prescribed that newly arrived prisoners transferred from camps near the front be placed on additional rations for one or one and a half months prior to putting them on the new reduced food rations of the wartime period. No doubt this would have been a fine idea, yet central Gulag offered no means to carry out its order. Local camps were informed that they must fund these extra food rations within their current food budgets for the average cost per prisoner per day.[56]

For its part, Karlag used the arrival of new contingents to deflect blame for the abhorrent death rates there. On April 7, 1943, Zhuravlev wrote to Sergei Kruglov to explain the growth of mortality rates at Karlag starting in November 1942. Zhuravlev attributed the rising mortality rates to the arrival, beginning in October 1942, of prisoners from areas near the front. These arrivals, he wrote, were as a whole very ill and physically exhausted, and many were close to death. For example, on November 15 a shipment of 880 prisoners arrived from Kamenlag.[57] Before they even arrived, some 70 prisoners had died; 3 more died immediately on arrival, and fully 430 of the 880 prisoners were immediately hospitalized for a variety of illnesses. Zhuravlev placed blame on the head of Kamenlag's sanitary section for sending too many prisoners who were hopelessly or too ill to travel. The majority of the prisoners were only partially clothed as well, and the conditions of their travel were highly unsanitary. Zhuravlev repeated such information for a number of additional groups of prisoners arriving at Karlag. In a mere two weeks during November 1942, Karlag received three large groups of such prisoners, or over 3,900 new arrivals sitting at once in the transit point Karabas. During November alone, 400 prisoners died at Karabas. In the second half of 1942, a total of 13,000 prisoners arrived at Karlag in poor physical condition, literally overwhelming the camp.[58]

As the mortality numbers show, the situation in Karlag during the war was simply horrific. Central Gulag authorities complained repeatedly about the high mortality rates at Karlag. While mortality rates soared throughout the camp system during the war, there is no indication that Karlag authorities knew or would have known about conditions in other camps. Consequently, Karlag chief Zhuravlev clearly feared for his job, and constantly sought in his correspondence to shift blame to others or explain Karlag's death rates away as a result of the camp's particularities. Zhuravlev found a fall guy in Georgii Mikhailovich Drevits, the head of the camp's sanitary department (sanotdel, or SANO).[59]

Zhuravlev had an ongoing feud with Drevits, so blaming him accomplished two objectives at once: evading responsibility for the disastrous mortality rates at Karlag, and settling a personal score. Drevits was a surgeon sentenced to five years in 1927. In 1930, he was released early and his conviction was removed (although the conviction was never forgotten, as it reappeared in every one of his job evaluations). Since 1935, Drevits had served as the chief of Karlag's sanitary department. It is not clear exactly when the troubles between Drevits and Zhuravlev began, but they were already apparent in an evaluation from January 2, 1942 of Drevits's work performance. The evaluation noted that his work had been good until recently, when he started to clash frequently with his superior, Zhuravlev. He had also reportedly begun to establish close ties with prisoners—a cardinal sin in the concentration camp world. "Considering himself irreplaceable, he has many times presented ultimatums that he be released from his position as head of SANO." Zhuravlev and the head of Karlag's political department, Egorov, concluded that keeping

Drevits in his position was not advisable.[60] Yet nothing changed. Drevits remained in his job throughout 1942. An evaluation from November 15, 1942 repeated the accusations of January 2 and also charged Drevits with using narcotics with prisoners.[61] It is not clear why he was maintained in his post after January 1942, or who had the authority to order his dismissal or transfer. What is obvious is that even as camp chief, Zhuravlev's power to hire and fire was quite limited.

On December 10, 1942, Drevits took his case to Moscow, where he reported in person to Gulag chief Nasedkin along with the head of the Gulag's central sanitary department on the conditions at Karlag.[62] He requested that the Gulag chief approve his transfer out of Karlag as well. According to Drevits's memo to the Karlag chief detailing his trip to Moscow, Nasedkin immediately agreed to transfer Drevits from Karlag to be the sanotdel's chief of the administration of corrective labor colonies for Kuibyshev Oblast. Furthermore, he informed Zhuravlev, Nasedkin had approved the promotion of a certain Terekhov, the sanotdel head of one of Karlag's subdivisions, to be the new chief of Karlag's sanotdel.[63]

Apparently as a direct result of Drevits's visit to Moscow, Nasedkin and Deputy NKVD Kruglov sent a letter to Zhuravlev on December 24, 1942, sharply criticizing Karlag for a decline in labor utilization, a decline in prisoner health, and overall poor living conditions in November 1942. Kruglov and Nasedkin provided recommendations for improving prisoner health and well-being, including such things as improving and ensuring the regular provision of meals along with appropriate clothing for the season, but they offered no specific assistance from the center to accomplish these tasks. Rather, Zhuravlev was ordered with an implicit threat against his job to ensure that conditions improved and to focus on the "preservation of the working force" through the winter months. He was also ordered to convene a special meeting of all Karlag employees to discuss the situation and the Kruglov-Nasedkin letter.[64]

Zhuravlev mounted a two-prong response to this criticism, first seeking to justify the conditions at Karlag and then seeking to shift blame to Drevits. On January 4, 1943, Zhuravlev responded that the primary reason for all the cited problems was the "unplanned and unsystematic" provision of prisoners to Karlag above the normal demands of production.[65] In essence, they were receiving more prisoners than they could utilize in economic activities. The provision of food products and housing was planned for a significantly smaller camp population, and even had camp populations been kept in the planned range of thirty thousand rather than the actual forty thousand or more, there would have been shortages. The overprovision of invalid prisoners proved especially problematic. Even newly arriving prisoners with some labor capacity were on the whole an unhealthy lot. According to Zhuravlev, of the sixty-six hundred prisoners arriving in the fourth quarter of 1942, fully 82 percent arrived in such poor physical condition that they were unable to work. Many required hospitalization, and nearly a hundred of these prisoners died immediately on their arrival at Karlag. From the beginning of 1942, he complained, Karlag had not received a single group of new prisoners who could be utilized at work immediately. Karlag also did not have adequate medical facilities to handle all the new sick prisoners.[66]

Finally, Zhuravlev leaned on Karlag's particularities, reminding central Gulag authorities of the agricultural and therefore seasonal nature of most work at Karlag. A drop in labor utilization rates in November was typical even under normal conditions. Zhuravlev offered an implicit criticism of the authorities' lack of knowledge about Karlag's locality when he pointed out that their recommendation that food provisions be supplemented by gathering mushrooms and wild berries in the steppe failed to take into account the dryness of the steppe around Karlag, essentially a semidesert, where mushrooms and berries were quite sparse.[67] While I have gone mushroom hunting in the steppe that comprised Karlag and can personally attest that finding edible mushrooms in the steppe is difficult, Semenova, as a former prisoner, writes of the drive for prisoners to collect mushrooms after the war began. She notes that they were successful in finding this "additional" food, which was used to make soup.[68] Nonetheless, it seems unlikely that mushroom hunting provided a real substantial dietary supplement for tens of thousands of prisoners.

Zhuravlev then went on the attack, writing a number of negative letters about Drevits and his associates, defending his turf by shifting blame for the conditions to Drevits himself and undermining Drevits's credibility as a conduit of information about Karlag to Moscow. Just a few days after his initial response to Nasedkin and Kruglov, Zhuravlev sent a personal letter to Nasedkin in which he cast aspersions on the performance of Drevits, and expressed his feeling that Drevits's reported approval for transfer to Kuibyshev and the promotion of Terekhov to new Karlag sanotdel chief was probably a provocation.[69] On February 11, 1943, Zhuravlev wrote the Gulag's assistant chief for cadres that Terekhov could not be promoted, because it had turned out that he had maintained close ties and drank with former prisoners. In addition, his work was poor, as he preferred gossip and drink over work. Zhuravlev also noted that the camp's internal surveillance and police section (the operative-Chekist department, or operchekotdel) was investigating Terekhov for spreading defeatist sentiments.[70] As well, Zhuravlev sent his superiors a report from the operchekotdel on Drevits. After his exit from Karlag on January 18, 1943, Drevits apparently took a leave of absence without proper sanction from Gulag authorities, during which time he worked as a surgeon in a Karaganda hospital and refused to report for duty in Kuibyshev. He even failed to let Karlag or Gulag authorities know of his location. The head of Karlag's operchekotdel recommended that Drevits be punished for desertion, and the investigative materials were sent to Karaganda's NKVD military tribunal.[71]

Zhuravlev clearly had a staunch ally in the chief of his surveillance and internal police department. On February 18, 1943, the head of Karlag's operchekotdel wrote to his superior in Moscow, addressing the rise in mortality at Karlag. The high mortality rate, in his opinion, was attributable primarily to coldlike illnesses (*prostudnye zabolevaniia*) and exhaustion (*istoshchenie*).[72] The former occurred because prisoners were sent out to work poorly dressed and without adequate footwear. They also lived in barracks that frequently lacked fuel for heat, so after working outdoors in freezing weather, they were not even able to thaw themselves at the end of the day. These conditions led to outbreaks of flu and other illnesses. Then, these ill prisoners were not brought to the camp hospital until their condition had become quite severe, and many died in the barracks without ever receiving medical assistance.[73]

The operchekotdel's report, following Zhuravlev's lead, laid most of the blame on improper work by the camp's sanotdel, especially its now-former chief, Drevits. Drevits, according to the operchekotdel investigation, was involved in falsifying causes of death and in particular trying to cover up cases of dysentery, which would have put the sanotdel's work in a bad light. Consequently, he refused to allow laboratory studies of dysentery cases and ordered his doctors to write pellagra in place of dysentery in all medical records.[74] The report further accused Drevits of cohabitation (as mentioned earlier, a Gulag euphemism for sexual relations, both consensual and nonconsensual) with female German prisoners working in the camp infirmary. These women, it stated, were unqualified for their positions, and their incompetence and misdiagnoses were to blame for the deaths of several prisoners. It was not uncommon for prisoners to earn the desirable jobs in camp hospitals and infirmaries through personal contacts, and without adequate training to fulfill their duties. Getting such jobs, in fact, was often presented by memoirists themselves as the key reason for their ability to survive the camps.[75] Bardach, who would become a celebrated plastic surgeon and medical school professor at the University of Iowa after his Gulag experience, worried greatly that he was doing harm to his patients with his lack of true medical experience. He thus spent much of his free time while serving as a medical assistant in the camps poring over medical textbooks trying to learn about the illnesses that he was treating.[76]

The operchekotdel's report went on to blame various doctors and employees of the sanitary sections of the various Karlag subdivisions for the high mortality and illness rates. The report promised to add new informants in an attempt to uncover thefts of camp food and supplies. As to the camp chief and politotdel, the report concluded that they had been informed of the problems and were taking the necessary measures to improve the situation.[77]

All of the blame shifting and justifying did little to ameliorate conditions at Karlag, as can be seen from an especially morbid Gulag policy handed down in 1943. On March 17, Zhuravlev and the new director of the camp's sanotdel informed their subordinates about a new Gulag policy allowing for the burial of multiple corpses in single graves. While the subordinates were denied permission to accumulate corpses for mass burials (all corpses had to be buried within one to four days of death), they were allowed to bury bodies without clothing or coffins.[78] The allowance of mass burial ended in September 1946, when once again all bodies were to be buried separately.[79] On April 24, 1943, Kruglov complained again to Zhuravlev about the conditions at Karlag. In particular, the barracks were reportedly too cold, access to medical treatment was poor, and camp employees were not doing enough to provide additional hospital beds. The camp failed to take prophylactic measures against scurvy, despite the provision of vegetables to the camp. Prisoners with pellagra were being treated too late, and many were dying before even getting into a hospital.[80]

No evidence indicates the slightest amelioration of living conditions in the Gulag as a result of the reams of paperwork spent on the issue of Gulag mortality rates. Zhuravlev was replaced on March 8, 1944, as Karlag chief by Vasilii Petrovich Sokolov.[81] Although I have not discovered an official explanation for his removal, it seems quite likely that either the disastrous mortality rates along with the conditions at Karlag during the war or Zhuravlev's constant blame shifting were contributing factors. Zhuravlev probably could have done little to better the conditions in Karlag without financial and supply support from central Gulag, and that was not forthcoming given the Soviet defeats in the early years of the war. Once again, outside events controlled internal Gulag developments; for only when the Red Army began to turn back the Nazi invader did conditions in the Gulag notably improve. As the Soviet Union overcame its early problems with industrial production and food supply, it started to turn back the overwhelming hunger and privation that struck Soviet society as well as the Gulag. Only then did Gulag death rates begin to return to their prewar levels.

The demographic changes wrought on the Gulag by the releases, deaths, and prisoner movement presented significant challenges to the wartime camps and colonies, as mostly young, healthy men were transferred to the Red Army from the prisoner population and Gulag staff. At a time when it was mobilized for a total war, the Gulag consisted of a smaller, less healthy, less politically reliable, older, and more female detained population maintained by a smaller, less experienced, older, and more female voluntary staff. During the war, the category of counter-revolutionary and other especially dangerous state criminals rose from 27 to 43 percent of the Gulag population. Prisoners deemed "fit for heavy labor" dropped from 36 to 19 percent. Female prisoners rose from 7 to 26 percent.[82] Meanwhile, 120,000 Gulag staffers, including 94,000 out of 135,000 guards, were sent to the front. The portion of the militarized guard between the ages of twenty and forty dropped from 86 to 38 percent, while a mere 20 percent of all Gulag staff had worked in the NKVD since the prewar period.[83] At Karlag, the situation was only slightly different, since the female and counterrevolutionary portions of its population were already significantly higher than the average Gulag camp. On March 1, 1939, 44 percent of Karlag prisoners were sentenced for counterrevolutionary crimes and 38 percent were women. By January 1, 1941, the counterrevolutionaries and women were 56 and 50 percent, respectively, of the Karlag population.[84]

Karlag faced other demands, which strengthened these trends in changing its prisoner population. On May 30, 1942, Deputy NKVD Kruglov ordered the camp authorities to send two thousand of their physically healthy prisoners along with 6 percent of their guard staff to Aktiubinlag. Under no circumstances were they to send prisoners sentenced for especially dangerous crimes, those with less than six months remaining on their sentence, or invalids, sick prisoners, juveniles, or women. Such an order even further skewed the Karlag population toward the politically unreliable, female, juvenile, old, and unhealthy.[85] These demographic challenges were by no means unique. The Soviet working population at large shifted even more strongly toward elderly, juvenile, and female contingents.[86] Central and local Gulag authorities themselves frequently complained that these changes in their staff and prisoner populations were interfering with their work. In fact, the rising portion of prisoners understood as politically unreliable posed significant challenges, as the Gulag's role as a detention institution isolating these individuals perceived as potentially dangerous directly interfered with the Gulag's role as an economically productive institution.

Besides these issues, the ongoing battle to cleanse the home front confronted the Gulag with the integration of tremendous new contingents and the creation of new institutions. Some 2 million Soviet citizens fell under the wartime mass ethnic deportations, discussed at length below.[87] These national deportations solidified an ethnicization of the Gulag's population—especially its exile contingent—that began well before the war. Three other new wartime prisoner groups required the creation of new detention institutions. First, once the Soviet Army went on the offensive, the Gulag began to integrate POWs into its detained labor force. By the end of 1944, 75 POW camps on Soviet territory held some 1.1 million POWs.[88] As early as June 26, 1941, Karlag kicked off preparations for the conversion of its Spassk division into a POW camp. Over the course of four days, Karlag prisoners were transferred out of Spassk, and Karlag provided many necessary materials and staff for the new POW camp.[89] Over 60,000 POWs passed through the Spassk camp, and more than 5,000 are buried in a cemetery there.[90] The creation of a POW camp at Spassk added to the strain that the arrival of evacuated prisoner populations was already placing on Karlag's resources.

Second, throughout and after the war the NKVD operated filtration camps, through which a large portion of Soviet citizens who had been POWs and many Soviet citizens living in areas under German occupation passed.[91] The Gulag literally followed on the heels of the Red Army as it made its westward drive. These camps were tasked with uncovering spies, traitors, and deserters from among these populations. Some six million Soviet citizens ultimately passed through filtration camps. No fewer than a half million were sent to the Gulag, and many were shot.[92] Even in this time of an unprecedented need for laborers and soldiers, the Soviet state continued to be preoccupied with cleansing its population. The Gulag created new special camp divisions later on, with an especially strict regime for housing a select number of the most dangerous state criminals—a development that will be discussed at length below.

## The Gulag's Wartime Economy

The Gulag was neither an economically efficient nor an economically profitable institution during the war. Perhaps it never could have been, if only because it was first and foremost a place of detention whose primary task was the isolation of criminals considered a danger to Soviet society. The Gulag constantly categorized its prisoner contingent according to the perceived level of danger that they presented to the Soviet state and people. The differing practices applied to different ranks on the hierarchy of danger militated against economic productivity even in the 1930s, but with the onset of the war the Soviet state demanded that the Gulag tighten the isolation of a detained population perceived as more dangerous, in a time perceived as more dangerous than ever before. The changes in the Gulag contingent along with the demands of strengthening isolation challenged Gulag economic production throughout the war. The camp and colony prisoner population—the backbone of the Gulag's labor production—dropped significantly.[93] The losses of nonpolitical prisoners were even more devastating in economic terms, as only they could officially be used in any type of Gulag work without restrictions or armed guard convoys.

Labor in the Soviet Union and the Gulag had always meant much more than mere economic output. This was true even under the demands of war. "To live means to work," declared a *Pravda* article in July 1943, echoing the old Bolshevik truth that labor was the defining characteristic of humanity and, in penal politics, the ultimate tool for the return of the prisoner to society.[94] The importance of prisoner labor was only reinforced in the atmosphere of Armageddon, the battle for survival itself in the Second World War. The life of a Gulag laborer was cheaper than ever, yet Gulag labor, as we will see, was not divorced from its roots as a transformer of people.

Throughout Soviet society, the period between the signing of the Nazi-Soviet pact and the German invasion of the Soviet Union saw significant enhancements of labor discipline. The labor laws of 1940 extended criminal penalties to labor infractions such as leaving one's job without authorization, shirking, or showing up late for work. Individuals convicted under these labor laws quickly filled the ranks of the Gulag during these years.[95] In 1946, the procurator's office reported to Stalin that between July 1, 1940 and January 1, 1946, over 8.3 million people had been criminally charged under these labor laws—over 7 million for absenteeism, and another 1.2 million for leaving their jobs without permission. Further, another 767,000 had been sentenced under a December 26, 1941 law that punished desertion from military industries. Over 7 million were charged for what the procurator's office described as "inadequate reasons (not showing up for work or showing up more than 20 minutes late)." Those sentenced under these laws had largely been released under the amnesty of July 7, 1945 celebrating the victory over Germany, but their ranks were quickly being filled again by those arrested under these continuing laws. The procurator's office argued that the punishment for such minor violations was losing its "social-educational and preventive significance." After the victorious conclusion of the war, the reasoning went, such punishment was undesirable "from the political point of view." The problem of absenteeism should be the domain of individual enterprises rather than the criminal system. The laws would not be changed until 1951, however.[96]

These laws were echoed inside the Gulag itself, as failure to work in the camps was punished severely. On September 5, 1940, three female prisoners, Ol'ga Pavlovna Gorelova, Matrena Vasil'evna Alaeva, and Domna Mikhailovna Sapozhnikova, were executed in Karlag after conviction in the Karaganda regional court for refusal to work, inciting other prisoners to refuse to work, sabotage at work, and inciting other prisoners to sabotage at work. Camp authorities informed all prisoners of the executions during roll call.[97] On September 30, 1940, Pavel Mikhailovich Gumeniuk was executed at Karlag under a sentence handed down by the Karaganda regional court for refusing to work in the camp, and here too the execution was announced to all prisoners.[98] Between January 1 and December 1, 1940, 112 Karlag prisoners were given additional sentences for refusing to work.[99]

Yet even during a period in which labor laws in the Soviet Union were strengthened and executions for labor refusal were announced inside the camps, redemption through labor was still held out to the prisoners as a possibility. Thus, execution announcements at roll calls were complemented by release announcements. For example, on September 11, 1940, Karlag authorities read aloud a list of 108 Kolyma prisoners who had been released early for "systematic overfulfillment of industrial tasks in the camps, good quality of work, exemplary behavior and discipline."[100] Throughout the history of the camps, Kolyma was notorious in the minds of prisoners as the worst possible locale in the Gulag. Threats to send prisoners from Karlag to Kolyma in response to one offense or another were frequent. Here, authorities signaled to the prisoners that if good labor production could lead to the release of prisoners from Kolyma, it could lead to their release from any camp.

While the period between 1939 and 1941 saw some tightening of the labor regime in the Gulag, it paled in comparison to the demands placed on camps and prisoners after the German invasion. The Gulag, like every other element of the Soviet economy, was pushed to do more with less, all the while maintaining its emphasis on the detention and isolation of dangerous state criminals. And like the rest of the Soviet Union, the Gulag's response was to work its prisoners and staff more mercilessly than ever. When the militarized guard faced a significant loss of personnel to the army, the staff left behind often worked thirteen to fifteen hours per day, usually without days off. But no matter how tired such a schedule made them, they were required to be on high alert to deal with a prisoner contingent now considered more dangerous than ever. The slightest lapse of vigilance allowing a prisoner to escape could lead to criminal charges. Unsurprisingly, suicide and alcoholism were common.[101]

On July 4, 1941, Karlag chief Zhuravlev ordered that all his prisoners work twelve-hour days to complete 20 percent higher daily production norms.[102] Similarly, on June 26, 1941, employers outside the Gulag were empowered to require three hours of overtime per day, and cancel leave and holidays.[103] After some months central Gulag authorities stepped in to order that throughout the camps and colonies, prisoners be given three days off per month and an eight-hour period of rest for sleep each day (these regulations were touted as attempts to ameliorate conditions in the camps).[104] In the Gulag, though, even minimal rest periods were frequently violated.

Intensive labor practices allowed the Gulag to make a large production contribution to the war effort. The Gulag's population was more readily transferred from place to place than the free population.[105] Utilizing this complete control, the Gulag authorities were able, with amazing rapidity, to convert their civilian industries to military-industrial tasks and create new camps to aid the reconstruction of evacuated industry.[106] The Gulag's experience with the rapid integration of newly detained populations allowed the Soviet authorities to quickly organize the labor utilization of both POWs and internal deportees. In addition to its own economic production, by 1944 the Gulag "rented" out the labor of over 900,000 prisoners, including 316,000 POWs, to other people's commissariats, and constructed special camps and colonies near their work sites. More than one-third of all rented prisoner labor was engaged in coal mining, many in the Karaganda coal basin.[107]

The Gulag's own wartime economic achievements were substantial but costly. Gulag prisoners provided much-needed labor on a wide range of important defense constructions, boasted Gulag chief Nasedkin, from oil refineries and aviation factories to railroad construction and coal mines.[108] Gulag industries produced food, clothing, and an array of military objects, including 25.5 million 82- and 120-millimeter mortars, 35.8 million hand grenades, 9.2 million anti-infantry mines, 100,000 air bombs, and over 20.7 million ammunition casings by 1944.[109] Excluding special settlers, Nasedkin reported the total output of Gulag industries for the first three war years in "exchange prices" (otpusknye tseny) at 10.67 billion rubles.[110] This represented a yearly net profit of 0.45 billion rubles in 1940, rising to 1.03 billion rubles in 1943.[111]

Yet comparing the Gulag's economic production to that of the entire Soviet Union reveals a less rosy picture. As a percentage of GNP, the Gulag was significantly unproductive per capita. During those same three years of the war in Nasedkin's figures, the inmate labor force averaged 3 percent of the total civilian Soviet working population.[112] Producing an estimated 3.56 billion rubles per year (Nasedkin's 10.67 billion rubles divided by three years), the Gulag produced a mere 1.9 percent of the average GNP for 1941–43, far below its proportional representation in the workforce.[113] As to the profit that Nasedkin claimed, one needs to be skeptical of its validity considering the low productivity of prison labor and tremendous expense of running the Gulag system. Even in the near absence of labor costs for the inmate population, the Gulag had to provide all means of subsistence—shelter, food, and clothing—along with the substantial amounts spent on surveillance, guards, staff, political education, bureaucracy, secrecy, and so on[114]

Despite constant attempts to increase productivity, the Gulag may never have been a profitable institution. As early as 1941, the Gulag chief recognized that the typical Gulag laborer produced 50 percent less than did the corresponding free laborer. The Gulag was such an inefficient institution that it could not even manage a profit when hiring out its labor force to other institutions.[115] Ironically, the institution that symbolized the maxims of Soviet mobilization hardly contributed to the most intense mobilization effort in Soviet history. If the Soviet Union won the war through economic production, it did so despite the Gulag, not because of it. Nevertheless, at no point during the war did the regime entertain the notion of dismantling this increasingly wasteful and inefficient institution. The Gulag, after all, was not a mere economic institution. It was a pillar of the polity as a whole.

## Politicized Labor in the Gulag

Soviet authorities went to tremendous lengths both before and during the war to re-create Soviet society within the Gulag. As Soviet society was intensely politicized, so was the Gulag. It was never enough for Gulag prisoners (or free Soviet laborers) merely to fulfill their labor norms; every prisoner was required to understand the significance and thus maintain the appropriate political attitude toward their task.[116] The central Gulag authorities declared that only if prisoners understood "the context . . . of their tasks"—that is, the international and domestic political context— would they "not only fulfill and overfulfill the norms but fulfill two to three times the norms."[117]

Students of the Gulag have argued that eventually ideology gave way to economic considerations in managing the Gulag.[118] Yet even during the war when the Soviet state was stretched to the maximum to meet the economic demands of total war, the ideological element of Gulag life was never lost. In fact, central Gulag authorities sharply criticized two subdivisions of Karlag in October 1942 for underestimating the value of cultural-educational work.

> As a consequence you are using cultural-educational workers on various secondary work having no relation to cultural-educational work.
>
> This has all happened, I think, because you misunderstand the significance of political-educational and cultural-mass work among prisoners, one of the principles of the corrective-labor policy of the Soviet State; you misunderstand that this work has great significance in the more complete and proper labor utilization of prisoners for fulfillment of important economic and defense work, assigned to the NKVD.

You do not know the basic provisions of the Corrective-Labor Code. . . . Like for example, in point four of these basic provisions:

"The constitution of the RSFSR enunciates the responsibility of all citizens to perform socially useful labor. Among those deprived of freedom it is required to carry out political-educational work. The labor of those deprived of freedom and carrying out among them political-educational work must serve the reeducation and habituation of them to work and life in the conditions of the labor collective and their entry into participation in socialist construction."[119]

The critique concludes that they were making an "egregious political mistake and in practice it will lead to a disruption of economic tasks."[120] Cultural-educational work and labor output were always intimately tied together in the Gulag, and this did not change in the conditions of war. Gulag authorities, like authorities in other Soviet institutions, treated every failure and success as political. Every problem was ascribed to insufficient political education and could only be solved by improving political literacy. Hence, when the surveillance and police department at one camp encountered poor discipline among the militarized guard, who were showing up to work inebriated, cohabiting with female prisoners, and engaging in drinking parties with the heads of prisoner detachments, it blamed the problem on the guard's insufficient political education by local Communist Party and Komsomol organizations.[121]

The Gulag authorities approached the tasks of labor productivity and discipline among the inmates with the tools available from their decade of prewar experience. While the political education of prisoners was the primary responsibility of the six thousand employees of the Gulag's Cultural-Educational Department, every Gulag employee was charged with the tasks of political education.[122] The Gulag's employees brought every major economic and political campaign of Soviet society to their inmates. The KVCh led political discussions, oral newspaper readings, and lectures among prisoners throughout the war to foster "feelings of patriotism among prisoners" as well as a sense of inclusion in the activities of the front. The topics of political discussions included "the heroic struggle of the Red Army," the partisan movement, the war and construction, the productivity of labor in a time of war, Lenin and Stalin as founders of the Red Army, and others.[123] Almost identical discussions took place among the nonprisoner staff of the Gulag. The most significant differences in the educational activities aimed at camp staff were the focus on "revolutionary vigilance" and the cultivation of a certain hatred for the enemies of the people populating the camps.[124] Gulag chief Nasedkin reports over thirty-two thousand lectures in the Gulag during 1943 alone.[125] Even POWs were subjected to considerable political "anti-fascist" education, as they were "acquainted with the methods of socialist construction."[126]

Similar means spread Soviet political education to every level of society, both before and during the war. "Red Corners" in factories, party cells, Komsomol organizations, trade unions, the press, radio, and cinema were all charged with spreading the message of "defense of the motherland."[127]

To some extent, the drive to involve Soviet prisoners emotionally in the battle at the front was successful. I began the tale of the war with the heroic exploits of Pilishchuk, who directly tied his labor activities to his desire to help the front. Ginzburg recalls the atmosphere in the camps at the start of the war. "We, the outcasts, racked by four years of suffering, suddenly felt ourselves citizens of this country of ours. We, its rejected children, now trembled for our fatherland."[128] Figes recounts how prisoners in the Gulag greeted victory with "patriotic pride: they felt that they had made their contribution to the victory."[129] In the same vein, Solzhenitsyn describes how Gulag prisoners became "caught up" in work for the front. "Coal for Leningrad! Mortar shells for the troops!"[130] Solzhenitsyn notes that many prisoners sought a transfer to the front, but in his typical manner, he concludes that they did not seek to fight for any "ideological principle." Rather, they believed that "it is better to die in an open field than in a rotten shed! To unwind, to become, even for just a short while, 'like everyone else,' an unrepressed citizen."[131] Yet this desire to be "like everyone else" was in large part an "ideological principle," as the content of Gulag political education during the war will show.

The particular content of political education in the Gulag reveals much about the operation of Soviet society and the Soviet penal system during the war. By illustrating the "ideal" of how a prisoner was to be redeemed, the Gulag's transformative activities offer a picture of the characteristics perceived proper for a true Soviet citizen. A brochure written in 1944 by a Gulag cultural-educational worker named Loginov is a rich source for such analysis. Titled *The Resurrected* (*Vozvrashchennye k zhizni*, or literally, "Those who have returned to life") and circulated throughout the Gulag for internal use only, Loginov's "notes of a cultural worker" provides anecdotal accounts of his alleged successful reeducation of Gulag prisoners to teach proper cultural-educational work to other Gulag workers.[132] Forty copies of the brochure were sent to Karlag's KVCh on September 13, 1944, to illuminate the "forms and methods of working with the difficult to educate contingents of prisoners."[133] Loginov understood his primary task as the reeducation of criminals, transforming them into "conscious and hard-working members of socialist society."[134] His words emphasize the close tie in the Soviet mind-set between proper political consciousness and productive labor.

All of Loginov's tales begin with a prisoner who violates camp discipline, refuses to work, and remains isolated from the collective of prisoners. Loginov takes a personal interest in the laggard, learning about their past, criminal activities, and political mood.[135] Then, based on this knowledge, he is able to determine an effective individualized method of reeducation. As a rule, every case required a liberal dose of conversation about political topics. The prisoners eventually recognize their mistakes, return to work, and typically take a place among the camp's best laborers.[136]

At the same time, Loginov revealed again that not all prisoners could be resurrected: "They often ask me if all who emerge from the ITL [corrective labor camps] are corrected into useful members of society? No, not all, but the majority is and this is our great service."[137] There was no need to elaborate on the fate of those who were not part of his "majority."

So what were the topics of Loginov's political conversations? First and foremost, they "conversed for a long time about the principles of socialism." No matter where discussions led—the war, the heroes of Stakhanovite labor, "every chapter" of the Stalin constitution, ethics and morals in Soviet society, or labor competition—Loginov related all these topics to the hopes and joys of living in the land of Soviet socialism, where convicted criminals had the capacity to become once again "conscious builders of socialism."[138] The war, referred to as a great campaign "in defense of the socialist fatherland," was also a frequent point of conversation. It should be stressed that Loginov never presented this as a war for Russia or Russians. His calls for patriotism were for a Soviet patriotism. Unfortunately, lamented Loginov, many people "did not understand the historic tasks of the patriotic war . . . continuing to live and work as in old times." Loginov urged cultural-educational workers to "call forth a feeling of hatred for the bloody and vile enemy." Prisoners, he wrote, must understand that their "weapon" in the struggle with the enemy was their "labor."[139] All of these conversations and propaganda activity were matched in every sphere of Soviet society during the war. Free workers were exhorted to "work in the factory as soldiers fight at the front" and "work not just for yourself but for your comrade who has gone to the front." The Stakhanovite movement and shock work so common in the 1930s were given new impetus as the Soviet population was called to heroic feats of labor.[140]

Historians have frequently noted the reemergence of Russian nationalism in the war years: Russian historical figures, especially those with military achievements to their credit, were rehabilitated and the Orthodox Church was allowed some latitude to reconvene its activities. Further, they argue, socialism and revolution played a much-diminished role.[141] Yet one of Loginov's stories gives some pause to such a presentation. Loginov writes about the prisoner Samuil Gol'dshtein, whose Jewishness is never specifically mentioned but is made obvious to Loginov's readers as one of only two individuals in the brochure identified by their surname. Gol'dshtein's story starts like every other. He refused to contribute his labor to the drive for military victory, "calmly holed up in a penalty isolator" for his repeated refusal to work and violation of the camp regime. Loginov began to work with Gol'dshtein, but his first several conversations were wholly unsuccessful. Then one day, Loginov finally discovered the key to rehabilitating this particular prisoner. Loginov explained to his charge: "A cutthroat, slaughterous battle is happening now at the front. . . . The best sons of our motherland are giving their lives for honesty, freedom, the independence of our country, for the lives of their families, friends and for you. You criminally sit in the isolator" and do not help the front. Gol'dshtein was unmoved. Loginov continued, "Do you know what kind of goals the fascists seek in the war with us? . . . I explained to him who this [Adolf] Hitler was, the kinds of goals he was seeking." Loginov described to Gol'dshtein the nature of the "fascist cutthroats" and their desire for "world domination." Still, Gol'dshtein remained silent. Loginov then explained "the essence of racial theory and Hitler's new order in Europe. . . . So why do you behave like a traitor? By your behavior, you play into the hands of the enemy." Finally he had reached Gol'dshtein, who "began to weep like a little boy." Gol'dshtein exclaimed, "Forgive me! . . . I never thought that refusal to work was traitorous. But now I understand that this is so. Give me the chance to wash away my sin." Gol'dshtein immediately returned to work and became one of the most productive laborers in the camp. Soon, with Loginov's support, Gol'dshtein was released into the Red Army.[142]

Gol'dshtein's story, whether true or not, reveals the rising significance of ethnicity in the Gulag and Soviet society before and during the war, and presages the development of ethnic politics in the postwar period. His particularity, the aspect of his identity requiring specialized attention from his cultural-educational worker, was his ethnicity. Loginov was certainly aware of the activities of Nazi concentration and death camps. As he wrote in his introduction, "In contrast to capitalist countries, where concentration camps are places of torture and death for people, the corrective labor camps of the Soviet state are singular schools for the reeducation of worldviews, bequeathed to us by capitalist society." Although he does not specifically mention Nazi concentration camps, his reference is clear.[143] Loginov's conversations with Gol'dshtein were shaped by this knowledge and the prisoner's Jewishness—"the essence of racial theory" obviously referring to the atrocities being committed against Jews by Hitler's regime, even though the particularity of the Jews in Nazi racial theory was never spelled out. Although he never did so explicitly, Loginov called forth universal feelings of Soviet patriotism through a veiled appeal to Gol'dshtein's Jewishness. Crucially, the story reflected the parallel erasure of Jewish particularity in official commemoration of the war out-side the Gulag.[144]

The story also reveals the great extent to which cultural and political education in the Gulag operated with a conception in which national patriotism (and not just Russian national patriotism) and devotion to a socialist, Soviet polity were not competing ideas. Perhaps Richard Overy put it best in describing the use of "heroes of the past viewed through red-tinted spectacles."[145] During the war, the evidence of calls to Russian national patriotism is clear and overwhelming, yet one should not lose sight of the rehabilitation of carefully chosen non-Russian historical figures during the same period (like the seventeenth-century Ukrainian Cossack Hetman Bohdan Khmel'nytskyi) or the limited reemergence of Islam in Central Asia.

Four months after Gol'dshtein's release, he wrote a letter to Loginov telling him about the seventy-seven fascists that he had destroyed near Kiev and asked Loginov to remind the prison laborers that their work was aiding the defeat of the enemy. After destroying another fifty-five "fritzes," Gol'dshtein died in battle.[146] Gol'dshtein's experience was emblematic of central Gulag reports of a widespread "growth of patriotic feelings" among prisoners.[147] In nineteen camps, cultural-educational workers had received letters similar to that of Gol'dshtein from 348 former prisoners fighting at the front. Of these former prisoners, 114 had received medals, 34 had become officers, and many had entered the party.[148] These letters were treated both as the ultimate proof of the Gulag's success in reclaiming prisoners for Soviet society and a weapon in the ongoing struggle to reclaim others. One Lieutenant Kravtsov, formerly a prisoner at the Nizhne-Amurskii camp, wrote:

> I have already killed 32 fascists, but this is not many.... The government awarded me a high honor—the order of Lenin. Receiving the order of Lenin, I must fight all the more with the German horde, with this robber-army.... Also I have been accepted into the ranks of the Bolshevik Party and they have rescinded my conviction. I have corrected my admitted offense to the state in the struggle with the German occupiers and if it is necessary, I will give my life for the interests of our great Motherland [Rodina], I will give my life for the fatherland [otechestvo], for the party of the Bolsheviks, for Comrade Stalin.[149]

Local Gulag officials and cultural educators read these letters to their prisoners in attempts to arouse their sense of patriotism and drive them to productive labor. As one Gulag central official wrote, the letters had "great moral and educational" value to raise labor productivity and strengthen discipline among prisoners.[150] One account asserted that the refusal to work decreased fivefold in the Gulag during the war.[151] Many former prisoners received medals or entered the Communist Party, while five—Aleksandr Matveevich Matrosov, Vladimir Efimovich Breusov, Aleksei Ivanovich Otstavnov, Ivan Iakovlevich Serzhantov, and Vasilii Mefod'evich Efimov—were awarded the exalted order of Hero of the Soviet Union.[152] Breusov was released early from Karlag on January 6, 1943, whereupon he joined the Red Army and in November 1943 was awarded the title Hero of the Soviet Union, the Order of Lenin, and a gold star. Twenty other former Karlag prisoners received medals for their service at the front during the war.[153] The former prisoners turned heroes were a great source of pride for the Gulag. The five former prisoner "Heroes of the Soviet Union" were mentioned time and again in official documents as the prime example of the "success" in rehabilitating prisoners.[154]

One final lesson from Loginov's brochure is the unit of measure for the success or failure of prisoner reeducation: labor. Loginov's wards were unreformed when they refused to work, and their transformation created in them a desire to work and do so well. Through their labor, they became participants in the grand struggle to build a new society and destroy the fascist enemy.[155] Once again, labor was much more significant than its economic output.

## The Hierarchy of Danger

The war represented an important turning point in the development of Soviet penal policy. Like previous major events in Soviet history, external events led to a substantial reconfiguration of Gulag society. During the war, the dividing line between Gulag prisoners and Soviet society became wider than ever before. While many *zeks* were released during the war, many others were subject to a rigidification of the Gulag regime. Denied a role at the front during the war—the new foundational experience for Soviet society—Gulag prisoners found themselves even further removed from the Soviet social body. Armageddon had in fact arrived, claiming the lives of twenty-seven to twenty-eight million people. In the midst of this epic battle, the Soviet polity's efforts to categorize and cleanse its population of internal enemies never wavered.[156]

By the beginning of 1942, the Germans had advanced deeply into Soviet territory. Three million Red Army soldiers had been taken prisoner, and at least 1.5 million were dead from all causes. The civilian economy was nearly ruined, and most of the Soviet government had been evacuated from Moscow.[157] In this atmosphere one of the first large-scale armed uprisings hit the Gulag. On January 24, 1942, 125 prisoners at the far north Vorkuta corrective labor camp disarmed the camp's militarized guard, attacked the nearby district center of Ust'-Usa, and captured the local telegraph office, cutting off communication with other regions. The rebel prisoners then executed the guard of the local militia's holding cell, freeing forty-two prisoners, twenty-seven of whom joined their band.[158] The battle to destroy the group lasted over a month, with sizable losses on both sides. The official accounts reported that forty-eight were killed, six committed suicide, and eight were captured among the prisoners, while thirty-three were killed or seriously injured, twenty were less seriously wounded, and fifty-two suffered from cases of serious frostbite among the NKVD forces. The resulting investigation blamed the uprising on a counterrevolutionary organization created in October 1941 by former alleged Trotskyites in the camp. For their part in the uprising, forty-nine prisoners were sentenced to death.[159]

Most important for other camps in the system, only three days after the uprising began, Beria, the head of the NKVD, personally sent a letter to all chiefs of corrective labor camps as well as republic and local level NKVDs describing this uprising, and prescribing measures to prevent further ones. Camp guards should be battle ready, and instructed that any violation or weakening of vigilance among them would be punished harshly. Free laborers should replace any prisoners or even former prisoners sentenced for counterrevolutionary or especially dangerous crimes serving the camp in positions of authority. Extra measures should be taken to protect weapons in the camp. The head of the camp surveillance system should check up on all agents and informants, and take measures to reveal any "rebellious-bandit moods" among prisoners. Any prisoners expressing terrorist moods or preparing armed escapes should be arrested.[160] Karlag authorities reacted swiftly, issuing their own order on February 9, 1942, to remind their subordinates of the need to introduce "iron discipline" in the face of the anti-Soviet activization of the prisoners.[161]

The uprising caught the authorities off guard, but it was not unexpected. From the first day of the war, the Soviets anticipated a battle on the home front. In Stalin's famed radio speech on July 3, 1941, he proposed, among other tasks for the Soviet people, "to organize remorseless struggle with all disorganizers of the rear, deserters, panic-mongers, circulators of rumors, and to destroy spies and saboteurs."[162] These words were repeated frequently in the wartime camps, where the authorities took their role in battling Soviet internal enemies quite seriously, isolating them and keeping their harmful influence from doing damage to the Soviet war effort. The battle at the front was to be matched by an intense battle to cleanse the rear. In the latter battle, the Gulag played a decisive part. Perhaps more blatantly than ever before, the Gulag was performing its role in weeding out the bad from the good—the redeemable from the hopeless. While releases of the "good" from the wartime camps occurred over a period of time, the intensified isolation of the "bad" was immediate.

On the very day of the German attack, the NKVD issued an order for the creation of special camp zones where counterrevolutionary and other especially dangerous criminals were placed under heightened guard. Deemed too dangerous to be allowed to fall into the hands of the advancing German armies, prisoners sentenced for counterrevolutionary and other especially dangerous crimes were the first to be evacuated from prisons, camps, and colonies near the front.[163] Some prisoners were even perceived as too dangerous to live in the face of the German onslaught. For example, on September 11, 1941, in the Medvedev forest, 157 political prisoners from the Orel prison, including the famous Left Socialists Revolutionary Mariia Spiridonova, were executed.[164] After the war began, political prisoners in western Ukraine were executed en masse. On the day of the German attack, the NKVD halted all releases of prisoners sentenced for betraying the motherland, espionage, terror, sabotage, Trotskyism, rightism, banditism, and "other serious state crimes." An even wider group of Gulag prisoners, including anti-Soviet agitators, serious military criminals, armed assailants and robbers, recidivists, socially dangerous elements, family members of traitors, and other especially dangerous criminals, were to stay in camps after the completion of their sentence, although they were granted all the rights of camp staff (except for the right to leave the camp vicinity). These "semi-released" prisoners lived in a nervous limbo, where any violation of discipline led to immediate reincarceration until the end of the war.[165]

These new instructions were carried out rapidly in Karlag, where orders were issued on June 23 and 26, 1941, to implement the demands of central Gulag authorities. In addition to the new practices already noted, Karlag authorities halted all visits and correspondence for all prisoners. Staff vacations were canceled. A "mobile group" (*manevrennaia gruppa*) composed of twenty-five members of the militarized guard was formed for use in "special situations." The camp's operchekotdel was ordered to arrest all prisoners involved in anti-Soviet activities. Furthermore, the camp was placed under "martial law" (*voennoe polozhenie*), as a strengthened guard was established for critical camp locations like investigation prisons, electric and radio stations, dams, food supplies, and weapons depots. The camp staff was formed into fighting groups, trained to fight and defend all-important camp objects at a moment's notice. In essence, the camp staff was taught to expect anti-Soviet or terrorist activity from its prisoner contingent. Staff members were ordered to be battle ready at all times, so much so that the camp's guards were ordered never to undress fully when sleeping. They were instead only to remove their boots and hats. Finally, as was typical of all Gulag orders, Karlag required an increase in political education work among the camp guards.[166]

On March 11, 1942, the Presidium of the Supreme Soviet formalized and strengthened the establishment of military order in the Gulag by extending all Red Army disciplinary measures to Gulag staff and guards.[167]

Throughout the war, additional measures were taken to further isolate concentration camp prisoners from Soviet society at large. On July 8, 1941, Karlag forbade its prisoners from sending money to their relatives.[168] On September 12, 1941, Karlag prisoners were informed of a central Gulag decision forbidding them from contributing to the defense fund.[169] On August 27, 1941, Karlag ordered the stricter censorship of incoming and outgoing prisoner correspondence. Letters "from freedom" could only be given to prisoners if they were of an "exclusively positive character." Outgoing letters from prisoners were only to be accepted in extraordinary circumstances, and then only from prisoners who had proven themselves trustworthy through high productivity and good behavior in camp life. Even in these cases, letters were only to be accepted from prisoners with the consent of both the camp director and chief of the operative section.[170]

With the disastrous retreats of the Red Army, Vorkuta uprising of 1942, and rising share of counterrevolutionary criminals in the Gulag population, the atmosphere inside the Gulag intensified. The war was going so badly for the Soviet Union that from January 15 to February 15, 1942, Karlag's militarized guards and camp staff attended a twenty-eight-hour training course on the destruction of enemy tanks in the event of a German advance as far as Karaganda.[171] Looking back, the Gulag chief portrayed the detained contingent as highly dangerous. Nasedkin wrote in his 1944 report that "from the first days of the war, enemy activity among the prisoners was significantly intensified. . . . Anti-Soviet activity manifested itself in the establishment of multi-member rebellious organizations and groups, preparations of armed and group escapes . . . , circulation among the prisoners of defeatist fascist agitation, strengthening of banditism and other criminal activities." Careful as ever to put the best face on the Gulag for higher authorities, Nasedkin did not mention the Vorkuta uprising at all, instead describing a litany of planned uprisings thwarted by Gulag authorities.[172] At Karlag, incidents ranged from the relatively minor to the decidedly serious. Minor incidents included the arrest in September 1941 of Nina Borisovna Bondareva-Dmitrieva, originally sentenced to five years as a socially dangerous element and sentenced three times previously for allegedly passing a flyer to a camp staff member that read, "Down with Stalin. Long live Hitler."[173] A much more major event was an armed escape in 1943. On May 2 a group of four especially dangerous criminals was being moved twenty-five kilometers when they attacked and strangled their convoy guard to death. They took his gun and thirty rounds of ammunition, and escaped. The disappearance of the guard and his prisoners was only discovered on May 4. The guard's body was found on May 5. On May 28, 1943, central Gulag authorities, unaware that the escape had been "liquidated" the day before, ordered the head of the relevant camp subdivision along with the head of its political section to be removed from their jobs and charged criminally for failing to provide the necessary minimum of two armed guards for convoying prisoners.[174]

In their battle against enemy activities and uprisings among the prisoners, Gulag authorities paid special attention to the call for increased surveillance, recruiting many more prisoners for their agent-informant network. While the number of prisoners declined, the agent-informant network grew by 186 percent, raising the proportion of informants among the camp population from 1.7 percent in 1941 to 8 percent in 1944.[175] An agent-informant network operated also among the special settlers, but on a much smaller scale, comprising approximately 2 percent of the population in 1944.[176] With the assistance of this network, the Gulag authorities carried out systematic "operative-prophylactic measures" against anti-Soviet activities. They maintained surveillance on 76,000 prisoners, Soviet ethnic Germans drafted into labor armies, and Gulag staff on suspicion of such crimes as espionage, wrecking, and anti-Soviet agitation. Within the camps and colonies, some 148,000 individuals were arrested from 1941 to 1944 for criminal activities, primarily for the refusal to work, escape attempts, anti-Soviet agitation, embezzlement, and other property crimes. For more serious crimes, 10,087 prisoners, 526 Soviet Germans in labor armies, and 245 voluntary staff were sentenced to death.[177]

Prisoners from the Baltic states, agents of the German occupiers, former military servitors sentenced for anti-Soviet activities, and Soviet Germans drafted into labor armies were all singled out for their alleged participation in rebellious organizations. The Gulag chief claimed to have uncovered and destroyed 603 rebellious organizations in the camps and colonies from 1941 to 1944, whose usual goal was the armed overthrow of the Gulag militarized guard and transfer to the side of the fascist military. All members of these organizations were "repressed."[178] In July 1942, for example, twenty-two members of an "insurrectionary counterrevolutionary organization" were arrested before they could carry out their goal of disarming the guard and "joining the fascists in battle."[179] One should, of course, skeptically evaluate the existence of such "rebellious organizations," particularly those liquidated before carrying out any actual rebellious activity. The Gulag authorities expected and were expected to uncover such organizations, and high pressure may have been placed on their agents to uncover such rebellious elements.[180]

The need for skepticism is highlighted by the data on escapes from corrective labor camps during the war. While the general tenor of Nasedkin's report would make one expect escapes to have risen greatly during the course of the war, the numbers themselves tell a different story. The total escapes as a percentage of the camp population rose slightly from 1941 to 1942, but quickly fell to all-time lows in 1943, 1944, and 1945. (The percentages for each year were 0.7, 0.83, 0.63, 0.54, and 0.3). Add in the declining overall camp population during the war years and it is clear that the absolute numbers of escapes diminished significantly.[181]

Nonetheless, the actual data of escapes rarely mattered throughout Gulag history. Even one escape was treated as one too many, requiring heroic efforts at prevention and liquidation. One high-profile or dramatic escape could bring a great deal of heat on a local camp chief. In 1943, as-sistant NKVD Chernyshov sharply criticized Karlag for its negligence in the battle with escapes. Zhuravlev replied in a letter dated June 12, 1943 that all necessary measures had been taken, but escapes had increased anyway, especially the number of escapees who had not been captured—twenty-nine as of June 10. In his letter, Zhuravlev recognized that poor work among Karlag's staff and guards contributed to the problems. Yet repeating old (and true) arguments about Karlag's particularity, and en-gaging in his typical search for excuses and blame shifting, he pointed out that the agricultural character of the camp made it difficult to isolate prisoners as fully as necessary to prevent escapes. During the growing season, fully three-quarters of the camp's prisoners (up to thirty thousand prisoners) worked and even lived in fields spread out over twenty-three thousand square kilometers that were not surrounded by any fences or other physical boundaries. The nature of the work also required prisoners to move frequently from place to place. To return all prisoners to a camp zone at night was by and large impossible. While during the winter the prisoners were concentrated in over three hundred places, during the sum-mer season they were spread out over nearly three thousand locations. Furthermore, he wrote, the composition of the prisoner contingent had changed so radically since the start of the war, especially with the arrivals in the second half of 1942 of prisoners from evacuated camps near the front, that Karlag could no longer complete its agricultural work without sending portions of the especially dangerous prisoner population out into the fields. Included in this group of prisoners were those with known ten-dencies to escape. Consequently, according to Zhuravlev, he had written to Gulag chief Nasedkin on May 15 requesting that they curtail future ship-ments of especially dangerous prisoners to Karlag. Zhuravlev then faulted central Gulag authorities for the fact that no representative had visited Karlag in four years to acquaint themselves with these conditions.[182]

These particularities of Karlag continued to occupy an important place in preparations to battle against escape. In a directive to all Karlag employees at the outset of the agricultural season in 1944, Zhuravlev emphasized the dangers presented by utilizing the changed contingent of prisoners in field work, especially considering the large number of brigades that were "self-guarded," lacking any permanent armed convoy to accompany them. In particular, he warned his employees to be vigilant about escapes and prisoners shirking their work duties. Authorities in the various camp points and subdivisions were to concentrate prisoners likely to attempt escape or disobey camp authorities in brigades with permanent armed guards, equipped with search dogs. Prisoners should also be housed every night in permanent or temporary summer zones. Trusted prisoners should be placed in brigades that would go out and work without guards. Armed guards should check on these prisoner brigades daily. Prisoners sentenced for especially dangerous crimes were forbidden from membership in such brigades. All brigades were to be placed on the system of collective responsibility wherein the entire brigade would face punishment for escapes or violations of discipline by any of its members.

Increased vigilance and concerns about loyalty extended beyond the prisoners in the wartime Gulag. As early as August 15, 1941, central Gulag authorities sent instructions to all Gulag camps warning of a dramatic rise in counterrevolutionary activity on the part of the militarized guard in the camps. Relating several instances of guards spreading rumors among their fellow guards and to inmates, the instructions required all camps to check up on their staff for counterrevolutionary activity and punish harshly anybody found guilty.[183] During the war, the Soviet secret police never lost sight of the need to educate and propagandize among its own staff. In 1943, the NKVD created its own "Higher School of the NKVD USSR" in order to educate the highest officials in all NKVD staffs in Marxist-Leninist theory, the specific tasks of the NKVD, and raise the level of those whose job it was to teach others in the organization.[184] Nasedkin prepared and delivered lectures at the school on the history and tasks of Gulag. The creation of the higher school was followed by the establishment of several schools within the Gulag apparatus to train the leading staff of Gulag camps as well as the chiefs of camp subdivisions and departments. The NKVD clearly intended to create a well-trained, young staff for leadership of the corrective labor institutions. As such, candidates for the schools had to be twenty to forty years old, and have at least a fifth-grade education, a good record of behavior and political outlook, and no compromising material in their files.[185]

## The "Return" of Katorga

Two particularities of the wartime hierarchy of danger need further discussion: the introduction of katorga camp divisions, and the exile of nationalities. For some so-called criminals, none of the regime enhancements of the first two years of the Gulag at war would suffice. For them, for the worst of the worst, the Soviets created new camp subdivisions with a regime stricter than any in Gulag history. As a sign of the harshness of these new divisions, the camps were emblazoned with the notorious tsarist term for forced labor: katorga. The Presidium of the Supreme Soviet issued a decree on April 17, 1943, creating katorga subdivisions to house German fascist villains, spies, and traitors to the motherland along with their associates. Katorga was described as "the strictest criminal punishment after the death penalty, combining deprivation of freedom with the necessity to carry out hard labor in favor of the state."[186] Katorga camp divisions were introduced as an alternative punishment for all sections of the criminal code under which a person could be sentenced to death. The authorities sought to use a small portion of the most dangerous and least redeemable state criminals at the harshest of all tasks, such as uranium mining, so as to protect the health of other Gulag prisoners.[187]

The katorga regime had a number of specific strict regime characteristics. Katorga prisoners were to be placed in independent camp subdivisions with zones surrounded by fencing with a height of 3.5 meters—that is, they were to be isolated from all other camp inmates. Barracks in katorga divisions had bars on their windows and were locked at night. Katorga prisoners worked one hour longer per day than the normal prisoner, had one less day of rest per month, and worked at the heaviest labor, especially in underground mining. If they failed to fulfill their work norms, their working day could be extended by up to two additional hours, they could be transferred to even heavier work, or they could be charged criminally. Katorga prisoners had to travel to work under strict armed guard. All of these "innovations" were introduced in a period when even regular labor camp prisoners lived at and beyond the edges of survival. All prisoners in katorga divisions wore special clothes clearly displaying their prisoner number. Katorga prisoners were subject to enhanced criminal penalties for crimes or violations of camp discipline while in katorga divisions. Katorga division chiefs could also punish entire brigades or barracks for the disciplinary violations or escape attempts of one individual. Katorga prisoners deemed especially difficult were transported to and from work in handcuffs. After a one-year period in which they were deprived of all correspondence and contact with the outside world, katorga prisoners could earn such privileges as writing to their family, receiving parcels and visits, earning cash premiums for their work, and working in their specialty.[188]

Writing about the creation of katorga divisions, Solzhenitsyn concluded that "little attempt was made to conceal their purpose: the *katorzhane* [katorga prisoners] were to be done to death. These were, undisguisedly, murder camps: but in the Gulag tradition murder was protracted, so that the doomed would suffer longer and put a little work in before they died."[189] Such an assessment was not inaccurate, as after less than two years of katorga, almost 50 percent of its inmates became invalids. Though I have not found specific figures on mortality in the katorga divisions, these health numbers indicate that death rates must have been high. Gulag authorities did not seek to improve the inmates' condition, only to bolster their ranks. In view of the rapid destruction of katorga laborers, a draft order from April 1945 requested "no less" than an additional sixty thousand katorga inmates.[190] Solzhenitsyn continued, noting that the katorga divisions combined "all that was worst in the camps with all that was worst in the prisons." He specifically had in mind the inability to move about freely within the zones of katorga divisions. Prisoners were not allowed to go to the latrine, attend the mess, or seek care in the medical section without permission. After the twelve-hour working day, lengthy roll calls morning and night, eating, and other camp business, the prisoners in katorga divisions barely got four hours of sleep per night.[191]

How could Gulag authorities, long emphasizing the progressive nature of Soviet penal policy in contrast to that of the tsarist past, accept the return of the loaded term katorga? It was, for them, a matter of great concern. Katorga had always represented the exploitative political imprisonments of the prerevolutionary era. The products of this concern are reflected in a lengthy internal Gulag study of the role of katorga in prerevolutionary Russia and several European countries, which also sought to rationalize the maintenance of the katorga system.[192] Nasedkin summed up the findings in September 1945:

> In the majority of states, katorga operates in special prison institutions with a strict regime. In several countries, in England, France, and Russia, katorga and exile were closely tied to carrying out not only penal but also colonial goals..... England in the seventeenth century introduced katorga exile in the newly opened lands—Australia, Africa, etc.... In the eighteenth century, France also introduced exile to katorga into its colonies.[193]

The historical note stressed the complete absence of corrective goals in European katorga.[194]

Writing about tsarist Russia's katorga practices, Nasedkin highlighted at length those factors that he believed cast Soviet katorga in a positive, progressive light. He focused on the tsarist use of katorga for colonial purposes, introduction of eternal katorga, application of corporal punishment to katorga prisoners, and counterrevolutionary use of katorga against Russian revolutionaries. In Russia, he observed, criminals had been sentenced to katorga as early as the late sixteenth century, when they were sent into exile for colonial purposes but without a forced labor component. In the seventeenth century, Peter I introduced the widespread utilization of forced labor. The abolition of capital punishment led Elizabeth to add eternal exile to katorga. In the eighteenth and early nineteenth centuries, katorga prisoners were branded and had their ears clipped. In the nineteenth century, katorga could be either time limited or eternal, and involve forced labor in mining, factories, and forts. To the end of the tsarist regime, all katorga prisoners regardless of their gender were shackled, their heads were shaven, and they were dressed in special clothes. In the late tsarist era, katorga prisoners were sentenced to terms of four to twenty years. They faced the deprivation of familial and property rights. For crimes committed while completing a sentence of katorga, individuals could be imprisoned for a hundred days on a diet of bread and water, face the extension of their katorga sentence, receive a hundred blows, or incur a number of other punishments. Nasedkin also noted the application of Russian katorga against political prisoners starting with the Decembrists and extending into the early twentieth century when it was used against representatives of workers' movements, especially in the wake of the revolution of 1905–6.[195] Ultimately, the study concluded, the failure of tsarist or European katorga to fulfill the state's penitentiary, colonial, or fiscal goals could be attributed to the complete absence of a "penitentiary pedagogy."[196] In a word, the Gulag chief sought the distinctions in both methods and goals, and more important, the political framework within which the katorga system operated. Historians of today certainly could pursue the comparison between tsarist and Soviet katorga, but in humanitarian terms the comparison, contra Nasedkin, would redound in favor of the tsarist system.

In Karlag, a katorga division was created to house those prisoners sentenced to katorga but ill and unable to work. All physically able katorga prisoners were sent to Vorkuta, Noril'sk, and Kolyma.[197] The katorga division at Karlag was closed in 1951, when its invalids were placed in the nearby special camp, and those few healthy katorga prisoners were sent to Vorkuta, Noril'sk, and Kolyma.[198] Only a tiny fraction of Gulag prisoners were in katorga camps; by July 1944, a mere 5,200 of 1.2 million camp and colony prisoners were classified as such. For those unlucky few, life was horribly difficult.[199] The number of katorga prisoners remained relatively small throughout the war, reaching 39,000 in September 1945 and 60,000 two years later.[200] Yet its significance lay in the imposition of the harshest hierarchies of penalties and paving the way for their application in 1948 to a much larger group of prisoners with the introduction of special camps.

## The Wartime Gulag and Soviet Nationalities

In the emerging wartime hierarchy of danger, the role of nationality occupied a special place. The shift toward a national definition of the internal enemy can be seen in a number of ways. While nearly all those exiled in the early 1930s were officially categorized as kulaks—that is, in terms of social class—by the mid-1930s Soviet authorities began to exile non-Russian peoples based solely on their nationality. By January 1945, fewer than 647,000 of over 2.1 million exiles were still classified as former kulaks. All the rest, except for a small group of religious sect members (numbering under 5,000), were classified exclusively in ethnic terms.[201] The ethnicization of camps, colonies, and prisons was less obvious in terms of prisoner demographics than in the practices of these institutions. While Gulag authorities differentiated prisoners by nationality throughout the 1930s, nationality became a primary category of Gulag identity among staff and prisoners in the latter 1930s and during the war.

The story of Soviet nationalities and the Gulag during the war is dominated by national deportations. While a number of 1930s' deportations had taken on national and ethnic tones, the shift in reference point for the hierarchy of redeemability from class to ethnic terms was solidified during the war. The wartime national deportations occurred in three waves: deportations from the newly annexed territories, deportations of nationalities matching external nation-states fighting against the Soviet Union, and deportations of "punished peoples."

The deportations from the newly annexed western territories were, on the one hand, a continuation of the types of policies typical throughout the Soviet Union during the Great Break of the early 1930s. In essence, these areas were being Sovietized through the same campaigns that previously happened elsewhere. Soviet authorities brought their entire range of "Sovietization tools" to bear on the new territories. As Bardach recalled, "Life in Wlodzimierz-Wolynski [a town just on the Soviet side of the new 1939 border] changed swiftly.... The intrusion of Soviet indoctrination and propaganda, mandatory political meetings, Soviet control of the radio and press, and the dissolution of religious activity transformed the city.... I absorbed the indoctrination and devoured the propaganda." Along with this propaganda and control of information came the need to cleanse the territories of enemies as well as a strong skepticism of the entire population. Bardach soon joined the Red Army to fight against the Nazis, but "as a former Polish citizen, I was still considered foreign and therefore suspected of political illiteracy and unreliability—this much was made clear on a daily basis."[202]

As shown earlier, the 1930s' deportation campaigns were largely organized on the basis of social class, and to an extent this continued to be true in the western territories. It was not difficult to integrate the selective deportations from the western territories into the Soviet focus on class enemies. It "made sense" in light of Soviet practices in the 1930s. While hostile class elements officially ceased to exist in the Soviet Union with the declaration of socialism built in 1936, these new territories had not undergone the processes of building socialism. Consequently, class enemies could and were presumed to exist, and thus present a danger to the Soviet state.[203] These territories were nonetheless marked as ethnically and nationally different from the remainder of the Soviet Union. Combined with the targeting of ethnonational movements and organizations for deportation from these territories, class and national enemies were often conflated. As such, during the deportations from the Baltics, one sees the use of such explicitly mixed class and national terms as "kulak-nationalist."[204] Yet unlike the wartime deportations, these operations in the newly annexed territories continued to operate in a differentiated fashion. Not every Lithuanian would be subject to deportation, but every German and Chechen would be deported during the war.

The place of nationality became firmer as the wartime deportations turned undifferentiated. Due to their numerical preponderance in the Karaganda region, I focus on the deportations of the Germans first and later the Chechens. The first and largest wartime deportation was of the Soviet Germans.[205] The heightened distrust of Soviet Germans was obvious in the camps even prior to the nationality's deportation. Ginzburg noted that only by convincing Kolyma camp authorities that she was of Jewish rather than German origin was she able to avoid the heightened security over prisoners with "German-sounding names."[206] Semenova recalled the attitude of the chief of the Department of Cadres at Karlag, a man named Monarkh. Since Jewish surnames often sounded like German ones, Monarkh refused to release Jewish prisoners during the war unless he was absolutely certain that they were "of the Jewish nationality."[207] The distrust of Soviet Germans even extended to the prisoners themselves. Many prisoners recounted the wartime emergence of a national hierarchy among Gulag prisoners, with Germans occupying the lowest rung. Buca related the serving of soup in his first prison: "The Russians got the first bowls, then the Ukrainians, then us Poles, and finally the two Germans." Not surprisingly, the Germans were forced to give one of their bowls to the Russians and thus receive only a half portion. "That's enough for Germans."[208] Scholmer concurred, stating that both Russian prisoners and camp authorities considered all Germans to be fascists. Germans therefore suffered worse punishment in disputes with other nationals.[209] Consider Lev Kopelev's outrage on his arrest in April 1945 at being placed in a cell with Germans. "'Don't you know there are Fritzes in here?' I bawled; I swore; I was furious. 'I'm a Soviet officer! I won't be humiliated like this!'"[210]

In the Soviet Union at large, this distrust of Germans was expressed in their undifferentiated deportation. It was just one of several moves directed against Soviet citizens whose official Soviet nationality matched that of a nation-state fighting against the Soviet Union. For example, lecturing on the wartime Gulag to the NKVD school in the early postwar period, Nasedkin stated that Soviet citizens whose nationality was that of countries fighting the USSR along with foreigners from countries fighting against the USSR were held until the end of the war regardless of their particular crime.[211]

On August 26, 1941, the Presidium of the Supreme Soviet issued its first decree on the forcible deportation of the Soviet Germans—in this case, those living in the German Volga Republic. The order required their resettlement in areas around Novosibirsk, Omsk, the Altai Krai, and Kazakhstan. The published decree presented a picture of the Volga Germans as a people concealing "thousands and tens of thousands" of spies and saboteurs who were awaiting a signal from Nazi Germany to engage in action against the Soviet Union.[212] Consequently, the Soviet government, the decree continued, found it necessary to undertake repressive measures against "the whole German population of the Volga region." Deportation was presented as a less disruptive and less bloody means of suppressing the possibilities of espionage and sabotage.[213] A subsequent series of decrees extended the deportations of Soviet Germans to those from other regions, while a decree from September 7, 1941 liquidated the Volga German autonomous republic, transferring its lands into the Saratov and Stalingrad regions.[214] The following day, September 8, 1941, a decree ordered the removal of Soviet Germans from the ranks of the Red Army.[215]

Figures differ, but somewhere between 950,000 and 1.2 million Soviet Germans were deported as a result of these decrees.[216] Some 420,000 Soviet Germans were deported to Kazakhstan.[217] While the Karaganda region was not the intended destination of the first major wave of Volga Germans, the area became involved in the latter deportations from other regions. Ultimately, the region housed some 20,000 Soviet German special settlers along with an already-existing Soviet German population of about 10,000.[218]

The deportation process was quick, chaotic, and often deadly. Soviet authorities gave deportees a short period of time to gather a limited amount of personal property to take with them or make arrangements to sell their remaining property. They also organized deportations by kolkhoz, and resettled deportees in existing kolkhozy and sovkhozy (state farms), or newly established kolkhozy and sovkhozy, which the deportees had to build by their own hands and at their own expense with the assistance of government loans. They resettled deported city residents into cities that were not regional centers.[219] Similar to the deportations of kulaks in the 1930s, the process left families together except in the frequent cases in which the head of household was arrested, usually as "anti-soviet or doubtful elements."[220]

The deportation operation and resettlement process was no doubt an expensive one. At a time when Soviet forces were collapsing at the front, Beria ordered 4,800 officers of the NKVD and police along with over 12,000 Red Army troops to do the initial round of deportations in an eighteen-day period. Those carrying out the deportations were ordered to conduct "explanatory work" among the deported population, informing them that the head of the family would be held criminally responsible for any illegal activities of family members. Any opposition was to be dealt with decisively and quickly.[221] Rail and water travel also had to be provided. On arrival, the Germans needed places to live and food to eat.[222] Kazakh government and Communist Party authorities hustled to gather the necessary financial, construction, and food resources to house the expected 415,600 Germans to be distributed among every region of the republic, except for the Gur'evskaia and Zapadno-Kazakhstanskaia regions. While these authorities made every effort to house the Germans in existing kolkhozy and sovkhozy, they determined that only 7,266 vacant homes existed in the republic. Kazakh authorities believed it necessary to construct an additional 100,000 homes to accommodate the arriving Germans. Yet they also determined that the republic was simply short of many of the necessary materials to complete such a task.[223]

The Kazakh Republic's resources—already strained by the Soviet war effort, resettlement of free peoples evacuated from the western regions of the country and wartime demands to accomplish more with less— were pushed beyond all capacities with the arrival of over four hundred thousand exiled residents. In their mind, these were not just any new residents, either. They arrived under a cloud of accusation. As the Kazakh Party Central Committee charged in a letter dated October 4, 1941 to all Kazakh party organs, these new arrivals were all to be considered potential Gestapo collaborators. Local party operatives should take actions to prevent the exertion of negative influence by the Soviet Germans on their local populations. They should be particularly wary of a variety of anti-Soviet agitation and even the formation of "counterrevolutionary fascist diversionist groups" with the goals of distributing fascist literature, disrupting work on kolkhozy, and agitating kolkhozniki (collective farmers) to hatred of the Soviet Union in hopes of fomenting an uprising in the rear. Consequently, local authorities were also required to increase their attention toward political education of the local populations to fight these negative influences. They were specially advised to provide instruction to the local Kazakh population in their native language.[224]

Warned to expect anti-Soviet activity from their German population, local authorities found this activity everywhere they looked.[225] The secretary of Karaganda's regional party committee, Kondratenko, reported to the Kazakhstan Central Committee on November 20, 1941 about the rise of a counterrevolutionary fascist group among the Soviet German population already living within the Karaganda region at the time of the German invasion. The group, he wrote, had the goals of murdering responsible party and Soviet workers, seizing secret documents, and organizing industrial and agricultural sabotage. More generally, he accused the Soviet German population of joy at the news of Nazi military advances and negative feelings toward Soviet power. He also warned ominously of rising ties between certain portions of the German population and Karlag prisoners, who had displayed a special interest in the arrivals of exiled Germans. Kondratenko proposed the resettlement of this Soviet German population within the Karaganda region so that they would be further from the Karaganda coal mines and railways.[226]

Local resources in Kazakhstan were strained to provide for the needs of an arriving unfree population considered to contain a significant number of spies, counterrevolutionaries, and fascists seeking to disrupt work in the Soviet rear. In this situation, can it be any surprise that local authorities frequently failed to meet the needs of Soviet Germans? As Kaidar S. Aldazhumanov notes, NKVD officials complained that some localities unapologetically squandered the funds that were provided for meeting the needs of special settlers. As one official in the Taldy-Kurganskaia regional executive committee (*oblispolkom*) declared, "He did not want to give anything to the special settlers, since they were 'traitors to the motherland' and should be shot." Following his lead, several other local officials completely stopped offering economic assistance to the exiles in their localities.[227]

Just as the Soviet German population began to settle into their new surroundings in winter 1941–42, new upheavals greeted a new year. On January 10, 1942, Soviet authorities drove a large portion of the deported Soviet German population into stricter forms of detention. On that date, the State Committee of Defense, the de facto central ruling authority in the wartime Soviet Union, responding to both the local inability to engage the deported population in useful labor and reports of anti-Soviet activity among the deportees, ordered all deported Soviet German males of working (and fighting) age (seventeen to fifty years old) and in condition to perform physical labor to report for "mobilization" into forced labor working columns for the length of the war. Initial estimates predicted the mobilization of approximately 120,000 men to labor in various NKVD concentration camps and economic enterprises ranging from forestry to railroad construction. The mobilization of Soviet Germans was expanded three times. On February 14, 1942, all Soviet German males meeting the conditions outlined above, but from regions where they had not initially been subject to deportation, were forced into the ranks of mobilized workers. On October 7, 1942, the order was extended to all Soviet German males between the ages of fifteen to sixteen and fifty-one to fifty-five, and all Soviet German females between the ages of sixteen to forty-five who did not have children less than three years of age. Children over the age of three were to be given to relatives or German kolkhozy, while their mothers were sent to the working columns until the war's conclusion. All men mobilized under the October 7 decree were sent to work in the coal mines of Cheliabinsk and Karaganda, while the women were sent to work at various enterprises of Narkomneft.[228] Coal in Karaganda had taken on a higher priority with the loss of the western coal-mining regions to occupation. The decision to send many of the mobilized Germans there occurred no doubt because of figures that revealed that by August 1942, Karaganda coal production was down by 40 percent.[229] Finally, on October 14, 1942, forced mobilization into working columns was expanded to Soviet citizens of "other nationalities of countries fighting with the USSR—Romanians, Hungarians, Italians and Finns."[230]

When reporting for forced mobilization, Soviet Germans were required to bring their own winter clothing, bedding, and dishes, along with food for their journey. The determination of those subject to forced mobilization was made with the use of data held by the passport division of the local police and local Soviet organs.[231] By December 1942, approximately one out of every eight Soviet Germans living in the Kazakh Republic had been mobilized.[232]

These mobilized workers were essentially Soviet labor camp prisoners. In many cases, the mobilized Germans were actually housed in separate divisions of existing Soviet corrective labor camps, where administrators were responsible for organizing both the living space and labor tasks for the Germans.[233] Even those mobilized Soviet Germans not officially held in labor camps were forced to live and work under the established concentration camp regime. The mobilized Germans were organized as a labor army, divided first into ranks of 1,500–2,000 for transport to individual locations. They were then further divided into production columns of 250–500 and then into labor brigades of 35–100, all depending on the particular needs of their economic activity. Labor brigades lived together in barracks, inside guarded zones. These zones were to be completely separate from those for regular Gulag inmates. While the mobilized Germans could move about freely within the zone, entrance or exit from the zone other than with one's labor brigade required a permit. Initially, mobilized labor brigades were not placed under armed guard during their march to or at their place of work. They were nevertheless subject to extremely strict labor discipline rules as well as roll calls each morning and evening. Already in March 1942, however, orders were handed down for keeping the mobilized Germans under armed guard twenty-four hours per day.

Mobilized workers were also placed under surveillance both at work and in the zones and barracks. Violations of labor discipline, failure to present oneself for induction into a working column, desertion of a working column, or refusal to work were all criminal offenses, with punishments ranging from several months in a penalty section to execution and the extension of criminal responsibility to one's family. An agent-informant network was created to monitor and quash counterrevolutionary groups and labor indiscipline. During the war, 6,918 individuals from among the mobilized nationalities received criminal convictions. Food norms were established on par with Gulag camps. Incentive systems offered financial rewards, unification with families, and short holidays in exchange for good behavior and high labor productivity.[234]

Even placing the mobilized Soviet Germans in concentration camp settings did not quell Soviet fears of their potential for enemy activities. The surveillance section of the Solikamskii corrective labor camp reported in September 1942, for example, on an increase in anti-Soviet activity among its contingent of mobilized Germans. Several Soviet Germans were arrested and accused of spreading defeatist rumors, anti-Semitic views, and profascist propaganda.[235]

At times, as the war progressed, Soviet authorities took steps to ease living conditions for at least some of the mobilized Germans. A Sovnarkom decree of August 23, 1943 required the reunification of the families of all mobilized workers in the coal industry. Yet even by July 1946, only 30 percent of the mobilized workers at Karaganda Coal (Karagandaugol') had been reunited with their families.[236] Typically, though, life in the labor army was difficult and often deadly. The health and welfare of these individuals was simply a low priority for Soviet authorities. In January–February 1944, a group of 297 mobilized workers was moved by rail from Gur'ev to Krasnokamsk. The journey lasted twenty-one days, and the group was without food for almost the entire trip. Of the 297 workers, 51 deserted during the trip, while 3 died.[237]

The most noteworthy aspect of the Soviet German deportations and accompanying labor mobilizations was their universal and undifferentiated nature along with their efficiency. While there is no evidence that Soviet Germans were disloyal to the Soviet Union during the war at rates significantly different from other Soviet nationalities, and while no doubt a great portion of the Soviet German population was deeply loyal to the Soviet Union's war effort, the deportation decrees made no effort to differentiate between the innocent and guilty.[238] The presence of some collaborators and the "failure" of the local population to uncover them led to a presumptive notion of collective guilt. Nobody was exempted, not even members of the Communist Party or Komsomol.[239] Mixed marriages provided the only real possibilities for avoiding the deportations.

If the head-of-household husband was not German, but the wife was, the family was not deported.[240] Russian women married to German men were deported, but were not subject to labor mobilization.[241]

As was to become a hallmark of Soviet wartime deportations of nationalities, the Soviet German deportations are notable for their speed and efficiency. Approximately 480,000 Volga Germans were deported from September 3 to 20, 1941. Another 300,000 Soviet Germans were deported from other areas from September 20 to October 10, 1941.[242] In just a little over five weeks, more than three-quarters of a million people were deported, all while the Soviet Union strained in defeat after defeat in a massive war effort. Nonetheless, the targeted regions were almost entirely emptied of Soviet Germans. While the Nazi military expected to find significant populations of *Volksdeutsche* on its entry to the Soviet Union, it instead found only small numbers of such people along with evidence of the hasty exit for the vast majority of the Soviet German population. Such efficiency was possible due to some eyewitness accounts of lists of Soviet Germans prepared long before the deportation operations (perhaps as early as 1934 due to Soviet mistrust of Hitler's intentions—a date corresponding to the Soviet clearing of the immediate borderlands of Soviet Germans).[243]

The initial deportation of the Soviet Germans was but one of many ways in which Soviet authorities expressed their doubts about Soviet nationalities whose nominal national homeland was among the Soviet Union's opponents in the war. Wartime releases of Gulag prisoners for service in the Red Army specifically excluded Germans, Finns, Romanians, Bulgarians, Hungarians, Italians, and all foreign-born prisoners.[244] More broadly, however, Soviet authorities expressed fear and mistrust of all Soviet citizens whose nationalities corresponded to a nominal non-Soviet nation-state. In a Gulag memorandum of 1939, the inmate population was categorized by nationality, split into two large subgroups: nationalities of Soviet citizens, and those of non-Soviet citizens. Three years later, a similar memorandum further divided the subgroup of nationalities of Soviet citizens into an unlabeled group of cleanly Soviet nationalities (Russians, Ukrainians, Belarusians, Georgians, Armenians, Estonians, Jews, and others) and a second subgroup labeled "nationalities of other countries." Here, the memorandum listed Soviet citizens belonging to nationalities with putative nation-state homelands outside the Soviet Union (Germans, Poles, Romanians, Iranians, Afghans, Mongols, Chinese, Japanese, Koreans, Greeks, Turks, and others).[245]

The final wave of wartime deportations, in 1944, involved the "punished peoples." These were Soviet nationalities without corresponding external nation-states collectively punished for alleged collaboration with the enemy. The largest nationality groups to wind up in Kazakhstan were the Chechens and Ingush. Although the level of anti-Soviet collaboration is disputed, there is no question that Moscow authorities perceived the Chechens and Ingush as guilty.[246] Yet Moscow authorities clearly perceived matters differently. Most likely, the deportation of the Chechens and Ingush was motivated by a long-standing history of opposition to Russian and later Soviet rule.[247] Such a history, no doubt, informed the tendency of central Soviet authorities to interpret a few cases of collaboration as a crime committed by an entire nation. Even as early as late 1942, mandatory military service in the region was suspended due to distrust of even those Chechens and Ingush who voluntarily served in the Red Army.[248] On February 23, 1944, the deportation of the entire Chechen and Ingush nations from their homelands to Central Asia began. Some 496,640 people were deported in just a few days.[249] While the deportations of Soviet Germans had been notable for their efficiency and speed, they paled in comparison to the Chechen-Ingush operation. By February 29, just six days after the operation's start, Beria reported to Stalin that nearly 480,000 people had already been dispatched toward Central Asia. This left just some 6,000 Chechens to be deported from the areas highest in the mountains that lacked roads or were unreachable because of snow. Beria noted that the operation had been completed without serious opposition or other incidents. NKVD authorities had arrested just over 2,000 Chechens and Ingush as "anti-Soviet element[s]" during the operation and had confiscated just over 20,000 guns. Even at a time when Soviet personnel were still needed at the front, the deportations used some 120,000 secret police operatives.[250]

As always, this was a huge logistical undertaking. Nasedkin, the Gulag chief, and Nikolai K. Bogdanov, the people's commissar of internal affairs for the Kazakh Republic, reported to Beria on February 29, 1944 that they were prepared to take 400,000 Chechen and Ingush exiles into the Kazakh Republic. They planned to place 309,000 in kolkhozy, 42,000 in sovkhozy, and 49,000 in various enterprises. They had commandeered 1,590 automobiles, 57,000 horses, and 103 tractors to take the newly arriving exiles from the train stations to their place of settlement—a distance reaching up to 250 kilometers. Nonetheless, they still expected the available means of transport to be insufficient. As they also anticipated the sanitary facilities to be insufficient at the train stations, they did not provide baths and clothing disinfection until the exiles arrived at their new place of residence. Even so, it was expected that sanitary measures at the place of exile would be insufficient, too, due to a shortage of soap, given that the officials' request for twenty thousand tons of soap had gone unfilled.[251] Some 38,000 Chechen and Ingush exiles were sent to the Karaganda region.[252]

The death rates were enormous, with some one hundred thousand deaths in the first three years after deportation, either from privation and disease during the deportation process itself, or from the general lack of preparation in terms of supply and employment in the exiles' new homes.[253] Much as during the deportation of the Soviet Germans, local Kazakh authorities refused to devote resources to the settlement of these new exiles. Even a visit from Deputy Commissar of Internal Affairs Kruglov in mid-1944 did little to ameliorate the situation.[254] Like the deportation of the Soviet Germans, the operation was undifferentiated. Even Chechens and Ingush who were Communist Party or Komsomol members were subject to deportation. Not even service at the front in the Red Army exempted members of the punished nationalities from exile. Chechens and Ingush in corrective labor camps were concentrated in Karaganda.[255] While Chechens and Ingush maintained a sense of national identity in their shared experience of exile and from conscious Soviet decisions to concentrate them in small national communities, they were forbidden from teaching and publishing in their native languages. The Chechen-Ingush Autonomous Soviet Socialist Republic was abolished. Chechen historical figures were erased from the *Great Soviet Encyclopedia.*[256]

Exiled peoples continued to be differentiated by nationality into the late war and postwar periods. Although the status of deported nationalities would only be officially extended in perpetuity after the war, it was clear that they were considered more dangerous and less redeemable to Soviet authorities. Furthermore, whereas the children of kulaks were potentially reclaimable, those of exiled nationalities could never escape from their national identity. A decree of August 8, 1944 set up a sharp distinction in policies toward the children of exiled kulaks and those of exiled national groupings. Children of former kulaks who were seeking industrial education could be removed from the status of special settlers and allowed to seek work in any part of the Soviet Union on graduation. But the children of special settlers of other categories (i.e., all the national groupings, including those from the Caucasus, Crimean Tatars, Kalmyks, and all those of a nationality fighting against the USSR) could not be removed from the rolls and could only seek work in the region of permanent exile.[257]

The focus on nationality in the Gulag, a category of identity that could not be changed, raised the specter of the Nazi-Soviet comparison, as it violated years of practice that treated the punished as at least potentially redeemable. This tendency toward treating certain prisoners and exiles as irredeemable was expanded in the postwar years.

•  •  •  •  •

After four years of brutal, exhausting warfare and a disastrous initial stage, the Soviet Union emerged from its Armageddon victorious. Despite any hopes that the Soviet people may have held for a loosening of the political regime in the early postwar era, the battle on the home front was far from over. The early postwar period offered no indication that the Gulag would cease to be a mass social phenomenon within fifteen years. Rather, the Gulag remained a pillar in the reestablishment of the Soviet system, following the Red Army into liberated territories, so that every liberated district received its own corrective labor colony.[258] By 1944, the camp and colony population began to grow again.[259] Filtration camps continued their work to cleanse the populations living under German occupation and Red Army soldiers captured by the German military. Executions, arrests, and exile greeted the opposition in the brutal guerrilla wars fought between Soviet NKVD forces and members of nationalist military groupings in western Ukraine and the Baltics. Soviet POW camps sought to educate an antifascist cohort for active participation in the postwar German state. Mass arrests and deportations marked the Sovietization of the reannexed western territories—the Baltic republics, western Ukraine, western Belorussia, and Moldavia. All these processes brought large new groups to the Gulag population—both ethnic and Red Army veterans—and they substantially affected life in the postwar Gulag, just as they affected life in postwar Soviet society.

*Chapter 5*

# A NEW CIRCLE OF HELL: THE POSTWAR GULAG AND THE RISE OF THE SPECIAL CAMPS

T HE GULAG PLAYED AN INTEGRAL ROLE in the construction of the Soviet system during the 1930s, and was bound to play a similar one in the reconstruction and reconfiguration of the postwar system. The Gulag followed hard on the heels of the Red Army as it conquered Nazi forces, reclaiming the occupied territories and making new claims throughout Eastern Europe. The Soviet Union emerged triumphant from the war it had so much dreaded and so long expected. Victory, however, came at a tremendous price. Millions and millions of Soviet people died. Millions of others experienced non-Soviet social systems, saw parts of Europe, and were transformed by their experiences at the front. New territories were annexed and then reannexed, bringing with them peoples and societies with distinct political and social backgrounds. The economy was thoroughly wrecked. Rebuilding Soviet society and the Soviet economy required as massive an effort as building that society and economy in the first place.

Remaking this world was a huge task, and the Soviet state approached it with experience and tools developed over nearly thirty years. The Gulag itself was one major weapon in the battle to reshape Soviet society in the wake of the mass transformative experience of total war. The Gulag had already existed as a mass social institution for some fifteen years, and it continued to refine and apply its practices designed to guard as well as shape the boundaries between Soviet society and its internal enemies. The postwar decade saw the Gulag reach its extremes in both population and the radical nature of the brutalities in the camps.

## Remaking Soviet Society

One tricky issue for the victorious Soviet Union was how to deal with those Soviet citizens who had lived, sometimes for several years, under Nazi occupation. In a polity fixated on the effects of the social environment on individuals, the potential for contamination of its citizens in the occupied territories from contact with the ideology and life practices of the Nazi occupier caused tremendous concern. As one camp political worker in Kazakhstan put it, "Tens of millions of people lived in the territories temporarily occupied by the German fascists. Many were driven into fascist forced labor in Germany. All were deprived of honest Soviet information. We must work with these people; we must discuss with them the policies of our [Communist] Party and the policies of the Soviet state."[1] Red Army soldiers who had spent time in Nazi POW camps were similarly suspect for not giving their life for the cause, their exposure to Nazi ideology, and their potential contacts with Andrei Vlasov's collaborationist Russian Liberation Army.

The official Soviet approach toward these citizens combined suspicion with a need to differentiate the honest from the enemy. The attitude is well stated in an October 22, 1945 letter on the return of Soviet citizens deported to Germany for forced labor. The letter to Vyacheslav Molotov from the chief of staff of the partisan movement and the first secretary of the Belarusian Communist Party, Panteleimon Ponamerenko, reads in part:

> Returning along with the deported Soviet citizens are former policemen, volunteers of the penal detachments and other German henchmen, who escaped to Germany with the retreat of the German army. The local population—workers, kolkhozniki and white collar workers—greet the repatriated citizens with a feeling of warmness and care, giving help in the reconstruction and adjustment of their lives. The returning . . . henchmen face the hatred of the Belorussian people, who have not forgotten the horrors of German occupation and the mean, treasonous activities of these traitors.[2]

The suspicious yet differentiated approach is clear. Some of those returning were honest people, but many others were "German henchmen." For the latter, the Soviet people, it was said, rightly expressed their hatred. Expressions of hatred for alleged collaborators were no doubt quite genuine. In the wake of the ferocious battle with the Nazis, Soviet soldiers and veterans were not in the mood to compromise with or feel compassion for those perceived to be their enemies. Kopelev recalls his moving field prison being overtaken by columns of soldiers shouting, "Where are you taking them? Hang 'em on the spot!"[3] The question for the Soviet state was how to delineate the honest Soviet citizens from the German henchmen.

Even before the war had ended, Soviet authorities created a system of filtration camps through which Soviet citizens in the occupied territories and Red Army soldiers who had spent time in POW camps passed. The word "filtering" describes precisely the mandate of these camps. They were to filter suspect Soviet populations to determine who had passed cleanly through the experience of occupation or capture, and who had compromised themselves by collaboration while under occupation or in a POW encampment. The war had become the new defining moment in Soviet history, and the actions of a Soviet citizen during the war defined whether they were worthy or not of the now-august status of Soviet citizen and victor. The filtration camps then carried out a particular version of the Gulag project of defining a Soviet citizen from an internal enemy among a population suspect merely because they had survived under Nazi occupation or in Nazi captivity. Soviet citizens and veterans passing through the filtration camps were either released or arrested, and then transferred to the Soviet secret police organs, where a further determination was made as to the appropriate sentence for their crimes.

According to one estimate, during the war and postwar periods, approximately 6 million Soviet citizens passed through the filtration camps and at least 500,000 were sent to the Gulag.[4] Indeed, not every Soviet citizen and army veteran who passed through the filtration camps was ultimately arrested. As Beria noted in a letter to Stalin and Molotov, 932,000 people had been detained for verification as of January 8, 1944, of whom 583,000 were military and 349,000 were civilian. They were detained for offenses including disorganized retreat from the field of battle, destroying or losing party cards, being in enemy prisons, and violations of the regime established for areas near the front. Document issues were by far the most common reason for detention. Of these 932,000 filtration camp prisoners, a total of 80,000 were then arrested for violations ranging from desertion to treason to regular criminal offenses.[5] The filtration camps continued to operate into the postwar era, focusing mainly on the verification of Soviet citizens repatriated from Europe. In January 1946, as their operations began to wind down, the filtration camps were transferred to the Gulag's administrative control.[6] In 1946, 228,000 people passed through the filtration camps. By mid-January 1947, only 29,000 remained inside.[7]

Throughout their existence, even though their inmates often remained for only a short period until their wartime activities were verified, the filtration camps operated similar to other Gulag camps. Filtration camp inmates were forced to work and were subjected to political propaganda work.[8] Most important, the very purpose of the filtration camps served as the initial arbiter of the wartime activities of individual Soviet people. Those passing the test were released; those failing it were sent ever deeper into the Gulag's throat for a further determination of their suitability for reintroduction into postwar Soviet society.

## Gulag Population Trends in the Immediate Postwar Period

In the Gulag proper, the immediate end of the war led to a small reduction in population as a result of a July 7, 1945 amnesty issued in celebration of victory.[9] In 1945, the population of corrective labor camps fell from 716,000 at the beginning of the year to 601,000 in early 1946. The amnesty was a temporary measure, though, as evidenced by the release in 1945 of 337,000 camp inmates compared to 152,000 released in 1944 and 116,000 released in 1946. The downward trend in camp populations was short-lived as the rate of camp growth turned sharply upward in 1946, reaching growth levels unknown since 1937–38.[10] The camp population jumped from 601,000 at the start of 1946 to 809,000 in 1947 and 1.1 million in 1948. Similar trends can be seen even more sharply in the corrective labor colonies.[11] Meanwhile, the official figures for deaths in camps and colonies continued the significant downward trend evident since the middle of the war. Only the effects of the postwar Soviet famine temporarily reversed the downward trend in 1946–47. The total camp deaths (excluding colonies) dropped from 249,000 in 1942 to 167,000 in 1943, 61,000 in 1944, 49,000 in 1945, and 18,000 in 1946. The downward trend was reversed in 1947, when camp deaths rose to 36,000. The total deaths of colony prisoners in each year were similar, although the temporary spike here came in 1946 rather than 1947: 56,000 in 1944, 37,000 in 1945, 73,000 in 1946, and 32,000 in 1947.[12]

In line with long-established practices, counterrevolutionary criminals were excluded from the postwar amnesty. As Solzhenitsyn angrily put it, the postwar amnesty was "for deserters, swindlers, and thieves. And Special Camps for the 58's. And the closer the war came to its end, the more and more cruel did the regimen for the 58's become."[13] The amnesty applied to those with sentences shorter than three years. For those with longer sentences, their terms of detention were cut in half. This provision, however, did not apply to those sentenced for "counterrevolutionary crimes, for stealing socialist property (the law of 7-VIII-1932), banditism, counterfeiting, murder and robbery." The amnesty also excluded recidivists.[14] Consequently, the relative weight of the politicals in the prison camp population rose in 1945. While overall prisoner populations dropped in 1945, the counterrevolutionary population grew from 289,000 or 41 percent of the camp population on January 1, 1945, to 334,000 and 60 percent on January 1, 1946.[15] As was typical, Gulag authorities complained of the increased difficulty in isolating a prisoner contingent that was made up of a higher proportion of so-called especially dangerous inmates. They attempted to improve the readiness of the guard for their job by removing the elderly, invalids, and women who had taken so many of these positions in the war years, and replacing them with demobilized Red Army soldiers.[16]

In the following years, the total number of counterrevolutionary prisoners failed to keep pace with the growth of the total prisoner population, for two main reasons. First, two 1947 decrees discussed below dramatically increased the number of nonpolitical inmates given long sentences. Second, the approaching ten-year anniversary of the terror led to the release of a number of counterrevolutionary prisoners given ten-year sentences during those bloody years. As a result, in 1947, the total number of counterrevolutionary prisoners in camps dropped even as the total prison camp population exploded. On January 1, 1947 and 1948, respectively, counterrevolutionary prisoners in camps totaled 428,000 or 54 percent of the camp population and 416,000 or 38 percent.[17]

And so following a brief spell of postwar amnesty, the Gulag population grew rapidly. Camps were overcrowded, and more prisoners kept arriving. On January 1, 1946, Karlag had an official capacity of 51,000 inmates but held 61,000, making it the fourth-largest camp in the entire Gulag system.[18] By August 1948, on the eve of a massive transfer of prisoners to the newly constructed special camps, the Karlag population had grown to 74,000. Karlag's population growth continued to outpace its capacity, affecting the conditions of camp life directly. Year after year, Karlag added new barracks and zones for its prisoners, but construction failed to keep up with population growth, leading to a reduction of the already-meager living space per prisoner.[19] Even after 1948, when the creation of special camps soon siphoned off a significant share of the Karlag population, prisoner overcrowding did not improve, since several Karlag subdivisions were also stripped away to form the new special camps.[20]

The Gulag as a whole continued to grow after the creation of the special camps, as new convictions greatly outpaced releases. The primary cause was a pair of laws issued in 1947. In the immediate postwar era, the Soviet Union suffered yet another famine. In one respect at least, the Soviet response to the famine drew on an earlier playbook. During the famine of the early 1930s, Soviet authorities issued the notorious law of August 7, 1932 on property theft that brought large numbers of arrests for relatively minor incidents of theft. The postwar famine brought two equally notorious decrees on June 4, 1947 that pushed the Gulag population to its highest levels in the institution's entire history. The decrees on theft of state, social, and individual property provided long terms of punishment (up to twenty-five years) for relatively minor incidents of theft. From 1947 to 1952, at least 20 percent of all court convictions fell under the June 4, 1947 decree. Over half of those convicted under the June 4, 1947 edict were peasants. The charges under these laws, even among all the injustice in the Soviet penal system, seem particularly outrageous in their lack of proportionality between crime and punishment. Just a few examples will suffice: collective farmers were given as much as a five-year sentence for stealing as little as 850 grams of rye, an invalid war veteran was given seven years in the camps for stealing 600 grams of pork to feed his four children between the ages of one and eleven, and a war widow with three children and working in a pasta factory received a seven-year sentence for stealing 800 grams of dough.[21]

The total camp and colony population peaked in 1950 at just over 2.5 million. The real quantitative leap, though, was made during 1947. On January 1, 1947, the camp and colony population was 1.7 million. By January 1, 1948, the figure had risen to 2.2 million, and it hovered between 2.2 and 2.6 million until the mass releases began after Stalin's death in March 1953.[22] The jump in Gulag population was largely attributable to the June 4, 1947 decree, as indicated by the lack of a corresponding leap in the numbers of prisoners sentenced for counterrevolutionary crimes.[23] On January 1, 1951, over a million Gulag prisoners were in camps or colonies for convictions under the June 4, 1947 decrees, with more than 600,000 of those spending their sentences in corrective labor camps and more than 400,000 in corrective labor colonies.[24] As prisoners were sent to corrective labor camps if they had sentences longer than three years, the vast number of convicts under these decrees housed in labor camps indicates the severity of the punishment and the length of the sentences handed out for such thefts.

## Politics of the Postwar Gulag Economy

For Solzhenitsyn, the "mocking" slogans greeting the postwar amnesty "smear[ed on] the internal archways and walls of the camps. . . . 'For the broadest amnesty we shall respond to our dear Party and government with doubled productivity'" were worse than the exclusion of the political prisoners.[25] The Gulag cultural-educational apparatus continued to operate in high gear after the war's end. Just as in Soviet society at large, the postwar period was met not with relaxation but with more campaigns—this time for rebuilding the ruined Soviet economy.[26] The Gulag continued to grind away at its economic tasks, engaging a growing portion of the Soviet workforce in comparatively expensive and unproductive work. Party workers in the Kazakh Republic administration of corrective labor camps and colonies (Kazakh UITLK) openly discussed their difficult financial situation and appeared especially vexed at the inability of their operations to turn a profit.[27] Gulag authorities made many attempts in the postwar period to make their system economically efficient. They tried to step up their political agitation of both their own staff and the prisoners themselves. They undertook a massive reorganization of camp life and the camp economy with the introduction of the special camps. They introduced specific changes in camp regime such as the introduction of paying prisoners for productive work. Still, none of these efforts could overcome the inherent unproductiveness of forced labor or the incredible costs associated with isolating prisoners from Soviet society. Just like in previous decades, the one move toward economic efficiency that was never contemplated was the reduction of the camps' militarized guard, surveillance apparatus, or supervisory staff. As a Kazakh UITLK party member who worked in the camp's internal police division put it, "Once again [I must] repeat, that it is necessary not only to review indices of productive significance, but we must also pay attention to the guarding of state criminals and the tightening of the regime in the [camp and colony] subdivisions."[28] Thus, despite all the efforts, the Gulag continued to stand out for its economic inefficiency even in a world of inefficient Soviet economic institutions, if only because it was not in the first instance an economic institution.

Nonetheless, economic productivity was always at the forefront of cultural-educational activity. The basic tasks of agitation work among Karlag prisoners in the postwar period were described as:

> The popularization of the battle of the laborers of our motherland for the restoration, the further development and the consolidation of socialist society, the explanation and study of the decisions of the Party and government, questions of the international situation, the policies of the Party and government in the sphere of the battle for peace, the exposure of the aggressive tendencies of the instigators of a new war, the policies of the struggle for a strengthening of the friendship of peoples and the further consolidation of the position of the new democratic countries.[29]

The postwar period required a turn toward the future. Victory was not allowed to slide into complacence. The first order of the postwar era, "a new historical stage," was the task "placed before the entire Soviet people, before every enterprise and institution, and that means also before our camps and colonies," to complete the Five-Year Plan and reconstruct the Soviet economy.[30] Contemplating these tasks in peacetime conditions, the chief of Karlag's cultural-educational apparatus wrote in late 1945 of a transition away from themes of the heroic activities of the Soviet people at the front and in the rear toward "episodes of the self-labor of our motherland's toilers working for the liquidation of the consequences of war." Above all, this work focused on the slogan "Complete Ahead of Schedule the Five-Year Plan for Reconstruction of the Economy" along with the celebrations of the twenty-eighth anniversary of the "Great October Revolution" and the twenty-fifth anniversary of the formation of the Kazakh Soviet Socialist Republic (SSR).[31] The chief lesson of the victory lay in the importance of prewar preparation, and the Soviet Union must immediately concern itself with preparations for the next war—a cause that seemed all the more pressing as the cold war heated up.

The cult of the war had definite ramifications for the postwar Gulag. Soviet society in the postwar period was increasingly viewed through the prism of the war experience. This was specifically encouraged among camp employees. Party meetings of Gulag workers ritualistically began with paeans to the war victory, especially to the significance of prewar preparations for the country's defense.[32] The focus on prewar preparations, of course, was intended to concentrate the necessary energies of the country on the postwar economic reconstruction and serve as a cautionary tale for the unfolding cold war. Kazakh UITLK Komsomol organizations often spoke with the war on their minds, calling their members to greatness in the name of Komsomol legends "Aleksandr Matrosov, Zoia Kos'modem'ianskaia, Oleg Koshevoi and hundreds of other young heroes" of the war.[33]

Having passed through the crucible of war, Soviet authorities and much of Soviet society were in no mood to compromise with their enemies. Consequently, Gulag prisoners were typically painted with the broad brush of the term fascist. The Russian Liberation Army, the Vlasovites who fought against Soviet forces, and the Ukrainian partisan armies, the Banderites who continued to fight bloody battles with the Soviet government well into the postwar period, tainted the political prisoner population in the eyes of Soviet authorities, society, Gulag employees, and even other Gulag inmates. Common criminals frequently tossed off the term fascist in reference to the counterrevolutionaries, emphasizing their own honesty and pro-Soviet loyalties.[34]

The important cult of action, of participation in battle, was also used to define the political criminals as outside the boundaries of true Soviet citizenship. When Kopelev attended his second trial in December 1946, he recalled one bit of testimony in particular: "There's no denying, he's [Kopelev's] an educated man, very educated. Wore out the seat of his pants reading books while others like us spent their lives working and fulfilling five-year plans and fighting the kulaks and enemies of the people."[35] The testimony played on popular conceptions of the educated as afraid of getting involved and getting their hands dirty. Even though Kopelev himself had been in the army, the testimony also played on his Jewishness in accord with the popular perception that Jews had sat out the war in Central Asia. The charges against Kopelev are especially ironic given that Kopelev himself was an active collectivizer.[36]

Mass political education was also frequent, if not ubiquitous. In the first quarter of 1947, the twenty-seven subdivisions of Karlag saw the publication of twenty-six hundred editions of twenty-one wall newspapers. The papers' main theme was tracking the progress of labor competition among camp prisoners and propagandizing for high labor productivity. Popularizing the methods of work of highly productive prisoners and criticizing, often through caricature or rhyme, the poor work of those refusing to labor was described as a key element in reclaiming a number of individuals from the ranks of the slackers and malingerers. Prisoner correspondents informed the camp press of problems in production and daily life.[37]

Even when Gulag employees talked about prisoner "labor utilization" as their "most important task," their understanding of this task was profoundly political. Raising prisoner labor productivity involved primarily the "mobilization" of prisoners, and teaching them a "conscientious attitude toward labor" through "mass cultural-educational work and the organization of labor competition."[38] Stalin was quoted on the subject from his speech at the party plenum in 1937, when he noted, "In life . . . in practice, politics and economy [khoziaistvo] are indivisible."[39]

The same was true in the political education of the camp workers themselves. Party and Komsomol functionaries were warned not to follow the improper path that relegated education to a secondary place behind production. Defects in educational work would lead to poor military discipline among the camp and colony employees.[40] Poor educational work was blamed for all kinds of negative events in the camps. As they quoted from Stalin, "In order to build, you must know. In order to know, you must learn."[41] Hence, poor mass education work was blamed for the suicide of a female armed guard after she contracted a venereal disease.[42] A lack of educational work was blamed for guards falling asleep at their posts.[43] Poor Komsomol education of young guards was faulted for such negative activities as "cohabitation and ties with prisoners."[44] Low-quality political education work was the cause when a guard allowed prisoners to move about without a convoy, live with the prisoners, accept things from them, and drink with them, all of which led to two group escapes.[45] As the head of the Kazakh UITLK political department summed it up, "Practice has shown that in those camp subdivisions where organizational-party, propagandist and mass-political work is shabby . . . there exists an atrophy of vigilance, mass escapes of state criminals, low production indices, manifest failures in economic activity, and large material losses in economy." In contrast, he continued, good party practices led to good local camp work.[46]

The exhortation to increased labor productivity was not left to political propaganda alone. On August 1, 1950, Gulag authorities reintroduced the payment of salaries to Gulag prisoners.[47] In addition, a certain amount of funds was reserved for the payment of bonuses for especially productive laborers. An effort was made to increase the number of products available in the camp commissary, so that prisoners would have somewhere to spend their new earnings. Some experiments were also made in the introduction of better living conditions or even making private rooms available to prisoners for cash payments.[48]

A Karlag report from early 1951 marked the payment of salaries to prisoners as a big success in increasing their productivity. The third quarter of 1950 saw the number of prisoners failing to fulfill their work norms drop from the figure of 4,330 in 1949 to 2,890. The report also noted an increase in the numbers of record-setting workers completing 200 percent of their daily norms or more. The average prisoner was receiving just over ninety-three rubles per month, although the failure to provide adequate products in the camp commissary was undermining the new system.[49] But there is no evidence that the introduction of payment for work led to a substantial improvement in the Gulag's financial condition. The Gulag continued to lumber along in its unwieldy, inefficient ways.

## Politicals, Criminals, and the Special Camps

Dolgun was an American employee of the U.S. Embassy in Moscow. He was arrested on the streets of Moscow in 1948 and spent nearly a decade in the camps, including many years in the newly created special camps in Dzhezkazgan, then part of the Karaganda region. Dolgun's memoirs are a careful and important contribution to our knowledge of life in the special camps—a new type of institution that shook up Gulag society and radically changed the way that the Gulag operated.

Prior to the creation of the special camps, most political prisoners understood Gulag society along the lines of Grigori Orlov, one of Dolgun's prison cell mates. Orlov had experience in the camps and set about educating Dolgun on the ways of survival there. First and foremost, he warned Dolgun to be careful of the "common criminals."

> They are truly very tough boys, Alex. They are organized all over the Soviet Union. They have their own code of rules . . . and if you find yourself in a camp where political prisoners and common criminals are mixed, be careful, because [they] live by stealing from the politicals. [They] call the political prisoners "fascists," you know, and they call themselves *urki*. . . . They consider themselves loyal Soviet citizens who happen to live by a different code, by the way. They think all the politicals are enemies of the people. . . .
>
> And the politicals?
>
> Entirely different! Entirely different! Every political is convinced of his own innocence and convinced of every other political's guilt. They have no street experience in cooperating for survival. . . . They distrust each other. They are completely incapable of organizing, you see. So they are the perfect victims for the *urki*.[50]

As Dolgun's experience and this chapter show, this binary opposition that neatly divided the camp population into politicals and criminals, if it ever fully existed, began to break down in the postwar period. Tensions within the criminal world came to the fore, and the politicals started to lose their timidity as the combination of a new type of postwar political and the creation of a new type of camp almost completely free of professional criminals allowed them to find a voice.

The key year in this postwar radicalization of the Gulag was 1948. During that year, two primary events changed the face of the Gulag in ways that reverberated into the post-Stalin era. First, Soviet authorities established a subset of the corrective labor camp system dubbed special camps. The special camps were designed to isolate so-called especially dangerous state criminals from the rest of the camp inmates. Second, for the first time, Soviet authorities explicitly created permanent punishments. The term of exile for all nationalities deported during the war was officially extended permanently during that year. All prison camp inmates who were or would have been subject to isolation in the special camp system, even those inmates who had already been released, were also subject to permanent exile on the completion of their terms in labor camps. The first of these two policy changes—the introduction of the special camps—was integral to the evolution of the political prisoner/common criminal axis of Gulag identity. The second—the introduction of permanent exile for the deported nationalities and released special camp inmates—was relevant particularly for national identities in the postwar Soviet Union and Gulag.

In February 1948, Minister of Internal Affairs Kruglov wrote to Stalin about the work of the Gulag. His report gives us a good picture of the Gulag's state on the eve of the creation of the special camps. On January 1, 1948, the Gulag held 2.2 million prisoners in sixty-three independent corrective labor camps and over a thousand corrective labor colonies. During 1947, this population had experienced a huge growth spurt, rising by nearly one-half million or 28 percent.[51] While the overall Gulag population grew, the number of prisoners sentenced for counterrevolutionary crimes, those typically understood as political prisoners, dropped some 25,000 to a total of 545,000, or 26 percent of the total Gulag population.[52]

While the Gulag population grew significantly, its duties remained the same. As Kruglov wrote, "One of the serious tasks, standing before the GULAG . . . , is the reeducation of prisoners, for which political-educational work is carried out in camps and colonies, set in the first place towards their enlistment in active participation in socially-useful labor and compliance with the established camp regime."[53] The Gulag's practices remained essentially unaltered; socialist competition, tying food norms to labor output, labor education, and the practice of earning credit toward early release through fulfillment and overfulfillment of labor norms were all credited as decisive elements in prisoner reeducation.[54]

The counterrevolutionary portion of the overall camp population had become smaller, but a major change in the lives of many of them was about to strike. On February 21, 1948, the USSR Council of Ministers issued its order to organize a system of special camps with strict regimes to hold especially dangerous state criminals. According to the implementation directive of the Ministry of Internal Affairs (MVD), this category was defined as "spies, saboteurs, terrorists, Trotskyites, rightists, Mensheviks, SRs, anarchists, nationalists, white emigrants and participants in other anti-Soviet organizations and groups and those presenting danger by their anti-Soviet ties and enemy activities."[55] Most important, special camps were forbidden from housing prisoners sentenced for any crimes other than those listed.[56] Even allowing special camp prisoners to work in the same location as general camp prisoners or non-MVD employees was in fact forbidden.[57] For the first time in Gulag history, a substantial number of political prisoners were held separately from their criminal counterparts.

According to the initial decree, special camps were to be established immediately in Kolyma, the far north, Noril'sk, Vorkuta, Karaganda, and the Mordovian autonomous republic. New special camps were also to be built in 1949 in the Irkutsk and Bratsk regions. The new camps were quickly filled with prisoners transferred from regular camps. Local MVD and Ministry of State Security (MGB) deputy directors, local prosecutors, and camp deputy directors in charge of surveillance were ordered to review the prisoners in their locality to determine which inmates were subject to transfer to a special camp or special prison. A central commission reviewed the individual prisoner files to make a final decision on transfer. Among prisoners whose crimes fit the criteria for transfer, only the most severely ill invalids or prisoners whose terms were due to expire in 1948 were to be left in regular camps. Even these prisoners, however, had to be isolated from other regular camp prisoners and placed under stricter guard so as to preclude the possibility of their escape. Regular camps were given an eight-month window in which to complete the transfers. All future penal sentences were to include a statement on whether the prisoner should be held in a special prison, special camp, or general camp.[58]

Once prisoners were sent to a special camp or special prison, the camp gate closed behind them. It was not possible for a prisoner to earn transfer from a special camp to a regular one. On the other hand, even special camp prisoners were allowed release at the conclusion of their sentence. Yet release from special camps was only partial, as all prisoners on release from special camps were subject to exile under MGB auspices in the Kolyma region, no less than fifty kilometers north of the Trans-Siberian Railway in the Krasnoiarsk and Novosibirsk oblasts, or the Kazakh Republic excluding the Alma-Ata, Gur'ev, south Kazakhstan, Aktiubinsk, eastern Kazakhstan, and Semipalatinsk oblasts.[59]

Special camps held a prisoner population, then, that to a large degree lacked hope. Few of their inmates had short sentences. For example, in December 1952, only 0.8 percent of special camp inmates had sentences shorter than five years, while 48 percent had sentences longer than ten years and 29 percent had a sentence of twenty-five years.[60] Incredibly long camp sentences combined with the prospect of only partial release after their sentence's conclusion created a sense of hopelessness among this portion of the camp population—a major factor in the wave of uprisings in special camps after Stalin's death.

In the Karaganda region, there were ultimately four different special camps. The first, largest, and longest lasting, authorized by the original order on special camps, was Steplag. Officially known as "special camp no. 4," it was originally built on the site of the Spasozavodkii POW camp, formerly the Spassk subdivision of Karlag, for a population of ten thousand prisoners.[61] Steplag grew, and soon encompassed and was centered in and around the city of Dzhezkazgan, another former Karlag division and one of its deadliest. Steplag survived for just over eight years, until 1956. Its maximum population was around twenty-eight thousand in 1950, and its main economic activity was mining, especially coal and copper mining.[62] The other special camps in the Karaganda region were Peschanyi lager' (Peschanlag) and Lugovoi lager' (Luglag), with planned populations in 1950 of seventeen thousand and eighteen thousand, respectively.[63] Finally, Dal'nyi lager' (Dal'lag) was formed in April 1952 in the Ekibastuz coalfields to hold eleven thousand prisoners. Only a portion of Dal'lag was in the Karaganda region, as Ekibastuz—its headquarters—was in the Pavlodar region of Kazakhstan.[64] Solzhenitsyn was himself a prisoner in the Ekibastuz special camp from 1950 to 1953. Unfortunately, his individual prisoner file is not in Karaganda's archival collection.

Dolgun described Steplag's Dzhezkazgan as "a living hell." Recalling his train trip to Steplag in 1950, Dolgun tells of the terrain after passing the city of Karaganda: "The grasses began to thin out and there was nothing to see but flat expanses of rock and sand. The guards told us maliciously that it was called Bet Pak Dala, the Dead Steppe, and that we'd all be part of it soon enough." Dolgun's train arrived at 3:00 a.m., and the extreme brutality of Dzhezkazgan confronted him immediately.

> When we came out, there was nothing but flat rock reaching off into the darkness, and milling dogs pulling at their leashes, and dozens of guards in tropical uniforms. . . . They sat us on the ground and came around to us with file folders and heard our prayers [more on the prisoner prayer below]. Several of us were judged too weak to walk the eleven kilometers to camp and were put into a truck. . . . We were unloaded beside a huge stone wall that seemed to stretch

for a half a mile in each direction. There were watchtowers and barbed wire on the top, and a great gate a hundred feet or so from where we were told to sit and wait for the rest of the prisoners, who were marching in convoy from the station. . . . Almost immediately after the sun appeared, there was some noise from inside the gates, and in a moment they swung open. A thin, tired horse appeared, drawing a flat farm wagon with wooden wheels. Ten or twelve corpses were stretched out on the wagon. Somehow I found this normal. I was watching indifferently until the wagon stopped and two guards appeared with axes. Then I felt quite sick. The guards methodically walked from corpse to corpse and swung the axes up and down. Soon each skull was split wide open. The man leading the horse tugged the reins and led it off. Each corpse had a small metal tag wired to a big toe and the metal tags waved back and forth as the wagon moved away across the steppe.[65]

The special camps were specifically designed to be more isolated, controlled, cruel, and deadly than the regular camps. The special camps operated under an especially strict disciplinary regime, modeled on practices developed since 1943 in the katorga camp divisions. Prisoners in special camps were held in the Gulag's most remote locations and subjected to its most physically demanding labor. Many prisoners in Steplag's Dzhezkazgan division worked in copper mines, where they often developed fatal cases of silicosis from breathing copper dust.[66] The special camp was the lowest circle of the corrective labor camp hell; the living conditions were worse than anywhere else, isolation was stricter than anywhere else, and its inmates were on the lowest rung of the ladder of potential redeemability.

Strict guard of special camp prisoners in camp zones, on their march to and from work as well as at the workplace, was designed at every instance to preclude the possibility of escape or maintenance of uncontrolled ties with the world outside the barbed wire. Internal surveillance, limits on and strict censorship of correspondence, and the total isolation of the special camp prisoner were all intended to prevent the prisoners from continuing their "enemy work" while in camps. Even those guards and camp employees who would have contact with special camp prisoners were supposed to be specially screened so that only the most politically trustworthy and proven could work in the special camps.[67] The enhanced guard and stepped up surveillance was effective, at least initially. From its creation through May 1949, a total of fifteen escapes occurred from a Steplag population of twenty-two thousand. Only three of those escapees had not yet been caught. During the same period, there were no prisoner-on-prisoner murders.[68] Yet as we will see later, the special camps would become the locus for the largest incidents of mass prisoner disobedience in Gulag history.

The general emphasis on increased security measures and total prisoner isolation had many specific manifestations that made life in the special camps especially brutal. From the construction of camp zones to the management and marking of the prisoner population, life in the special camps was decidedly different from that in the regular ones. Dmitri Panin recalls his Ekibastuz special camp zone, at the time a part of Peschanlag, in late summer 1950:

> Besides the guardhouse—a stone structure with damp, unheated punishment cells—the camp also had a barracks with barred windows which was surrounded by watchdogs and barbed wire. This was the so-called BUR, a special punishment block. All the other barracks also had barred windows and the doors were kept locked throughout the night. . . . The camp and another zone around it were both surrounded by barbed wire. Man-traps consisting of sharp-pointed stakes were set into the ground and tilted at forty-five degree angles in the direction of the prisoner's living quarters. Between the two barbed-wire fences there was a wire with leashes for specially trained shepherd dogs. A strip of earth just outside the fences was always kept plowed so that anyone trying to escape would leave clear prints on the freshly upturned earth. . . . [A]ll this had a permanently depressing effect on the weaker spirits among us.[69]

Dolgun describes one special camp zone of Steplag in a similar fashion:

> [It] had stone walls two meters thick and nearly six meters high. About one and a half meters from the wall there was a barbed-wire fence almost as high as the wall. Sloping down from the top of the fence on the inside was a kind of tent of barbed wire, which stretched to the ground at a point nine or ten meters from the bottom of the fence. Two and a half meters farther in from the barbed-wire tent was a single thick wire on short posts, marking a forbidden area between the compound and the barbed wire. This area was known as the fire zone, and we were repeatedly told that anyone stepping over the wire into the fire zone would be assumed to be attempting escape and would be shot without warning from the watchtowers. In the space between the wall and the barbed-wire fence another thick wire was strung about five feet above the ground from wall to wall around the camp. Every night German shepherds were leashed to the wire as an additional precaution against escape. . . . Occasionally, it was said, a watchtower marksman had been known to relieve the monotony of his job by shooting down a prisoner who had strayed close enough to the wire for the guard to be able to tell his commanding officer that he had warned him to stop running into the fire zone before he shot him.[70]

All incidents of shooting required that the local MGB commandant be summoned, but Dolgun wrote that he was known to throw a prisoner's corpse into the fire zone "to create a legitimate reason for the killing."[71]

The similarity of the different camp zones portrayed by Panin and Dolgun is no surprise, as strict regulations governed their construction. Regular barracks were designed for one to two hundred prisoners and were organized by brigades. In stark contrast to regular labor camps, the barrack windows of special camps were equipped with bars and the barrack doors were locked at night. Prisoner movement from barrack to barrack was forbidden.[72]

For especially malicious and continual violators of the special camp regime, each special camp subdivision was equipped both with a punishment barrack with a general cell for fifteen to twenty prisoners and a separate solitary confinement internal prison. Regulations required that two layers of barbed wire surround the punishment facilities.[73] Prisoners in the punishment barracks were led to work daily in handcuffs. They were denied all correspondence and packages. Prisoners in solitary confinement were only allowed to sleep six hours per night and were denied sheets. They were kept in their cells twenty-four hours per day. They were not allowed to go out for work or to smoke. Prisoners were limited to three hundred grams of bread per day along with water. Every third day, they were given a small amount of thin soup. Camp authorities were allowed to sentence a prisoner to solitary confinement for periods up to fifteen days. If prisoners continued to violate the camp regime, they were subject to transfer to special prisons.[74]

Special camp prisoners were guarded just as strictly on their march to work. Their path was watched by machine guns, and movement of special camp prisoners outside the camp zone without an armed convoy was strictly forbidden.[75] Every morning the prisoners were warned of the dire consequences for attempted escape on the march to work: "Prisoners! On the way to the work site you will keep close column. Hands behind your back. One step to the right or one step to the left will be considered an attempt to escape, and the convoy has orders to shoot without warning. Remember! One step to the right, or one to the left!"[76]

The special camp prisoner population was managed and controlled in a similarly detailed fashion. Male and female special camp prisoners were supposed to be strictly isolated in separate camp zones (though these zones were sometimes adjoined). Prisoners convicted as coconspirators in the same crime were housed in either separate camp subdivisions or entirely separate special camps. They were to be searched on their arrival at a special camp. Prisoners were then medically reviewed and placed in quarantine for at least twenty-one days.[77] The medical examination, such as it was, could be the defining factor in a prisoner's survival of the special camp experience. Dolgun attributes his survival to the fact that his initial Steplag medical examination showed that he "had almost no buttocks. . . . [T]he medical examination . . . consisted almost entirely of having your buttocks squeezed." He thus managed to avoid work in the copper mines and instead was sent to a rock quarry, where the work was comparatively easier and safer.[78]

No less than once a week, the camp subdivision staff was ordered to make a full search of prisoners and the camp zone for forbidden items. Prisoners were also individually searched every time they left or reentered the camp zone on their way to and from work. Those prisoners found to possess forbidden items were punished by temporary isolation in the punishment barrack. Collective punishment could apply if forbidden items were discovered in a barrack and the individual owner was not identified.[79]

Special camp prisoners were allowed to submit a petition for review of their conviction only once a year. They were allowed to receive packages of food and other items from relatives, although this privilege could be removed as punishment. They could also receive money from relatives to be placed in their personal account to be used at the camp commissary. They were limited to seventy-five rubles of expenditures per month, however. Prisoners were only permitted to send one letter per month, although this privilege too could be taken away. They were only allowed to receive letters from their closest relatives. All other letters were to be confiscated, and all correspondence was strictly censored.[80]

Special camp prisoners were visually marked as distinct from their regular camp counterparts. Regulations required them without exception to wear only clothing issued by the camp and emblazoned with their prisoner number.[81] The numbers were painted in large figures, increasing the ability of guards to punish individual violations of camp order even when they occurred at such a distance from the guards that ordinarily they would be unable to determine the offender's identity.[82] As Dolgun recounts, there seemed always to be a guard around to write down a prisoner's number for violations of the camp regime.[83] Regulations required guards and camp staff to use only a prisoner's number and never their name, although memoirists widely agree that this was not universally practiced.[84] Nonetheless, the mere regulation indicates the degree of dehumanization imagined in the special camp regime.

While Gulag attitudes toward cultural-educational activities among the special camp prisoners were ambivalent at best, at some level the practices continued. In September 1950, the MVD and MGB both worked to create a revised set of regulations governing the camp regime in special camps. The organizations, given their responsibilities, had different visions of what the special camps were to be like. The MGB, which was responsible for determining which prisoners were sent to a special camp, recommended that special camp prisoners be as thoroughly isolated as possible. The MVD, which had the task of running the special camps, sought to operate the camps in a fashion more like regular corrective labor camps.[85] The two organizations had two particular disagreements reflecting the ambivalence about the level of danger and capacity for redemption of the special camp prisoners. First, the MGB believed that no special camp prisoners should be allowed to work as engineering or technical personnel. Such work in special camps, in the MGB's view, had to be performed by MVD employees. The MVD disagreed, arguing that such a scheme was too costly. Second, the MGB thought that no cultural-educational activities should be carried out among the special camp prisoners. The MVD disagreed, contending that cultural-educational work increased labor discipline and tightened the camp regime, thus belonging within the menu of options for establishing order in the camps.[86] It would seem that the MVD won the argument, as official documentation attests to the continued existence of cultural-educational work and sections in the special camps.[87] Dolgun recalls political indoctrination meetings at Steplag "from time to time."[88]

Prisoner identity in the postwar Gulag was a complex phenomenon shaken to its core by the radical reorganization of Gulag life. Beyond the physical marking of special camp prisoner identity—the painted numbers and special clothes—inmates were required frequently and repeatedly to recite "the prisoner's prayer . . . consisting of full name, date of birth, length of sentence, and section of the criminal code under which they have been convicted."[89] Special camp prisoners were therefore forced to declaim their identity in precisely those terms dictated by camp authorities. The guards had their own prayer that ritualistically reemphasized the danger presented by their inmates. As Dolgun writes, a guard coming off duty would shout, "Sentry number forty-one. Post number three. For the defense of the Soviet Union. Guarding terrorists, spies, murderers, and enemies of the people. Sentry forty-one delivers the post." The replying guard coming on duty repeated the phrase.[90] While the recitation of the prisoner prayer compelled the inmate to give a self-declaration of identity in categories chosen by camp authorities, the prisoners themselves used such terms of identity in their relations with one another. Dolgun recalls some of his first meetings with fellow prisoners: "After we had talked for a while, he asked me about my case. That was always the way. . . . And within minutes of any encounter you were always launched on an elaborate version of your prayer. It was credentials. It placed you, so the other person knew who he was dealing with."[91]

Nearly all memoirists, and none more so than Solzhenitsyn, write of the significant impact that the special camps had on the lives of political prisoners. As Solzhenitsyn puts it, "In the Special Camps we raised the banner of the *politicals*—and politicals we became."[92] Dolgun remembers how "many of the prisoners spent their entire free time talking politics and cursing the Soviet system."[93] Many memoirists identified the isolation of political prisoners from common criminals as the key element of this new outlook. Prisoners, according to Solzhenitsyn, were no longer divided into the crude binaries of trusty/worker and nonpolitical/political prisoners. Rather, their social identities became more complex, based on region of origin, religion, people of practical experience, people of learning, and so on. He maintains that in the absence of thieves, the prisoners of special camps began to trust their fellow prisoners and for the first time look at themselves as politicals.[94]

Solzhenitsyn describes a special camp in his *One Day in the Life of Ivan Denisovich*. This led one former party member to remark in memoirs sent to the Central Committee in the 1970s about the stark difference between regular and special camps. In the regular camps, he notes, the "thief and gangster world" did anything with the counterrevolutionary prisoners that they could imagine, because they knew that nobody would stand up for the counterrevolutionaries. Life in the special camps was different, because they held only the counterrevolutionaries.[95]

While a few professional thieves made their way into the special camps, mainly after the commission of crimes in the camps that fell under statutes calling for detention in special camps, they found themselves there in an entirely different position. Thus, Artem Fel'dman tells of a prisoner called "Uncle Vasia" in Steplag's Kengir division. Uncle Vasia was a former professional thief, a *vor v zakone*, who had been transferred to Steplag on a twenty-five-year sentence for terror after killing an informer in a regular camp.[96] He was in quite a different position in Steplag, though. Rather than ruling over the politicals, as the professional criminals had done in the regular camps, he was initially isolated due to the near total lack of his fellow criminals at Steplag. Consequently, he attached himself to a different group, joining a religious sect as a repentant sinner.[97]

Some memoirists even indicate that the professional criminals had been politicized to at least some extent during the years following 1948. Dolgun compares his transit camp experiences in 1950 and 1951. During the latter trip, he

> was put in a cell with twelve or fifteen older *urki* [professional thieves]. I was afraid that they would take what little I had left . . . but when they saw the black Dzhezkazgan prison uniform with the numbers they treated me with respect and consideration. They had heard about Dzhezkazgan. They seemed more politically aware in this summer of 1951 than Valentin and his cohort a year ago. We had many thoughtful discussions about the system. They were more cynical. One had SLAVE OF STALIN tattooed on his forehead. STALIN had been partly obliterated but was still legible.[98]

The removal of a large portion, though not all, of the political prisoners from the general corrective labor camps led to a significant change of atmosphere there as well. Without many of the political prisoners to prey on, the divisions between different groups of criminals became sharper and more violent. The main division was between the so-called thieves and bitches. The former, the vory v zakone (thieves-in-law; hereafter vor or vory) characterized themselves as the "honest thieves." They lived according to a certain unwritten law—the most important element of which was the categorical refusal to cooperate with camp authorities. On this account they distinguished themselves from the suki, the bitches, who for them were all those willing to cooperate in running the camps.

A criminal acquaintance of Dolgun describes his understanding of the emergence of the bitches. The professional criminals, he notes, had set up a system of cooperation with the camp guards to sell items they had stolen from newly arriving prisoners. The proceeds were split with the guards, to buy good food, tobacco, and other necessities for the criminals. The camp and prison commanders had tried to interfere with the system by punishing the guards, but they had not been successful, so they took a new approach.

> They went into the camps and began to terrorize some of the less staunch *urki* by violence and threats, you know, until they had some of the poor guys so cowed they'd do anything. Then they were very cunning, those bastards. They forced some of these *urki* to do jobs that were absolutely against the code of the underworld. . . . Anything that helped the prison. You must never help build a prison wall or put up barbed wire. No self-respecting *urka* will ever do that; the rest would rub him out. So they forced them to break their own unwritten laws, do you see? Forced them to be a foreman in a work project. Absolutely taboo. Every *chelovek* [person] knows that. Accept a job like that and you've practically committed suicide. These were the suki, then. They had to be separated from the rest of the criminals or they'd have been rubbed out fast. The suki are the MVD's converts. The *chestnyagi* [the honest thieves], the unconverted, hate their guts. So the MVD always separates the two groups when there's an *etap*. They don't want their precious converts wiped out. All the same the war goes on in camp. Any time a *suka* is discovered, he usually loses his head. . . . Or [somebody] strangles him. It's the code.[99]

The vory maintained their unwritten laws through collective and often bloody punishments. Kopelev remembers the call for the "breaking" of one vor who had been caught cheating a fellow vor at cards:

> To be "broken," in their parlance, was to be found in violation of the thieves' law and deprived of the rights and privileges of their world. A broken thief lost his natural right to "pluck the pigeons." . . . [H]e no longer had a right to every other thief's assistance when in trouble; and, in fact, he was no longer immune to violence or death at the other thieves' hands. The elders, in this case, refused to break the Bomber, but Goga wouldn't be mollified, and he was supported

secretly by the other minors, who felt that their leaders, in forming a work team, had entered into a compact with the "vipers," the thieves' term for the camp authorities.[100]

The code of conduct for the vory was complex, but the most fundamental element remained the refusal to cooperate with authorities. Serving as an informer was the ultimate violation. As Kopelev's "Bomber" observes, "A thief cannot squeal on another thief to a viper. If he does, he's not a thief; he's a bitch."[101]

Most political prisoner memoirists acknowledge a distinction between the honest thieves and bitches. Solzhenitsyn disagrees. "People will object that it was only the *bitches* who accepted positions, while the 'honest thieves' held to the thieves' law. But no matter how much I saw of one and the other, I never could see that one rabble was nobler than the other. . . . No, you'll not get fruit from a stone, nor good from a thief."[102] Here, Solzhenitsyn's self-understanding as a political prisoner and his desire to render the political prisoner/common criminal divide in as clean a fashion as possible led him to dismiss this major rift within the criminal world. In a way, of course, Solzhenitsyn was correct. In regard to their relationship with political prisoners, there was often little practical difference between the two groups. After all, these honest thieves had the right, in Kopelev's telling, to "pluck the pigeons." That is, they were explicitly allowed under the "laws" to exploit any prisoner in the camp who was not a member of the vory. These pigeons were often the politicals. Yet even Solzhenitsyn acknowledges that the division was real, even if it lacked significance for the political, when he wrote about the "bitches' war" during the period after the creation of the special camps.[103]

Even among those cooperating with camp authorities, there were subtle gradations. Some prisoners served as "informers," attempting to gather incriminating material from other prisoners to pass on to authorities. Others were the "trusties," the prisoners holding privileged positions in the camps—such as kitchen workers, barrack supervisors, and the like. While they did not necessarily serve as informants, they maintained control over the camp through their control of access to food, living space, and other necessary elements of survival. As Kopelev writes, "Inside the camp—in the barracks, the yurts, the dining room, the bathhouse, the 'streets'—our lives were under the direct control of the trusties." But Kopelev himself maintains that the trusties were somehow not as bad as the informers. Kopelev even befriended a few of the trusties, and it worked to his advantage. When his suit was stolen, his acquaintance trusties, careful not to leave behind bodily marks as evidence of their work, engaged in torturous interrogations to secure its return.[104]

Kopelev's friendship with one trusty provided him a particularly interesting inside view of the bitches' war. In the words of this trusty, "We want order in the camp. That means we must keep the thieves in their place. But they're pretty strong right now, so we've got to move carefully."[105] Kopelev, of course, is not the only memoirist to write of the bitches' war. Buca recalls the murder of a criminal-made-hut-boss in Vorkuta under the slogan, "Death to the bitches!"[106] Yet Kopelev, through his access to this trusty, had a perceptive vantage point on this bitches' war.

One day the trusty told him:

> "Looks to me like you're scared of me or something. I'm your friend. . . . I don't care if you're a Fifty-eighter. I can see through people better than any investigator. . . . I'm no informer for the Oper [the camp police and surveillance department]. I've got my own informers. I know things about you that maybe you yourself don't know. . . . [W]e bitches, as the thieves call us, we're going to make it hot for the thieves pretty soon. More and more bitches among the new arrivals, did you know that?"

The trusty had it wrong, it seems, as he told Kopelev on a different evening, "Bad business at the BUR [strict regime barrack]. . . . Cut off one of the zek's heads and stuck it on a pole outside the door. Just like old times." The trusties, fearing the thieves, refused to go in until the next morning.[107]

Clearly the bitches' war raged from camp to camp, as the frequent relocation of prisoners from one camp to another carried this underground battle around the Gulag. As Kopelev describes, another battle happened soon among "two newly-arrived groups—a bunch of thieves and a crew of 'bitches' who had tangled in another camp. . . . Sasha [Kopelev's trusty acquaintance] gave me a lively account of how the combatants hacked away at each other with axes, knives and bits of glass and bashed each other's heads in with bricks and shovels."[108]

The whole situation was driving the trusty mad. "Things were getting worse and worse, he claimed—worse than at the front. At least at the front you know who's your enemy and who's your friend, but here you don't know what to expect, from what quarter. Some night some raggedy-ass kid will lose everything at cards in some barracks and will start betting with blood. You know what that means? He loses, he's got to pay by spilling blood—the first man he sees when he goes outside the next morning. . . . They tell us to maintain order; they let us have sticks, but what good are sticks against knives, axes, crowbars?"[109]

The camp's head doctor gave Kopelev his perspective, asserting, "The camp's in a state: war between the thieves and the bitches. Two more men killed last night. A trusty strangled in the toilet, stuck his head down in the hole. And the goner beaten to death with the shepherds' staves by the garbage dump. The trusties have gone berserk, and the commandant's backing them up."[110]

In official camp documentation, specific manifestations of the bitches' war at Karlag are apparent. While individual incidents are discussed, the bigger picture of the bitches' war is rarely mentioned. Karlag documentation identifies three criminal groups fighting one another: the vory, the *otoshedshie* (a splinter group of former vory), and the *otkolovshiesia* (another splinter group of former vory). While the latter two groups are portrayed as distinct from one another, the line of battle clearly lies between these two groups and the vory. In some cases of prisoner-on-prisoner murder, the participants and/or the victim are identified merely as bandits. It seems likely in these instances that the participants were members of a particular criminal group, but the camp administrators had either been unable to uncover this information or had simply neglected to record it.

On February 21, 1950, a member of Karlag's "criminal-bandit element" murdered a prisoner "belonging to the category 'otoshedshie.'" As a result of the effort to stop this incident, a camp employee was inadvertently shot by a camp guard.[111] A document from May 1950 notes a number of recent "bandit murders" between vory and otkolovshiesia. In one division medical clinic, four invalid prisoners were killed in one day.[112] On May 30, 1950, two so-called bandit prisoners beat another prisoner to death with a piece of iron. At the time, the murdered prisoner was helping camp employees in the barrack get the other prisoners out for work. When the two bandits began their attack, the camp employees fled, leaving their prisoner assistant at the mercy of the attackers. The employees were reprimanded for "cowardice."[113]

While in this last case the employees working inside the zone would have been unarmed and their cowardice may have been nothing more than it appeared, in a number of murders the role of the camp employee may have been more sinister. Many cases of prisoner-on-prisoner murder were facilitated by camp employee incompetence so blatant that it may indicate complicity in the murders themselves. Thus, on May 23, Aleksei Gerasimovich Podsokhin was murdered inside the penalty isolator of one Karlag subdivision. Podsokhin was a member of the otoshedshie. He had been placed in the penalty isolator on May 9 for a ten-day term. On May 14, he and other prisoners were caught trying to breech the cell wall. Podsokhin was given another ten-day term in the isolator for this offense. Two of the isolator's supervisors for unknown reasons transferred Podsokhin into a cell with members of the vory. On May 23, one of the supervisors who reportedly knew of Podsokhin's membership in the otoshedshie placed a vor, Andreev, in the cell with Podsokhin and left the two alone, whereupon Andreev strangled Podsokhin. The isolator's supervisors were each given ten days of house arrest for their actions.[114]

If the isolator supervisors were complicit in this murder, it raises one issue that should be reemphasized. It may seem wrong that camp employees assisted murder committed by a vor, the criminal group supposedly defined by its refusal to cooperate with the camp administration. Nonetheless, cooperation with the camp administration and the establishment of ties with individual camp employees and guards were two different things altogether. Recall the tale of the bitches' origin as told by Dolgun's acquaintance. The vory v zakone had established contacts among the guards to facilitate their thefts of property inside the camps. These contacts did not violate the vory laws. Working in the camp administration or serving as an informant—basically serving in any kind of role that would assist the camp—were the types of activity that violated the thieves' code.

While camp authorities frequently transferred prisoners from one subdivision to another to try to prevent murders, this tactic was generally unsuccessful. In late December 1950, the prisoner Tarasov was transferred out of his camp zone after a serious enmity developed between him and the prisoner-cook Iakovlev from whom Tarasov had been extorting extra food. On January 21, 1951, a nurse sent Iakovlev to Tarasov's new camp zone so that he could visit a dentist. Tarasov learned of Iakovlev's arrival and rushed to the dentist's office, where he stabbed Iakovlev to death with a handmade knife.[115]

Sometimes, although less often, murders occurred among female prisoners. On February 16, 1951, prisoners Reshtanenko and Ostrikova were murdered inside the zone of a strict regime camp division. On their arrival on February 12 in the strict regime division, Reshtanenko and Ostrikova had informed the head of the zone supervisors that they had a hostile relationship with several of the zone's prisoners and should therefore be sent somewhere else. They even brought a document with them from an administrator in their previous camp subdivision that attested to the dangers of putting them in the same zone with these other prisoners. The warnings were ignored. On February 16, their adversaries first suffocated Reshtanenko with a sheet and then beat Ostrikova to death with a piece of gridiron. The head of this camp zone was even reportedly aware of many prisoners' possession of gridiron as early as February 14, but had not performed a search.[116] All of these prisoner-on-prisoner murders point to the complete failure of the frequent searches in camps to remove weapons from prisoners.

Some prisoners certainly believed that camp employees were complicit in the commission of prisoner-on-prisoner murders. This belief even led to incidents of mild resistance. On March 28, 1951, a group of vory in a penalty camp division protested the actions of camp staff toward two of their number. These two vory had been placed in confinement cells located in a part of the camp populated by otoshedshie members. The vory raised their voices at the possible murder of these two vory by the otoshedshie. When camp employees went to remove the vory from their cells, they found evidence that the otoshedshie were trying to break into the cells. Order among the vory was only restored after one of the camp supervisors fired his pistol several times, wounding one vor. In response, most of the vory mounted a hunger strike demanding to see the camp's leading staff.[117]

The camp authorities' primary response to the rash of prisoner-on-prisoner murders followed a script that had been rehearsed many times over the years. Prisoners from different criminal groupings were to be isolated from one another in separate camp divisions.[118] They also demanded better and more frequent searches of the camp zone for forbidden items. In January 1953, a decree was issued to intensify the battle against criminal behavior inside the camps. All prisoners had to sign a statement that they had been made aware of the new enhanced penalties for crimes committed while in the camps.[119] According to Ivanova, fifty-two prisoners were executed for banditry under this law.[120]

The violence in the camps carried particular weight to the extent that it was a battle against informers. This phenomenon occurred in both regular and special camps. When prisoners reportedly started killing informers, informers reportedly stopped informing. Dolgun even writes of an informal prisoners' "committee."

> [The] People's Council of Justice [was] a sort of special soviet that undertook on behalf of the camp as a whole to execute these destructive people. The commonplace saying in camp was, "The stool pigeon walks with an ax at his back," and it was not just a figure of speech. . . . When a professional was assigned executioner by the People's Council, consistent with the ethic of audacity among the coloreds [another term for the professional criminals], he would sometimes take the severed head immediately to the nearest guard and say, "Here! I got the dirty stool pigeon. He's one of yours!" Then he would hand over the head and stoically take his three months in hard punishment.[121]

Many memoirists note the killing of informers. Panin estimates that forty-five informers were killed in Karaganda in an eight-month period during 1950–51. Fel'dman writes of his arrival at Steplag, when a young frightened prisoner approached and asked that Fel'dman inform "the intelligenty" that he was no stoolie (stukach). A brick from a "Bandera" man (a Ukrainian nationalist) killed this young man in his bunk that very same night.[122]

As the camp administrators lost their sources of information about prisoners and their weapons of control over prisoners, Panin reports that they sought other means of control, including "clumsy attempts to provoke bloodshed among prisoners of different nationalities." Still, Panin adds that "we saw through their plan and brought it to nothing. The man in charge of all the camp guards, Lieutenant Mochekhovski, a Chekist who had served with Kovpak's Red Partisans, worked especially hard to arrange a St. Bartholomew's Night. We often saw him nosing around in the camp. But for the time being at least, the prisoners were out only for the blood of the informers in their own ranks."[123]

The absence of informants, in the appraisal of memoirists, broke down the camp authority structure. By mid-1951, observes Panin, tension in the camp was high. "It was clear that the guards were receiving stronger doses of indoctrination at their political classes." Yet some prisoners continued to exhibit a new sense of voice, grabbing the rhetoric used against them for so many years and turning it on its head. One prisoner brigade leader "in effect" yelled at the camp administrators the following: "We are the revolutionaries, not you. We're fighting against your jailhouse fascism. For thirty-four years you've been calling yourselves revolutionaries. But it is *you* who are against *us*. It is *you* who are the real counterrevolutionaries. Stuff that in your pipe and smoke it." Not only did this prisoner speak out; his fellow prisoners also stepped in to prevent his seizure by camp guards.[124]

Local camp administrations were apparently reluctant to report the dearth of informants to central authorities because they were afraid it would cost them their own jobs.[125] Some informants were placed inside the internal camp prison as a method of protecting them from the general camp population. At Ekibastuz, trying to handle the problem locally, some prisoners suspected of killing informers were placed into prison cells with these informers. Other prisoners heard the screams of pain from the subsequent torture of these informer killers. According to Panin, on January 21, 1952, a group of prisoners tried to break into the camp jail to kill the informers taking refuge there. The guards in the watchtowers opened fire. "Most of the prisoners participating in the operation had seen service in the war and they immediately scattered, zigzagging and keeping their heads down, just as they must have done during an attack at the front." Panin reports that fewer than a dozen were killed.[126]

After the military veterans' actions and subsequent shootings, nearly the entire remaining population of Panin's camp division refused to work the next day, and some three thousand prisoners began a hunger strike. The prisoners demanded the arrival of the Kazakh Republic's general procurator to investigate the incident and punish those guilty of administering torture in the internal camp prison. They also demanded a halt to such repressive actions. Their strike was weakened, however, because the adjacent camp zone of Ukrainian nationalists did not join the action. The work stoppage and hunger strike lasted five days, until top camp administrators and the republic general procurator agreed to the prisoners' demands. While the prisoners celebrated, Panin claims that they "could clearly see that it was all bluff and that they would most surely have their revenge." In just two weeks, revenge was served as interrogators arrived from Karaganda. Gulag authorities shipped hundreds of prisoners off to other camps. While it was a long-established Gulag practice to split up prisoners after incidents of group resistance or misbehavior, in this case the practice truly seemed to backfire. Spreading the prisoners out among the extremely small group of special camps carried news of the hunger strike to every corner of the special camp system. Panin himself saw evidence of the Ekibastuz strike's fame when he was transferred to Steplag's Spassk subdivision. In this division known as the "Camp of Death" for its role in camp executions along with its concentration of sick and dying prisoners, Panin recalls, "It gave our hearts a lift to read on the walls of all the toilets, 'Greetings to the heroes of Ekibastuz!' or similar inscriptions. . . . The echo of what we had done quickly resounded throughout the Empire of Gulag, eventually making possible the uprisings at Dzhezkazgan, Vorkuta, and elsewhere. All this made great inroads in the slave-holding system in our country."[127] The arrival of prisoners with experience in and news of previous incidents of prisoner resistance was important in the development of the mass post-Stalin uprisings in the special camps.

The continued refusal of access to archival materials on the internal camp surveillance system renders impossible the evaluation of the relation between these murders and the killing of informers reported so widely in memoirs. Frankly, the scale of prisoner-on-prisoner murders even during this period was relatively low, if official statistics are to be believed. In Karlag's 192 subdivisions, prisoners murdered a total of fifty-one other prisoners in 1949, and another fifty-eight were murdered in sixty-four bandit incidents in 1950.[128] Such events, then, were still uncommon, and in 1951, they all but disappeared as prisoner-on-prisoner murders were reduced to seven.[129]

The particular facts of some of the prisoner-on-prisoner murders potentially fit a pattern in which informers could have been the victims. On January 22, 1951, the five prisoners Chernichkin, Kochetkov, Kilius, Tolkov, and Burgeev at one Karlag subdivision were locked up in the zone's penalty isolator for stealing the money, food, and belongings of other prisoners. The same night, the prisoners broke into the corridor of the isolator, where they then "created an uproar." Supervisors in the camp zone heard what was happening and went to open the door of the isolator. They had not realized that the prisoners were already in the corridor, though. When they unlocked the exterior door of the isolator, the prisoners rushed them and ran out into the zone. The camp staff took no measures that night to detain the prisoners and return them to the isolator. Later that night, armed with handmade knives, Chernichkin, Kochetkov, and Burgeev entered the prisoner barracks, stabbing to death the sleeping prisoners Gofman, Tregubenko, and Bezborodov.[130] The report does not mention any motivation for the murders. Presumably, these five prisoners had been able to move freely among the zone's population prior to their detention in the zone's penalty isolator. They thus could easily have killed these prisoners on other nights. The coincidence of the murders' timing and their detention in the penalty isolator indicates that their victims were chosen for at least some presumed relationship to their new punishment.

Available official documentation indicates that the "absence" of informants and/or reduction of informing activities noted so frequently in memoirs may have been a figment of the prisoners' collective imagination. Even if a significant number of stoolie murders occurred, available Gulag documentation provides a numerical picture of surveillance work that looks quite improved in the postwar era. As of July 1947, from a total camp and colony population of just over 2 million, central Gulag officials claimed to have 9,958 "residents," 3,904 "agents," and 64,905 informants, plus another 60,225 "anti-escape agent-informants."[131] According to Zemskov, this represented a growth of informers to 8 percent of the total Gulag population from a mere 1 percent in 1940.[132] Of course, we cannot exclude the possibility that individual Gulag camps engaged in their own brand of *tufta* (the ubiquitous prisoner strategy of cheating on fulfillment of norms) when reporting on the numbers of active informants in their camps, and Gulag officials complained of informants who were out of touch with their handlers and were offering no useful information. Despite the numerical growth in the informant apparatus, Gulag officials in the postwar period were unhappy with the poor working of the network, especially in regard to fighting against the theft of socialist property.[133]

As the 1950s approached, the special camps thrived. By July 1, 1949, seven special camps held 132,000 prisoners, employed primarily in underground mining and other heavy work.[134] By January 1, 1950, the total number of special camps grew to nine, with a population of 171,000.[135] The total hit 206,000 on January 1, 1951.[136] Much of the growth of special camps occurred in the Karaganda region. As Steplag grew, its subdivisions spread far and wide through central Kazakhstan from Ekibastuz to Karaganda to Spassk to Dzhezkazgan. In mid-1949, Steplag included camp subdivisions spread as far as six and eight hundred kilometers (Spassk and Balkhash, respectively) from the camp administration.[137] Soon thereafter, some of its subdivisions broke off to form other special camps: Peschanlag "special camp no. 8," Luglag "special camp no.

9," and Dal'lag "special camp no. 11." Of these, only Peschanlag lasted more than two years; Luglag and Dal'lag were soon folded back into the other special camps in the region.[138] As of January 1, 1954, Dal'lag, Peschanlag, and Steplag held a total of just over 47,000 prisoners, guarded by 7,300 militarized guards, or one guard for approximately every sixth prisoner.[139] While the post-Stalin era was marked by massive instances of special camp prisoner disobedience, on the issue of prisoner escapes, the special camps must be marked as a major success. On February 8, 1954, from a total special camp prisoner population of 209,000, only two instances of prisoner escape without recapture remained outstanding.[140]

While the battle against escape was typically at the forefront of special camp activity, no document reveals precisely why the introduction of special camps was deemed necessary. Escapes from camps were at all-time lows and declining, so this seems not to be the explanation. By 1948, the counterrevolutionary prisoner population had fallen in both relative and absolute terms, so the special camps cannot be explained as a response to a growth in this part of the camp population. In a February 1949 report, Minister of Internal Affairs Kruglov attributed the creation of the special camps to the rising number of prisoners with long sentences "in conjunction with the abolishment of the death penalty, and also the strengthening of criminal responsibility for embezzlement of state and social property and robbery."[141] Even this explanation, however, is unrevealing. He never makes it clear why a growing camp population, let alone one in which the counterrevolutionary population was declining, necessitated the creation of the special camps.

Nothing indicates that the individual regular camps were clamoring for the creation of special camps. In some respects, existing regular camps even objected to the loss of a portion of their prisoner labor force. Transfers out of regular camps proved burdensome both administratively and economically. In August 1948, Karlag was preparing for the transfer of over seventeen thousand of nearly seventy-four thousand prisoners into special camps and prisons. Karlag worried about meeting its obligations to provide prisoners as contract labor to non-Karlag industries. A "significant portion" of Karlag's seventeen thousand prisoners contracted out to other industries came from the contingent marked for transfer to special camps. Karlag worried whether its population after these transfers would include enough prisoners in adequate physical condition to meet its obligations to supply laborers. Even if it could provide enough contract laborers, this would leave Karlag without a large enough number of physically fit prisoners to complete its own economic work.[142] Between August 1948 and February 1949, the Karlag prisoners dropped in number from seventy-four to fifty-seven thousand, half of whom were classified as physically weak or invalids.[143]

It seems rather that the origin of the special camps must be understood mostly as a response to external events in the Soviet Union and world shaped by long-term trends in Gulag practice toward an ever-finer sorting of the prisoner population into ever-more-specialized detention institutions. The ongoing bloody battles with the Ukrainian and Baltic partisans, the terror of 1948, fears of a new world war, worries about inmates as a potential fifth column in such a war—all of these events created an atmosphere inside the Soviet Union that demanded no compromise with the internal enemy. The atmosphere, especially in the face of the ban on capital punishment, contributed to the creation of the special camps and the introduction of exile in perpetuity.[144] Yet the special camps were also a product of a long-term trajectory of Gulag practice that shaped the particular response to this uncompromising environment.

The creation of the special camps was driven in part by the long-term Soviet drive to sort its population into ever-finer categories. The special camps operated as yet another new circle in Dante's hell.[145] In the 1930s, the entire Gulag system had evolved into a hierarchy of detention that meshed well with a developing hierarchy of redeemability. Individuals deemed more dangerous, and less likely or less desirable for return to Soviet society, were subjected to harsher conditions along with stricter isolation. While execution offered the extreme in the hierarchy, obviously by definition excluding the possibility of return to the Soviet social body, other forms of detention from prisons down to the noncustodial refusal of passports to Soviet villagers and collective farms operated within a continuum of trust. Over the Gulag's history, Gulag authorities had frequently added new levels at all points in the hierarchy of detention institutions. The sorting of prisoners thus became ever finer, and the introduction of the special camps was just a particularly important event in this extended process. The special camps were not even fundamentally innovative, as they simply expanded on the practices developed since 1943 in the katorga camp divisions.[146] The main differences were that special camps operated as independent camp complexes (whereas the katorga divisions had been subdivisions of larger camp complexes) and housed a substantially larger number of inmates.

Finally, the creation of the special camps should also be understood at least in part as an attempt to make labor in the regular camps productive. The existence of the special camps as a potential destination for the most malicious violators of camp discipline could be used as a means to motivate prisoners in regular camps to complete their labor tasks. In this respect, the brutality of special camps directly served a purpose, as news of their conditions spread in the camps throughout the Gulag system. In creating a reputation for brutality, if not in motivating regular camp prisoners to work hard, they were successful. The creation of the special camps, in a much broader but similar fashion to the creation of katorga camp divisions during the war, also sought to protect the health of regular camp prisoners by condemning the most hated and least re-deemable Gulag prisoners to labor longer hours in the most dangerous Gulag industries.

Even if the special camps had been created for economic reasons, their operation undercut any positive benefits. The regime in special camps was not economically motivated; it was designed without much regard to cost to prevent escapes and isolate its prisoners completely from Soviet society and regular camp prisoners. The enhanced guard and more elabo-rate camp zone constructions were expensive, but they were the reasons for the special camps' existence.

Ultimately the creation of the special camps backfired, as it created a new social atmosphere in both the special and regular camps of the Gulag. While the special camps were successful at preventing escape, starting with the hunger strike at Ekibastuz and extending into the post-Stalin era, the special camps experienced the largest incidents of prisoner unrest in Gulag history.

## Nationality and Postwar Exile

Memoirs from the postwar Gulag attest time and again to the importance of national identity in the organization of postwar prisoner society. As Fel'dman, a prisoner at Steplag, describes it, the camps had a distinctly multinational hue. Ukrainians, Belarusians, Balts, Chinese, Japanese, Germans, and citizens of the people's democracies—these were the na-tions of the Gulag. He even remembers "one black man," a U.S. Army tank captain captured outside the American section of Germany in his tank and given seven years.[147]

A number of factors explain the particular significance of national identity during the postwar period. First, Soviet authorities starting in the 1930s and especially during the war had shifted toward a conception of the internal enemy that was defined ever more frequently in national terms. Prisoners and deportees increasingly found themselves in camps or exile not for their class status but rather for their nationality. Nationality became a primary organizing principle of Gulag practice. Second, the in-tegration of the western territories and Baltic states into the Soviet Union brought vast new populations to the Gulag that had spent the interwar period in polities organized on the nation-state principle. Nationalism, often in its integral nationalist form, was a dominant ideology in these regions. Many from these regions who found their way into the Gulag were members of nationalist underground organizations and nationalist partisan armies that had fought fiercely against all comers, including Soviet power, in the name of nationality. Third, postwar Soviet policy, especially starting with Stalin's famous toast to the Russian people, increasingly operated on the basis of a hierarchy of nationalities that raised primarily the Russian and secondarily the other Slavic nationalities above all others.

Nationality was certainly recognized by camp and colony administrators as an crucial element of camp life to be addressed in the postwar era. As one camp and colony Communist Party functionary in Kazakhstan put it in 1946, "In our ideological work, a large place must be taken by the national question."[148] The exact nature of work on "the national question" was never quite clear. Frequently, when talking about their work, camp and colony party members emphasized the necessity of propagandizing the ideas of "Soviet patriotism."[149] At the same time, the actual practices of camp employees generally privileged Russians over other nationalities.

Gulag prisoners and exiles, struggling for survival, latched on to various forms of community as ways to organize their lives in detention. Nationality in the Gulag worked in a number of different ways—first as a positive tie between prisoners on the basis of which they offered help to one another. According to Scholmer, a German Vorkuta inmate attuned to the national groupings in the Gulag, prisoners working in the kitchens tended to favor their conationals.[150] Members of various nationalities attempted to find space to continue some cultural traditions that defined their national existence. Thus, in the mines of Vorkuta, where the camp guards refused to go, Lithuanians reportedly performed religious services.[151] Western Ukrainians often refused to speak Russian, preferring their native language.[152] These national communities were not, of course, undifferentiated. Scholmer notes that German Nazis generally had less to do with the German Left than with members of other nationalities.[153] Nonetheless, for the prisoners in special camps, where the political prisoner/common criminal nexus had broken down, nationality was the primary organizing principle of Gulag society.

Among different groups, national identity operated as a shorthand identity vouching for a prisoner's character. Buca describes his experiences trying to engage in shadowy business dealings in the camp. One engine driver, approached by Buca, "looked me over carefully, glanced around, and asked me what nationality I was. He seemed relieved when I said I was Polish. . . . 'Usually you can trust the Poles in a deal.'"[154] He faced the same question from some Georgians, who replied, "The Poles aren't usually double-crossers."[155] In fact, Buca's Polishness seems to have given him a wider social circle than many prisoners. Usually, he observes, prisoners did not help those of other nationalities, but since there was a shortage of Poles around, he had wider contacts with prisoners of various nationalities than most.[156] His depiction certainly implies that the nationalities largely kept to themselves, providing social contacts and resources only for conationals and not for members of other nationality groups.[157]

Intriguing, though, is that it was the largest and smallest national groupings that failed to find cohesiveness exclusively within their own numbers. For Buca, it was the lack of fellow Poles. Many foreigners in the camps described a similar phenomenon. On the other hand, Russians typically did not form a single, coherent group.[158] The population of Russian prisoners was simply too large to make such a grouping effective in organizing systems of mutual assistance in the camp world. After all, if you were in a camp that was largely Russian, how would you decide which Russian you would help because of shared nationality and which you would not? Other factors of prisoner identity like political attitude, region of origin, or veteran status were more likely to structure prisoner society in this case.[159] A prisoner's Russian identity, then, was most likely to come to the fore when dealing with prisoners of a non-Russian nationality.

Panin thus was not terribly focused in his memoir on his position as a Russian in the camps. Rather, he was clearly more concerned with his religious identity. Nonetheless, when evaluating non-Russians, in particular Chechens, he offered an essentialized (though positive) perspective. Of the Chechens behind barbed wire, he writes that "they were reliable, brave and strong-minded people. You didn't find stool pigeons among their kind. If one did crop up, he was doomed to a short life."[160] Panin was also a great admirer of the uncompromisingly anti-Soviet and proreligious life led by Chechens and Ingush in exile.

> The Chechens and the Ingush are closely related Moslem peoples of the Caucasian region. Most of them are determined and courageous. They had at first believed that Hitler would free them from the shackles of Stalinism, and when the Germans were finally driven from the Caucasus, Stalin ordered their resettlement. . . . Many . . . perished. But the Chechens were very tenacious of life and liberty and were thus able to survive this barbarous deportation. Their chief strength lay in their religious faith. They settled down in closely knit communities and in each village the most educated man among them took upon himself the duties of the mullah. They tried to resolve their differences and quarrels by themselves, without resorting to the Soviet courts. Despite government-imposed fines, Chechen girls were not sent to school at all, while the boys went only for a year or two, long enough to master the rudiments of reading and writing. Thus a protest of the simplest kind, made in a direct, palpable manner, enabled the Chechens to win a victory for their nation. Their

children were brought up to have some idea of their religion, if no more than the most basic customs. They were taught to hate atheism.[161]

Panin's positive evaluation was not shared widely, although his essentialized view of the Chechen and Ingush peoples was. Soviet authorities singled them out among the exiles in Kazakhstan as the most malicious violators of labor discipline and the most likely to refuse to work.[162] In 1952, Kazakh authorities requested that the Chechens be deported again, this time to move them to the more distant areas of Kazakhstan. Although the MGB considered the Chechens and Ingush in exile to be "totally incorrigible," it denied the request, stating that such a move would not "solve the problem."[163] Bloody battles between Russian and Chechen or Ingush prisoners were quite common.

While Buca's Polish identity provided him with access to other groups, nationality also supplied the organizing principle for much camp antagonism. The great number of non-Russian prisoners blamed the Russians for their plight. The most virulent conflict, according to Buca, was between Russians and Ukrainians. This, of course, mirrored the bloody battles between Soviet NKVD troops and Ukrainian partisan guerrillas that continued for several years into the postwar period. As Buca writes, the Russians regarded the Ukrainians in the camp as Banderites, enemies of the Soviet homeland, aliens who did not deserve to be fed and who should be worked until they dropped dead. He also points to the important role of guards in fomenting these feelings. Guards threw around the term Bandera as a derogatory curse. One morning, Buca recalls the wake-up call, "Up, you fascist bastards! You Bandera dirt! Are you waiting for your fucking mother . . . ?"[164] National disputes also occurred among the non-Russian nationalities. According to Scholmer, these disputes often mirrored larger geopolitical rivalries. Thus, he comments on the animosity at Vorkuta between Lithuanians and Poles motivated by the disputed status of Vilnius.[165]

Numerous memoirists testify to the role of Soviet officials in facilitating animosity among the national groups. Scholmer believes that the camp administration tried to use its Russian population to keep the other nationalities in their place.[166] Dolgun remembers the local secret police commander in Dzhezkazgan as "chiefly occupied with creating internal conflict in camp, setting the Ukrainians against the Russians (which was not hard) by spreading rumors and so on, on the divide-and-rule principle."[167]

Even when not specifically seeking to foment hatred among the nationalities, the actions of Gulag authorities reinforced the ties of nationality. The strong sense of national identity among Ukrainians was only strengthened by the conscious decision of camp authorities to concentrate

Ukrainian inmates in particular camp sections. Buca recalls the prisoners at Peltevna as being 85 percent Ukrainian.[168] The Kengir camp division of Steplag, a Karaganda region special camp to be discussed further below, had a population at the time of Stalin's death that was 72 percent Ukrainian and Baltic nationalist.[169] The intense concentrations of Ukrainian prisoners led to persistent feelings that the Ukrainian people had been targeted entirely out of proportion to other Soviet nationalities.

To some extent, the Ukrainians were correct. They had been targeted, if not exclusively for their nationality, then at least for living both in regions that had not been part of the Soviet Union during the prewar period and those areas that were occupied by the Nazis. On both accounts, the Ukrainians, especially those from western Ukraine, were treated as suspect. The same was true of western Belarusian, Baltic, and Bessarabian (now Moldovan) peoples. Not only had these peoples been exposed to non-Soviet ideology during their wartime occupations, raising all the issues of contamination addressed in the filtration camps, but they had also lived outside the Soviet Union in the prewar period in polities operating on very different bases. Furthermore, they had not undergone the intense Sovietization and purification experienced in the Soviet Union during the interwar period. Beyond these issues of socialization and exposure to non-Soviet ideology, the peoples of the western territories and Baltics were also in large numbers participants in nationalist organizations and partisan armies with explicitly anti-Soviet agendas. The bloody battles between Soviet and nationalist partisan forces continued well into the postwar era, and defined Soviet distrust of the peoples from these regions.

The Sovietization of the newly integrated western territories was a critical part of the Gulag story in the postwar era. Between 1944 and 1947, the labor camp population of Ukrainians rose 2.4 times, Belarusians rose 2.1 times, Lithuanians 7.5 times, Latvians 2.9 times, Estonians 3.5 times, and Poles 1.8 times. All of these peoples saw their proportional weight in the total corrective labor camp population rise significantly during this period. In addition, these same nationalities were much more likely to spend their period of imprisonment in corrective labor camps than in corrective labor colonies.[170] This certainly indicates that prisoners from among these nationalities were more likely to be handed longer sentences. Distrust on the basis of nationality was not limited to the peoples from the western territories and Baltic republics. The same preponderance of their numbers in corrective labor camps over corrective labor colonies was true for members of deported nationalities, members of nationalities with corresponding non-Soviet nation-states (Soviet citizens who were ethnically Chinese, Mongols, Turks, etc.), and foreigners.

Much as it had during the war, national identity played a particularly important role in shaping postwar exile practices. In 1945, the Council of

People's Commissars codified the legal situation of special settlers. These exiles existed at the margin between the prisoner and the free Soviet citizen. Special settlers were given all the rights of Soviet citizens, except they were not allowed to leave their locality without express permission of the political police organs. The failure to comply with this requirement was treated as escape and punished criminally. The special settlers were required to engage in "socially useful labor," which was supposed to be organized for them by the local NKVD. They were also required to report any changes in family status (birth, death, or escape) to the local NKVD within a three-day period.[171] The living conditions for exiles were still difficult. In 1945, Beria himself wrote to Nikolai A. Voznesenskii, the chair of the state planning agency (Gosplan), about the "extremely difficult daily-living conditions" faced by exiles in the Kazakh, Kyrgyz, and Uzbek republics. More than twenty-six thousand families had no fit living structure.[172]

Deportations in the postwar era continued to operate largely on a national basis. From 1945 to 1948, an additional 120,000 Soviet Germans, mostly postwar repatriates from Germany and Austria, were sent into exile.[173] They likely had been in territories occupied by the Nazis prior to the mass deportations in 1941. In 1946, Gulag and MVD directives emphasized that any labor camp or colony prisoners due for release who were members of those nationalities deported during the war were only to be released into exile either with their families or at least to those regions where their conationals had been deported.[174]

The main thrust of postwar ethnic deportations was from the reannexed territories in the Baltic republics, western Ukraine, western Belorussia, and the new Moldovan Republic. Between 1944 and 1947, over a hundred thousand Ukrainians were sent into exile for being members of the Organization of Ukrainian Nationalists (OUN). In 1945 and 1948, nearly fifty thousand were exiled from Lithuania. Another ninety-five thousand were exiled in 1949 from the three Baltic republics combined, and fifty-seven thousand were exiled from the Moldovan Republic.[175] Further postwar national deportations targeted Basmachi (alleged Central Asian nationalists), Poles, Turks, Greeks, Dashnaki (alleged Armenian nationalists), and Iranians.[176]

These national exiles were all based on a specific combination of class and national factors. Unlike the wartime deportations of Germans, Chechens, Ingush, and others, these postwar deportations were not undifferentiated and were not total. Only a portion of the national populations of these republics was sent into exile. The differentiation was officially based on either alleged membership in nationalist and/or profascist organizations, or class status as a kulak.[177]

There were two main "nonnational" exile groups in the postwar period: the 16,000 agricultural workers deported for leading "anti-social and parasitic forms of life," and the nearly 150,000 deported for a term of six years as members of the All-Russian Liberation Army, the Vlaso-vites.[178] When Stalin ordered the release of the latter after six years, all those who were members of any of the deported nationalities were left in exile "permanently." The remainder were released, with restrictions forbidding them to live in Moscow, Leningrad, Kiev, border zones, re-stricted areas, and the western territories—the Baltic republics, the Mol-dovan Republic, and the western zones of the Ukrainian and Belarusian republics. The individual enterprises in which they had worked in exile were urged to conclude agreements with these exiles to remain in place in their jobs.[179]

By the postwar era, a sharp distinction had arisen between the treat-ment of the ever-shrinking number of former kulaks in exile and the na-tional deportees sent into exile during the war. This is especially evident for exile youths. Among the national exiles, children on reaching the age of sixteen were personally placed on the rolls of exiles. For kulak exiles, children under the age of sixteen were released from exile, and on reach-ing the age of sixteen only a small number were placed on the rolls of exile.[180] For the national deportees' children, placement on the rolls of ex-iles had become a matter of blood, of parental lineage. For kulak exiles' children, a presumption of their necessary subjection to exile on reaching the age of majority was not present. This obviously accords with the dif-fering conceptions of enemy status placed on the differing contingents. Being an enemy according to nationality was an inescapable definition, while being an enemy according to class left the potential open for mov-ing away from the parental background. The entire postwar period saw a gradual expansion of the terms under which various exiles from the former kulak contingent could be released. By the time of Stalin's death, and the ensuing mass releases from camps and exile, few former kulaks were left to be freed. For the national exiles, the postwar period saw the tightening up and extension of their terms of exile forever. Those who had been sent into exile as kulaks yet belonged to any of the nationalities exiled during the war were not subject to release but instead were merely transferred officially on to the rolls of the national deportees.[181]

Despite the releases of former kulaks from the rolls of special settlers, the combination of the continued postwar exile of nationalities and grad-ual regularization of exile life to the point that births began to outnum-ber deaths led the total exile population to reach its maximum only on January 1, 1953, when 2.8 million people lived in internal Soviet exile. By the late Stalin era, new exiles primarily came from indigenous popula-tion growth—that is, the new children of exiled peoples officially became exiles themselves.[182]

The introduction of permanent exile was the second major Gulag historical event in 1948. This was the first official application of any punitive measure other than execution without a theoretical end. Eternal exile first appeared in the resolution on the creation of special camps. All special camp prisoners on their release from special camps were registered as permanent deportees in some of the Soviet Union's most isolated regions. At least some 37,900 people had been sent into permanent exile after completing their sentence as of May 1953. Moreover, all inmates who had been released since the end of the war but who would now be subject to permanent exile on release were rearrested in order to change their legal status. Over 20,000, particularly among those arrested in 1937 and released after ten-year sentences, were rearrested for the purpose of placing them in permanent exile.[183] Many of them were not rearrested until 1949—a year that Ginzburg calls the "twin brother of 1937."[184] While the bloodiness of 1948 and 1949 were no match for their 1937 and 1938 cousins, these rearrests affected many people who had become Gulag inmates in the earlier terror. As Ginzburg writes of her 1949 rearrest, "They confronted me with no new charges. They required no 'confessions.'" They had been rearrested "merely in order to have our status regularized to that of permanent, lifelong exile by a decision of the MGB's Special Conference." Ginzburg herself was limited to living and moving about within a seven-kilometer radius of Magadan and was under the open surveillance of the MGB, to whom she was required to report twice a month for life.[185]

Ginzburg's story is similar to many others. Vasillii Nikoforovich Lazarev, a former member of the Central Committee of the Communist Party of Kazakhstan, had been arrested during the terror. He was released on September 7, 1946, and returned to Kazan, where he was allowed to register and live in nearby Vasil'ev. Lazarev was rearrested in July 1949. An MGB representative specifically told him that they had no new evidence against him, but had nonetheless decided to exile him to Krasnoiarsk.[186] The same happened to Nikolai M. Busarev, who was told that his second arrest was based on the same crimes as his first arrest. He was sent for lifelong exile into the far north.[187]

Yet intriguingly, permanent exile—an official declaration that a person could never be fully reintegrated into Soviet society—did not imply that a person had been totally removed from society. Perhaps the most surprising part of Ginzburg's story was the arrival of an agitator five years after her deprivation of rights ended, but while she was still in permanent exile. The agitator wanted to make sure that Ginzburg got out and voted. She said:

> "I want first of all to congratulate you . . . and to welcome you back with all my heart to the family of the workers. . . . " She was a Stalinist of the effusively emotional variety. She simply oozed enthusiastic benevolence, and a fervent

desire to induct me, a heathen, into that harmonious world in which she lived so fruitfully. She spoke to me more or less in the manner in which gentle, patient missionaries doubtless address primitive African tribesmen.[188]

Even as a permanent deportee, Ginzburg was a subject to be reclaimed by some fervent Stalinist for the "family of the workers." Of course, her status as a permanent exile revealed that she could not be fully integrated into that family.

In late 1948, permanent exile was extended to many of the deported nationalities. On November 26, 1948, the Presidium of the Supreme Soviet of the USSR issued its decree detailing the criminal penalties for escape from exile of any peoples deported during the war. The nationalities deported during the war were now officially informed that their exile was permanent. Anyone among these national exiles who escaped (that is, who left their region of exile without permission) was subject to a twenty-year term in Gulag camps. All those subject to permanent exile were required to sign an affidavit attesting that they understood that their term of exile extended forever and that they faced twenty years in camps for escape.[189] In June 1949, the permanent exile status was extended to Latvians, Estonians, and Lithuanians exiled in 1949.[190] In April 1950, those exiled as members of the OUN were subjected to permanent exile.[191]

When their exile was made permanent, over five thousand adult OUN exiles lived within the bounds of Kazakhstan, most in the Karaganda region. According to official reports, not one of the five thousand refused to sign the affidavit on their permanent exile and criminal liability for escape. Informers and political police reported on the "moods" of the OUN members about this momentous change in status. They ran the gamut. Some meekly accepted their situation. One woman reportedly said, "If they resettled us from western Ukraine to Karaganda, then it means we must live and be employed here and submit to the laws of Soviet power." Another woman echoed the comments, "I thought that after two to three years I would return to western Ukraine, but now as much as there is a law on us staying here forever, we must live and work here. If you escape, they will nonetheless capture and convict you." Some even expressed more positive evaluations of life in Karaganda, especially since their pre-Soviet western Ukraine had ceased to exist. The arrival of collective farms in western Ukraine came in for particular abuse. "Here in Karaganda we live much better [than in the Stanislav region], we should call on our families to move from western Ukraine to Karaganda." Or another woman commented, "If they let us leave Karaganda, there would nonetheless be no reason to go to the western Ukraine, where they are now organizing kolkhozy. It is better to live here and work in industry than to enter a kolkhoz."[192]

Others had more decidedly negative attitudes. Hopes that external events, especially a war between the United States and the Soviet Union, would intervene and change their position were common. "Soon there will be war, we will fall under the power of America and only this will relieve us from exile." Another asked, "Why don't England and America start a war with the Soviet Union? What are they waiting for?" Some expressed their plan to return to western Ukraine anyway. "I did not kill anyone in Ukraine, I did not steal, therefore, I shall leave after my six-year term, despite whatever laws, I will leave for western Ukraine." These declarations of "anti-Soviet moods" were turned over to the organs of the MGB for investigation.[193]

Some of the exiles from the Baltic republics sent to other regions were even more virulently anti-Soviet. As an informant reported, one Estonian woman spoke with excitement about the war in Korea. "It's good that the Americans bomb all the cities and villages of North Korea.... They should at the same time bomb the cities and villages of the Soviet Union and destroy the Communists. I hate the Communists such that if the Americans today started to bomb us, then I would be prepared to die if only they destroyed the Communists for how they torment us."[194]

The training of a keen ear on the international situation for events that could alter their status was common in the camps as well. Solzhenitsyn remarked on the eagerness in a transit prison about reports from Korea. Rumors abounded that "Stalin's blitzkrieg had miscarried. The United Nations volunteers had by now been assembled. We saw in Korea the precursor, the Spain, of the Third World War."[195] War, the prisoners hoped, could bring a new fate, perhaps their release, or even the overthrow of the Soviet government itself. Scholmer also noted that prisoners were constantly talking about war and what would happen if it were to come. They asked Scholmer repeatedly whether the Allies had tried to save Nazi camp prisoners after the war.[196]

Prisoners' focus on the international arena was no surprise. On the one hand, during the war they had already seen how international events of such a magnitude could directly affect camp life. On the other hand, the international situation was a constant subject of discussion in the Soviet world. The cold war was echoed not only in the prisoners' hopes but also in the camp employees' discussions of their work. Conversing about the coming election campaign of 1948, the chief of the political department of Kazakhstan's Administration of Corrective Labor Camps and Colonies (UITLK) reminded his local party workers that the "socialist power [derzhava] was moving forward to communism as the vanguard of all progressive humanity in the struggle with the forces of the black reaction led by American imperialism and its lesser partner the English bourgeoisie.... Our country stands as the herald of peace, freedom and the national independence of all peoples."[197] Or as he said following the attack on the journals *Zvezda* and *Leningrad*,

> The bourgeois world does not like our successes both inside our country and in the international arena. . . . The question of socialism has become the order of the day in many countries of Europe. The imperialists do not like this. . . . In these conditions, the task of ideological education consists not only in answering blow for blow all of these heinous smears and abuses leveled at our Soviet culture, but also to lash out and attack boldly bourgeois ideology. . . . The spiritual riches of our people are no less important than the material riches.[198]

A knowledge of foreign affairs, or at least a knowledge of the official Soviet version of foreign affairs, had always been a requirement for a good Communist. This was no less true in the postwar era. Criticisms of party political education in the Gulag system included those "who could not speak about what is happening now in Paris, events in China, and other international questions."[199]

Karaganda continued to serve as a deportation locale for many exiles in the postwar period. As of March 25, 1949, the region held 111,000 exiles, including 30,000 men, 42,000 women, and 39,000 children under the age of sixteen. The major statistical categories were based largely on the exile contingents—that is, with whom or for what reason these people were sent into exile. The largest group consisted of Soviet Germans and their families, comprising over 57 percent of the region's total. The second largest, encompassing nearly 35 percent of the exiles in Karaganda, were those exiled from the northern Caucasus, an overwhelming proportion of whom were Chechen. The final large groups were those sent into exile for particular reasons, mostly former members of the OUN, former members of the Russian Liberation Army (listed as Vlasovites), and Poles exiled in 1936.[200] While the numbers of class-based exile groups like former kulaks were small in the Soviet Union as a whole by 1949, they were entirely absent in the Karaganda region. The overall breakdown by contingent for the Kazakh Republic, where over 828,000 exiles were being held in 1949, is roughly similar to that in Karaganda, with the exception of a sizable 3.5 percent from among those exiled from the Georgian Republic. No former kulaks remained in exile in the Kazakh Republic.[201]

The totals had changed little by 1952, when the exiles in the Karaganda region numbered 130,000, including 42,000 children under the age of sixteen. Germans, Chechens, Ukrainians, and Ingush continued to occupy, respectively, the four largest national groups of exiles in the region. The total exile population of the Kazakh Republic in early 1952 was over 940,000.[202] The main growth in the number of exiles in Karaganda and Kazakhstan during the 1949–52 period seems to be an indigenous population growth of the exile community itself—that is, new births were added to the roll of exiles faster than deaths removed names from the rolls.

Reviewing data on the locations of individual special settlements in the Karaganda region reveals only the slightest evidence for concentrating exiles from a particular contingent or nationality group in one location. For the most part, the exiles were freely mixed with one another. Since the exiles of Karaganda region fell almost exclusively into four contingents (Germans, northern Caucasians, former OUN members, and Poles), however, and the vast majority of those were either German or Chechen, the special settlements were overwhelmingly comprised primarily from these groups.[203] The concentration of just a few exile groups in the Karaganda region should temper any argument that Soviet authorities were attempting to break national groups apart and thus destroy their national identities. Living mostly around their conationals, these peoples maintained their cultures, languages, and national identities. If Soviet authorities had truly wanted to denationalize these peoples, they would have been better off trying to disperse them widely among existing populations of other nationalities.

Finally, anti-Semitism in the postwar Gulag highlights some elements of national identity behind the barbed wire. The history of anti-Semitism, official and unofficial, in the postwar Soviet Union has been well documented. From the destruction of the Jewish Anti-Fascist Committee, to the barely veiled anti-Semitism of the anticosmopolitan campaigns and the indications of a major purge of Soviet Jews emerging from the "doctors' plot" at the end of Stalin's life, anti-Semitism became a ubiquitous element of postwar Soviet life. The same was true of the Gulag.

Officially at least, the immediate postwar era continued to see denunciations of outbursts of anti-Semitism.[204] Nevertheless, the increasing interconnections between Soviet identity and Russian, or at least Slavic, identity became quite obvious. In Kopelev's presentation, Soviet and Russian identity are so inseparable that he almost unproblematically identifies himself as Russian, despite being "officially" Jewish. After complaining bitterly about being placed in a cell with Germans, another prisoner called out, "We've got some Russians here too." Of this, Kopelev notes, "It's interesting how meeting your own kind in a political prison calms you down and brings you out of yourself." Kopelev reflexively sees the self-proclaimed Russian as his "own kind" without considering for a moment whether his "own kind" meant Russian specifically, or whether by Russian he was simply referring to Soviet or at least non-German.[205] Later, Kopelev even denies much real significance to his Jewishness as part of his identity as a Soviet man. He was interrogated about his complaints of Soviet commission of brutalities against Germans. You are "too kind," he was told, yet, "Still, you're a Jew. How can you love the Germans? Don't you know what they've been doing to the Jews?" Kopelev responded, "What is 'love'? I hate the Fascists not as a Jew—I haven't had much occasion to be reminded of that—but as a Soviet man, a Kievite, a Muscovite, and, above all, as a Communist. And that means my hate cannot find expression in rape or pillage."[206]

Despite Kopelev's self-understanding as Soviet (or perhaps Russian) first and Jewish second, his fellow prisoners and Gulag authorities thought differently. Scholmer recalls the arrival of official anti-Semitism in Vorkuta, where *Pravda* suddenly became popular in the camp. The guards began making anti-Semitic remarks. Political officers engaged in anti-Semitic discussions while reviewing the latest *Pravda* articles with prisoners in the barracks, and anti-Semitic comments became common in the mess hall and at work. Thus it is clear that anti-Semitism extended well beyond camp officials themselves. Scholmer opined that "anti-Semitic feeling in the camps at Vorkuta is more intense than it ever was even among the anti-Semitic German middle classes under Hitler. The Jews in these camps are living side by side with many of their most brutal persecutors." He singled out the Ukrainian prisoner population as especially prone to anti-Semitism.[207]

The doctors' plot had specific ramifications in the Gulag. Fel'dman recalls, "After the doctors' plot, the camp administration decided that all Jews were terrorists, therefore they began to blame Jewish youth for recent murders."[208] Ginzburg specifically recalls the doctors' plot as bringing anti-Semitism to Kolyma. "Until then," she writes, "we had been, as far as the authorities were concerned, a single, uniform mass."[209]

In the postwar Gulag, nationality had risen to the forefront as both an organizing principle for prisoners' and exiles' construction of their own societies and networks of relationships, and a primary means by which Soviet authorities defined their enemies. The postwar Gulag saw the introduction of populations with committed and explicit anti-Soviet nationalist ideologies. Soviet practices intensified national identities among the prisoners and exiles.

## War Veterans

As we have seen, many Red Army veterans and Soviet partisans passed through filtration camps, and then found their way into the Gulag. Even though they all carried the potential taint of collaboration with the enemy, they occupied a high place in Gulag society, just as they did in postwar Soviet society. Shumuk remembers a fight in a prison cell. His opponent, indignant, yelled: "Do you know who I am? . . . I'm a 'repeater.' I've been sentenced three times, saw all the labour camps of Russia, and then was taken from the camps and transferred to Kovpak's detachment, behind German lines. I was with Kovpak [the legendary Soviet Ukrainian partisan commander] until he reached the Carpathian mountains, and here you've dared to raise your hand against me!"[210] The outburst speaks to two of the most important elements of Gulag status in the postwar period: being a repeater with long camp experience, and being a former Soviet partisan. It also speaks to the pride and sense of entitlement felt by those veterans.

Gulag authorities and guards had an ambivalent attitude toward those with army experience. The ambivalence arose from significant uncertainty about the nature of prisoners' wartime activities. Were they Soviet patriots or traitorous Vlasovites? Furthermore, the assertiveness of military veterans was a potential threat to order in the Gulag society. Consider again the indignant tone of the Kovpak partisan. "Don't you know who I am?" he cried. The boldness of the veteran has been noted throughout postwar Soviet society. These people had risked their lives in defense of the Soviet Union, and had a corresponding sense of entitlement and empowerment.

Kopelev recalls a scene played out in front of his prison train in Gorky. Two drunken locals were being shooed away by the train's guards. "And who are you?" cried one of the drunken men. "I fought for the Motherland." On the same train platform, it became apparent that imprisoned Soviet veterans called forth the same ambivalence from Soviet citizens as they did from Gulag guards. A disabled veteran hobbled up to the train, "Vlasovites, eh? We spilled our blood, and you, you rats, you worked for the Fritzes. To the gallows—all of you." Yet two women approached with a completely different response to the prisoners. One of the women asked the prisoners if any had been "front-liners." A guard came to send the ladies on their way, but they soon returned with arms full of food, shouting, "Hey, boys, front-liners—catch!" The train commander approached the ladies, warning them that they could be shot for such actions. They finished throwing the food, as one said, "They're from the *front*! Whom did *you* ever fight? . . . Who're you going to fire at—women? And for what—for showing a little mercy? Who are you—Germans?" At this point, the disabled veteran who had just harangued the prisoners as Vlasovites approached the guards, saying, "Go ahead, shoot *me*, riffraff, if you dare! I'll flatten you with this crutch! I captured Warsaw, fuck your mother!"[211]

Kopelev himself felt this sense of entitlement based on his own involvement in the Soviet military. After his arrest, he was tossed in a cell with Germans. This was an affront to his sense of dignity. "'Don't you know there are Fritzes in here?' I bawled; I swore; I was furious. 'I'm a Soviet officer! I won't be humiliated like this!'"[212]

The ambivalence on the part of Gulag employees toward Red Army veterans was pronounced. On the one hand, Gulag practices often were designed specifically to remove any dignity from former Red Army officers. Buca recalls civilians entering his barracks and asking for Red Army officers, who were then forced to carry out the "shit bucket" as a reminder that they were now prisoners and nothing more.[213] Yet in spite of the hostility to imprisoned veterans, whether on account of their presumed role as traitors during the war or assertiveness in places of imprisonment, where authorities expected passivity of their prisoners, Red Army veterans were also frequently granted privileges over their civilian or non-Russian fellow prisoners. Solzhenitsyn himself remembers his appointment as a camp foreperson as based on his officer experience in the army during the war.[214]

The prisoners themselves held frontline soldiers in high regard and with high expectations, although Solzhenitsyn regards them as abject failures. Writes Solzhenitsyn, "High hopes were placed in the front-line soldiers when they arrived—they would go after the stoolies! Alas, the military reinforcements were a disappointment to the camp warriors."[215]

Red Army and/or partisan veteranship presented certain difficulties as itself an organizing principle of group identity. After all, some veterans really were traitors of one sort or another. Some had in fact fought with Vlasov's army, and other had in actuality cooperated with the Nazis in POW camps and under occupation. For the proud, honest war veteran, it was impossible to know for sure if the other veterans in the camp were also honest veterans or whether they had fought against you on the other side. Nonetheless, something of a "community of warriors" did develop among those who had fought during the war, even among those who had fought against one another.

## The Gulag in Stalin's Last Years

In the early 1950s, the Gulag system—now fully developed and at its population peak—continued to grind away. A report on Karlag's work for 1951 emphasized the camp's now-familiar primary objectives: the tightening of the camp regime, the isolation and guard of prisoners, and through the tightening of the regime, the completion of the camp's economic tasks.[216] Party conferences, meetings of the camp activists, political education meetings of camp employees—the protocols developed over twenty years of Karlag's history continued unabated. Prisoner-on-prisoner violence and violations of the camp regime were down significantly in 1951, while escape attempts were essentially unchanged, and were still blamed on a lack of vigilance among the guard and the particularities of agricultural work.[217] Karlag had definitely run out of ingenuity in problem solving. The "solution" proposed for every problem identified in various reports from 1952—and none of the problems were new—merely rehashed long-established practices. The morale and vigilance of the guard was inadequate, so they had to have political meetings of the officers and party-Komsomol conferences among the rank and file, and they had to improve their living conditions as well as organize cultural and sporting events for them.[218] Escapes were (as always, no matter the figures) too frequent, so they had to review the prisoners living outside the zone to remove those sentenced for especially dangerous crimes.[219]

In some respects, the Gulag operated more efficiently than ever. By the early 1950s, the Gulag held its all-time largest populations of prisoners and exiles. The system continued a losing battle for economic efficiency, but this battle had been waged since its first days. Prisoner deaths and prisoner escapes had reached historic lows despite the burgeoning camp population. There was no particular crisis.

Some camps were even celebrating their "success." In 1952, Karlag celebrated the twentieth anniversary of the founding of its educational camp point (*lagpunkt* "Uchebnyi Kombinat") for the preparation of agricultural specialists. During those twenty years, the camp point's director bragged, they had trained over ten thousand specialists ranging from veterinarians and agrotechnicians to tractor drivers and bookkeepers. These former delinquents had, he continued, "found their place as citizens of the great country of socialism—the USSR." In every part of Karlag, educational camp point trainees worked as specialists, "expiating their guilt before socialist society" while assisting in "the transformation of the wild Karaganda steppe into an advanced, cultured, enormous agricultural enterprise."[220]

Still, Gulag society had changed significantly in the postwar period. New prisoner populations of war veterans, nationalist guerrillas, and peoples with significant life experience outside the Soviet Union provided a potentially combustible mix. The isolation and concentration of many of these prisoners in a small number of special camps raised even further the potential explosiveness of the population. The Gulag was a political institution, though, and it was only the death of the system's founder that would set off the explosions.

# Chapter 6

# THE CRASH OF THE GULAG: RELEASES AND UPRISINGS IN THE POST-STALIN ERA

So I finally made it to that day in March when all the sudden we heard this heavenly music on the loudspeakers. Bach, Handel, Beethoven, and then we heard the health announcement. I remember how we all ran to the camp infirmary and the doctors discuss this among themselves and tell us what we could hope for. So the chief doctor, his assistant and the male nurse all of whom were convicts of course, went into the bania to hold their meeting. Meanwhile we're all huddled in the changing room, our teeth chattering with anticipation. They met for about 20 minutes, then the chief doctor walked out. He was a professor, a very well educated man. He was beaming, and he said, you guys, the bastard is finished. No hope for him. And we began kissing one another.
    —Lev Razgon on news in the Gulag of Stalin's illness

O N JUNE 26, 1954, at 3:28 a.m., a brief radio message warned the prisoners of the Kengir division of the Steplag concentration camp that an assault was about to begin.[1] For forty days, the prisoners had controlled the camp division, located just outside the city of Dzhezkazgan. A mere two minutes after the first radio announcement, five armed tanks followed by armed military personnel entered the camp zone to suppress the longest uprising and mass strike in Gulag history. The tanks fired blanks, and physically crushed the zone's barricades, trenches, and barracks during the assault. One tank ran over the communal toilets, fell into the cesspool, and became stuck. Some prisoners were crushed under the tanks' tracks. Meanwhile, the soldiers entered the breaches in the prisoners' defenses and on orders opened fire on the rebels. Teargas was tossed into the barracks. The prisoners, armed with handmade knives and other nonfiring weapons produced during the uprising, were no match for the heavily armed soldiers. Four hours later, the camp zone was in ruins; dead and wounded prisoners littered the grounds. No fewer than forty-six prisoners died as a result of the assault.[2]

The Kengir uprising in 1954—the last and longest of a string of prisoner revolts in 1953 and 1954—was a moment and place where authorities and inmates assessed the declining Soviet penal system as well as each other following the death of Stalin, execution of his most visible henchman, Beria, and the renunciation of mass terror. Soviet actions in relation to the uprising are remarkable for their restrained nature, at least as compared to the likely response only a short time earlier.[3] This chapter takes the uprising and mass releases—the two were interconnected, since the partial nature of early post-Stalin amnesties fueled the uprisings, while the uprisings contributed to the expansion of the scope of release—as a starting point to explore how Soviet authorities and Gulag prisoners coped with the lingering legacy of these brutal penal institutions in the post-Stalin Soviet polity along with the enduring impact on the lives of its (soon-to-be-former) inmates.

By the time of the Kengir uprising, the Gulag had already entered its years of decline. The prisoner population changed so radically that the system was virtually unrecognizable by the end of the 1950s. None of this could have been imagined before Stalin's death, however. In Stalin's waning days, the population of the Gulag—that institution that became one of the pillars of the system associated with his name—reached its peak. On January 1, 1953, the total population of camps, colonies, and internal exile reached its maximum of 5.2 million. Over 2.4 million of this total came from corrective labor camps and colonies.[4] By the end of the decade, the camp and colony population was some 40 percent of its 1953 total, and the population of exiled special settlers was reduced to several thousand. The total number of political prisoners—sentenced for counterrevolutionary crimes—was reduced on January 1, 1959 to a mere 11,000.[5] The Soviet concentration camp and exile system had not ceased to exist, but it was forever altered, and it would never again be the type of mass social institution that it was during the Stalin era.

While there had been proposals within the Gulag apparatus to dramatically reduce the size of the camp population in the late 1940s and early 1950s, no one was willing to make these proposals to Stalin, and they remained a dead letter.[6] Only Stalin's death made the near-total destruction of the Gulag system possible—a fact that is strangely easy to forget when considering the Gulag's demise. Typically, the Gulag's decline has been attributed to two important factors: the dire economic situation in the Gulag, and a series of prisoner uprisings in the special camps, including the uprising at Kengir. Writers have argued that the Gulag was in a deep systemic crisis at the time of Stalin's death. The changing nature of the postwar Gulag population—the tremendous growth of the prisoner population, and especially the rising numbers of prisoners who were either active opponents of the regime or had experience in the past in armed battle—led to the formation of underground organizations among prisoners, murders of informants, and specific prisoner countermeasures to destroy the administration's surveillance system in the camps. As the authorities' control over the camps diminished—a situation exacerbated by a severe shortage of armed guards—acts of mass disobedience, escapes, and mass refusals to work occurred more frequently. Along with the historically low productivity of Gulag labor, these incidents, these authors contend, led to a broad crisis throughout the Gulag.[7]

On the one hand, this explanation of the Gulag's decline is irreproachable. The Gulag was a tremendously unproductive institution, and a series of mass uprising did occur and did lead to specific changes in the Gulag regime—all of which will be discussed further below. On the other hand, this situation can in no way be understood as a crisis. The Gulag had long been unproductive. In fact, in some ways, conditions in the Gulag were as good as they had ever been. Mortality rates had reached all-time lows. Escape attempts had also reached all-time lows in both absolute and relative terms. No increase in the numbers of deaths or escapes relative to the total camp population had actually been registered since 1948.[8] If the Gulag was in a crisis, it is hard to determine by any objective measures, nor can one even see any real increase in administration complaints about the situation in the Gulag.

The crisis explanation for the Gulag's demise underemphasizes the simple fact that had Stalin continued to live, no crisis in the Gulag was likely big enough to bring the system down. Furthermore, many of the signs of crisis cited by the authors were endemic to the Gulag and had been for years. Ivanova along with Marta Craveri and Khlevniuk have themselves provided some of the most significant evidence yet that the Gulag was never an economically profitable institution. As Craveri and Khlevniuk wrote, the low productivity of prison labor had always been a problem, and had been discussed repeatedly in the government and Central Committee, but it was only after Stalin died that anyone dared speak openly about the problems of Gulag productivity.[9] While the factors identified by Craveri and Khlevniuk combined to convince Stalin's successors that the system should be radically altered, Stalin's death was the necessary precipitating factor. Before the dictator died, no level of economic loss or amount of systemic crisis could cause a serious reevaluation of the need for this mass social institution. Yet his death almost immediately ushered in a radical change in the size of the system. While the Gulag was too integral to the Soviet system to die as definitively as did the dictator, its decline marked by fits and starts, a direction was set in place that over a number of years, resulted in a paroxysm of mass disobedience throughout the system and finally the system's almost total collapse.

## The Death of the Dictator

When Stalin died on March 5, 1953, prisoner reactions were mixed. Some obviously saw his death as a momentous event, potentially signaling an end to their sufferings. In Steplag, "cries and yells of celebration [were heard] throughout the camp."[10] The prisoners even celebrated in poetry, as Fel'dman recalls:

> Mourning from scarlet and black ribbons.
> Both Stalin and Klement Gottwald died.
> The steel faces trembled.
> When will the rest die?![11]

Of course, the poem's question of "the rest" offered a note of caution that Stalin was not the sole cause of the prisoners' troubles, but another prisoner remembers the dictator's death as joy without reservation:

> The unforgettable spring of 1953!
> It was not the pleasure of arable land and sowing, nor the pleasure of free work!
> A miracle has come to pass!
> The locks were taken from the barracks and the zeks have seen the sunrise!
> The unforgettable spring of 1953![12]

On the other hand, many prisoners seemed to believe quite truly that Stalin was not the source of their problems but rather their hope for a reversal of the injustices they had faced.

> I didn't just cry. I thought that our lives would collapse. And how could we live without Stalin? I bawled my heart out. I wasn't just crying. I sobbed for several hours. Cried and cried, because I never blamed him for anything. The idea never crossed my mind. You know, many people thought he didn't know about anything that was happening. But in spite of everything, I thought, well no matter what, this must be just another mistake.[13]

More than a few in the camps and exile responded with grief and tears to the news of Stalin's death.[14]

The optimism showed by so many Gulag prisoners at Stalin's death was severely tested as the next several years saw halting and unsteady steps toward emptying the Gulag. Nonetheless, it is chronologically quite clear that Stalin's death marked the beginning of the Gulag's demise. As early as March 18, 1953, Georgii Malenkov, chair of the Council of People's Commissars and widely believed to be the likely successor to Stalin, signed an order transferring nearly all the economic activities out of MVD and into the ministries in charge of the corresponding industries.

By March 28, the responsibility for housing all prisoners except those in special camps and special prisons was transferred to the Ministry of Justice. The Ministry of Justice was then expected to provide workers to the relevant industries on the basis of contracts—effectively extending to almost the entire prisoner population a practice that had long been used for a portion of the prisoners.[15]

Most significantly, on March 27, 1953, a mere three weeks after Stalin's death, Soviet authorities declared a wide amnesty, under which over 1.2 million prisoners were released from the camps and colonies.[16] Most writers—both historians and memoirists—focused as ever on the Gulag's political prisoners, have written mostly about the shortcomings of this amnesty, particularly its explicit and effective denial of its applicability to political prisoners.[17] These complaints, in fact, were a key element to the rising tensions, which led to the Gulag's major uprisings. Yet such a focus misses the radical change of the Gulag system heralded in this one decree. Beria knew when he reported to the Central Committee Presidium on March 26 that the proposed amnesty would release around 1 million prisoners. He and the Central Committee Presidium knew that this one amnesty alone would radically change the scale of the Gulag operation. Not only did that fail to deter them from taking the action, it was clearly their motivation for doing so. Under the March 27 amnesty, nearly 50 percent of the Gulag population was released.[18] Granted, nearly all Article 58 prisoners were excluded from this amnesty, but it still represented a sweeping alteration in the magnitude of the operation and set in motion the precipitous decline of the system.[19]

It has been widely recognized that Beria himself was one of the main initiators of these radical changes.[20] He played a critical role in the promulgation of the amnesty, reporting the day before its announcement to the Central Committee Presidium on the Soviet Union's prisoner population. Beria emphasized that it was not a "state necessity" to continue to imprison such a large population when "a significant portion were convicted for crimes not presenting a serious danger for society." Especially, noted Beria, a large number of prisoners in recent years had been convicted under the 1947 laws on strengthening punishments for property crimes. Those convicted under these crimes alone, he wrote, accounted for over 1.24 million prisoners. Beria further criticized a June 15, 1939 law that prohibited early release and the practice of accounting for productive workdays as a means of achieving early release. He also warned that if the laws of 1939 and 1947 were not changed, the amnesty's effects would prove short-lived. Based on the then-current rates of imprisonment under these laws, Beria estimated that the prisoner population would again approach 2.5 to 3 million in just a few years.[21]

Beria's proposal did not spell the ultimate end of the Gulag, however, as he left behind many for whom he apparently thought it was still a state necessity to isolate and punish in the camps. Over the next several years, the new leadership's and especially Nikita Khrushchev's commitment to the idea that communism could be built without what they termed Stalin's "excesses" would finally bring release to most politicals.

Implementing the 1953 amnesty was, on the one hand, a rather routine task for the experienced bureaucracy of the Gulag. Karlag employees quickly threw their administrative experience into the task of a differentiated implementation of the amnesty, determining who could and could not be released. Twenty groups of five employees from the camp's spetsotdel along with a medical commission reviewed prisoners and their files individually to establish the applicability of the new amnesty to their cases as well as to discover which prisoners qualified for release as incurably ill or pregnant. Medical examinations were performed on all prisoners subject to release. The ill prisoner was not allowed to leave the camp until healthy. Under the terms of the amnesty, invalids who had no family to support them were to be placed in appropriate medical or psychiatric institutions.[22]

The consequences of release were not so easily handled. The only previous occasion on which releases of this magnitude occurred was during the early years of the war. During that time, though, most released prisoners were immediately enrolled in the armed forces. In the wake of the March 27, 1953 amnesty, a tremendous mass of prisoners had to be returned to Soviet society—a logistical and social nightmare. The moment of actual release was treated as one of high danger. At Karlag, a group of twenty-eight soldiers was gathered to help ensure order at the moment of release. Those released were subjected to a final thorough search to ensure that they left with nothing that would reveal the working of camp life: no camp food, no notes that described the camp regime and nothing else related to camp life.[23] The prisoners were also required to sign a statement that they would not reveal any information about conditions in the camps, camp rules and regulations, or the work that they performed there after their release. They were also required to declare that they would not take out any notes or messages from their fellow inmates. Failure to abide by this pledge would lead to criminal prosecution.[24]

Problems with the releasees arose immediately. By late April 1953, Karlag administrators had already released or were about to release some eighteen thousand prisoners. Every day, over two thousand people gathered at the Karabas train station, awaiting transportation back to their homes. Incidents of hooliganism, theft, and banditry were reportedly frequent, leading Karlag administrators to call on the Karaganda Oblast Administration of the Ministry of Internal Affairs (UMVD) to establish a militia post at the rail station to restore order.[25] Reports from around the Soviet Union indicated a wave of crime, including a significant number of murders committed by the prisoners released under this amnesty. Much of the Soviet citizenry responded to the amnesty not as the beginning of a period of awaited reform and relaxation but instead as a grave danger to Soviet society.[26] Yet even these dire consequences did not lead to a reconsideration of the need for the amnesty. Those committing new crimes were reincarcerated when caught, but the new Soviet leadership remained firmly committed to a significant reduction in the Gulag's size. Primary blame for the resulting crime wave was laid on local officials who failed to provide released inmates with employment along with the camp system itself for failing to adequately reeducate and prepare its inmates for socially usefully labor.[27]

The loss of such a large portion of the prisoner population left a gaping hole in Karlag's capacity to carry out its economic functions. Local officials tried to adjust, following the instructions of central Gulag chief Ivan Dolgikh that they should close the least profitable camp subdivisions first, especially those where it was not possible to rent out prisoners as contract workers to other agencies.[28] Karlag's production staff was ordered to determine what remained of the camp's prisoner-specialists and organize courses in specialties to train enough of the remaining prisoners to fill the necessary jobs. Efforts were also made to convince released prisoners to stay on as voluntary workers, especially those prisoners in hard-to-replace specialties.[29] Karlag staff was told during a gathering on July 3, 1953 that they should not expect a replenishment of their prisoner population. Rather, they had to make their economic plans based on the new, reduced prisoner population. As such, they were urged to make sure that every single prisoner was constructively engaged in the work of the camp.[30]

Gulag authorities saw not only the reduction of the prisoner population as a hindrance to their work. In accord with a long-entrenched mentality, they also anticipated problems due to the new profile of that population. The March 27 amnesty had released the common criminal sentenced for relatively petty crimes—the backbone of Soviet conceptions of an eminently redeemable convict population, and also the source most often tapped for trusties and informants.[31] Left behind were the murderers, recidivists, bandits, and politicals—the lowest rungs on the Gulag's ladder of redeemability. Comparing January 1, 1953 with January 1, 1954, one sees a sharp rise in the relative numbers of prisoners sentenced for counterrevolutionary crimes—from 21.9 percent of the total camp and colony population to 34.8 percent.[32] Typical of this mentality, Karlag authorities observed in mid-May that the March 27 amnesty had left the camp with a much more dangerous contingent, necessitating extra attention in guarding prisoners as well as the cleansing of the camp's staff to remove "the morally decayed, formerly sentenced, former repatriates and those not wishing to continue their service."[33] Furthermore, Gulag-wide, the amnesty had released a great many prisoners who had been working in the camp guard itself. Replacing these prisoner-guards from among a more "dangerous" prisoner population was perceived as a tough task.[34]

Even the camp's "socially friendly" elements who had been released and were now hired to work on a voluntary basis were still suspect in the eyes of Gulag authorities. On the one hand, even as Karlag authorities ordered their staff to hire former prisoners as much as possible to help fill the economic void left by their departure, they blamed, on the other hand, disciplinary infractions on the hiring of these very same former prisoners. In June, Karlag authorities issued an order complaining of a rise in violations of the camp's disciplinary regime, particularly among those recently released prisoners who stayed on as free employees of the camp. A certain former prisoner Stroganov, for example, was working in the camp despite the fact that he was from the camp's "criminal-bandit element." It was charged that the division chief's negligent hire of this former prisoner led to Stroganov getting drunk, killing two local residents, and wounding two others. As a result, all division chiefs were ordered yet again to review all former prisoners who had been hired, and fire any who had in the past been sentenced for banditism, robbery, or other malicious violations of camp regime. They also were to ensure that all newly released prisoners were housed separately from current prisoners and that segregation by gender be maintained.[35] In July, Karlag authorities suggested that all former prisoners hired as voluntary workers should be prohibited from working in the camp division where they sat as inmates.[36]

Despite the partial nature of the amnesty, those prisoners left behind noted a definite improvement in their material condition following Stalin's death. At the same time, a pervasive sense of unease seemed to hang in the air.[37] Nobody—neither prisoners nor Gulag employees—seemed to know what the change in leadership was going to bring. The immediate aftermath of Stalin's death generated a great deal of uncertainty and fear on both sides. One Steplag prisoner, Dolgun, wrote that rumors spread around the camp—rumors that Zhukov had surrounded the Kremlin with tanks to subdue the MVD, talk of Malenkov being imprisoned by Beria, speculation about the causes of Stalin's death, and even wild rumors within the MVD that Beria had arranged a special signal to the prisoners to rise up simultaneously.[38] Fel'dman, another Steplag inmate, recalled the day that Stalin died. A certain particularly mean camp administrator, Mednikov, later one of those who shot prisoners during the Kengir uprising, came into the camp's prison, saying, "There's been a coup in the country, and you [prisoners] are its organizers."[39] A former prisoner remembered that "everyone was frightened when Stalin died. . . .

People feared that Beria would come to power, and they were scared of him. The Gulag system was associated with Beria and the MVD, not with Stalin, who many people thought had not even known the truth about the camps."[40]

Nonetheless, as Dolgun recounted, the same dynamic of uncertainty also led to changes for the better. Many camp personnel treated prisoners with a new kindness for fear that they would soon be released en masse and would possibly seek vengeance against their tyrannical overseers.[41] Optimism increased among the prisoners when they read the announcement in newspapers of the rehabilitations of those caught up in the doctors' plot.[42] Over time, Dolgun also noticed real systemic improvements— the introduction of wet mining, where the spraying of water removed excess dust from the air and reduced the number of fatal cases of silicosis, while the replacement of manual labor by large mining machines reduced the number of deaths due to exhaustion and increased economic output. Work hours were cut from twelve to ten, rations were slightly improved, and the time for rest and recreation was increased. While prisoners still died, "fewer died, because survival took a little less skill."[43]

Karl Riewe, another former Steplag prisoner, also recalled great improvements in prisoner life after Stalin's death. British government officials interviewed Riewe after he left the Gulag. In their report, Riewe drew on one of the rumors so common in the camps that concluded Stalin's death was not the key event at all. As his interrogator summed up:

> [Riewe] was very impressed by the changes which took place in the administration of the camps in 1953 and 1954. . . . Although some of these changes, such as the imposition of the death penalty for murder, had the effect of strengthening camp discipline, the over-all result was to introduce a more humanitarian regime and to improve the living conditions of the prisoners. Source is convinced that these revisions had nothing to do with the death of Stalin, because in the summer of 1952 a rumor passed through the camps that one Captain Kozlov, (fnu), commander of Camp Group 2 in Dzhezhazgan-Rudnik [sic], while in an inebriated condition, had told certain prisoners that they would soon receive cash payments for their labor, that the strict guarding of the barracks enclosures would be eased, and that their relatives would be allowed to visit them. In April 1953, the changes predicted by Captain Kozlov began to be put into effect. Source does not know the real reason for the decision to ameliorate camp conditions, but he was told by one prison official that it was because the USSR had signed the UN convention on genocide. Whatever the reason, the changes were publicized in such a way that credit for them went to the new leadership in the Kremlin after Stalin's death.[44]

Others recollected major improvements only by spring 1954, when as Dolgun noted, the barracks, even in the katorga divisions, were unlocked

and the bars were torn out of the windows. The gates between the katorga and the adjoining camp divisions were torn down. A culture brigade was formed, and Sundays became work-free days all the time. Rumors of camp mutinies in Siberia reached Dzhezkazgan, and the prison
staff became "noticeably more friendly." The numbers were taken off the
prisoners' clothing—a particularly happy day.

> I came out into the Zone one morning to find hundreds of prisoners yelling
> and laughing and ripping the linen patches off their sleeves and breasts and
> backs and caps and trouser legs. The air was filled with a snowstorm of num-
> ber patches. No official order had been received in the camp, but the prison
> telegraph had brought the news that it was about to happen and so we all just
> went ahead without the order, and Belyakov, the commandant, let it happen
> without any reprisals or even threats of reprisals. . . . This seems like a small
> matter, but for all the prisoners of Dzhezkazgan the number was the prime
> symbol of our slavery, of our demotion from human being to object. Its disap-
> pearance was like the beginning of a fresh new day.[45]

At the same time, Dolgun observed a "sense of lack of equilibrium, as
if the changes could swing around and blow the other way. The camp
personnel were manifestly anxious all the time and wiser heads among
us . . . said that anxious men do not react well in critical situations and
that, with so much change going on around us all the time, there could
be a crisis, a totally unpredicted and unpredictable crisis, at any time."[46]

Official Gulag documentation offers a muddled picture of this eased
regime. In fact, the memoir literature even presents a "softer" picture of
life in the camps during this period than does the official documentation.
For example, during the days of the Presidium conference at which Beria's
fate was sealed, the upper administration and operative staff of Karlag
met to discuss the need to tighten the camp's regime. As it had for several
months, the focus remained on the deleterious effects of the March 27
amnesty. As one participant in this meeting on July 3, 1953 stated, "After
implementation of the decree on amnesty, the contingent changed, the
bandits, the counterrevolutionary element and other dangerous prisoners
are left, recently a number of escapes have occurred. . . . With the goal of
introducing order in the camp and to eliminate escapes, we decided to
convene the present conference."[47] The conference recommended that all
prisoners sentenced for escape, having long terms, or having committed
dangerous crimes be placed inside the zone and taken out to work only
under strong guard. This regulation was to be applied even to such prisoners who had worked well for several years without guards. This regulation was not new, however, as one conferee noted, having existed since at
least 1947.[48] As so many times before, another conferee complained that
the particularities of agricultural work meant that prisoners employed in

the fields almost always worked without convoy.[49] Here again we see the Stalinist mind-set embodied in the notion that one could work well for years, hiding one's wrecking activities behind a veneer of party membership, proper politics, and high productivity. A prisoner could never be judged exclusively on their activity in the camp. Rather, their article of conviction always hung over them like a dagger.

Further unsettling the atmosphere in the camp, on July 23, 1953, Karlag authorities circulated among prisoners the decisions from three other camps to execute prisoners who had committed serious violations of camp order, including group escape and murder of fellow prisoners.[50] This tense atmosphere provided the foundations for the Gulag uprisings.

## The Forty Days' War: The Kengir Uprising

The Kengir uprising in 1954—forty days of Gulag prisoner resistance ending in a bloody massacre of inmates by Soviet forces—has become a near-mythical moment.[51] Yet the truly remarkable aspect of the Kengir uprising lies in the apparent moderation of the prisoners' demands, and the comparatively measured and delayed response of Soviet authorities. The Kengir uprising occurred in a camp zone overwhelmingly populated by Westerners—that is, former members of the nationalist movements and partisan armies of the recently annexed western borderlands. These Gulag prisoners had well earned the term anti-Soviet after fighting a lengthy, brutal, and bloody civil war with Soviet military and secret police forces.[52] Still, the uprising was fronted not by a Baltic or Ukrainian leader but rather by a former Red Army officer, and the uprising proceeded not under slogans such as "Long live independent Ukraine" but instead under banners reading "Long live the Soviet Constitution!" and "Long live the Presidium of the Central Committee!"

Why in one of the most brutal outposts of Soviet power would committed anti-Soviet Ukrainian and Baltic nationalists allow their uprising to be led by a Red Army veteran, an ethnic Russian, and exhibit the characteristic proregime, antilocal official outlook uncovered in studies of other mass Soviet disorders?[53] Some might make this merely a matter of tactics, but it requires a more complex explanation. In addition to its fiercely anti-Soviet prisoner population, Kengir held a substantial number of former Red Army veterans who had recently risked their lives for the Soviet Union, and thus had developed a sense of both deep loyalty to the regime and entitlement to redress the wrongs committed by local officials, particularly for what many of them saw as a wrongful conviction. It was the leadership of one former Red Army officer—Kapiton Ivanovich Kuznetsov—that largely carried the day in putting the public and pro-Soviet face to the events at Kengir. The nationalists, who had effective control over the uprising, consented to Kuznetsov's leadership. Even if the nationalists had not begun to "think Bolshevik," the overwhelming power of the Soviet regime and its discourse had taught them the value of at least "speaking Bolshevik."[54]

In Gulag history, the wave of major uprisings that struck in 1953 and 1954 after Stalin's death is not remarkable; rather, what is noteworthy is the relative paucity of such incidents earlier in its history. Given its massive scale, supposedly anti-Soviet population, or at least the seeming likelihood that its inmates would become anti-Soviet based on their Gulag internment itself, the Gulag experienced remarkably little mass resistance throughout its history. Of course, individual and small group escapes occurred constantly, though with greatly reduced frequency and success over the course of Gulag history. Prisoners continually engaged in *tufta*, or padding and falsifying their work output, as a strategy to meet often-impossible work norms. Many prisoners refused either individually or in small groups to work. On occasion, even small outbursts of violence against Gulag guards happened. Truly significant mass resistance nonetheless awaited the postwar period and especially the death of Stalin. Even then, mass resistance was largely limited to the small group of special camps created in 1948.[55]

The string of Gulag uprisings emerged in part from the specific conditions of the post-Stalin Gulag, yet they also represented the culmination of a number of changes in the Gulag's population and institutions dating to the war and postwar eras. From 1939 and into the postwar era, a new generation of prisoners entered the Gulag. People from the annexed western territories had never been exposed to socialism in power, and carried with them the social memory of different systems of government and different penal institutions. Unlike those living in the Soviet Union before the war, they had not undergone years of political education and socialization into the Soviet polity. Their exposure to "bourgeois ideology" made them particularly hostile in the mind-set of Soviet authorities.[56] Members of these regions' partisan armies and nationalist organizations brought with them to the Gulag a history of struggling with authority despite the odds. Members of the OUN and the guerrilla fighters of the Ukrainian Insurgent Army formed the largest anti-Soviet movement since Soviet power had become firmly established. They had a well-articulated anti-Soviet, nationalist ideology and had engaged Soviet authorities in ferocious, bloody battle.[57] Remnants of these organizations took a leading role in the uprising at Kengir.

Even the longtime Soviet citizens sent to the Gulag in the postwar era were different than their prewar brethren. Red Army veterans (many of whom had spent time in Nazi POW camps), Soviet partisans, and members of the Russian Liberation Army (Vlasovites) all carried new experiences of power and struggle into the Gulag.[58] Representatives from these groups also played an important role in the Kengir rebellion.[59] While their personal histories as armed combatants helped make their participation in such a rebellion possible, their long exposure to Soviet ideology, as we will see, rendered them a far different type of "rebel" than their fellow prisoners from the western territories.

Institutionally, the war saw the first attempt by Gulag authorities to segregate a small portion of the political prisoners from all other prisoners, creating segregated camp divisions emblazoned with the old tsarist moniker katorga. While these katorga divisions only held several thousand inmates during the war, they provided significant experience for the similar but much larger system of special camps created in 1948. These special camps featured a particularly strict regime, forcing the so-called especially dangerous state criminals to wear numbers on their clothing, eliminating nonworking days, adding bars to windows, and locking all barracks at night. In 1948, several subdivisions of Karlag were turned into an independent special camp called Steplag. In the special camps, political prisoners were for the first time fully segregated from the criminal population.[60] In the absence of the criminals' reign of terror over them, the politicals finally had the security and capability to look on themselves as politicals. Gaining a sense of their own power, the politicals began to punish, and often even kill, collaborators with camp authorities and informants.[61] The special camps also indicated to some groups of inmates that they could barely ever hope for reintegration into Soviet society. Twenty-five-year sentences and the emerging practice of exiling prisoners permanently after their release from the special camps drove home the point of their irredeemability.

While these factors led to a number of small-scale uprisings before 1953, the largest ones awaited the death of the dictator.[62] Both Stalin's death and Beria's execution raised hopes among the special camp prisoners for an amnesty or a review of their cases.[63] When they were excluded from amnesties and their cases were not reviewed, the prisoners grew increasingly agitated. In this state, especially considering their backgrounds, the special camp populations were not inclined to react to events passively.[64] The ground for the uprising was laid.

The basic events of the Kengir uprising are well known thanks to an entire chapter of Solzhenitsyn's The Gulag Archipelago titled "The Forty Days of Kengir" and a more recent article in which Craveri made the first attempt to review the events utilizing official Soviet sources. This chapter only briefly reviews these basic events before moving on to a more in-depth discussion of two subjects that provide significant insights into the society that entered the post-Stalin era inside Soviet concentration camps and the Soviet Union: the propaganda war between the prisoners and the authorities, and a critical look at Kuznetsov, the leader of the prisoners' commission during the uprising.

## The Uprising

The Kengir camp zone was a subdivision of the Steplag special camp located just outside the city of Dzhezkazgan. Its physical structure included a large rectangle surrounded by a double wall of bleached brick at least three meters tall, and topped by another meter and a half of barbed wire. Illuminated by hundreds of electric lamps, the white color provided great visibility of any prisoner entering the "firing corridor" near the wall, where they could be—and all too frequently were—shot for attempted escape. Armed guards stood watch in a number of towers rising above the wall. Two additional parallel lines of barbed wire expanded the guarded perimeter beyond the wall. Inside, the camp zone was subdivided by internal walls into an internal prison, two men's camp points, one women's camp point, and a service yard, which housed industrial workshops and food stores for the entire camp division.[65]

The prisoner population at Kengir totaled 5,392, of whom 43 percent were women. Over 72 percentof the prisoners were identified as former members of Ukrainian and Baltic nationalist organizations, while more than 46 percent had sentences over twenty years.[66] Life in this special camp was particularly harsh. The Kengir camp division was primarily engaged in urban construction, and its prisoners worked without days off. Filthy, dirt-floor barracks—locked at night—were completely congested, housing three to four hundred prisoners each. Attempted escape was met with gunfire. Dead prisoners were often left hanging from the camp walls for several hours until the camp administration and the local prosecutor arrived to verify that the shooting occurred in the forbidden zone at the camp wall. Even killings taking place elsewhere in the camp were usually deemed legal if the shooter declared that they were either defending themselves or attempting to prevent an escape. Simple murders of prisoners could easily be covered up under such vague rules.[67]

Tensions among camp staff were high after Beria's arrest. Prisoners were unafraid to invoke the unholy trinity of arrested Cheka leaders—Iagoda, Nikolai Ezhov, and Beria—as proof of their innocence.[68] In this tense atmosphere, the camp guards opened fire on the Kengir prisoners a number of times in 1953 and 1954.[69] In spring 1953, the camp population responded to the killing of six prisoners with a three-day strike.[70] The reintroduction of criminal inmates—in particular, the arrival of six hundred hardened criminal recidivists—into this special camp heated the already-tense situation to a full boil. The authorities apparently believed that the criminals would resume their terrorization of the politicals and dampen their spirits. The criminals, however, refused to clash with the politicals and actually served to radicalize the camp's atmosphere.[71] The conditions for the uprising were set.

From May 16 to 18, 1954, some male prisoners scaled the internal walls of the camp several times, entering the service yard and the women's camp zone.[72] The chronology of events is convoluted in the many accounts, with control of the camp passing back and forth between the prisoners and authorities during these first several days. Nonetheless, the outcome is clear. The prisoners had gained complete control of the camp zones and expelled all camp authorities by May 19. During these days, camp guards opened fire on prisoners several times, killing no fewer than eighteen prisoners and wounding no less than seventy.[73]

In protest, the prisoners declared a universal strike. They breached the zone's internal walls, uniting all the camp points. The camp's internal prison was liberated, freeing several prisoners who became the most important leaders of the uprising, including Red Army veteran Kuznetsov as well as Red Army veteran and alleged participant in Vlasov's Russian Liberation Army Engel's Ivanovich "Gleb" Sluchenkov, both ethnic Russians.[74] The camp authorities, meanwhile, called in one hundred soldiers from Karaganda to form an armed guard of the camp perimeter.[75]

Representatives of the USSR and Kazakh MVDs, USSR Procurator, and central Gulag administration flew to Dzhezkazgan, where they began negotiations with a commission elected by the prisoners and headed by Kuznetsov. Minister of Internal Affairs Kruglov was kept constantly informed of events by telegraph and along with USSR procurator Roman Rudenko made all the significant decisions relating to the uprising.[76] Negotiations led to a brief break in the strike, and the prisoners returned to work from May 21 to 24. The camp authorities then violated the negotiated agreement by rebuilding the internal camp walls and transferring prisoners involved in the disorders to other camps. In response, the prisoners renewed their strike on May 25 and again tossed the camp staff from the zone.[77]

After further negotiations failed to end the uprising, Kruglov and Rudenko issued an order on June 4 denying permission to suppress the strike by force. Here we find a major difference with the Stalin-era Gulag, when there would have been little hesitation about the use of massive violence to quell the uprising. The uncertain atmosphere of the post-Stalin, post-Beria Gulag left central authorities less certain in their use of violence, and they tried for an extended period of time to end the uprising through peaceful means. Kruglov and Rudenko's order set forth a strategy that held until the final assault on the prisoners' compound. The camp zone was to be guarded. Armed force should only be used if facing an attack from the prisoners, and all possible measures should be used to break down the prisoners' resolve and unity.[78] Under this strategy, Soviet authorities waged a propaganda battle, seeking to convince the prisoners to abandon their rebellion. Yet they were unwilling to allow the uprising to continue indefinitely. The MVD ordered five tanks to Dzhezkazgan on June 15.[79] Their patience ended after local industrial leaders complained to the Council of Ministers on June 20 that the uprising was interfering with the provision of workers necessary to fulfill their production plans. Three days later, Malenkov forwarded their complaints to Kruglov, ordering him to take the necessary measures to end the strike.[80] The tanks arrived in Kengir on June 24, and plans for an assault were immediately prepared.[81]

Inside the zone, two groups led the uprising: a commission elected by the prisoners, and a "conspiracy center" controlled by criminals and Ukrainian nationalists. The conspiracy center also forced the inclusion of their representatives on the prisoners' commission.[82] The prisoners created a quasi-government to run the zone during the uprising. Besides establishing control over basic food and medical services, they formed military, security, and propaganda departments.[83] The military department fortified the prisoners' defenses, building barricades and laying barbed wire around every gate and breach in the camp's outer walls. Prisoners were assigned to patrol the zones and guard all the entrances, while a special department worked to produce weapons from the various materials available in the zone. They even hung signs around the barricades warning that they had set up a minefield.[84] The security department provided bodyguards for the uprising's leading members, and established a system of passes and passwords to control movement around the camp zones and into the buildings of the uprising's central staff.[85] Prisoners who did not support the uprising or wanted to leave the zone were arrested and tossed into the internal prison, where members of the security department interrogated, beat, and tortured them. The uprising's security department arrested as many as forty prisoners during the uprising.[86] None of the security and military measures made much difference when the authorities began their assault. Resistance was minimal, and injuries on the side of the authorities were few and minor.

### The Propaganda War

"There were weeks when the whole war became a war of propaganda," noted Solzhenitsyn.[87] Following the strategy laid out in Kruglov and Rudenko's order of June 4, 1954, the Soviet authorities engaged in a propaganda barrage aimed at breaking the prisoners' unity and resolve. The propaganda's content, in its appeals to the entire prisoner population as well as particular prisoner subgroups, reveals Gulag society in 1954 as seen through the eyes of Gulag authorities. The most intriguing aspect of the authorities' propaganda war was their general regard of the prisoners, even the fiercely nationalist Westerners, as an integral part of Soviet society, prone to its same system of values and responsive to similar appeals, be they appeals to the heroic struggle against fascism during the war or the equally heroic struggle to build socialism and then communism in the Soviet Union.[88]

The authorities set up loudspeakers around the camp, over which they played local radio programs, political discussions, and a variety of appeals aimed directly at the prisoners of Kengir.[89] The appeals followed a number of different strategies. Appeals to the entire prisoner population sought to convince them that their situation was hopeless, and that the only chance to avoid a dark ending to the whole affair was to bring the strike to an immediate end. They also promised to meet several of the prisoners' demands and submit the remainder to higher authorities for review, but only if the uprising was brought to a swift conclusion.[90] Less often, they threatened punishment if the uprising was not ended, depriving prisoners of the few privileges they had, or preparing materials to charge the rebels criminally. They even threatened to send all participants in the uprising to prisons or Kolyma, with the promise that those who ended their strike would be left at Kengir.[91]

The Gulag had many years of experience in the field of political education and propaganda—its solution of choice for nearly every problem. The Kengir uprising was no different. At one of the negotiation sessions, Viktor Mikhailovich Bochkov, assistant director of the central Gulag administration, "replied to the prisoners' requests with a lecture on the building of socialism, the unprecedented rapid progress of the economy, and the successes of the Chinese revolution."[92] Radio programs broadcast to the prisoners during the uprisings included political lectures on such topics as "the role and significance of socialist ideology in the transition period from socialism to communism," "the moral guise of Soviet man," "on the reasons of my break from the Ukrainian nationalists," and "more completely utiliz[ing] the technology of industry."[93] Perhaps it seems strange that Gulag authorities would respond to prisoners' concerns about illegal shootings by discussing events in China, but in the world of the Gulag, this was quite predictable. The Gulag from its earliest days operated on the idea that reeducating prisoners involved giving them a "proper" consciousness of the political world and their place in it. Such "education" was also, of course, designed to demonstrate the invincibility of the Soviet system and thus ensure the acquiescence of the prisoner population. In this case, the discussion of China may have been intended to emphasize that the tide of history was on the side of Communism.[94]

The authorities viewed the prisoners' refusal to work as thoroughly anti-Soviet and indicative of their failure to reform their criminal ways. At the same time, they continued to declare confidence in the clean conscience of the majority. "We are convinced that the majority of you burn with the desire to purge your guilt through honest labor, to liberate yourself more quickly from camps and to return to the monolithic family of our socialist society. . . . Going out to work and reestablishing order in the camp will be the confirmation that you recognize your mistake and are ready to correct it."[95] This idea of socialist society's "monolithic family" proved one of the major points at which Gulag authorities and prisoners could not understand one another. In the mind-set of Soviet authorities, the party, the MVD, the Gulag, and even the Soviet Union itself were indivisible. To be anti-MVD or anti-Gulag necessarily meant to be anti-Soviet. Perhaps this notion was best expressed in the speech of a prisoner who had left the zone: "You are building barricades. You are arming yourself for what? Against whom? Against the Soviet Union?"[96] As we will see below on "Soviet" grounds, however, the prisoners would argue for a differentiation of these various levels of Soviet authority.

Soviet authorities sought to paint the uprising as the folly of a few "adventurists." Most of the prisoners, they declared, did not support the uprising and wanted to return to work, but were prevented from doing so due to threats, arrests, and beatings administered by the uprising's leaders. The authorities even breached the camp's outer walls in numerous places, while they broadcast their appeals for those prisoners not supporting the uprising to exit through the breaches, where they would be protected from reprisals by the prisoner rebels and would not be punished for their part in the uprising.[97]

In support of this strategy, Gulag authorities directed their appeals not merely at the prisoner population as a whole but also at particular prisoner groups in hopes of breaking unity inside the zone. Not surprisingly, the differentiated appeals from Soviet authorities were directed along the main axes of identity in Gulag society: war veteranship, political prisoners versus common criminals, nationality, and gender. The specific use of these categories of identity showed how Gulag authorities had come to understand the fissures running through Gulag society.

The war, and one's role during it, had become such a defining element of postwar social identity that Gulag authorities were bound to cast aspersions on the war record of the uprising's leadership as a means of destroying prisoner unity. One radio address rehashed the facts of Kuznetsov's conviction for allegedly collaborating with his German captors in POW camps. The authorities charged that Kuznetsov was following up his collaboration with the fascists by "now leading a fascist regime in your camp division." Sluchenkov, they declared, had spent his whole life associating with criminals and traitors. During the war, he allegedly showed "cowardice" and went over to the fascist side, where he "fought against the Soviet people." During his camp term, they said, he had personally committed murders and robberies.[98] Aleksei Filippovich Makeev, one of the original members of the prisoners' commission who subsequently left the zone during the uprising, in an appeal to his fellow prisoners after leaving the zone, denounced Sluchenkov, who "screams about 'freedom' but personally acts like a wild Gestapo man."[99]

For years, Gulag authorities had driven a wedge between political and common criminals, but the political prisoners of the special camps had long been isolated from the common ones. As noted above, the reintroduction of common criminals into the zone at Kengir failed to re-create this sharp division, but the authorities maintained hope that they could reopen hostilities between the two groups. On the one hand, the authorities tried to convince political prisoners that the criminals wanted only "to rape your wives and daughters."[100] When that failed to provoke a reaction, they called on a criminal prisoner who left the zone to broadcast an appeal. "You all know that in the camp we were all fixed up well. . . . We, common criminals [bytoviki], were happy . . . but a group of arch enemies of our state from the very first day pushed us into provocative actions."[101] The authorities were quite obviously offering to place blame for the uprising on the politicals and return the common criminals to the position they had long held—the group of prisoners most trusted by Gulag authorities, ruling over the politicals—if only the criminals would help end the uprising.

Since at least the late 1930s, nationality had risen to the fore as a primary category of identity in Gulag society. Given the national makeup of the Kengir camp zone and bloody history of struggle with the Westerners, nationality played a particularly important role during the uprising, especially after the authorities' agents reported that the prisoners were divided into two camps: Russians and western Ukrainians, with the latter using weaponry to dictate their will to the former.[102] The authorities reportedly approached Sluchenkov, a Russian, urging him to provoke clashes between Russians and Ukrainians. If the clashes could lead to ten to fifteen corpses, the authorities would have a sufficient excuse to enter the camp with force. In return, Sluchenkov was purportedly offered freedom and his choice of places to live anywhere in the Soviet Union.[103]

Not only does this indicate the importance attached to nationality but it also reveals a certain impatience on the part of the local camp officials, who were apparently looking for an excuse to get around Kruglov and Rudenko's order and quell the uprising by force.

During the Karaganda regional court's initial investigation of the criminal cases brought against many of the uprising's main participants, many of the defendants had alleged "provocative actions" from the camp's employees during the uprising intended to create national divisions among the prisoners.[104] While all sources indicate that the various nationalities at Kengir maintained separate centers of authority during the uprising, open clashes between nationalities were avoided.

Even though internal documents consistently pointed to the Ukrainian nationalists as the uprising's true leaders, the authorities did not forego particularistic appeals to the Ukrainian prisoners. These appeals were directed in part to provoke disunity between the Ukrainian prisoners and the uprising's formal Russian leaders. One Ukrainian prisoner who left the zone spoke to the prisoners:

> I, above all, am addressing my countrymen. . . . I want to remind you, that the majority of us Ukrainians from the West fell into the camp leading or supporting a hopeless struggle. We must not now repeat the same mistake. . . . Dear countrymen, they see us Westerners as the main authors of the strike's continuation. I well know that very many of us want to work. . . . [Y]ou have nothing in common with Kuznetsov and Sluchenkov [both Russians]. They are only using you and will force the Ukrainian youngsters to take responsibility for their [Kuznetsov's and Sluchenkov's] actions.[105]

Here, the nuanced differences in the authorities' appeal to western Ukrainians must be stressed. Rather than appealing to them as Soviet citizens, as individuals who had made their peace with the Soviet regime, they are addressed with emphasis on the hopelessness of the uprising. In particular, they are pointed toward their own history of defeat in their armed battles with Soviet power as a reason to rethink the wisdom of following the Russian leadership of the uprising, which would no doubt be able to place blame on the Ukrainians themselves for the entire affair.

Kruglov and Rudenko's communiqué of June 4 specifically ordered Steplag authorities to take special measures with the female prisoners.[106] From the authorities' perspective, one of the most concerning aspects of the uprising was the free association of male and female prisoners.[107] Rhetoric of mass rape and sexual depravity can be found throughout the official documentation. The camp administration felt sure that left alone, "the prisoners would drown in their debauchery."[108] Several radio addresses were directed to the imprisoned women, including a lengthy address from Gulag chief Dolgikh himself.

> Believing their provocations, you vote for their anti-Soviet resolutions.... [You] spend nights in the men's barracks and foul your maiden purity, the purity of mothers and wives. Children and husbands impatiently await your return from temporary isolation into your family. Can you really not know the best traditions of Soviet women, who are fighting for the purity of the family and the women of the USSR—the vanguard of the world's women.... They are raping your girlfriends.... We know that those raped do not speak about this at the meetings, because they are afraid that if they speak about this, they will be killed.... In the camp are girls, whose mothers and fathers await them at home. Why don't you guard their purity ... ? Remember that only under the Soviet socialist structure are the spiritual riches of women fully revealed.... [Women] together with their husbands, sons, and brothers established our socialist state and fought for victory over the enemy in the Great Patriotic war. 2,346 women were awarded the titles of Hero of the Soviet Union and Hero of Socialist Labor.... What will your husbands, mothers, and fathers say if they learn about the orgies and outrages?[109]

Dolgikh's speech provided a picture of the ideal multifaceted Soviet woman—war hero, laborer, mother, wife, sister, and defender of purity and family. It must have been bitterly ironic to women facing twenty-five-year sentences, many of whom had been subject to rape at the hands of Soviet authorities during the postwar battles in the western territories.[110] In many ways, the speech seemed completely oblivious to the particular national makeup of the Kengir camp. These women from the western territories had certainly not "established our socialist state" nor had they "fought for victory over the enemy in the Great Patriotic war" (unless that "enemy" included Soviet power itself.)

Dolgikh's speech also served as counterpropaganda to the residents of Kengir and Dzhezkazgan as well as their own employees and soldiers. For these external audiences, the picture painted of a camp zone overrun by impurity and sexual depravity evoked the strongest reactions. After the uprising was suppressed, married Russian women gathered at the roadside to shout at the female prisoners, "Prostitutes! Dirty whores! Couldn't do without it, could you!"[111]

Nonetheless, all accounts of the uprising seem to agree that the prisoners did not engage in "debauchery." Solzhenitsyn writes that "witnesses agree that the thieves behaved *like decent people*" and that such depravity as mass rapes did not occur. For Solzhenitsyn, this uprising was the pinnacle of the political prisoners' coming-of-age as politicals, even to the point that they purified the common criminals whom he typically depicts as virtually subhuman, and he presents an almost implausibly purified account of the criminals' behavior. His account is substantiated by other sources, including official investigations after the uprising that failed to substantiate the dire predictions of mass rape. If Solzhenitsyn is correct, the authorities were dismayed to learn, based on medical examinations, that many of the female prisoners were still virgins after the uprising.[112]

Finally, Soviet authorities directed their propaganda at prisoners of Steplag's other divisions in an effort to prevent the uprising from spreading. Thus, according to Riewe's testimony, an official from the Kazakh Ministry of Internal Affairs appeared in his camp at Dzhezkazgan during the uprising and attempted to defuse potential tensions there, especially by promising a review of sentences handed out under Article 58.[113] Whether or not it was a result of such speeches, Soviet authorities successfully isolated the uprising in the Kengir camp division.

•  •  •  •  •

Kengir's prisoners were active participants in the propaganda war. Under the direction of the prisoner Iurii Al'fredovich Knopmus, the prisoners' department of propaganda published bulletins, programmed internal radio broadcasts, spoke at gatherings of the prisoner population, and issued leaflets.[114] It attempted to spread its leaflets among the local free population using kites and balloons, and rumors even abounded that the department was building its own radio transmitter to broadcast prisoners' messages to foreign countries. The prisoners' internal radio broadcasts were made through low-powered amplifiers, which the prisoners had built themselves, though they were often drowned out by the authorities' higher-powered broadcasts. They also raised banners over the camp zone such that they were readily visible to the local population. The prisoners' propaganda department hoped that it could convince local residents to pass the prisoners' demands directly to a member of the Central Committee.[115] The propaganda department also stationed individuals near the gates to pass its messages verbally to the soldiers surrounding the zone, with the goal of convincing the soldiers not to enter the zone or shoot at the prisoners.[116]

The most significant element of the prisoners' propaganda message was the list of demands. The prisoners' demands reveal a fascinating picture of the prisoners' understanding of "speaking Bolshevik" and the limits of the uprising's possibilities. They included, among other demands, the punishment of those responsible for the shootings of May 17 and a full investigation of shootings earlier in 1954, the termination of the permanent exile of all prisoners released from special camps, the reduction of sentences for all those who received twenty-five years, a raise in prisoners' pay to a level on par with free workers, the introduction of an eight-hour working day, an increase to five days' credit toward completion of prisoners' sentence for each day's work, allowance of free association between male and female prisoners, and the arrival of a member of the Presidium of the Central Committee or a secretary of the Central Committee to resolve the prisoners' demands.[117]

These demands were not particularly radical. The prisoners were not asking for unconditional release. Rather, they were making demands that had in many ways been conditioned by years of official Soviet propaganda in and out of the Gulag. These demands can be understood according to three strains of thought. First, years of political education in the history and politics of the socialist Soviet Union led the prisoners to formulate their demands as those of a workers' strike.[118] Thus, they sought higher pay, better working conditions, and an eight-hour workday.

Second, the demands reveal a desire to be treated as normal Soviet citizens. These demands were also conditioned by years of Gulag propaganda stressing that prisoners were temporarily isolated from society but could be reeducated and reintegrated into that society. Practices in the special camps seemed to undercut this rhetoric, and the prisoners sought to overturn them. Consider the demands to reduce the sentences of those with twenty-five years and to end the permanent exile of former special camp inmates. The introduction of permanent exile in 1948—not only for former special camp inmates but also for the many nationalities deported during the war—was a particularly traumatic event. Soviet authorities, for the first time, declared some elements of Soviet society, other than those directly executed, incapable of redemption and reintegration into society. Never before had they imposed any penalty that officially lasted forever. The prisoners wanted a sense of hope that someday they could return to society.

Finally, in a manner quite common in Soviet society, the prisoners expressed faith in the upper echelons of Soviet power, especially the Communist Party, while lacking confidence in local authorities. The prisoners were not resisting the party; they were resisting in the name of the party.[119] Contrary to the attempts of Gulag authorities to present Soviet society as monolithic and indivisible, prisoners responded to years of rhetoric and practice that showed everyone except those in the highest echelon of power to be a potential enemy. Since they understood their oppressors to be part of the state organs, they looked to the state's watchdog—the party. The hopes aroused by Beria's arrest still resonated among the prisoners. If the party had seen Beria for the criminal that he was and had removed him, surely they would see the criminality of the local camp authorities and the justness of the prisoners' demands. In fact, these two elements—the call for a representative of the top party organs to come to Kengir, and references to Beria's criminality—were the most frequent subjects of prisoner propaganda.

Some prisoners, especially the Ukrainian and Baltic nationalists, wanted a more radical approach during the uprising, particularly in the heady early days of the rebellion. Immediately after forcing the camp staff from the zone, prisoners covered the cafeteria with proclamations: "Arm yourselves as best you can, and attack the soldiers first!" "Bash the Chekists, boys!" "Death to the stoolies, the Cheka's stooges!"[120] Yet Kuznetsov, the Red Army veteran, was the glue holding the rebellion's pieces together—the criminals, the stridently resistant Westerners, and the Red Army veterans who had risked their lives for the Soviet Union and had thus gained a sense of entitlement that they identified in Soviet terms. Kuznetsov soon convinced the rebels to moderate their rhetoric, arguing that provocative actions or slogans deemed anti-Soviet would serve as an excuse for the authorities to crush the uprising. Solzhenitsyn quotes Kuznetsov: "Our salvation lies in loyalty. We must talk to Moscow's representatives *in a manner befitting Soviet citizens!*"[121] The banners that were raised over the camp during the course of the uprising read: "Long live the Soviet Constitution!" "Long live the Presidium of the Central Committee!" "Long live the Soviet regime!" "The Central Committee must send one of its members and review our cases!" "Down with the murdering Beria-ites!" "Wives of Steplag officers! Aren't you ashamed to be the wives of murderers?"[122]

Prisoners also aimed their propaganda at the prisoners surrounding the camp zone, hoping to convince them not to fire on prisoners when the inevitable assault came. One female prisoner was overheard at 9:25 p.m. on June 18 declaiming to the soldiers,

Help us not to die from hunger. They have not given us letters and packages for over a month. . . . The bread ration has been reduced to five hundred grams. . . . Don't let the Beria followers think that they will destroy our will. We will die, but we will not give in to the Beria-ites. . . . Don't listen to them, don't fall for the Beria-ite provocations . . . and don't commit crimes. . . . You will be brought to answer for this not only before us but also before the entire Soviet people. . . . And a crime against unarmed people . . . will be punished harshly. Soldiers! We are not afraid of you and we request that you not enter the zone, don't shoot us. . . . We are not afraid of death. . . . Comrade soldiers! Help us achieve the arrival of a member of the Presidium of the TsK [Central Committee].[123]

Though ultimately the prisoners were unsuccessful at preventing the guards from using force against them, the approach had possibilities. Given that so many secret police apparatchiks, including Beria himself, had been arrested since Stalin's death, the threat of punishment may not have seemed an empty one.

The prisoners' actions were as important as their written and spoken propaganda. They tore their prisoner numbers off their uniforms. Men and women who had managed in some way to correspond with each other between the camp points finally met one another. Religious believers freely held prayer services. Foreigners found and conversed with their compatriots. Prisoners stripped off their prison uniforms and replaced them with their street clothes, which had been stored by the camp. Kuznetsov and Sluchenkov took to wearing their military uniforms. As Solzhenitsyn describes it, "Some of the lads crammed fur hats on their heads; shortly there would be embroidered shirts, and on the Central Asians bright-colored robes and turbans. The gray-black camp would be a blaze of color."[124] And it is no surprise that this "blaze of color" carried distinctly multinational hues. In short, the prisoners, through their actions, declared themselves humans, not prisoners. Finally, invoking their blood brothers of Vorkuta, Noril'sk, and Kolyma, the prisoners stated emphatically, in the words of a Ukrainian hymn composed by prisoners and sung several times a day by the entire camp population, "We will not be, will not be slaves."[125]

The propaganda war ultimately was not successful for either side. The authorities never convinced the prisoners to end the uprising peacefully. The prisoners never succeeded in bringing a member of the Central Committee Presidium to Kengir, and they clearly did not convince the soldiers to refuse to fire on the prisoners.

## The Case of Kuznetsov

How could those thoroughly anti-Soviet veterans of the Ukrainian and Baltic nationalist guerrilla armies have allowed themselves to be part of an uprising expressing such seemingly moderate, even pro-Soviet demands? It has been acknowledged time and again in official documents and memoirs that these nationalists had effective control over the course of the uprising. If these demands could be embraced by such stridently anti-Soviet groups, could they have really have been so pro-Soviet? The answers to these questions lie, at least in part, with perhaps the most written about figure from the Steplag uprising: Kuznetsov. No matter how nominal his leadership of the uprising, Kuznetsov was of fundamental importance for its public face in negotiations with Soviet authorities. Kuznetsov's background, especially his membership and frontline experience in the Red Army, is crucial to understanding the path of the uprising.

Kuznetsov was an enigma for Solzhenitsyn, who could not quite understand this leader of the prisoners' commission during the Gulag's biggest uprising.

> Kapiton Kuznetsov! Some future historian of the Kengir mutiny must help us to understand the man better. What were his thoughts . . . ? What stage did he imagine his appeal to have reached . . . ? His pride in keeping the mutinous camp in such good order—was it only the professional pride of a military man? Had he put himself at the head of the movement because it captured his imagination? (I reject that explanation.) Or, knowing his powers of leadership, had taken over to restrain the movement, tame the flood, and channel it, to lay his chastened comrades at their masters' feet? (That is my view.) In meetings and discussions, and through people of lesser importance, he had opportunities to tell those in charge of the punitive operation anything he liked, and to hear things from them. . . . Did Kuznetsov exploit such opportunities? Perhaps not. His position may have been a proud and independent one.[126]

Kuznetsov left behind more documentation than any other participant in the uprising, even those who wrote memoirs. He reported to authorities quite fully on the events a mere three days after the final assault and was a prodigious writer of appeals until his final release in 1960. The Kuznetsov who emerges from his prisoner file was something more and less than Solzhenitsyn surmised. It is more appropriate to consider that Kuznetsov, in a hopelessly complicated situation, was both "proud and independent" and thoroughly loyal to Soviet rule—positions held by Solzhenitsyn to be contradictory, but embraced by Kuznetsov. His story, on its own and compared with some other key figures of the uprising, is quite revealing of the postwar and post-Stalin Gulag.

Kuznetsov, born in 1913 in Saratov Oblast, was a Russian from the peasantry, a former member of the Communist Party, and an agronomist. During the war, Kuznetsov was captured by the Germans and held in a series of POW camps. On December 15, 1948, Kuznetsov was arrested in Rostov Oblast and accused of being a traitor to the homeland for acts allegedly committed while in German captivity. He supposedly accepted the post of commandant of a POW camp, recruited Soviet POWs for cooperation with their German captors in ferreting out Polish partisans among the local population, and attempted to uncover any antifascist mood or escape plans among the prisoners. On November 17, 1949, Kuznetsov was found guilty by an MGB tribunal and sentenced to twenty-five years in the camps.[127] Four months after the uprising's conclusion, Kuznetsov's original conviction was overturned for lack of evidence. He was not released, however, because he now faced charges arising from the uprising itself.[128]

After a stint at Dubrovlag from February 1950 to June 1953, Kuznetsov was transferred to Steplag.[129] From his file, Kuznetsov appears to have led an ordinary existence in Steplag until some time before May 15, when according to one witness he was tossed in the internal camp prison for attempting to sneak a letter past the censors to his wife in which he described conditions in the camp with complete candor.[130] The rebelling prisoners liberated Kuznetsov and all other inmates of the internal prison on May 19, whereupon Kuznetsov was elected to head the prisoners' commission. We have no specific evidence telling us why Kuznetsov was chosen for leadership or what part he played in Kengir society before the uprising.

Kuznetsov's role in moderating the prisoners' demands has already been noted. As Solzhenitsyn observes, it was only through the force of Kuznetsov's will that the rebels "adopted the line of those orthodox Soviet citizens who were not very numerous in Kengir and were usually pushed into the background."[131] "Orthodox Soviet citizen" certainly seems to be an apt description of Kuznetsov. A proud Red Army veteran who denied charges of collaboration with the Germans, Kuznetsov supported order and hierarchy. Kuznetsov took to wearing his Red Army uniform during the uprising. He was known to treat Gulag authorities with a deference accorded to one's superiors, and he bragged incessantly of how during the uprising, he established order in the camp for food and medical distribution along with other necessary services. Kuznetsov's desire to prevent the prisoners from escalating the uprising into an anti-Soviet action was probably more than just a tactical decision. Despite all this, he sincerely felt that he had been wronged and sentenced for crimes he never committed. In this respect, too, he was typical of other Red Army veteran prisoners who expressed the feeling that Soviet authorities owed them more consideration for their services to the Soviet homeland.[132] Kuznetsov spoke frequently at prisoners' meetings, and urged the inmates to stay strong and maintain their unity. According to one memoirist, Kuznetsov's heartfelt speeches were absolutely critical in convincing the prisoners to hold out until the end, notwithstanding the growing nervousness among them about a predictable violent assault.[133]

In spite of his reputation and position, Kuznetsov maintained no more than a tenuous control over the uprising.[134] He usually clashed with representatives of the criminal world and members of Ukrainian nationalist organizations, particularly Sluchenkov and Gersha Keller. In official documentation, Keller, referred to as Mikhail by Solzhenitsyn, was a Jew from western Ukraine sentenced to ten years in 1944 as a member of a German Ukrainian nationalist organization. He was twice given additional sentences for crimes committed while in the camps, including the murder of a camp cook.[135] According to one former Kengir prisoner, Keller was actually a Ukrainian named Pendrak who claimed to be a Jew named Keller when first arrested.[136] If this is true, Keller managed to maintain his false identity throughout Gulag documentation about him. The radical actions and statements of Sluchenkov and Keller stood in stark contrast to Kuznetsov's. It was Sluchenkov who stood at the camp gates on May 24 as the prisoners returned from work and urged them to reignite the uprising in response to the authorities' violation of the negotiated agreement.[137] On May 25, Sluchenkov, Keller, and Knopmus declared their unwillingness to recognize the commission as their representatives, and forced the inclusion of their candidates Sluchenkov and Knopmus on the commission.[138]

Sluchenkov directed the prisoners' security department, and it was he who allegedly threatened to murder any prisoner attempting to leave the zone.[139] It was also Sluchenkov who made provocative statements while negotiating with authorities. While Kuznetsov treated them with a level of deference, Sluchenkov, on hearing one of them speak of the prisoners as "enemies," jumped in with, "How many of your sort turned out to be enemies? Yagoda . . . Yezhov . . . Abakumov . . . Beria . . . How do we know that Kruglov is any better?"[140]

Keller controlled a tight-knit group of forty Ukrainian prisoners designated to provide constant watch over and control the actions of the prisoners' commission.[141] He also served as head of the internal prison, and allegedly took a personal role in the beatings and torture of those prisoners placed under arrest by Sluchenkov's security department.[142] Solzhenitsyn, too, suspected that authority really centered in the national communities, particularly the huge Ukrainian population headed by Keller.[143]

In all of his declarations after the uprising, Kuznetsov consistently placed himself in opposition to the other prisoners who led the rebellion.[144] He claimed that his activities as the leader of the prisoners' commission was solely to maintain order within the camp, provide assistance to the investigators of the illegal shootings of prisoners, and serve as the prisoners' representative in discussions with authorities.[145] In a later appeal, he even claimed that he approached the authorities at the camp gates several times during the uprising, requesting that he be allowed to leave the zone, but they urged him to stay since only his presence assured the safety of their representatives entering the zone for negotiations.[146] Kuznetsov consistently asserted that the prisoners' commission was created solely at the behest of the local negotiating team of Soviet authorities, who requested that the prisoners appoint representatives to facilitate the functioning of negotiations. Furthermore, his assumption of the leadership, he later alleged, was also at the request of authorities.[147]

Ukrainian bodyguards armed with knives constantly accompanied Kuznetsov throughout the uprising. While Solzhenitsyn posited the possibility that they were with him to settle scores, Kuznetsov asserted that the guard was actually set up to keep an eye on him, to prevent him from leaving the zone or passing information to authorities. It should be noted, though, that other uprising leaders also had bodyguards accompany them throughout the uprising. Even Solzhenitsyn also allows for the possibility that the bodyguards were actually just Kuznetsov's defenders.[148]

A fellow member of the prisoners' commission, Makeev, clearly believed that Kuznetsov did not support the actions of Sluchenkov and his companions. As Makeev stated in one of his radio addresses after leaving the zone, "I know that Kuznetzov does not say what he thinks, but what he has been compelled to say. He understands that nothing good will come from this situation."[149] A surprising witness also testified in support of Kuznetsov's version of his role in the events. In one of his final appeals against his death sentence, Sluchenkov wrote to the chair of the Presidium of the Supreme Soviet, Kliment Voroshilov, that neither Kuznetsov nor Knopmus were guilty in any way of the crimes alleged in the case. Kuznetsov, in particular, according to Sluchenkov, attempted to get the prisoners to return to work, and "the fact that the prisoners did not listen to him was not his fault." Sluchenkov closed, "If it is necessary to kill somebody as an example, then shoot me alone—not seven people!"[150] Kuznetsov could never find such magnanimity. He consistently blamed the entire affair on others.[151]

Ultimately, Kuznetsov's story demonstrates the need to further complicate our understanding of postwar Gulag society. The relationship between Red Army veterans and nationalist partisans is neither clear nor simple. While they had fought on opposite sides, they also had a shared background experience of battle and struggle in seemingly hopeless situations.[152] Of course, the differences between the groups were just as significant. Red Army veterans, after all, had been socialized in the Soviet Union. The Ukrainian and Baltic nationalists were more at ease with the notion of struggling against Soviet power.[153] Yet the influence of the same Red Army veteran, Kuznetsov, and years spent in an environment saturated with Soviet ideology led even these nationalists—these inveterate and uncompromising enemies of Soviet power—to accede to Kuznetsov's notion of presenting their uprising in a manner "befitting Soviet citizens."

## The Aftermath

In the period following the uprising, thirty-six prisoners deemed to be active participants were arrested, four hundred were transferred to prisons, and a thousand were transferred either to Kolyma or Ozerlag in Taishet Oblast.[154] Of the thirty-six prisoners arrested, a verdict has been found for only thirteen. The Kazakh SSR Supreme Court under Article 2 of the law of June 4, 1947, Article 59-2, part 1, and Article 59-3, found Sluchenkov, Keller, Viktor Petrovich Riabov, Knopmus, Kuznetsov, Valentin Vladimirovich Ivashchenko, and Vitalii Petrovich Skiruk guilty. In accord with the decree of January 13, 1953 on strengthening the fight against banditism in camps, all were sentenced to death. Zaidula Khamidilovich Ibragimov, Anatolii Ivanovich Zadorozhnyi, Anatolii Kostritskii, Boleslav Adamovich Gerin'sh, Mariia Semenovna Shimanskaia, and Iozac Kondratas were all found guilty under the same sections, but the law of January 1953 was not applied, and they received ten years in corrective labor camps with their term counted from June 26, 1954. Due to her advanced age, Shimanskaia's sentence was reduced in accord with Article 51 to five years.[155]

All seven sentenced to death submitted an appeal to the Presidium of the Supreme Soviet of the Kazakh SSR on November 30, 1955. On December 20, 1955, all appeals were denied except for Skiruk's, whose sentence was changed from death to twenty-five years in corrective labor camps. On August 27, 1956, the Presidium of the Supreme Soviet of the Kazakh SSR affirmed its denial of petitions for leniency from Sluchenkov, Keller, Riabov, Knopmus, and Ivashchenko, but agreed to reconsider Kuznetsov's petition. Taking into account the reversal of Kuznetsov's original sentence in 1949, the Presidium agreed to Kuznetsov's petition and changed his sentence from death to twenty-five years.[156] The five condemned were executed on September 18, 1956.[157]

Kuznetsov was subsequently transferred to the MVD prison in Semipalatinsk and then finally to Karlag. After a stint in a strict regime Karlag camp division, Kuznetsov earned a transfer to a general regime division for good behavior. He even received official declarations of gratitude for his conscientious attention to his work and active participation in the sociocultural life of the camp.[158] Throughout his remaining years in camps and prisons, Kuznetsov submitted a variety of complaints and appeals for either pardon or a review of his case to all manner of authorities. Time and again his appeals were denied, until March 14, 1960, when the Supreme Court of the USSR overturned his conviction. Kuznetsov was released from Karlag on April 8, 1960, and moved to Novorossiisk.[159]

The Gulag authorities studied the events at Kengir rigorously and made a number of changes in the concentration camps' regime in hopes of preventing any future such problems. These changes included moving all female camp points at least three to five kilometers from male camp points, reducing the number of prisoners held in any one camp point, the complete isolation of prisoners with twenty-five-year sentences from other prisoners, and the complete isolation of political prisoners from other prisoners.[160] In addition, the final assault on the uprising was seen as an unqualified success, and its lessons were taught to the armed guards in all Gulag camps.[161]

Over the next several years, political prisoners finally received widespread review of their cases and release from concentration camps. While it would be presumptuous based on the material presented here to make the uprising into the decisive factor bringing the Gulag system down, the fact remains that in the several years that followed the events at Kengir, the Gulag was irreversibly altered. The mass uprisings in the special camps doubtless weighed on the minds of Soviet authorities as they considered the question of how to deal with the newly released inmates along with the millions of deportees still living far from their homeland. In particular, the prominent role of Ukrainian and Baltic nationalists in the uprising indicated to the Soviet regime a continued high level of hostility among this population. Gulag authorities had determined during their investigation of the events at Kengir that the long exposure of these peoples to so-called bourgeois ideology before the annexations of their territories into the Soviet Union made them especially hostile and in need of special reeducation efforts to make them into Soviet citizens.[162]

Among the prisoners, news of the Kengir uprising spread quickly, and it became a memory much larger than life. Solzhenitsyn made the Kengir uprising the climax of his multivolume exploration of Gulag history, but even much earlier rumors of the uprising exaggerated the results of the prisoner actions. The victims of the assault on the uprising were hailed as martyrs, and the female Ukrainian victims were raised as national heroes. Riewe even reported rumors that Khrushchev came to the Karaganda region in May 1954 at the request of the prisoners' committee.[163] While these rumors were wrong, the uprising was the longest and one of the largest incidents of mass prisoner disobedience in Soviet history.

Gulag society after the war had changed significantly. The relatively quiescent populations of the 1930s had been replaced by aggressive, assertive veterans of the Second World War as well as the bloody battles between nationalist guerrillas and Soviet forces throughout the Soviet Union's new western territories. It is unsurprising that such people would react violently and forcefully in the midst of the turbulence surrounding Stalin's death along with the uncertainties injected into the Gulag system by the unsteady steps toward its dismantling. What is surprising, though, are the terms in which such resistance occurred. The prisoners of Kengir rebelled not against the party or the Soviet regime but rather in the name of both.

It can be objected that these were merely tactics, and that the nationalists did not truly "believe" in the way that Kuznetsov was presenting their uprising. This is a more significant development than some might allow. The nationalists had never seen a need to moderate their rhetoric while engaged in a civil war with Soviet forces throughout the late 1940s. The Gulag had in at least this small way accomplished its goal. It had transformed the nationalists. It had broken them just enough that they began to mouth the words.[164] Of course, the existence of the uprising itself evidenced the incomplete nature of this breaking of their will, but the language they used (or allowed to be used) was evidence of a small Soviet success. The overwhelming power of the Soviet system to control the political discourse was never more apparent than when these overtly anti-Soviet nationalists not only showed a facility for speaking Bolshevik but also accepted the desirability of speaking publicly in that language.

## The Politicals Get Their Release

While conditions in the camps seemed to be improving before summer 1954, the time following the uprising and through 1956 was hailed even by Solzhenitsyn as "an era of unprecedented indulgences, perhaps the period of greatest freedom in [the Gulag's] history."[165] The changes in the aftermath of Kengir were almost immediate. On July 10, 1954, a law from the Presidium of the Supreme Soviet ordered the end of the super strict katorga regime in the special camps that had mandated, among other things, locked barracks with barred windows, extra-long working days, fewer nonworking days, and numbers on prisoner clothing. A review in 1956 by a commission of the Presidium of the Supreme Soviet noted substantial improvements in health, behavior, and productivity among Steplag prisoners in the wake of the easing of their camp regime.[166] Nikolai L'vovich Kekushev, a prisoner who remained in Steplag following the Kengir uprising, wrote that momentous changes took place immediately after the uprising. Some prisoners began to be released. For the first time in his experience at Steplag, select prisoners were moved about without a convoy. Prisoners were allowed to write as many letters as they liked, even to other camps, and receive visitors.[167]

Riewe recalled many changes in the camp atmosphere in the post-Stalin period. The introduction in 1953 of at least some modicum of pay for prisoners had far-reaching consequences. Thus, the improvements in the prisoners' lots were embodied not only in the removal of prisoner numbers and the unlocking of barracks but also in the appearance of kiosks from which prisoners could purchase "food, tobacco, clothing, toilet articles, stationery, and musical instruments." While alcohol was officially prohibited, prisoner demand and money led to widespread smuggling of *kvas*—the mildly alcoholic fermented drink. The smuggling became even easier when the mandatory inspection of all prisoners entering and leaving the camp zone was discontinued. Local camp officials turned a blind eye to the drinking of alcohol "so long as the prisoners were orderly and did not engage in fights."[168]

The creation of a three-tiered system of camp regime—strict, general, and light—mirroring the early 1920s' corrective labor code was also ordered on July 10, 1954. Prisoners were required to complete one-third of their sentence in a general regime division before becoming eligible, on the basis of good behavior and labor productivity, for transfer to a light regime. If prisoners successfully showed themselves to be capable of living in light-regime divisions, they were allowed to live outside the zone and even have their family come live with them. Strict-regime divisions were reserved for especially dangerous criminals, including counterrevolutionaries, bandits, murderers, recidivists, and those committing severe violations of the camp regime. The main goal was the isolation of these prisoners from the rest of the camp population. Still, Steplag prisoner Riewe observed little difference in practice between the general- and strict-regime divisions, as many of the officially mandated restrictions on the latter were not put in place. On July 14, 1954, the Presidium of the Supreme Soviet introduced conditional early release for prisoners who showed their "correction" through honest labor and exemplary behavior.[169]

Solzhenitsyn quite accurately summarized the changes in the Gulag during this period, when the special camps saw the removal of bars from windows and locks from doors, the renewed allowance of correspondence, and even visits and free choice of individual hairstyles. The distinction, he writes, between the special and corrective labor camps no longer held. Even in the regular camps, conditions were becoming notably easier—prisoners were paid for their labor, newspapers and radios abounded, women were removed from timber work, and so forth. Light-regime camp sections were created where prisoners only slept in zones but went to work without escort. Finally, even the possibility of living outside the zone entirely was introduced. Such prisoners only had to report periodically to the camp authorities.[170]

As with nearly all innovations in Gulag practice, the determination of which prisoners were to be allowed to live outside the zone was largely made based on behavior and labor activity in the camps. For example, consider the case of Khristian Georgievich Shmidt. Shmidt was a prisoner at Karlag, sentenced to ten years under Article 58-10 for anti-Soviet propaganda. On December 31, 1955, Karlag authorities issued an order allowing Shmidt to live outside the camp zone. "For his time in the camp, he showed himself in daily life and at work in an exclusively positive manner, has earned 651 'accounted days,' has not violated the camp regime and has no administrative reprimands." Therefore, "for exemplary behavior and conscientious relations to labor," he was given the right to live outside the zone.[171] Such examples of prisoners transferred to light-regime divisions or for living outside the zone altogether appear frequently in the Karlag records, and all of them include a specific consideration of the subject prisoner's labor activities and behavior in the camp.[172]

The period following the uprising saw the continued diminution of the Gulag's population as Soviet authorities extended amnesty, case review, and release to many categories of prisoners excluded from the initial post-Stalin amnesty.[173] The prisoner population in the camps and colonies on January 1 of the years 1953 to 1956 dropped from 2.4 million to 1.3 million, then to 1 million, and finally to 780,000, respectively.[174] From 1953 to 1958, over 4.1 million inmates were released from the camps and colonies.[175]

The releases began with political prisoners determined not to be guilty of their alleged crimes. Later, a far wider group of political prisoners was released regardless of their supposed guilt. Under a decree from May 19, 1954, Soviet authorities reviewed the cases of a select portion of prisoners convicted of counterrevolutionary crimes. The reviewing authorities were empowered to release inmates, when prisoners' convictions were unjust or unfounded. Under this decree, some ninety thousand political prisoners were released in 1954 and 1955.[176] In September 1955, an amnesty released nearly all those Soviet citizens sentenced to less than ten years for collaboration with the occupying Germans during the war. Those sentenced to ten years or more saw their terms reduced by half.[177]

Merely acknowledging the wrongful conviction of a significant number of political prisoners marked an extraordinary new path for Soviet penal politics, but the most astonishing events were yet to come. After Khrushchev's secret speech on February 25, 1956, the pace of release for the politicals picked up considerably. On March 24, the Presidium of the Supreme Soviet authorized the review of cases of those convicted of "crimes of a political character" and all juveniles in the labor colonies. The decree authorized the commissions to decide not merely whether the inmates were truly guilty but also "the advisability of keeping incarcerated those persons who, although guilty of anti-soviet crimes, do not present any danger to the state or to society." The commissions could make final decisions about release or commutation of sentence on the spot.[178] According to Nanci Adler, liberation commissions were formed as early as February 7, when Procurator Rudenko presented a draft directive on their operations. The directive "emphasizes that cases should be examined for 'their essence and the data that characterizes the personality of the prisoner.' Furthermore, the commissions were obligated to speak with every prisoner."[179] Solzhenitsyn described the commissions. Prisoners were called in individually.

> A few factual questions are asked about each man's case. The questions are perfectly polite, and apparently well meant, but their drift is that *the prisoner must admit his guilt.* . . . He must be silent, he must bow his head, he must be put in the position of one forgiven, not one who forgives! . . . What of those who out of incomprehensible pride refused to acknowledge their guilt to the commission? *They were left inside.*[180]

Even in times of broadest amnesty, the Soviet authorities insisted on differentiation and individual attention to individual prisoners.

On April 11, 1956, the Karlag administration issued an order to begin preparatory work for these commissions. First, all personal files of prisoners falling under the Presidium's directive were gathered and materials characterizing prisoners' behavior in the camp were attached. All movement of prisoners among camp divisions was prohibited during the course of the review except in extraordinary cases. The order charged heads of individual camp divisions with providing all necessary documentation to released prisoners along with returning to prisoners all personal property and money. The order set up a fund for the help of released prisoners, which was to supply released prisoners without money with means to survive until they got a new job. Camp employees were required to assist released elderly, invalids, women with young children, and pregnant women in travel to their chosen place of residence. These categories of prisoner were to be given seats in reserved train compartments. Those unable to travel alone were even supposed to be provided with escorts, either by calling on their relatives to come travel with them or, in exceptional cases, offering them escorts from among the camp's employees. Invalids without relatives were to be placed in invalid homes. All released prisoners were also to be provided with quality clothes, shoes, and socks. The provision of passports to released prisoners was the decision of the special commissions.[181]

While a high percentage of prisoners who had their cases reviewed by these commissions were released, every individual case of release specifically characterized the individual prisoner's labor production, behavior, accumulation of accounted working days, and frequently their participation in political and cultural activities in the camps. While I have found no precise statistics on this question, my review of a selection of individual prisoner files revealed only one case of a prisoner who was refused release by these commissions. Evdokiia Arsent'evna Novikova had served as a nurse in the Red Army during the war and was captured by the Germans. She was convicted on December 10, 1948 for allegedly enlisting in the service of the German intelligence and gathering information on Soviet troop movements around Taganrog. Although her twenty-five-year sentence had been reduced by half in accord with the September 1955 law, and despite her consistent ratings of excellent in behavior and production in the camps, the commission determined that there was no basis for reviewing her case under the March 1956 order. She was ultimately released in April 1957, however, under terms set up for conditional early release in exchange for good behavior and outstanding labor performance.[182]

The broad latitude given to the commissions to not merely determine whether an individual was or was not guilty of their purported crimes but also to determine the state necessity of their continued isolation led them to seek out information on behavior and labor activity in the camps to decide whether the prisoner presented an ongoing danger to the state. In fact, even in cases in which a prisoner was determined not to have committed their alleged crime, their behavior and labor production in the camps was still weighed in deciding whether they should be released.[183]

Dolgun, one of the few memoirists not terribly laconic when discussing his release, writes that the "reliable prison telegraph" had informed him of the special commissions on releases. "The bad part was that the only ones who were not released were those who had not had a trial but had been sentenced by committee or tribunal or special procedure," as he had.[184] In Kengir, they heard, releases had closed one camp after another through February. The atmosphere at Dzhezkazgan was "electric." In March 1956, the commission arrived in Dzhezkazgan, and Dolgun's case was postponed. "We can't review your case. . . . We have nothing but a slip of paper with your charges. We have to send to Moscow for your full file from the KGB. It will take between one and two months, and we will call you back." Although it was nearly another four months, Dolgun's day finally came. On July 13, 1956, he was released, although he was forced to agree that he would never try to contact the American Embassy and to live under constant KGB surveillance.[185]

Reviewing individual prisoner files in Karaganda, the veracity of Dolgun's account is apparent. In the records of those sentenced by courts and military tribunals, the file included a complete narrative sentence of the court describing the circumstances surrounding the alleged criminal activity along with the sentence and frequently a recitation of the "evidence." When the organs of the MVD, MGB, NKVD, or other nonjudicial organ had sentenced a prisoner, the prisoner file only included a brief note indicating the article of conviction and the sentence without any details. Clearly, in cases like Dolgun's, the commissions wanted to know the circumstances of the crime so that they could make their determination as to the "necessity" of continuing to detain the prisoner.

The scope of the mass releases is indicated by the closure of the camps and camp divisions. Steplag was disbanded on May 24, 1956 due to its falling population. Its subdivisions were transferred to the control of the Kazakh MVD's UITLK.[186] On April 7, 1956, owing to the reduced prisoner and staff contingent, their unlikely replenishment, and the consequent unprofitability, the Temir-Tau camp subdivision of Karlag was closed.[187] From 1953 to 1958, the prisoner population at Karlag fell from forty-two to nineteen thousand.[188] Camps and camp divisions were closing throughout the Gulag system.[189]

The period following the uprising saw not only the numerical reduction of the prisoner population. At the same time, a fundamental transformation of the Gulag social hierarchy occurred. These decrees, reviews of cases, and amnesties led to significant releases of prisoners sentenced for counterrevolutionary crimes. While the effects of the March 27, 1953 amnesty, which excluded most political prisoners, led to a rise in the counterrevolutionaries' proportion of all inmates from 21.9 to 34.8 percent on January 1, 1953 and 1954, respectively, the tide turned immediately thereafter. On January 1, 1955, their proportion fell to 28.7 percent, and the number dropped to 14.6 percent on January 1, 1956. The total number of prisoners sentenced for counterrevolutionary crimes had dropped from the 460,557 on January 1, 1954 to 113,735 on January 1, 1956, and then 11,000 on January 1, 1959.[190] The Gulag administration's attention had turned from counterrevolutionaries to hard-core organized, professional criminals.[191] Quite suddenly, the political prisoners were removed from their perch as the least redeemable and most dangerous citizens of Soviet society. This transformation, even more than the quantitative reduction in the size of the Gulag, was perhaps the most fundamental alteration of the post-Stalin penal system.

## Release from Exile

Alongside the release of prisoners from the corrective labor camps and colonies was a parallel process of release from exile. In the first half of 1952, nearly 130,000 exiles, including over 42,000 children under the age of sixteen, were confined to the Karaganda region. The largest groups included well over 50,000 German adults, over 25,000 adults exiled from the northern Caucasus (more than 23,000 of whom were Chechen), over 5,500 adults of the OUN, and nearly 2,000 adult Poles who had been exiled in 1936.[192] This picture changed dramatically by the end of the decade.

On January 1, 1955, just over 90,000 exiles remained on the rolls in the Karaganda region, with most of them working in agriculture or the coal industry.[193] During the course of 1954, nearly 3,800 new exiles arrived in Karaganda Oblast, all after release from the camps, including 2,000 from Peschanlag and 750 from Steplag. The vast majority of these former prisoners were put to work building mines for Karaganda Mine Construction (Karagandashakhtstroi). A small number of specialists worked for Karaganda Coal (Karagandaugol') or in agriculture, and a few of these former prisoners were considered physically unfit for mine-building labor.[194] During the same year, 55,000 were removed from the rolls of exiles. The vast majority of these, some 42,000, were children removed from the family roll in accord with a law from July 5, 1954 freeing all children of special settlers under the age of sixteen and all those over the age of sixteen who were studying in educational institutions.[195] In total, some 875,000 exiles were officially removed from the rolls as a result of the July 5 law, but as Zemskov makes clear, the significance of this release was limited since the parents of these children, with whom most of them continued to live, remained exiles.[196]

Well over 10,000 Karaganda exiles were released on the basis of an August 13, 1954 resolution of the Council of Ministers, including some 4,000 who were former kulaks exiled between 1929 and 1933; 6,000 who were Germans from the Far East, Siberia, Central Asia, Kazakhstan, and other places from which exile was not supposed to apply; 525 who were freed as improperly exiled; 160 who were Vlasovites completing their sentences; and around 30 who were from the mobilized Germans.[197] The question of allowing these exiles to return to their homes was not addressed.[198]

The law of July 5, 1954 did more than allow for the release of children from the exile rolls and was the subject of a propaganda campaign directed at all exiles. Under its terms, special settlers who were engaged in socially useful labor could freely move within the oblast, krai, or republic to which they were exiled, were only required to register with local authorities once per year, and could take official business-related trips anywhere in the Soviet Union. These measures, significantly, did not apply to those sent into exile after serving time in the camps for especially dangerous state crimes, or to Ukrainian nationalists and their families, or to nearly all other categories of exiles from western Ukraine, western Belorussia, Pskov Oblast, Lithuania, Latvia, and Estonia, thus making it quite clear whom the Soviet authorities feared the most among the exiled peoples.[199] Soviet authorities attempted to explain the importance of the law to the special settlers—above all, "that their further fates and terms spent on the rolls of special settlement will depend on them, first on their behavior and their relationship to socially useful labor." The local minister of internal affairs of the Karaganda region, Sergei Aleksandrovich Konovalov, reported that this had a positive influence on the exiles there.

He quoted several exiles, such as Israil Nal'giev, born in 1881, who said, "We should thank the Soviet government for the show of faith in special settlers. We old ones should exert influence on the youths, so that nobody violates the new situation established for us." The German exile Ol'ga Kun reportedly declared, "I am now happy that my children are liberated from the special settlement." And the exile V. O. Bentsin observed, "For the children it is now good. They can study in any educational institution in any city of the USSR. They can enter the Komsomol and the party." The affirmative comments about the capacity to study anywhere in the Soviet Union are repeated by many other exiles. Furthermore, noted Konovalov, "a certain portion of the special settlers, not carrying out socially useful labor, having in the past violations of the regime, after explanation to them of the role of the law from the Council of Ministers and revelation of the new legal condition, started on the path of correction."[200]

Despite the high tide of reportedly positive responses among the Karaganda exile community to the changes in their status in 1954, a few exiles from the particularly feared Chechen-Ingush and Ukrainian nationalists exhibited negative attitudes in the eyes of local Soviet authorities. Among many Chechens and Ingush, the law was supposedly thought of as a half measure, but hopes were high that soon these people would be released and allowed to return to the Caucasus. As Konovalov added ominously, however, some exhibited "nationalist and terrorist moods." Many purportedly made statements similar to the Chechen Magomet Alkhoev, who declared that if the Chechens were freed, "All of us Chechens and Ingush would go to the Caucasus, and like water flows in a river, so would flow the blood of those who are living in our homes."[201] Similarly, OUN members reportedly "brooded" over the fact that they had no limitations removed, and exhibited "anti-Soviet" and "nationalist" feelings. For example, Nikolai Andreevich Proniuk allegedly stated, "They are liberating a large part of the special settlers. We don't need this joy. Soon will come a time when we will liberate ourselves and go to our 'independent Ukraine.' Soon these Communists will stop drinking our blood."[202] Such opinions must have given Soviet authorities great pause about allowing the exiled nationalities to return to their homelands in the event of their release from exile. The nationalists from the western borderlands, who had already shown themselves as unrepentant enemies of the Soviet order during the Kengir uprising and were now heard to make such provocative statements, would be the last of the internal exiles to be removed from the ranks of exiles. Yet given the vehemence of their anti-Soviet ideology, it perhaps should be surprising not that they were the last to be released but rather that they would be allowed to return to their homes at all.

The Chechens, in particular, continued to show themselves to be a potentially problematic group on release, both from the statements of exiles like those noted above, and by the behavior of certain Chechens and Ingush in the camps and in exile. In 1953, 698 special settlers in the Karaganda region were brought up on criminal charges, 487 of whom were Chechen or Ingush. In 1954 the numbers were 431 and 307, respectively. These numbers were completely disproportionate to their total of just over 20 percent of the region's exiles.[203] Actual mass fighting between the Chechen-Ingush and Russian populations was common. On November 7, 1954, a fight broke out during a film screening in a club in the village of Elizavetinka in the Akmolinsk Oblast between mostly drunken Russian and Ingush villagers. One man was put in the hospital for ten days after the battle.[204] Throughout the 1950s, despite efforts to house Chechen prisoners in special camp divisions along with other innovations intended to prevent contact between Chechen-Ingush and prisoners of other nationalities, reports continued to appear of mass fighting between national groups inside the camps.[205] On May 28, 1954, a fight took place at camp division number 16 of the camps and colonies under the direct supervision of the Kazakh Republic MVD between a Chechen and a Russian prisoner. The fight quickly expanded into a large melee between Russian and Chechen-Ingush prisoners. Eight prisoners were wounded. The central MVD issued an order to the Kazakh Republic MVD to improve educational work among the prisoners there and blamed the local camp staff for failing to draw the "necessary practical conclusions from the particularities of the contingent of prisoners held in the division"— namely, the prisoners' nationality.[206] In November 1955, a large fight erupted in Karlag between the Chechen and Russian prisoners of the Samarskoe camp division's camp point Severnyi. Eighteen prisoners were transferred to strict-regime divisions and deprived of 180 accumulated workdays each as a result.[207]

Even in the wake of the release of the Chechen and Ingush population from exile, and the re-creation of the Chechen-Ingush national homeland, those Chechen and Ingush prisoners still in concentration camps continued to battle with their Russian counterparts. On the night of March 23–24, 1958, in the zone of Spassk camp division's camp point 1, a fight occurred between Russian and Chechen prisoners. In the point's hospital zone, two Chechens, Umarov and Kanaev, were recovering from venereal diseases. These prisoners also sold narcotics in the camp zone. In their dealing, they reportedly perpetrated a fraud on some Russian prisoners, leading to hostile relations. On the evening of March 23, a fight broke out between Umarov and a Russian prisoner, Grankin. Grankin then provoked the other Russian prisoners into tossing the Chechen prisoners out of their barrack, during the course of which one Chechen, Ibragimov, was struck in the back with a stick. These Chechens went to the acknowledged leader of the Chechen prisoners, Baryshev, who decided to avenge Ibragimov's injury. Armed with sticks, pokers, and one crowbar, a group of Chechen prisoners entered barrack 22 and began beating Russian prisoners. The fight lasted a half hour before the camp authorities put it down. Ten Russian prisoners were injured to varying degrees, and one was killed due to serious head wounds. The camp division's operative staff and leadership were faulted for allowing the fight to happen—especially for their failure to carry out adequate searches, which should have revealed the presence of weapons and the trade in narcotics in the zone. Moreover, many of the fighters were actually healthy and should not have been in the hospital zone. The head of the camp point was relieved of duty.[208]

Despite the high levels of hostility, the Chechens and Ingush were released from exile, as will be noted below, in a fashion similar to all other exiled nationalities. The Soviet government sought to create autonomous regions for the Chechens and Ingush in either Kazakhstan or Uzbekistan to prevent them from returning to the Caucasus. This, too, was the typical story of the release of nationalities, who were initially prevented from returning to their homes, but with few exceptions were ultimately allowed to do so. The Chechen and Ingush leaders refused to accept the construction of these national regions in Kazakhstan or Uzbekistan, and many members of these nationalities began to return to their homes on their own. On their arrival, reports abounded of fighting and armed clashes among the returnees and those living in their homes. Nonetheless, not only did the Soviet authorities not return the Chechen and Ingush nationalities into internal exile, they also relented on the prohibition of a return to their former homes, and even reestablished the autonomous Chechen and Ingush national republic. The Chechens and Ingush continued to provide problems to Soviet authorities throughout the Soviet period, and individual and social memories of the deportations fueled the fury of post-Soviet Chechen fighters against Russia.[209] The period of mass deportations was over, though, regardless of the consequences.

Prior to the appearance of mass releases by nationality and in addition to the 1954 releases from exile described above, 1954 and 1955 saw a significant number of individual petitions for release from or changes in the status of exile. During the course of 1954, for exiles living in the Karaganda region alone, over 29,000 complaints and petitions were submitted, nearly 20,000 of which were petitions either for release or reuniting family members living in separate locales.[210] A review of some of these release petitions is instructive of the situation for exiles in this period. The most likely route to release from exile was a change of one's official nationality. For example, a letter of October 1954 from the Kazakh Republic MVD to the Main Administration of the Militia (GUM) of the central USSR MVD included the eighty-one-page personal file of Iusip

Abdulaevich Abdulaev. The reason for the petition was the recent change of nationality on Abdulaev's passport from Chechen to Kalmyk. As such, according to the petition, he was mistakenly exiled in 1944 along with the Chechens and Ingush. In January 1955, the Passport Registration Department of GUM replied with no objection to Abdulaev's change of nationality. Abdulaev was thus released from exile.[211] Children of mixed nationality families could also sometimes gain release from exile, if only one family member was of a nationality subject to exile, and that family member was no longer living. Mariia Ivanovna Fogel' had been exiled from Moscow to Karaganda in 1941 on account of her father being German. In April 1954, she was released from exile because her father had died in 1944 and all the rest of the family was Russian.[212] The end of marriages to spouses of an exiled nationality could lead to release as well. Ekaterina Nikitichna Dran'ko was a Russian who had been exiled to Karaganda due to her marriage to a German. In January 1955, she was released from exile because she had not lived with her German husband since 1943 and she had no compromising materials in her file.[213]

In some cases, being an invalid or related to an invalid allowed for some change in an exile's position. A petition sought to allow a daughter, a former member of the OUN in exile in Magadan, to be transferred to Karaganda, where her ill mother was in exile. This move was allowed, but the petition's additional request that the mother be released from exile was denied, as it was determined that "as a member of the family of a participant of the band 'OUN,' [she] was exiled justly."[214] In cases where invalids sought not to be relocated to join other family members in exile but instead to be released to join family living in freedom, such petitions were denied.[215]

Cases dealing with family members of those sentenced as participants in the OUN could lead to strange outcomes. I. Ia. Maksimchuk was arrested in 1944 and sentenced to five years in the camps under articles 58-1a and 58-2 as a member of the OUN. On his release, he was exiled to Karaganda, where his wife had been exiled in 1948 as a relative of an OUN member. On the basis of the amnesty of March 27, 1953, Maksimchuk was freed from exile, but there was not "at the present time any basis for the release of [his wife] from special settlement."[216] So the supposed OUN member himself was freed, but his wife was not because she was a relative of an OUN member. Such were the absurdities of a bureaucracy blindly applying irrational regulations. Nearly all petition denials were accompanied with this formula: a "lack of basis" for release.[217]

Finally, some petitions were granted even when similar petitions had been denied. It seems that the distinction may have been the origination of such petitions outside the boundaries of the MVD. For instance, Antonina Nikolaevna Galkina was released from exile in Karaganda in

January 1955, despite the fact that her exile from the Leningrad region in 1938 resulted from her husband's execution. She was officially released because she had been in exile for a long time and had a positive record of labor activity. Yet the real distinctive element of her case was that her petition was sent not directly to MVD authorities but instead was submitted to the USSR procuracy, who then passed the petition on to the MVD.[218]

These cases were all quite different from what would come later in the way of mass releases, yet they are quite revealing on their face. Most significant, each case was dealt with individually and almost always by a figure as high up as the head of the exile system, the chief of the Fourth Special Department (Spetsotdel) of the MVD B. V. Novikov. Furthermore, all petitions included the exile's personal file for review by the central authorities making the decisions. Novikov and others frequently recorded the exile's attitudes, behavior, and labor productivity as part of the justification for the decision made on a given petition. Consideration of these criteria calls to mind the typical process of appeal or petition for clemency from sentences in the corrective labor camps.

In 1955, two selective releases—that is, releases not of entire nationalities but rather of specific persons from among the exiled nationalities—occurred, leading up to the era of mass release of entire nationalities. These releases are particularly interesting for their commentary on social hierarchy in the post-Stalin Soviet Union, for it was certain Soviet notables who were released prior to the all-encompassing mass releases of December 1955 to July 1956. After exiling national groups as a whole, regardless of class membership, party membership, or military service, in the days leading up to the mass releases, it was as if the Soviet government needed to declare that an entire nationality was not equal and would not henceforth be treated as such. Occupying primacy of place, Communist Party members and their families were released in May 1955. A laundry list of Soviet notables were released in November, including veterans of the Great Patriotic war, holders of USSR orders and medals, family members of those who perished at the front, and teachers in educational institutions. Ensconcing in legislation the reasoning behind some of the individual releases already noted, the November decision also allowed for the release of the Russian, Ukrainian, or other national wives who were exiled because of their marriages to Crimean Tatars, Chechens, or other exiled nationalities, but whose marriages had subsequently ended. The order also released women who had married local nonexile residents. Finally, incurably ill invalids who could not support themselves were released.[219]

There were only two other releases that were not of national groups. On September 17, 1955, those exiled for cooperation with the fascist occupiers were released from exile, with the exception of those who were still subject to exile based on their nationality (Germans, Chechens, Crimean Tatars, etc.).[220] On March 10, 1956, all those especially dangerous state criminals who had been sent into exile after the completion of their camp terms under the 1948 law were released, although those whose families had been sent into exile were sent to join them.[221] This release of the especially dangerous state criminals was delayed for nearly three years due to Beria's removal. Already in May 1953, a proposal had been made to release these individuals from exile, but it would not actually happen until March 1956.[222]

According to the numbers gathered by Zemskov, between July 1, 1954 and July 1, 1957, over 2.5 million people were released from exile, reducing the special settler population to just over 178,000 by July 1, 1957. Other than the releases discussed to this point, and the just over 109,000 exiles released on the basis of executive or judicial decisions in individual cases, all releases were made by national group. Most of these national releases were made between December 1955 and July 1956.[223] Significantly, however, release did not necessarily mean freedom of movement. Rather, being removed from the rolls of special settlers merely entitled the former exiles to cease periodic reporting to local MVD authorities. Released exiles were specifically forbidden from returning to their homeland and denied any recompense for lost property. As Zemskov quite correctly noted, these releases should be understood as an act of clemency and not one of rehabilitation. The Soviet government even required those released to sign statements agreeing to these conditions, although the rate of those refusing to sign was high, reaching nearly one-third of the Chechen exiles. Thousands of people ignored these conditions and returned to their homelands, even though many did choose to stay in their locales of exile, which had become home.[224]

Recognizing what was occurring, the Communist Party Central Committee in November 1956 attempted to slow down and control the return of these peoples to their homelands. Consequently, it made plans for the reestablishment of autonomous regions for the Kalmyk, Karachai, Balkar, Chechen, and Ingush peoples, while specifically informing local authorities to do all in their power to prevent the independent return of these peoples to their homelands before spring 1957, so that preparations for their return could be made. The Central Committee also discussed and rejected the idea of granting an autonomous homeland to the Crimean Tatars based on the logic that they were merely one nationality in a multinational region that was now settled by others and part of the Ukrainian Republic.[225]

The first major release of national groups was the liberation of the remaining 695,000 Soviet Germans, who did not come under the release of August 13, 1954. They were freed from exile on December 13, 1955, but specifically denied the right to return to their homes.[226] It was not until 1964 that the Soviet Germans were officially cleared of the accusations of 1941, but their national republic was never restored. They were given the right to free choice of residence in 1972, however. The impetus for their release seems at least in part to have been a visit in September 1955 by German chancellor Konrad Adenauer to the USSR, during which he inquired into the conditions of Soviet German exiles.[227] Shortly after the release of the Soviet Germans, local MVD officials were besieged with complaints from other exiled nationalities as to why they should be held in exile if the Germans had been freed.[228] Other releases quickly followed. Keeping in mind that their numbers had already been greatly reduced by the removal of children under age sixteen and other categories from their ranks, the releases of the nationalities went as follows: On January 17, 1956, 23,000 Poles who had been exiled in 1936 from regions close to the Polish border were removed from the rolls of special settlers. On March 17, 1956, the 49,000 exiled Kalmyks were released. Their homeland was restored in January 1957.[229] On March 27, 1956, 22,000 Crimean Greek, Bulgarian, and Armenian exiles were removed from the rolls of special settlers. On April 28, 1956, 178,000 Balkar, Crimean Tatar, Turk, Kurd, and Khemshil exiles were released. They were explicitly forbidden from returning to their homelands. The Crimean Tatars were not cleared of their alleged collective guilt until 1967 and were not allowed to return to their homeland until the 1980s.[230] On May 15, 1956, an order released 14,000 families of Ukrainian and Belarusian nationalists from exile.[231] On July 16, 1956, the 245,000 Karachai, Chechen, and Ingush peoples were released from exile, although they were expressly forbidden from returning to their homelands. Many disobeyed this order, and faced with the return of thousands to the Caucasus, the Soviet government restored their homelands in January 1957.[232]

These releases radically changed the size and composition of the Soviet exile community. Of the 178,000 remaining on the lists of special settlers on July 1, 1957, the vast majority of them were from the western territories—Ukraine, Belorussia, and the Baltic republics. Piecemeal reductions of the rolls took place throughout 1958, releasing those deemed less guilty and less dangerous of offenses of nationalism, but refusing to allow them to return to their homes. By January 1, 1959, the number of exiles was reduced to 42,000. Most of these were released on January 7, 1960, yet they were still not allowed to return to their homelands. Several thousand people sent into exile by individual judicial sentence remained officially in exile. On January 1, 1959, less than 300 such individuals remained in exile in Karaganda Oblast.[233]

## Life after Release

The prisoners' responses to their release were varied. Many of them stayed in their locale of imprisonment. As Dolgun notes, "For many of the released there was no home to go back to.... Many of the released still had terms of exile to serve. There was an acute need to keep the mines of Dzhezkazgan functioning, and the work force would largely be made up of ex-prisoners."[234] Riewe observes that releases from Steplag created no apparent serious labor shortages for local enterprises, since he estimates that one-third to one-half of those released remained in the area. He speculates on the reasons why former prisoners would stay to work in the region of their detention:

> In the first place, prisoners who signed an agreement to stay on as free workers were released sooner than the others. Moreover, many prisoners had managed to obtain for themselves fairly responsible positions, which paid them well once they were free. In return for signing an agreement to work for a definite period, a released prisoner might receive a bonus ranging up to ten thousand rubles, and living quarters would be provided for him.[235]

For others, release was a tremendously disorienting event. As Dolgun explains,

> It was clear that many of [the released] had no sense at all of how to manage on the outside. There were many deaths from drunkenness, and from accidents arising out of drunkenness, or because people just stepped in front of trucks, without seeming to see them, when they had not been drinking at all.... It was the suddenness of it, combined with the anxiety. One moment you were a prisoner. The next moment you might be free but you dared not count on it because life had dealt so many blows you were conditioned by disappointment.[236]

The release of some of the most hardened criminals injected a dangerous element into life around many Gulag localities. "We heard that the towns of Nikolsky and Dzhezkazgan were overrun with professional criminals taking advantage of the horde of unworldly and innocent new arrivals who knew so little of the world," writes Dolgun.[237]

Gulag survivors faced many difficulties wherever they moved after their camp experience.[238] Saddled with official documents noting prisoners' time in the camps, local authorities frequently either resisted release altogether, or resisted the reintegration of former inmates and exiles into their communities. For example, secret police authorities in the Kemerovo region complained to central authorities about Karaganda's release of exiled UPA and OUN members for reunion with their family members in Kemerovo Oblast. In this case, the central authorities in charge of exile ordered Karaganda to cease such releases.[239] At other times, locals them-selves were able to prevent the reintegration of former Gulag inmates. Employers refused to give them jobs. Police authorities refused to give them residency documents. An MVD report from 1956 on a proposed reorganization of the work of camps and colonies complained about the unwillingness of local industries and authorities to provide work and living permits to former prisoners. Left without means and a place to live, the report argued, former prisoners were being forced back into a life of crime.[240] Even the signs coming from the Central Committee were ambivalent as to whether these former prisoners could ever be fully trusted as members of Soviet society. Extremely telling is a Central Com-mittee letter warning local party organizations in December 1956 "there are people among the returnees who are unfavorably disposed to Soviet authority, especially among the former Trotskyites, right opportunists, and bourgeois nationalists. They . . . try to renew their hostile anti-soviet activity."[241]

Former prisoners themselves long remained ambivalent as a group about their own reintegration into Soviet society. Many criminals con-tinued their lives of crime. Many nationalists from the western territories continued to be vehemently anti-Soviet. And many members of the small dissident movement of the 1960s–80s were former prisoners themselves. Yet at the same time, many former Communist Party members sought rehabilitation and party reinstatement after their release from the camps. Adler writes that in some cases, the desire to return to the party was "utilitarian," but "sometimes the motivation was ideological. . . . Many victims considered themselves to be the 'builders of socialism' and thus had abiding faith in the party."[242] Ivanova strongly disputes this notion, quoting one prisoner writing in 1956, "I don't know why you need com-plete rehabilitation. . . . This kind of false restoration of honor cannot right the wrongs committed against you as a citizen." For Ivanova, this is proof that "the former inmate of the Gulag had absolutely no illu-sions as to the 'triumph of justice.'"[243] Adler ultimately agrees, even de-ideologizing and reducing to mere self-interest such an intensely ideo-logical statement from a former prisoner as the following: "Only after I got Party membership did I feel like a full-fledged citizen of my mother-land!" Adler immediately follows up this comment: "The power to grant or withhold privileges proved to be an effective way of forcing support of the Party."[244] Still, the deeply ideological pronouncement implicit in the tie between reinstatement in the party and reattainment of the sta-tus of "full-fledged citizen" was by no means an uncommon one. In the wake of the Twenty-second Party Congress, a number of former and re-instated party members submitted lengthy memoirs to the Central Com-mittee. These memoirs detailed the shattered lives as well as the suffering inflicted through false arrests, interrogations, torture, prisons, and camps. Intriguingly, these stories generally climaxed with claims about the essential truths and triumph of "Leninist" justice. Consider, for example, the letter of Ol'ga Krishevna Roga, a Communist Party member since 1917. She was able to survive "all these horrors" because in her heart "not for a minute, not even the most agonizing did I lose faith in the great belief that Leninist truth would triumph." Leninist justice triumphed, these memoirists write, when they were released, rehabilitated, and/or reinstated into the party.[245]

No doubt, though, many returned from the Gulag with their spirits and bodies destroyed. Their personalities and bodies had so changed that they were often almost unrecognizable. Many relatives were devastated at the condition of their returning relatives. Many returning prisoners refused to talk about their lives in the camps, and exhibited a constant fear of informants and police authorities. They found it incredibly difficult to reconnect with their old life and acquaintances. As a result, many former prisoners found one another for comfort.[246]

The mass releases, Khrushchev's secret speech, public acknowledgment of the falsehood of such cases as the doctors' plot, and the publication of Solzhenitsyn's *One Day in the Life of Ivan Denisovich* began to blow apart the wall of secrecy that had surrounded the Gulag.[247] Nonetheless, simultaneous actions tried to shore up that very wall. Dolgun, while waiting for his case to be reviewed, saw the arrival of a trainload of Komsomol members as part of Khrushchev's virgin lands campaign. The press immediately started covering their activities and attributing to them the construction of "the new city of Dzhezkazgan, building it from the 'virgin soil' where nothing had stood before, and so on." They were giving the Komsomol credit for the construction projects already completed by prisoners.[248] Prisoners who were released from the Gulag also were required to sign an oath that they would not reveal any details of their life in the camps. They were given new clothing and were searched to prevent them from taking anything from the camp that could expose what took place inside the barbed wire.

One particularly touchy subject was revealing the cause of death for both repressed individuals who had been executed and those who had died in the camps. In the case of those who had been executed, especially in 1937–38, MVD officials ordered the maintenance of a long-held policy to inform relatives that their loved one had been sentenced to ten years in camps without the right of correspondence and had died in their place of imprisonment. The only easing of these procedures was to allow MVD authorities to register these deaths with ZAGS (civilian registry offices) so that relatives could receive official death certificates.[249] In the case of deaths in the camps, local Gulag officials were specifically forbidden from revealing such causes of death as exhaustion (*istoshchenie*) or vitamin deficiency, which would expose the failures to provide adequate food to prisoners in camps. For instance, on May 21, 1957, an employee of the Kazakh MVD responded to a query from the daughter of Kanzafar Valeev about the reason for his death while in Karlag. The official camp death certificate in his file states "vitamin deficient exhaustion" (*avitaminoz istoshcheniia*) as the cause of death. But the letter to Valeev's daughter listed the cessation of cardiac function as the reason.[250]

Even the relative openness to talk about the Gulag was short-lived. In the wake of Khrushchev's ouster, life in the Soviet concentration camps returned to the world of taboo and secrecy that it had occupied from the early 1930s until Stalin's death, and would not emerge again until Mikhail Gorbachev's time, when the subject became an open topic and would never again be closed.

## The Gulag Is Dead, Long Live the Gulag

Solzhenitsyn writes of the camps' continued existence into the 1960s under Khrushchev: "Rulers change, the Archipelago remains. It remains because *that particular* political regime could not survive without it. If it disbanded the Archipelago, it would cease to exist itself."[251] It would be wrong to say that the Gulag disappeared entirely by the end of the 1950s. In fact, the population of corrective labor camps and colonies still totaled nearly one million. Yet the makeup of this population had changed quite radically. The total incarcerated population convicted of political offenses had been reduced to eleven thousand by 1959. The total population in exile was reduced to a measure of thousands. Similar to Solzhenitsyn, Adler argues that the Soviet system did not "renounce repression," as officials continued making arrests even during the course of releases. She explains that "while the victims of repression of the thirties and forties were being rehabilitated, new political prisoners were being created. Such contradictions could not continue indefinitely, and it was the rehabilitation process that was curtailed." The new arrests of political prisoners convicted under the new Article 70 for anti-Soviet agitation and propaganda in 1958, though, totaled just over fourteen hundred people. Adler notes that this number is "low by historical standards," but contends that it proves "an ongoing policy of official repression."[252] On the one hand, she is certainly correct, and the diminished overall numbers are no comfort for those being repressed. On the other hand, the quantitative difference was so radical that it entailed a qualitative change as well. The qualitative change is evident from the shift of priorities implicit in 1956 proposals for the reorganization of the work of Soviet corrective labor camps and colonies.

On April 5, 1956, the central MVD sent a report to the Central Committee, proposing a reconfiguration of the corrective labor camp system. The solutions should seem familiar, echoing long-established Gulag practices. Yet one element of the new proposals merits significant attention. The report recognized a new situation in Soviet corrective labor policy. The political prisoners no longer occupied the bottom rung of the camp hierarchy. In fact, they were almost totally absent from the camps altogether. In the eyes of Soviet authorities, the least redeemable and most dangerous prisoners were now the recidivists and criminal gangs. The report found the requisite Lenin citation to assert that it was necessary to battle the "petty criminal" (*zhulik*), who along with the bourgeoisie was the main enemy of socialism.

> The rich and the petty criminals, these are two side of the same coin, these are the two main forms of parasites reared by capitalism, these are the main enemies of socialism. These enemies must be taken under the supervision of the whole population, we must finish them ruthlessly for the smallest violations of the rules and laws of socialist society. Any weakness, any vacillations, any sentimentality in this regard would be a great crime before socialism.[253]

The new strictness with nonpolitical criminals implied in selecting this passage from Lenin was echoed time and again in the Gulag. In 1956, a commission of the Presidium of the Supreme Soviet conducted a review of the camps, colonies, and prisons, including Steplag. Its report noted that in the midst of the ongoing releases of political prisoners, a significant number of prisoners properly convicted of serious crimes sat in Steplag. The commission warned against allowing such prisoners quick access to the privileges of the lightened regime, even when they showed a proper attitude toward work and high production figures. These prisoners might be performing well only to receive such privileges, leading to cases where even some convicted of murder are transferred to a light regime in just a few months.[254]

In its April 5, 1956 report to the Central Committee, the MVD USSR noted that over 25 percent of all inmates in the camps and colonies were recidivists, who negatively influenced the life of the entire camp—committing robberies, murders, and other serious crimes, and leading "a parasitic way of life on the backs of the labor of honestly working prisoners."[255] To reduce the harmful influence of recidivists and other socially dangerous criminals in Soviet places of detention, the central MVD proposed their complete isolation in special corrective labor prisons organized in the most remote and unpopulated regions of the country.[256]

The removal of certain prisoners from camp society and its elements of corrective labor indicated a sense that certain criminals were hopelessly lost to society. The report made this point explicitly:

> All possible measures of an administrative and educational influence have been applied, but nonetheless, they persistently wish neither to work nor to refuse their criminal habits. Among them are many who have been convicted ten or more times and have committed five to ten murders. . . . Accustomed to conditions in places of confinement, these criminals establish various criminal gangs, constantly fighting among themselves. Inside these criminal gangs strict conspiracy is observed and special rules of behavior operate, violations of which result in strict punishment up to murder. . . . The gangs engage in robberies, murders, escapes, provoke insubordination among other prisoners and lead a parasitic way of life, stealing things, money and packages from the honestly working prisoners.

Furthermore, they beat any prisoners opposing them, and engaged in "drunkenness, drug addiction and sexual perversions [*polovye izvrashcheniia*]."[257]

While some of these hardened criminals and recidivists were treated as hopelessly irredeemable, the MVD report still placed blame on local camps, suggesting a failure to teach prisoners specialized work skills as a primary cause of the high rates of recidivism. Prisoners used exclusively at unskilled heavy labor were unprepared on their release to take an active part in Soviet society and thus, it was argued, returned to the criminal path. Production interests, the report went on, were allowed to govern the operation of the camp system, leading to the formation of extremely large camps in remote regions—factors inhibiting the capacity to reeducate and correct criminals. The MVD proposed that all corrective labor camps be abolished, that prisoners serve their sentence in corrective labor colonies in the region where they lived before their arrest, that specialties be taught in the camps, and that no prisoners be used in forestry, mining, or other difficult and unqualified work.[258] The report also blamed failures in reeducation on the frequent subordination of the proper isolation of criminals based on sex, age, crime committed, attitude toward labor, and level of correction achieved to production interests. The primary blame, according to the MVD report, for this privileging of production over reeducation was the new system of financing camps wherein each camp was denied funds from central state coffers and was required to meet its expenses solely from the income derived from the labor of its prisoners. This also led to a tendency to release invalids and other prisoners of questionable labor worth before the completion of their sentence, regardless of the seriousness of their crimes.[259]

The MVD report was sharply criticized by the chair of the Committee of State Security in a report to Leonid Brezhnev dated May 10, 1956, which argued for the preservation of the existing system.[260] Ultimately, however, many of the requested changes were implemented. In April 1959, the central MVD reported on the condition in corrective labor institutions in 1957–58 and noted that the transfer of all prisoners in accord with the prior directive to colonies in their home region was proceeding quite slowly due to difficulties creating all the new colonies necessary for such a transfer. The total prisoner population held in camps rather than colonies had fallen from 71.3 percent in 1956 to 45 percent in 1959.[261] On June 13, 1956, Karlag issued a stern order on the reorganization of strict-regime camp points in the Spassk camp division to separate members of rival criminal gangs, and also isolate the Chechen and Ingush prisoners from the rest of the camp population. Special searches were to be made of all prisoners to remove all weapons from among them. The prisoners were required to wear camp clothing and get short haircuts as well. Furthermore, the "criminal-bandit element" from among them was to be removed and placed in prisons.[262] In 1957–58, as part of the battle against criminal gangs, and to isolate recidivists and hardened criminals from first-time offenders, seventy-two thousand prisoners throughout the Gulag were transferred from general-regime colonies to strict-regime colonies and an additional nineteen thousand prisoners were transferred to prisons. Yet the process of isolation of prisoners according to their crimes was characterized as incomplete.[263]

The new changes were credited with reducing mass disturbances, murders, and other crimes committed by inmates. Part of the credit was handed to assigning prisoners to groups of between seventy-five and two hundred prisoners, in which the colonies' staff could study each individual and tailor a program of educational measures for each individual. Typically, though, officials were criticized because escapes and other crimes continued to exist.[264] In terms of labor education, they claimed some successes, reducing the number of prisoners released without preparation in a production specialty from forty-eight thousand in 1956 to nineteen thousand in 1958.[265] But many prisoners, they complained, were still unable to find work or were refused living permits in their home cities, leading them back to a life of crime.[266] Still, any notion that colonies should not be self-funding was put aside in the enthusiasm surrounding the "initiative" of Corrective Labor Colony No. 14 of the Kazakh Republic MVD to eliminate its need for government financial support.[267]

The shift in focus toward recidivists was echoed in prisoner population statistics for corrective labor camps and colonies. On January 1 of the years 1957 to 1960, the portion of the prisoner population comprised of those convicted more than once rose from 33.7 percent to 43.8, 45.9, and finally 52.6 percent, respectively. Meanwhile, the remnants of the former counterrevolutionary contingent, the especially dangerous state criminals, had been reduced to a mere 1.6 percent of the prisoner population on January 1, 1960. The change in focus is also reflected in the national makeup of the prisoner population, where significant percentage drops occurred among the "nationalist" nationalities—Ukrainian, Belarusian, Lithuanian, Latvian, and Estonian—along with a significant rise in the Russian portion of the prisoner population.[268]

By the end of the 1950s, corrective labor camps and colonies, and to a limited extent the practice of internal exile, continued to operate in the Soviet Union. The period following Stalin's death, however, saw a steep decline in the quantitative scope of the operation. In qualitative terms, the Gulag would never be the same. The release of the overwhelming majority of the political prisoners combined with a new focus on recidivists and criminal gangs altered the nature of the Gulag in ways so fundamental that daily life in the Soviet concentration camps, colonies, and exile resulted in an institution that differed in fundamental ways from its analogue in the Stalin era. While repression would continue to play a role in the Soviet political system, it would never again be as ubiquitous as it was during Stalin's lifetime.

# CONCLUSION

THE GULAG WAS THOROUGHLY INTEGRATED into the fabric of the Soviet Union, touching the lives of nearly every Soviet citizen whether directly or through the fate of a friend, colleague, or family member. Millions of prisoners were held in a variety of forced labor concentration camps, prisons, and internal exile. The Gulag served as the Soviet penal system. On the one hand, the Gulag held the types of prisoners incarcerated in virtually any country—robbers, rapists, murderers, and thieves. But the Gulag was also a system of detention for political opponents of the regime, potential political opponents of the regime, suspect classes, and punished national groups. The Gulag was also filled with the millions of victims of draconian legal campaigns that harshly punished individuals for the pettiest of crimes, like leaving a job without permission, chronic absenteeism or tardiness from work, and minor theft. It was a system of forced labor as well, requiring all able-bodied prisoners and exiles (and many who were not really able) to work. The theory of reeducation through labor, the evaluation of prisoners through their labor output, and the economic needs of the Soviet state all mutually reinforced the participation of the Gulag in the opening of new and remote regions to economic exploitation. Gulag inmates contributed substantially to the Soviet economy, though at tremendous cost and with low efficiency, by mining gold, copper, and coal; building cities, railroads, canals, and highways; felling trees; and operating vast agricultural enterprises.

For prisoners, the struggle to survive motivated their lives in the Gulag, and survival was difficult, although not impossible. For authorities, the Gulag served as the institution that would define whether or not a prisoner was fit for return to society. Soviet authorities operated within a framework that accepted the potential redeemability of all prisoners who entered the gates of the Gulag, but that redemption was never guaranteed. Given the radicalism of their project to build a socialist utopia, their ready acceptance of violent means to achieve that goal, and their predetermined belief in the existence of implacable enemies opposed to that perfect future, Soviet authorities were not inclined to "reforge" their prisoners peacefully. Soviet authorities directly executed hundreds of thousands of Soviet citizens, while millions more died in transit to the Gulag, in the camps, and at places of exile, yet some 20 percent of the Gulag population was released every year. Thus, the Gulag operated as a place of both mass death and mass release. The story of the Gulag, in many ways, revolves around the efforts of prisoners to be among that 20 percent and the efforts of Gulag authorities to determine who should be among that number.

Gulag institutions, practices, and identities operated to define and enforce the boundary between death and redemption. Gulag prisoners were never treated in an undifferentiated fashion. The institutions and practices of the Gulag were designed and implemented based on a categorization matrix placing prisoners into a hierarchy according to their perceived redeemability, danger to society, and level of reeducation. The length of sentences combined with complex hierarchies of living and working conditions, differentiation of food rations, and practices of early release to tie survival directly to a constant reevaluation of prisoners according to an intricate set of criteria, including who they had been prior to their arrival in the camps (their gender, nationality, class background, alleged crime, military service, etc.) and who they had become while in the camps (labor performance, political attitudes, health, etc.) The Gulag served as a crossroads, continually redefining the line between those who could be reclaimed for Soviet society and those who were destined to die in the camps.

The line between death and redemption shifted constantly throughout the Gulag's history, as the defining features of the honest Soviet citizen, and hence the most important categories of prisoner evaluation, were constantly reconfigured by the major events and turning points of Soviet history.

Not surprisingly, the Gulag emerged as a mass social phenomenon hand in hand with the "great breakthrough" of the First Five-Year Plan. The arrests and deportations associated with collectivization and dekulakization filled the Gulag in the late 1920s and early 1930s. The Gulag's rise to prominence during this crucial period was a product not merely of the economic demands of industrialization but also of the all-encompassing social and cultural transformations accompanying the building of socialism. Soviet authorities attempted with great haste to cleanse their newly emerging society of the criminals, class enemies, and political opponents they believed contaminated the new world. The builders of socialism thought that they either had to remove the unfit permanently or make them fit again.

The 1920s and early 1930s represented the acme of Soviet belief in the capacity to rehabilitate prisoners by means of corrective labor. Crime was understood as an outgrowth of the oppressive conditions of capitalism, and criminals, it was held, only needed to be shown through labor that work was no longer exploitative under Soviet rule. Corrective labor camps were not only openly discussed but were even a source of pride too. In the mid-1920s, the newspaper and journal of the Solovetsky prison

camp were even open to national subscription. In the early 1930s, paeans
to the building of the White Sea–Baltic Sea Canal proudly announced the
use of convict labor in its construction in a volume published not only in
the Soviet Union but also in an English translation in the United States.
The Bolsheviks were transforming humans as proudly as they were transforming nature, or at least that is what they claimed.

As the 1930s progressed, optimism and openness about penal practices
gave way to skepticism and secrecy, yet the practices of differentiating
prisoners, mass release, and even reeducation continued throughout the
system's history. The early 1930s saw the initial restriction on the publication of criminal statistics in the open press.[1] Prisoner transports were
hidden as "special equipment." Prisoner correspondence was severely re-
stricted. Released prisoners signed secrecy agreements forbidding them to
talk about the camps. Nobody could enter regions like Kolyma without
special entrance permits. After 1936, the continued existence of criminality was an embarrassment for a polity that explained such problems
in terms of the social milieu. A crossroads had been reached in 1936,
when the adoption of the Stalin constitution was accompanied by the announcement that socialism had been built. The Soviet Union, though not
a classless society, was now in official parlance a socialist state of workers and peasants. The class enemy had officially been destroyed. Consequently, capitalism could no longer offer a legitimate excuse for crime,
and the Soviet penal system became notably less compromising toward
enemies and lawbreakers. The years of the Great Terror saw a massive
number of executions inside and outside the Gulag, as many of those who
had failed to prove their rehabilitation during the transition period were
annihilated.[2]

Meanwhile, massive additions were made to the Gulag population. In
accord with the declaration in 1936 that the Soviet Union was a state
comprised of two nonantagonistic classes, the categorization of Soviet
enemies increasingly turned from the terms of class toward those of nation. Although the focus on class identities never disappeared, the path
was cleared for a major wave of ethnonational group deportations that
would continue right through the war. The exile in 1937 of the Far Eastern Soviet Koreans, though not the first ethnic deportation, did offer the
first instance in which an entire undifferentiated national group was deported from a particular territory. The deportation of the Soviet Koreans
provided an example for the coming wartime exile of entire nationalities,
when, among others, every last German, Chechen, Ingush, and Crimean
Tatar was subject to internal exile regardless of their geographic location
or class position in the Soviet Union.

The war represented another crossroads. In addition to the exile of
entire nationalities, the annexations in 1939–40 of western Ukraine,

western Belorussia, and the Baltic states changed the face of the Gulag. These Westerners entered the Gulag with utterly different life experiences. They had never been exposed to socialism in power, and carried with them the living memory of different systems of government and different penal institutions. The years 1941 and 1942 saw the largest prisoner releases at any time other than the post-Stalin amnesties. Around one million inmates sentenced for relatively minor crimes, especially violations of the harsh labor laws of 1940, were released into the Red Army during those years. The criminal past of these soldiers did not prevent a number of them from earning orders and medals for their deeds during the war. Not all inmates could join the Red Army, however. While some prisoners were released during the war, the suspect counterrevolutionary ones were further isolated and forced to try to endure through the deadliest years in the Gulag's history. They were also excluded from the broad postwar amnesties. A small subsection of political prisoners, the so-called especially dangerous state criminals, were subjected to a new type of severe isolation in the harshest climatic conditions, performing the most dangerous labor in the katorga camp subdivisions. The onset of war also intensified the division among nationalities in the Gulag, particularly for the German prisoners, who unsurprisingly found themselves harassed by both camp authorities and fellow prisoners.

Two new postwar prisoner contingents reshaped Gulag society. First, the arrest of many thousands of Red Army veterans introduced a new and often-prestigious element into the camps. Just as veterans gained respect, prestige, and positions of leadership in Soviet society, so they did in the Gulag. Their firsthand experience with the standards of life outside Soviet borders, along with an assertiveness and sense of entitlement earned on the battlefield, rendered these postwar inmates less docile than their prewar predecessors. The second postwar contingent was even more assertive and combative. These prisoners from among the nationalist organizations and partisan armies of the western territories and the Baltic states brought to the Gulag a strong sense of national identity, well-developed and explicitly anti-Soviet ideologies, and combat experience fighting Soviet power against overwhelming odds. Both Red Army veterans and the nationalist guerrillas played substantial leadership roles during the mass Gulag strikes of the 1950s.

The late 1940s held no indication that the next decade would see the radical shrinkage of the Gulag. Rather, the Gulag regime of the late Stalin era underwent a certain rigidification. In 1948, new special camps were created to hold a much-expanded group of so-called especially dangerous state criminals. For the first time, many political prisoners were largely isolated from the Gulag's regular criminal population. Their isolation led to a new political consciousness that would be a strong contributing factor to the post-Stalin strikes. The postwar period also saw the application of permanent, lifelong exile to all those nationalities deported during the war, and the permanent deportation of all those prisoners released from the special camps.

Stalin's death heralded major changes in the Gulag system. Long troubled by the economic inefficiency of the system and the overwhelming presence of the most petty of criminals among its population, the new post-Stalin leadership made immediate moves toward releasing these petty thieves and reducing the size of the institutions substantially. Within three weeks of Stalin's death, the first major amnesty was declared, releasing those prisoners deemed the least dangerous to the state. The partial nature of the amnesty, especially its near-total exclusion of political prisoners, touched off a wave of prisoner uprisings of a size and scope unprecedented in Gulag history. Soon after the strikes and as a result of Khrushchev's political steps toward de-Stalinization, the Gulag's political prisoners and its exiles were released almost in their entirety. By the end of the 1950s, the Gulag as the massive phenomenon containing millions of prisoners and exiles had come to an end.

The system took a terrible toll on Soviet society, with victims numbering into the millions, and even those who survived often crushed by the experience. Yet after Stalin, the Soviet state decisively moved away from the use of mass terror as a normal, permanent feature of the political system. The state would, of course, engage in numerous incidents of violence and political repression in its final thirty-five years, from the bloody suppression of uprisings within its borders and the countries of the Warsaw Pact, to the use of labor camps and psychoprisons to devastate the small but vocal human rights dissident movements of the Brezhnev years. Nonetheless, the Gulag never reemerged as the mammoth complex of its heyday.

# NOTES

## INTRODUCTION

1. Aleksandr I. Solzhenitsyn, *The Gulag Archipelago, 1918–1956: An Experiment in Literary Investigation*, trans. Thomas P. Whitney (New York: Harper Perennial, 1991), 1:582.

2. Alexander Dolgun with Patrick Watson, *Alexander Dolgun's Story: An American in the Gulag* (New York: Knopf, 1975), 164. Of course, Nazi camps were also known for greeting new prisoners with music—only one of many comparisons that can be made between the two systems. For more on this comparison, see Steven A. Barnes, "Soviet Society Confined: The Gulag in the Karaganda Region of Kazakhstan, 1930s–1950s" (PhD diss., Stanford University, 2003).

3. Gulag is actually an acronym for Glavnoe Upravlenie Lagerei (Main Administration of the Camps), a particular Soviet central bureaucratic institution responsible for running the concentration camp system. Here and throughout the book, I have opted to use the term in its broadest sense, common since the publication of Solzhenitsyn's works, as shorthand for the entire Soviet penal detention system, including everything from prisons to labor camps and colonies to internal exile.

4. Anne Applebaum has done a good job of sifting through historians' best understanding of the Gulag's overall demographic figures. By their nature, the numbers will always be somewhat imprecise, but it is unlikely that they are off by orders of magnitude. See Anne Applebaum, *Gulag: A History* (New York: Doubleday, 2003), 578–88. For execution figures, see V. P. Popov, "Gosudarstvennyi terror v sovetskoi Rossii, 1923–1953 gg. (istochniki i ikh interpretatsiia)," *Otechestvennye Arkhivy*, no. 2 (1992): 20–31.

5. The phrase comes from Robert Conquest, *Kolyma: The Arctic Death Camps* (New York: Viking Press, 1978).

6. On this point, see Leona Toker, *Return from the Archipelago: Narratives of Gulag Survivors* (Bloomington: Indiana University Press, 2000), 3.

7. For a sample of this, the project of the Hoover Institution Archives and the State Archive of the Russian Federation to microfilm the central Gulag archive came to more than 1.5 million frames. (These materials are now available at the Hoover Institution Archives and in several other libraries.) Numerous volumes of central administrative Gulag documents have been published in collections and are used extensively throughout this book. The archives in Karaganda include individual prisoner files and administrative materials related to the camps there, and number hundreds of thousands of pages. I have put a number of the documents used in this book on the archive of the *Gulag: Many Days, Many Lives* Web site, available at http://gulaghistory.org, under "Karlag documents" or "Karaganda." An Italian Web site created by Moscow's Memorial Society and the Fondazione Giangiacomo Feltrinelli, available at http://www.gulag-italia.it/gulag/frameset_biblio_generale.html, has a bibliography of nearly six hundred

published Gulag memoirs. The Moscow Memorial Society lists some three hundred unpublished memoirs in its collection; see http://memo.ru/history/memories/index.htm. Orlando Figes has also put a portion of the hundreds of interviews and family archives related to the terror and Gulag that he and the Memorial Societies of Moscow, Perm, and Saint Petersburg gathered online; see http://orlandofiges.com/index.php.

8. This has been most strongly and recently argued by Orlando Figes, who offers up oral testimony as a preferable source for the subjective experience of terror and camps. He writes that oral testimonies, on the whole, are more reliable than literary memoirs, which have usually been seen as a more authentic record of the past. Like all memory, the testimony given in an interview is unreliable, but, unlike a book, it can be cross-examined and tested against other evidence to disentangle true memories from received or imagined ones." Orlando Figes, *The Whisperers: Private Life in Stalin's Russia* (New York: Metropolitan Books, 2007), 636–37. Figes is off base here, though, as memoirs are also subject to cross-examination and testing through the use of complementary sources—both official and unofficial—to verify their accounts. Of course, Figes makes precisely such careful use of published and unpublished memoirs throughout his text. Although J. Arch Getty is well known for his critique of the use of memoir sources, he does not recommend their dismissal entirely. Rather, he encourages a critical approach to their use, and dismisses those memoirs that opine on aspects of high politics through second- and thirdhand accounts or rumors, and were treated uncritically by some early scholars of the terror. Speaking of camp memoirs in particular, Getty notes, "They can tell us what the camps were like but not why they existed." J. Arch Getty, *Origins of the Great Purges: The Soviet Communist Party Reconsidered, 1933–1938* (Cambridge: Cambridge University Press, 1985), 213. It is precisely for that "what the camps were like" that memoirs are used in the present study.

9. Toker, *Return from the Archipelago*, 6–8.

10. This differs at different points in time, but the most notable influences are the publications of Solzhenitsyn, the *samizdat* (underground) circulation of manuscripts, and the writings of Varlam Shalamov and others. On this point, I agree with Figes, but it is still a solvable problem through the use of multiple types of sources. See Figes, *The Whisperers*, 634–36.

11. On recent neuroscience research that reveals "that we alter our memories just by remembering them," see Kathleen McGowan, "How Much of Your Memory Is True," *Discover Magazine*, July–August 2009, available at http://discovermagazine.com/2009/jul-aug/03-how-much-of-your-memory-is-true (accessed September 4, 2009). McGowan observes that "until recently, long-term memories were thought to be physically etched into our brain, permanent and unchanging. Now it is becoming clear that memories are surprisingly vulnerable and highly dynamic. . . . Already it corrodes our trust in what we know and how we know it. It pokes holes in eyewitness testimony, in memoirs, in our most intimate records of truth. Every time we remember, it seems, we add new details, shade the facts, prune and tweak. Without realizing it, we continually rewrite the stories of our lives. Memory, it turns out, has a surprising amount in common with imagination, conjuring worlds that never existed until they were forged by our minds."

12. See especially chapter 6 on the Kengir uprising, which Solzhenitsyn discussed in significant detail; most of his findings are now confirmed by official documentation to which he had no access.

13. Based on a study of criminal statistics, Popov contends that "a new stage of terror accompanied each stage in the development of a new power, representing in fact the planned extermination of various social structures and groups." Popov, "Gosudarstvennyi terror v sovetskoi Rossii," 29–30. While it will become clear below that I disagree with the characterization of the Soviet penal system as solely an instrument of annihilation, Popov is right to emphasize the direct tie between developments in the penal system and the broader course of Soviet history.

## CHAPTER 1: THE ORIGINS, FUNCTIONS, AND INSTITUTIONS OF THE GULAG

1. Even works from critics of these early studies continue to examine Soviet penal policy without reference to life inside the camps themselves. See Gábor Tamás Rittersporn, *Stalinist Simplifications and Soviet Complications: Social Tensions and Political Conflicts in the USSR* (Chur, Switzerland: Harwood Academic Publishers, 1991), 237.

2. David J. Dallin and Boris I. Nicolaevsky, *Forced Labor in Soviet Russia* (New Haven, CT: Yale University Press, 1947), ix. For a lengthy discussion of the Gulag in historical comparison with slave-holding economies throughout history and around the world, see especially ibid., 88–107. For other accounts that tie the Gulag's growth to rapid industrialization, see Edwin Bacon, *The Gulag at War: Stalin's Forced Labour System in the Light of the Archives* (London: Macmillan, 1994); James R. Harris, "The Growth of the Gulag: Forced Labor in the Urals Region, 1929–1931," *Russian Review* 56 (April 1997) 265–80; Orlando Figes, *The Whisperers: Private Life in Stalin's Russia* (New York: Metropolitan Books, 2007), 111–12. Applebaum treads this well-established ground, noting that "the primary purpose of the Gulag, according to both the private language and the public propaganda of those who founded it, was economic." While she recognizes that Soviet forced labor camps were inefficient and unprofitable, she argues that they were "*perceived* to be profitable." Anne Applebaum, *Gulag: A History* (New York: Doubleday, 2003), xxxviii, 54. Meanwhile, David J. Nordlander, in his archival-based study of Kolyma, maintains that the economic factor was primary in the early 1930s while the political factor—the elimination of "enemies"—assumed prominence in the latter 1930s. David J. Nordlander, "Capital of the Gulag: Magadan in the Early Stalin Era, 1929–1941" (PhD diss., University of North Carolina at Chapel Hill, 1997); see also "Origins of a Gulag Capital: Magadan and Stalinist Control in the Early 1930s," *Slavic Review* 57, no. 4 (Winter 1998): 791–812. Applebaum follows Nordlander in her interpretation of the later 1930s, although she believes that economics returned to the fore after the Great Terror of 1937–38.

3. See, for example, the conclusions in Iurii Nikolaevich Afanas'ev, et al., eds., *Istoriia stalinskogo Gulaga: Konets 1920-kh–pervaia polovina 1950-kh godov: Sobranie dokumentov v semi tomakh* (Moscow: Rosspen, 2004), 1:54–55. While

each volume of *Istoriia stalinskogo Gulaga* carries a separate title, I will refer in the notes to the general name and volume number.

4. Applebaum, *Gulag*, 56. The fixation on Stalin—at times assuming the role of historical mind reader—and the assumption that no other individual or institutional interest in the Soviet Union had the capacity to shape the Gulag, is prevalent throughout the book.

5. Robert Conquest, *The Great Terror: A Reassessment* (New York: Oxford University Press, 1990), 333. Conquest, of course, does not deny the economic uses of the prisoners, and he too equates them with slaves. The economic factor was secondary, however; internment and death was primary. As he writes, "A man killed by squeezing a year or two's effort out of him is of more use than a man kept in prison." Ibid., 333. In his more recent introduction to *Istoriia stalinskogo Gulaga*, Conquest's stance seems to have changed somewhat. "The Gulag itself, and comparable institutions, was designed with two main objectives—the penal isolation of the victims, and their use as slave labor in Soviet economic projects. Both aims were always kept in mind, but at times one or the other predominated." Yet it remains that "the whole terror operations can, in fact, be understood as a conscious effort, on what were seen as Marxist grounds, to eliminate or crush all those categorized as unamenable to the new order." Afanas'ev, et al., *Istoriia stalinskogo Gulaga*, 1:30.

6. Conquest, *The Great Terror*, 338.

7. Ibid., 339. As we will see below, the assumption that releases from the Gulag were "very rare" was one of the major mistakes of the first generation of Gulag historians. The reason for this mistake will be explored later. Nevertheless, the work of Conquest, Dallin, and Nicolaevsky is particularly impressive given that it was completed not only prior to the opening of the archives but prior to the publication of Solzhenitsyn's magnum opus as well.

8. Rittersporn develops a lengthy critique of Solzhenitsyn's work, describing his history as "a series of rumours ... which then developed into an oral tradition and put down deep roots into the collective consciousness." Thus, he views Solzhenitsyn's work (and by implication the work of other Gulag memoirists) as a "mixture—and often an inextricable one—of indisputable facts and of their trace, sometimes very imprecise or distorted, preserved by a collective memory that has been more concerned about elevating a memorial to the martyrdom of its guardians then [sic] with the authenticity of its traditions." Rittersporn, *Stalinist Simplifications*, 16. My research reveals the bankruptcy of such a notion. Solzhenitsyn, as will be seen repeatedly, was right much more often than he was wrong, and now the availability of official sources allows the confirmation of many of his findings. Rittersporn's dismissal of Solzhenitsyn significantly weakens his own work. The unwillingness to wade through Solzhenitsyn's work to find its contributions leaves an analysis seriously flawed by its deliberate inattention to the conditions of life in the Gulag. Soviet penal practice simply cannot be fully understood with an exclusive focus on legal codes and official documentation.

9. The accuracy of Solzhenitsyn's presentation of the Kengir uprising in 1954, discussed at length in chapter 6, is particularly impressive.

10. Aleksandr I. Solzhenitsyn, *The Gulag Archipelago, 1918–1956: An Experiment in Literary Investigation*, trans. Thomas P. Whitney (New York: Harper Perennial, 1991), 1:174.

11. One of the few works to seek a broad approach to the subject is Applebaum's Pulitzer Prize–winning *Gulag*. While important for drawing the attention of the educated reading audience to the Gulag, Applebaum's book is of limited use to scholars. Her use of archives is so unsystematic that the book is more valuable for its cataloging of memoir testimony than for its few archival notations. Furthermore, Applebaum has added little to the well-established debate on the Gulag's origins and significance, and ultimately offers little more than Solzhenitsyn did some thirty years earlier. Scholars working on the Gulag have largely limited their work either chronologically, or to a single type or even a single Gulag institution. As will be shown below, in order to fully understand the Gulag, one must look at all its variety of institutions.

12. Oleg Khlevniuk, *The History of the Gulag: From Collectivization to the Great Terror*, trans. Vadim A. Staklo, ed. David J. Nordlander (New Haven, CT: Yale University Press, 2004).

13. Lynne Viola, *The Unknown Gulag: The Lost World of Stalin's Special Settlements* (New York: Oxford University Press, 2007).

14. A portion of this extensive work includes: Nicholas Baron, "Conflict and Complicity: The Expansion of the Karelian Gulag, 1923–1933," *Cahiers du Monde russe* 42, nos. 2–4 (2001): 615–48; "Production and Terror: The Operation of the Karelian Gulag, 1933–1939," *Cahiers du Monde russe* 43, no. 1 (2002): 139–80; Nordlander, "Capital of the Gulag"; "Origins of a Gulag Capital"; Nicolas Werth, *Cannibal Island: Death in a Siberian Gulag* (Princeton, NJ: Princeton University Press, 2007); Viktor Berdinskikh, *Istoriia odnogo lageria (Viatlag)* (Moscow: Agraf, 2001); Liubov' Gvozdkova, *Prinuditel'nyi trud. Ispravitel'no-trudovye lageriakh v Kuzbasse (30–50-e gg.)*, 2 vols. (Kemerovo: Kuzbassvuzizdat, 1994); V. M. Kirillov, *Istoriia repressii v Nizhnetagil'skom regione Urala. 1920-e–nachalo 50-kh gg. Tom 1: Repressii 1920–1930-kh gg., tom 2: Tagillag 1940-e–nach. 50-kh gg.* (Nizhnii Tagil: Nizhnetagil'skii gosudarstvennyi pedagogicheskii institut, 1996); Sergei Aleksandrovich Krasil'nikov, *Serp i molokh. Krest'ianskaia ssylka v Zapadnoi Sibiri v 1930-e gg.* (Moscow: Rosspen, 2003); Ol'ga Aleksandrovna Nikitina, *Kollektivizatsiia i raskulachivanie v Karelii* (Petrozavodsk: Karel'skii Nauchnyi tsentr RAN, 1997); Viktor Iakovlevich Shashkov, *Repressii v SSSR protiv krest'ian i sud'by spetspereselentsev Karelo-Murmanskogo kraia* (Murmansk: IPP "Sever," 2000); Nikolai Alekseevich Morozov, *Gulag v Komi krae* (Syktyvkar: Izd-vo Syktyvkarskogo Universiteta, 1997); S. A. Pankov, "Lagernaia sistema i prinuditel'nyi trud v Sibiri i na Dal'nem vostoke 1929–1941 gg.," in *Vozvrashchenie pamiati. Istoriko-publitsisticheskii al'manakh. Vyp. 3*, ed. Irina Vladimirovna Pavlova (Novosibirsk: Novosibirskoe knizhnoe izdatel'stvo, 1997), 37–67.

15. Paul R. Gregory and Valerii Vasil'evich Lazarev, eds., *The Economics of Forced Labor: The Soviet Gulag* (Stanford, CA: Hoover Institution Press, 2003). See also Leonid I. Borodkin, Paul Gregory, and Oleg V. Khlevniuk, eds., *GULAG: Ekonomika prinuditel'nogo truda* (Moscow: Rosspen, 2008).

16. J. Arch Getty, Gábor Tamás Rittersporn, and Viktor N. Zemskov, "Victims of the Soviet Penal System in the Pre-war Years: A First Approach on the Basis of Archival Evidence," *American Historical Review* (October 1993): 1017–49. The critical question of which inmates were released is not addressed in this statistics-driven piece based primarily on the research accomplished by Zemskov in the late 1980s and early 1990s. For Zemskov's work, see the various articles cited herein along with Viktor N. Zemskov, *Spetsposelentsy v SSSR* (Moscow: Nauka, 2005). The characterization of the Gulag's door as a revolving one has been pursued not only in my own work but also in Golfo Alexopoulos, "Amnesty 1945: The Revolving Door of Stalin's Gulag," *Slavic Review* 64, no. 2 (2005): 274–306.

17. Hannah Arendt, *The Origins of Totalitarianism* (Cleveland: Meridian Books, 1958), 468–72. Also significant here is Michael Walzer's use of the term: "The power of an ideology . . . lies in its capacity to activate its adherents and to change the world. Its content is necessarily a description of contemporary experience as unacceptable and unnecessary and a rejection of any merely personal transcendence or salvation. Its practical effect is to generate organization and co-operative activity." Michael Walzer, *The Revolution of the Saints: A Study in the Origins of Radical Politics* (New York: Atheneum, 1972), 27. Michael David-Fox usefully describes ideology as "outlooks deriving from disseminated doctrine," and understands it not as a "discrete variable or factor" but rather as "a more diffuse phenomenon." Michael David-Fox, "On the Primacy of Ideology: Soviet Revisionists and Holocaust Deniers (in Response to Martin Malia)," *Kritika: Explorations in Russian and Eurasian History* 5, no. 1 (2004): 103.

18. Bacon, *The Gulag at War*, 47.

19. David-Fox, "On the Primacy of Ideology," 104.

20. Maksim Gorky, Leopol'd Auerbach, and Semen Firin, eds., *Belomor: An Account of the Construction of the New Canal between the White Sea and the Baltic Sea*, trans. Amabel Williams-Ellis (New York: H. Smith and R. Haas, 1935).

21. The key work on *Belomor* is Cynthia Ruder, *Making History for Stalin: The Story of the Belomor Canal* (Gainesville: University Press of Florida, 1998). See also Solzhenitysn and Applebaum, among others, for expressions of moral outrage at this whitewashing of history. For a particularly enlightening commentary on the volume, and in particular on the relationship of the famed Soviet writer Konstantin Simonov and the construction of the canal, see Figes, *The Whisperers*, 192–207.

22. For an enlightening argument on the relationship between circumstances and ideology in historiographical considerations of the Soviet period, see David-Fox, "On the Primacy of Ideology."

23. Soviet authorities used the term kulak for the peasantry's "class enemy"—officially, the "rich" peasants. The term was applied quite broadly to potential opponents of the collectivization of agriculture in the late 1920s and early 1930s, when the Soviet government embarked on "the destruction of the kulaks as a class," sending millions into internal exile or to other institutions of the Gulag. For the classic statements on the Soviet meaning of the term kulak and peasants resistance against the term, see Moshe Lewin, "Who Was the Soviet Kulak?" in *The Making of the Soviet System: Essays in the Social History of Interwar Russia*

(New York: New Press, 1994), 121–41; Viola, *The Unknown Gulag*; *Peasant Rebels under Stalin: Collectivization and the Culture of Peasant Resistance* (New York: Oxford University Press, 1998).

24. Solzhenitsyn, *The Gulag Archipelago*, 2:9.

25. Aspects of this transformative vision of politics can be traced back at least to the Calvinists in European history. On the Calvinists break with ways of thinking based on the Great Chain of Being, see Walzer, *The Revolution of the Saints*. It should be emphasized again that the roots of many individual characteristics of modernity can be traced deeply into the historical past. Nonetheless, modernity as a fundamentally new compilation of characteristics into a coherent, new epistemology can be traced to the nineteenth and twentieth centuries. Arendt also recognized this "tremendous intellectual change which took place in the middle of the last century ... the refusal to view or accept anything 'as it is' and in the consistent interpretation of everything as being only a stage of some further development." Arendt, *The Origins of Totalitarianism*, 464.

26. The emergence of modernity occupies an important place in a broad range of European historiography. For the intellectual roots of the above discussion, see especially James C. Scott, *Seeing Like a State: How Certain Schemes to Improve the Human Condition Have Failed* (New Haven, CT: Yale University Press, 1998); Michel Foucault, *Discipline and Punish: The Birth of the Prison* (New York: Vintage Books, 1977); David G. Horn, *Social Bodies: Science, Reproduction, and Italian Modernity* (Princeton, NJ: Princeton University Press, 1994), especially 18–34; Arendt, *The Origins of Totalitarianism*; Zygmunt Bauman, *Modernity and the Holocaust* (Ithaca, NY: Cornell University Press, 1989); Wolfgang Sofsky, *The Order of Terror: The Concentration Camp* (Princeton, NJ: Princeton University Press, 1997); Amir Weiner, ed., *Landscaping the Human Garden: Twentieth-Century Population Management in a Comparative Framework* (Stanford, CA: Stanford University Press, 2003). For modernity in the Soviet context, see especially Stephen Kotkin, *Magnetic Mountain: Stalinism as a Civilization* (Berkeley: University of California Press, 1995); Weiner, *Landscaping the Human Garden*, 1–18; Peter Holquist, "State Violence as Technique: The Logic of Violence in Soviet Totalitarianism," in *Landscaping the Human Garden: Twentieth-Century Population Management in a Comparative Framework*, ed. Amir Weiner (Stanford, CA: Stanford University Press, 2003), 19–45; David L. Hoffmann, *Stalinist Values: The Cultural Norms of Soviet Modernity* (Ithaca, NY: Cornell University Press, 2003); David L. Hoffman and Yanni Kotsonis, eds., *Russian Modernity: Politics, Knowledge, Practices* (New York: Palgrave Macmillan, 2000; Daniel Beer, *Renovating Russia: The Human Sciences and the Fate of Liberal Modernity, 1880–1930* (Ithaca, NY: Cornell University Press, 2008).

27. From Gorky, Auerbach, and Firin, *Belomor*, we learn that "there were still enemies within the new world" (19).

28. It is quite interesting that Solzhenitsyn, despite his radical hatred of the Bolsheviks, himself operates in the same ethos imagining a contaminated society—sure enough contaminated by the Bolsheviks themselves as opposed to the class enemy, but contaminated nonetheless. "What kind of disastrous path lies ahead of us if we do not have the chance to purge ourselves of that putrefaction rotting inside our body?" The similarities between Solzhenitsyn and the

Bolsheviks continue: "We have the duty to *seek them all out and bring them all to trial!* Not to put them on trial so much as their crimes. And to compel each one of them to announce loudly: 'Yes, I was an executioner and a murderer.'" Solzhenitsyn, *The Gulag Archipelago*, 1:176–77.

29. I have adopted the translation in Robert Service, *Stalin: A Biography* (Cambridge, MA: Belknap Press of Harvard University Press, 2005) 273. The same quote appears with a slightly different translation in Gorky, Auerbach, and Firin, *Belomor*, 18.

30. Igal Halfin captured the Bolshevik spirit of violence in the name of utopia: "Communists ended up committing bloody deeds they hardly expected would follow from the lofty principles they thought shaped their project. The dream of universal emancipation spun out of control precisely because those who dreamed of 'human perfectability' or 'classless society' never imagined that a vision so perfect, so utopian, could embrace slaughter and systematic persecution. But once entrenched in the tissue of power, messianic dreams that structured the Communist discourse and provided it a frame of moral reference that set standards of conformity could not be easily curbed, even when some of their horrific implications asserted themselves with a vengeance." Igal Halfin, *Terror in My Soul: Communist Autobiographies on Trial* (Cambridge, MA: Harvard University Press, 2003), 6.

31. Gorky, Auerbach, and Firin, *Belomor*, 37.

32. Ibid., 338.

33. Ibid. quotes Stalin's reference to writers as the "engineers of the soul" (337). Reforging was generally the preferred term for the work of the Gulag. Shock workers at Belomor had their portraits made and hung in the camp bearing the decisive caption: "Reforged." Ibid., 153. Reforging was also the most popular name for newspapers in the corrective labor camps. On humans as material, see ibid., 151.

34. On the use of engineering and surgical metaphors in Gulag memoirs, see Leona Toker, *Return from the Archipelago: Narratives of Gulag Survivors* (Bloomington: Indiana University Press, 2000), 35.

35. On the relationship between Bolshevik visions and the early formation of the Gulag, see the prearchival but fantastic study in Michael Jakobson, *Origins of the Gulag: The Soviet Prison-Camp System, 1917–1934* (Lexington: University Press of Kentucky, 1993). It was believed that the failure to combat bourgeois influences would lead to the corruption of the proletariat, like engineer K. M. Zubrik at Belomor, "the classic story of the proletarian who is tempted by bourgeois culture and who makes bourgeois ideology his own, together with the knowledge he receives in the bourgeois school." Ibid., 163.

36. On Soviet state violence as more than merely repressive, see Holquist, "State Violence as Technique."

37. Quoted in Solzhenitsyn, *The Gulag Archipelago*, 2:144–45.

38. Kotkin, *Magnetic Mountain*, 75.

39. Gorky, Auerbach, and Firin, *Belomor*, 256.

40. Not even the "small peoples of the north" remained marginal during the Soviet era. See Yuri Slezkine, *Arctic Mirrors: Russia and the Small Peoples of the North* (Ithaca, NY: Cornell University Press, 1994). On the inclusion of every

individual in modern state projects for refashioning society, see Weiner, *Landscaping the Human Garden*, 2.

41. "Stakhanovskoe dvizhenie–Marksizm v deistvii," *Putevka*, January 21, 1936, plate 429, in *The GULAG Press, 1920–1937* (Leiden, Netherlands: IDC Publishers, 2000).

42. Cited in Solzhenitsyn, *The Gulag Archipelago*, 2:67.

43. Ibid., 2:13.

44. Eugenia Ginzburg, *Within the Whirlwind* (New York: Harcourt Brace Jovanovich, 1981), 24.

45. On the Marxist understanding of labor as the key feature of humanity, see Leszek Kolakowski, *Main Currents of Marxism: Its Rise, Growth, and Dissolution, Volume I: The Founders*, trans. Paul S. Falla (Oxford: Clarendon Press, 1978) 133–34. In the context of the Gulag, see Gorky, Auerbach, and Firin, *Belomor*, 340: "Man has developed throughout his mammalian history; he is human in as far as he is a worker, so when he is put into conditions which allow free development of his various abilities, it is natural for him to begin unconsciously to accept his real calling."

46. Ibid., 244.

47. Solzhenitsyn's work was far more complex than many of his readers thought. While he clearly understood the array of institutions, readers have often reduced his work and, thus, their concept of the Gulag to the labor camp alone.

48. V. P. Popov, "Gosudarstvennyi terror v sovetskoi Rossii, 1923–1953 gg. (istochniki i ikh interpretatsiia)," *Otechestvennye Arkhivy*, no. 2 (1992): 20–31.

49. For some of the protocols allowing for an increase in quotas, see Afanas'ev, et al., *Istoriia stalinskogo Gulaga*, 1:290–93.

50. See Solzhenitsyn, *The Gulag Archipelago*, 1:185. The ideal situation in the eyes of Soviet authorities was the maintenance of interrogation prison inmates in solitary confinement. Periods of mass arrest rendered this impossible. Yet even in such times, they attempted to negate as far as possible any contact of the prisoner with the outside world.

51. Ibid., 1:478.

52. Cited in Afanas'ev, et al., *Istoriia stalinskogo Gulaga*, 1:270.

53. Cited in Solzhenitsyn, *The Gulag Archipelago*, 3:289.

54. Eugenia Ginzburg, *Journey into the Whirlwind* (New York: Harcourt, Brace and World, 1967), 211. In the text, I chose to use Eugenia rather than the proper Evgeniia for her first name given its wide English usage since the translated publication of her memoirs.

55. Ibid., 206, 209, 214.

56. Ibid., 280.

57. Ibid., 348.

58. See Arkhivnyi Otdel Tsentra Pravovoi Statistiki i Informatsii pri Prokurature Karagandinskoi Oblasti (Archive Department of the Center for Legal Statistics and Information under the Procurator of the Karaganda Region; hereafter AOTsPSI), Karaganda, fond (f.) Karlaga, sviazka (sv.) 2, delo (d.) 44, list (l.) 15.

59. Quoted in Ginzburg, *Journey into the Whirlwind*, 333. Nikolai Ezhov (sometimes spelled Yezhov) was the people's commissar of internal affairs, or the secret police chief, for the People's Commissariat of Internal Affairs during the

worst years of the Great Terror in 1937–38. His name became synonymous with this dark period.

60. Quoted in ibid., 280.

61. The exact term used to described Soviet internal exiles varied, but *spetspereselentsy* was the most common. I will use the terms "special settlers" and "exiles" interchangeably throughout the text.

62. With the appearance of Viola's *The Unknown Gulag*, the special settlements will likely be increasingly integrated into a consideration of the Gulag in the future.

63. Gosudarstvennyi Arkhiv Rossiiskoi Federatsii (State Archive of the Russian Federation; hereafter GARF), Moscow, f. 9414, opis (op.) 1, d. 28, l. 17.

64. See the report from September 5, 1944, in "Spetspereselentsy v SSSR v 1944 godu ili god bol'shogo pereseleniia," *Otechestvennye arkhivy*, no. 5 (1993): 103.

65. Rachel Rachlin and Israel Rachlin, *Sixteen Years in Siberia* (Tuscaloosa: University of Alabama Press, 1988), 25, 238–40.

66. See the report from October 5, 1932, in Nicolas Werth and Gael Moullec, eds., *Rapports Secrets Sovietiques: La Societe Russe Dans Les Documents Confidentiels, 1921–1991* (Paris: Gallimard, 1994), 369–72.

67. See the 1932 report in Werth and Moullec, *Rapports Secrets*, 358–61; see also another report from 1931 on the unsatisfactory cultural work among the special settlement youths at Magnitostroi, in ibid., 363–66.

68. Rachlin and Rachlin, *Sixteen Years in Siberia*, 31, 34. Some exiles lived in specially constructed special settlements, where exile populations were concentrated and to a certain extent isolated from the surrounding populations. Often, however, they mixed right in with the local population, as did the Rachlins.

69. AOTsPSI, f. Karlaga, sv. 2, d. 43, ll. 18–22.

70. See Werth, *Cannibal Island*.

71. Rachlin and Rachlin, *Sixteen Years in Siberia*, 100. Both Ginzburg and Solzhenitsyn, after their release from camps into exile, also worked as teachers.

72. Ibid., 124, 174.

73. Ibid., 34.

74. Ibid., 44–45, 110–11.

75. Kotkin, *Magnetic Mountain*, 133, 234–35.

76. AOTsPSI, f. Karlaga, sv. 2, d. 43, l. 22.

77. Ibid., sv. 4 URO, d. 32, ll. 47–48.

78. Ibid., sv. 2, d. 43, l. 22.

79. Ibid., sv. 2, d. 21, l. 28. Clearly, the special settlement administration and Kazitlag authorities jousted over their relative responsibilities during this transfer of authority. In July 1931, central Gulag chief Kogan intervened with a five-page, twenty-two-point order laying out the authority and responsibilities of the two organizations. He placed his deputy Naftalii Frenkel' in charge of any further disputes. Ibid., sv. 2, d. 43, ll. 18–22.

80. GARF, f. 9414, op. 1, d. 1154, l. 4. The colony prisoner population in the Kazakh Republic did grow throughout 1940, but it still numbered a relatively small 11,500 in November. Ibid., l. 90.

81. See Kotkin, *Magnetic Mountain*, 134.

82. Ibid., 134, 230–34.

## CHAPTER 2: RECLAIMING THE MARGINS AND THE MARGINAL

1. Militsa Cheslavovna Stefanskaia, *Chernoe i beloe* (Moscow: Suzdalev, 1994), 22.

2. Nauchno-Informatsionnyi i Prosvetitel'skii Tsentr "Memorial" (Scientific Information and Enlightenment Center "Memorial"; hereafter NIPTs), Moscow, f. 2, op. 3, d. 60, memoir of Galina Aleksandrovna Semenova, str. 6, 83–84. (Page numbers are listed according to the pagination of the memoir.)

3. Cited in GARF, f. 9414, op. 2, d. 108, l. 4.

4. Andrei Sergeevich Elagin, A. K. Ivanenko, and B. N. Abisheva, *Karaganda* (Almaty, Kazakhstan: "Nauka" Kazakhskoi SSR, 1989), 5–6; R. N. Nurgaliev, ed., *Karaganda, Karagandinskaia oblast': Entsiklopediia* (Almaty, Kazakhstan: Kazakhskaia sovetskaia entsiklopediia, 1986), 4–6.

5. Galina Mikhailovna Ivanova, *Labor Camp Socialism: The Gulag in the Soviet Totalitarian System*, trans. Carol Flath (Armonk, NY: M. E. Sharpe, 2000), 70–71. Originally published as *Gulag v sisteme totalitarnogo gosudarstva* (Moscow: Moskovskii obshchestvennyi nauchnyi fond, 1997).

6. Mikhail Borisovich Smirnov, *Sistema ispravitel'no-trudovykh lagerei v SSSR 1923–1960: Spravochnik* (Moscow: Zven'ia, 1998), 278–79. Diusetai Aimagambetovich Shaimukhanov and Saule Diusetaevna Shaimukhanova *Karlag* (Karaganda: Poligrafiia, 1997), 15–16, place the amount of land allocated to the camp far lower, at about 110,000 hectares.

7. Cited in GARF, f. 9414, op. 2, d. 108, l. 6.

8. AOTsPSI, f. Karlaga, sv. 2, d. 43, ll. 18–22.

9. On specific mortality rates in Karlag and the camps generally, see below. On the famine in Kazakhstan, see Niccolo Pianciola, "The Collectivization Famine in Kazakhstan, 1931–1933," *Harvard Ukrainian Studies 25*, nos. 3–4 (2001): 237–51; "Famine in the Steppe: The Collectivization of Agriculture and the Kazakh Herdsmen, 1928–1934," *Cahiers du monde russe 45*, nos. 1–2 (2004): 137–92.

10. For the instructions on dismantling Kazitlag, see AOTsPSI, f. Karlaga, sv. 2, d. 43, ll. 45–51. Shaimukhanov and Shaimukhanova *Karlag*, 16, date the transfer from Kazitlag to Karlag as December 1931. All documentary materials relating to Kazitlag were transferred to the Karlag administration and can be found today among the materials at AOTsPSI. On the transfer, see GARF, f. 9414, op. 1, d. 1156, l. 205.

11. Shaimukhanov and Shaimukhanova, *Karlag*, 16.

12. Elagin, et al., *Karaganda*, 5–6.

13. GARF, f. 9414, op. 2, d. 108, l. 5. Prisoners frequently likened the territory of Karlag to the size of France. The porousness of its borders and the geographic separation of one camp division from another make the evaluation of such a statement nearly impossible.

14. Cited in ibid. It is no surprise in this self-promoting work that Karlag summed up its four years as a time of unremitting and persistent struggle, of great victories as well as the actions of Chekist and prisoner heroes.

15. On official conceptions of the steppe as empty and the reality that the steppe was not empty but emptied, see Kate Brown, *A Biography of No Place: From Ethnic Borderland to Soviet Heartland* (Cambridge, MA: Harvard University Press, 2004), 176–77.

16. Cited in GARF, f. 9414, op. 2, d. 108, l. 8.

17. Iurii Nikolaevich Afanas'ev, et al., eds., *Istoriia stalinskogo Gulaga: Konets 1920-kh–pervaia polovina 1950-kh godov: Sobranie dokumentov v semi tomakh* (Moscow: Rosspen, 2004), 3:74–79.

18. Ibid., 3:100–101.

19. Ibid., 3:123–24, 525–26.

20. Ibid., 3:525.

21. Shaimukhanov and Shaimukhanova, *Karlag*, 17–18.

22. Cited in GARF, f. 9414, op. 2, d. 108, ll. 4b–5.

23. Cited in ibid., ll. 4–4b.

24. Afanas'ev, et al., *Istoriia stalinskogo Gulaga*, 1:114–15.

25. Ibid., 115–16.

26. Viola makes this point clearly. See Lynne Viola, *The Unknown Gulag: The Lost World of Stalin's Special Settlements* (New York: Oxford University Press, 2007). On peasant resistance, often including violent resistance, to collectivization, see Lynne Viola, *Peasant Rebels under Stalin: Collectivization and the Culture of Peasant Resistance* (New York: Oxford University Press, 1998).

27. Applebaum points this out, but nevertheless maintains that the camps' growth was primarily economic in nature. Anne Applebaum, *Gulag: A History* (New York: Doubleday, 2003), 56. The point perhaps is made most clearly in Nicolas Werth, *Cannibal Island: Death in a Siberian Gulag* (Princeton, NJ: Princeton University Press, 2007), which reveals the utter devastation wreaked on special settlers due to the complete unpreparedness of local authorities. The same is true in Viola, *The Unknown Gulag*.

28. Oleg Khlevniuk, *The History of the Gulag: From Collectivization to the Great Terror*, trans. Vadim A. Staklo, ed. David J. Nordlander (New Haven, CT: Yale University Press, 2004), 24. This lies at odds with the statement from the editors (one of whom was Khlevniuk himself) in the introduction to *Istoriia stalinskogo Gulaga* that arrests seemed at times driven by political concerns and at other times the Gulag's "economic considerations appeared paramount, such as during the construction of major infrastructure projects in the early 1930s or the return to an economic orientation in 1939 during [Lavrenty] Beria's reforms of 1939, which were closely connected to the growing economic activities of the NKVD." See Afanas'ev, et al., *Istoriia stalinskogo Gulaga*, 1:55. Perhaps this apparent contradiction in Khlevniuk's thinking about the early 1930s is indicative of disagreement among the volume editors. As will become clear throughout the present volume, I believe the history shows that Gulag economic concerns were never the driving factor behind campaigns of arrest.

29. All of these campaigns are covered in ibid., vol. 1. On the passport campaign and the removal of socially dangerous elements, see Paul Hagenloh,

"'Socially Harmful Elements' and the Great Terror," in *Stalinism: New Directions*, ed. Sheila Fitzpatrick (London: Routledge, 2000), 286–308; Paul Hagenloh, *Stalin's Police: Public Order and Mass Repression in the USSR, 1926–1941*, (Washington, DC: Woodrow Wilson Center Press, 2009); Werth, *Cannibal Island*. See also Oleg Khlevnyuk, "The Economy of the Gulag," in *Behind the Façade of Stalin's Command Economy*, ed. Paul R. Gregory (Stanford, CA: Hoover Institution Press, 2001), 113–18. Khlevniuk (the author's surname has been transliterated Khlevnyuk and Khlevniuk in his English publications) even argues that the great number of death sentences handed out in 1937–38 was in part an effect of the critical overcrowding in Gulag camps that rendered the economic use of such large new prisoner populations impossible.

30. Applebaum, to her credit, acknowledges a number of these counterarguments, but attributes most of the rationale to the category of inefficiency in the arrests and contends that "none of these explanations for the growth of the camps is entirely mutually exclusive either." Yet here again, she finds it necessary to return to Stalin as the sole motive force behind the system. See Applebaum, *Gulag*, 56–57.

31. This is from a monograph prepared by Gulag central authorities in 1940 or 1941 about the Gulag's history and practices. GARF, f. 9414, op. 1, d. 28, l. 8. (The monograph contains no archival numbering, so the reference is to the monograph's page numbers.) This was also a primary rule for the internal exile population.

32. Aleksandr I. Solzhenitsyn, *The Gulag Archipelago, 1918–1956: An Experiment in Literary Investigation*, trans. Thomas P. Whitney (New York: Harper Perennial, 1991), 3:8–10.

33. On the latter, see Natalia Kuziakina, *Theatre in the Solovki Prison Camp*, trans. Boris M. Meerovich (Newark, NJ: Harwood Academic Publishers, 1995), 14.

34. Maksim Gorky, Leopol'd Auerbach, and Semen Firin, eds., *Belomor: An Account of the Construction of the New Canal between the White Sea and the Baltic Sea*, trans. Amabel Williams-Ellis (New York: H. Smith and R. Haas, 1935), 20–21. This slogan frequently appeared in camp propaganda in the form of posters, wall newspapers, and newspapers in general, and it even adorned the camp gates.

35. Edward Buca, *Vorkuta* (London: Constable, 1976), 140.

36. Solzhenitsyn, *The Gulag Archipelago*, 2:106.

37. Andrei Vyshinsky, ed., *Ot tiurem k vospitatel'nym uchrezdeniiam* (Moscow: Gosudarstvennoe izdatel'stvo Sovetskoe zakonodatel'stvo, 1934), quoted in Solzhenitsyn, *The Gulag Archipelago*, 2:13.

38. Quoted in Solzhenitsyn, *The Gulag Archipelago*, 2:14.

39. Gorky, Auerbach, and Firin, *Belomor*, 104. "By March, 1932, the basic camp population in the fourth division knew what part of the work it was doing, why this work was being done, and what would happen when the whole construction was finished. And this, of course, could not but show first and foremost, in the work itself. The productivity of labour rose. People worked more eagerly, and in a more comradely spirit." Ibid., 175. Notice that work is measured not only in the productivity of labor but also in the attitude of the laborer.

40. Gorky, Auerbach, and Firin, *Belomor* relates the story of one Belomor prisoner who had performed the labor of Sing Sing, but he was only redeemed in a Soviet labor camp. Ibid., 207. Of course, the White Sea–Baltic Sea Canal was ultimately of so little value that its prisoner laborers accomplished little more than the Sing Sing prisoner.

41. For one particularly strong argument in this vein, see Edwin Bacon, *The Gulag at War: Stalin's Forced Labour System in the Light of the Archives* (London: Macmillan, 1994), 78. See also Applebaum, *Gulag*, 185, 221, 231–41.

42. The classic statement on the politicization of labor in Stalin's Soviet Union is Stephen Kotkin, *Magnetic Mountain: Stalinism as a Civilization* (Berkeley: University of California Press, 1995).

43. Hannah Arendt, *The Origins of Totalitarianism* (Cleveland: Meridian Books, 1958), 430.

44. Afanas'ev, et al., *Istoriia stalinskogo Gulaga*, 1:54.

45. Applebaum, *Gulag*, 29. This work further shows that Solovetskii's supposed economic success in the later 1920s under Naftalii Frenkel was an illusion, even if many believed it. Ibid., 35.

46. Ivanova, *Gulag v sisteme*, 102.

47. Ibid., 125.

48. Sergei A. Krasil'nikov, ed., "Rozhdenie Gulaga: Diskussiia v verkhnykh eshelonakh vlasti," *Istoricheskii arkhiv* 4 (1997): 142–56.

49. For an example of this argument, see Applebaum, *Gulag*.

50. Cited in AOTsPSI, f. Karlaga, sv. 2, d. 43, l. 10.

51. Applebaum, *Gulag*, 89, drawing on Ginzburg's shock and admiration at the rapid growth of the city of Magadan. For the classic statement on extending the revolution to the remote regions of the union, see Yuri Slezkine, *Arctic Mirrors: Russia and the Small Peoples of the North* (Ithaca, NY: Cornell University Press, 1994).

52. This does not, of course, mean that mass cases of prisoner and exile death would not be investigated. See, for example, Werth, *Cannibal Island*. Nonetheless, it seems clear that excessive deaths would never be a reason to slow down the Gulag's growth or operation.

53. AOTsPSI, f. Karlaga, sv. 4 URO, d. 32, ll. 9–25.

54. Bardach's memoir of his experience in the Kolyma camps was written long after he became a renowned medical school professor in the United States. The memoir is frequently remarkable for its willingness to discuss topics that Russian memoirists shy away from, including, as we will see, homosexual rape and a more sympathetic rendering of professional criminal inmates. See Janusz Bardach and Kathleen Gleeson, *Man Is Wolf to Man: Surviving the Gulag* (Berkeley: University of California Press, 1998). In addition, with the publication of his second volume, *Surviving Freedom*, Bardach explores his life after the Gulag—a topic rarely covered by Russian memoirists. Janusz Bardach and Kathleen Gleeson, *Surviving Freedom: After the Gulag* (Berkeley: University of California Press, 2003). On the limitations of topics in Gulag memoirs, see Leona Toker, *Return from the Archipelago: Narratives of Gulag Survivors* (Bloomington: Indiana University Press, 2000).

55. See especially Elena Osokina, *Our Daily Bread: Socialist Distribution and the Art of Survival in Stalin's Russia, 1927–1941*, trans. Greta Bucher, ed. Kate S. Transchel (Armonk, NY: M. E. Sharpe, 2000).

56. AOTsPSI, f. Karlaga, sv. 6, d. 108, l. 173.

57. See Applebaum, *Gulag*, 206–15. For numerous examples of prisoner food rations and their tie to different levels of labor productivity, see Afanas'ev, et al., *Istoriia stalinskogo Gulaga*, vol. 4.

58. Afanas'ev, et al., *Istoriia stalinskogo Gulaga*, 3:71.

59. AOTsPSI, f. Karlaga, sv. 2, d. 44, l. 16.

60. Again, there were equivalents outside the Gulag of individuals living around rather than through the differentiated ration system. See Osokina, *Our Daily Bread*; Julie Hessler, *A Social History of Soviet Trade: Trade Policy, Retail Practices, and Consumption, 1917–1953* (Princeton, NJ: Princeton University Press, 2004).

61. Bardach and Gleeson, *Man Is Wolf to Man*, 135.

62. Stefanskaia, *Chernoe i beloe*, 23–24.

63. Vladimir Petrov, *Escape from the Future: The Incredible Adventures of a Young Russian* (Bloomington: Indiana University Press, 1973), 90.

64. Stefanskaia, *Chernoe i beloe*, 26–27.

65. Ibid., 28. Karlag was by no means the only Gulag camp in which prisoners lived without barbed wire. See, for example, Applebaum, *Gulag*, 82.

66. Stefanskaia, *Chernoe i beloe*, 29.

67. Cited in AOTsPSI, f. Karlaga, sv. 14, d. 230, l. 19. By no means was this a phenomenon exclusive to Karlag. Allowing prisoners in any camp to leave their camp or production zones freely, even for short periods of time, created a breach in the camp censorship system. Petrov recalls his own experience in Kolyma, where exceptional labor performance earned him a permit to live outside the camp zone. While he felt that his situation was precarious, because any negative report from a local resident could lead to the withdrawal of the permit, he also noted an incredible sense of freedom, as nobody bothered to prevent him from going to the telegraph office to send telegrams to anybody he wished. Petrov, *Escape from the Future*, 133–34.

68. AOTsPSI, f. Karlaga, sv. 6, d. 108, l. 31.

69. In a brief report short on details, two Karlag prisoners went to the city of Karaganda on March 30, 1934, and got drunk. When they tried to steal an automobile, a garage employee named G. Bochek tried to stop them, whereupon the prisoners began to beat him. While it is unclear what exactly happened and where the weapon came from, the outcome is plain enough: in the midst of the struggle, one of the prisoners shot and fatally wounded Bochek. Ibid., l. 73. For other decrees and reports critical of the failure to isolate Karlag prisoners from the surrounding populations, see ibid., sv. 3, d. 51, ll. 38–39, 54; sv. 4, d. 75, ll. 26–27.

70. Ibid., sv. 13, d. 220, l. 24.

71. Afanas'ev, et al., *Istoriia stalinskogo Gulaga*, 2:258, 453.

72. Aleksandr Kokurin and Nikita Petrov, "Arkhiv. GULAG: Strukture i kadry," *Svobodnaia mysl'* no. 3 (2000): 105–23.

73. The UNKVDs were local and regional departments of the NKVD.

74. AOTsPSI, f. Karlaga, sv. 9, d. 155, ll. 20–22.

75. GARF, f. 9414, op. 1, d. 28, l. 10.

76. Afanas'ev, et al., *Istoriia stalinskogo Gulaga*, 2:280. It seems perhaps a bit much, though, to write as Applebaum does that the guards performed their work "often with only the dimmest idea of why they were doing it." Applebaum, *Gulag*, 260.

77. GARF, f. 9414, op. 1, d. 28, l. 10.

78. AOTsPSI, f. Karlaga, sv. 2, d. 43, l. 10; Afanas'ev, et al., *Istoriia stalinskogo Gulaga*, 2:81–82.

79. Petrov, *Escape from the Future*, 176. See also David Nordlander's discussion of the privileges required to recruit guards to Kolyma. David J. Nordlander, "Capital of the Gulag: Magadan in the Early Stalin Era, 1929–1941" (PhD diss., University of North Carolina at Chapel Hill, 1997), 39.

80. The Soviet secret police changed its name several times over its history. Thus, VChK (or Cheka), OGPU, and NKVD all refer to the Soviet secret police.

81. AOTsPSI, f. Karlaga, sv. 6, d. 108, ll. 179–82.

82. See, for example, AOTsPSI, f. Karlaga, sv. 7, d. 114, l. 1.

83. Petrov, *Escape from the Future*, 176–77.

84. Rossiiskii Gosudarstvennyi Arkhiv Sotsial'no-Politicheskoi Istorii (Russian State Archive of Sociopolitical History; hereafter RGASPI), f. 560, op. 1, d. 44, ll. 1–2. The existence in the camps of so-called real enemies and Solzhenitsyn's failure to write about them was not an uncommon topic in letters to *Novyi mir* responding to the publication of *One Day in the Life of Ivan Denisovich*, even in letters from former prisoners themselves. See Denis Kozlov, "The Readers of *Novyi Mir*, 1945–1970: Twentieth-Century Experience and Soviet Historical Consciousness" (PhD diss., University of Toronto, 2005), 335–36. On katorga camp divisions, see chapters 4 and 5 herein. The term Vlasovites refers to those who fought alongside General Andrei Vlasov in the Russian Liberation Army, cooperating with Nazi Germany against the Soviet Union. The term Banderites refers to members of Ukrainian nationalist partisan armies who fought against both Soviet and Nazi forces.

85. Quoted in RGASPI, f. 560, op. 1, d. 44, ll. 3–4.

86. The key study on official corruption in the Gulag system is James Heinzen, "Corruption in the Gulag: Dilemmas of Officials and Prisoners," *Comparative Economic Studies* 47, no. 2 (2005): 456–75.

87. As we will see in chapter 5, sometimes prisoners were shot and then their bodies were arranged so that it appeared as if they were attempting to escape. Applebaum is particularly solid in discussing the guard-prisoner relationship. See Applebaum, *Gulag*, 256–79.

88. See, for example, the report in Afanas'ev, et al., *Istoriia stalinskogo Gulaga*, 4:184–87.

89. AOTsPSI, f. Karlaga, sv. 2, d. 16, l. 1.

90. Ibid., sv. 1 URO, d. 1, ll. 8–9; sv. 4, d. 75, l. 30.

91. Ibid., sv. 1 URO, d. 1, l. 20.

92. Cited in ibid., sv. 2 URO, d. 5, l. 62.

93. Ibid., sv. 1 pr., d. 3, l. 129.

94. Cited in GARF, f. 9414, op. 1, d. 28, l. 11.

95. Margarete Buber, *Under Two Dictators* (New York: Dodd, Mead, 1949), 27. One sometimes sees this author's name as Buber and sometimes as Buber-Neumann.

96. See Michel Foucault, *Discipline and Punish: The Birth of the Prison* (New York: Vintage Books, 1977). Note also that the panopticon was actually developed in eighteenth-century Russia by the brothers Samuel and Jeremy Bentham in an attempt "to improve the surveillance and labor efficiency of English wage laborers" working in Russia on Grigorii Potemkin's estate. Jeremy Bentham took these ideas with him when he left Russia in 1787 and developed the panopticon as a general means of supervision, whether in hospitals, prisons, or schools, or for labor. See Alessandro Stanziani, "Free Labor–Forced Labor: An Uncertain Boundary," *Kritika: Explorations in Russian and Eurasian History* 9, no. 1 (2008): 27–52, especially 43–47.

97. On gathering the mood of the population and on surveillance in Soviet society at large, see Vladlen Izmozik, *Glaza i ushi rezhima: gosudarstvennyi politicheskii kontrol za naseleniem Sovetskoi Rossii v 1918–1928 godakh*, (Saint Petersburg: Izdatel'stvo Sankt-peterburgskogo universiteta ekonomiki i finansov, 1995); Peter Holquist, "'Information Is the Alpha and Omega of Our Work': Bolshevik Surveillance in Its Pan-European Context," *Journal of Modern History* 69, no. 3 (1997): 415–50.

98. The central Gulag collection in GARF (f. 9414) is entirely declassified with the exception of two subsections. The first classified section includes Gulag personnel files that remain off-limits due to official restrictions on access to individual information. The second classified section includes the materials of the Gulag's surveillance section, its Third Department. In the central collection of the administration of special settlements (f. 9479), the materials of the surveillance section are not separated out into an easily classified subsection. Initially, the entirety of this collection was declassified and made available to scholars. The discovery of surveillance section materials subsequently led to the reclassification of a large number of previously available files in the collection. In Karaganda, at AOTsPSI, I was provided access to any document I wished in Karlag's archive, yet all requested photocopies and my notes on the issue of surveillance in the camps were taken from me prior to leaving the archive.

One can do little more than speculate about the reasons for the continued sensitivity toward this subject in both post–Soviet Russia and post–Soviet Kazakhstan. In both cases, I have actually seen some of the classified materials on surveillance. In the case of Moscow, some of the materials on surveillance were provided as photocopies to scholars prior to the reclassification. Several of these documents are used in chapters 5 and 6 below. The Moscow documents report various expressions revealing the mood of individual exiles. One suspects that the inclusion of actual information on individual exiles and possible clues to the identity of the informants may explain the sensitivity. Certainly some camp and deportee informers must still be alive, and contemporary authorities would no doubt be reluctant to have them identified. Yet the documents in Karaganda were quite different. All of the documents that I read in Karaganda prior to their confiscation from my notes and photocopy requests were mere administrative and regulatory documents, without any information about individual prisoners or informers. They simply laid out the nature of the surveillance operation, the means to recruit informers, and the like. In this case, one also suspects that current institutions of detention in former Soviet states may continue to operate similar forms of internal surveillance, and therefore do not wish such information to become public.

99. Quoted in AOTsPSI, f. Karlaga, sv. 6, d. 94, l. 21.

100. The inverse of the belief in the enemy's ability to become an honest citizen was the ability of the honest citizen to become an enemy.

101. Bardach and Gleeson, *Man Is Wolf to Man*, 113–14.

102. AOTsPSI, f. Karlaga, sv. 9, d. 155, l. 58.

103. For these figures, see J. Arch Getty, Gábor Tamás Rittersporn, and Viktor N. Zemskov, "Victims of the Soviet Penal System in the Pre-war Years: A First Approach on the Basis of Archival Evidence," *American Historical Review* (October 1993): 1048–49.

104. See chapter 4 herein.

105. Afanas'ev, et al., *Istoriia stalinskogo Gulaga*, 4:188.

106. See, for example, AOTsPSI, f. Karlaga, sv. 4, d. 75, ll. 26–27.

107. Ibid., sv. 5, d. 83, ll. 28–29. Unfortunately, I was unable to determine what happened to those responsible.

108. Arendt, *The Origins of Totalitarianism*, 431.

109. Quoted in AOTsPSI, f. Karlaga, sv. 2, d. 44, l. 3.

110. Quoted in ibid., sv. 3 prikazy, d. 7, l. 229.

111. Ibid., sv. 5 prikazy, d. 11, ll. 110–11.

112. See, for example, ibid., sv. 3 prikazy, d. 7, l. 229.

113. Many historians have made the mistake of assuming that the official commitment to reeducation (whether real or not) was abandoned in the mid-1930s with the Great Terror. While it is certainly the case that prisoners were no longer a topic of public discussion as they were when *Belomor* was published, the Gulag's indoctrination activities never ceased, as we will see in subsequent chapters. How real this commitment to reeducation was is, of course, a matter open to debate, but that the apparatus itself continued to operate is not. For these arguments, see Michael Jakobson, *Origins of the Gulag: The Soviet Prison-Camp System, 1917–1934* (Lexington: University Press of Kentucky, 1993), though the author did not have access to archival materials; Applebaum, *Gulag*, 100, even though the author should have known better.

114. This is the main problem for Applebaum in her section on the KVChs. She treats their activities in complete isolation from the question of release and looks at labor in isolation from reeducation. As such, she cannot understand the KVChs' enormous efforts. See Applebaum, *Gulag*, 216–41.

115. Kuziakina, *Theatre in the Solovki Prison Camp*, 30.

116. Buca, *Vorkuta*, 93.

117. Cited in Kuziakina, *Theatre in the Solovki Prison Camp*, 90.

118. Cited in Solzhenitsyn, *The Gulag Archipelago*, 2:67.

119. See ibid., 2:470. The failure of the KVCh at Svirlag to involve a significant percentage of the inmates in socialist competition and shock work was criticized by the assistant chief of the Gulag in a report on June 1, 1935. See Nicolas Werth and Gael Moullec, eds., *Rapports Secrets Sovietiques: La Societe*

*Russe Dans Les Documents Confidentiels, 1921–1991* (Paris: Gallimard, 1994), 374–76.

120. Quoted in GARF, f. 9414, op. 2, d. 108, l. 7.

121. Kotkin, *Magnetic Mountain*, 232.

122. Solzhenitsyn, *The Gulag Archipelago*, 2:106.

123. Gorky, Auerbach, and Firin, *Belomor*, 156–59.

124. The classic work is Lewis H. Siegelbaum, *Stakhanovism and the Politics of Productivity in the USSR, 1935–1941* (Cambridge: Cambridge University Press, 1988).

125. Kotkin, *Magnetic Mountain*, 232.

126. Quoted in AOTsPSI, f. Karlaga, sv. 9, d. 155, ll. 20–22.

127. "Glavnoe—eto liubit' svoiu rabotu," *Putevka*, January 19, 1936, plate 429, in *The GULAG Press, 1920–1937* (Leiden, Netherlands: IDC Publishers, 2000).

128. "Rekordnaia vyrabotka zaboishchikov shakhty 'Dubovka' Kurmanbaeva i Gol'tsmana," *Putevka*, January 5, 1936, plate 429, in *The GULAG Press, 1920–1937* (Leiden, Netherlands: IDC Publishers, 2000).

129. Various articles in ibid.

130. On Karlag's response to the USSR Sovnarkom, and calls from the Communist Party's Central Committee to liquidate illiteracy entirely in 1936 and 1937, see AOTsPSI, f. Karlaga, sv. 5 prikazy, d. 11, ll. 110–12.

131. Solzhenitsyn, *The Gulag Archipelago*, 2:474.

132. Ibid., 2:471.

133. Applebaum states that no photographs of Stalin or other leaders were allowed on the walls of camps or prisons. This seems contradicted by the photograph from Belomor available at http://gulaghistory.org/items/show/287, part of the International Memorial Society, Moscow collection. Leaders did certainly appear in camp newspapers. See, for example, the photograph of Lenin on the tenth anniversary of his death in Karlag's newpaper, *Putevka*, January 21, 1936, plate 429, in *The GULAG Press, 1920–1937* (Leiden, Netherlands: IDC Publishers, 2000).

134. On Gulag newspapers as a means to instill "culturedness" among the prisoners, see Wilson Bell, "One Day in the Life of Educator Khrushchev: Labour and *Kul'turnost'* in the Gulag Newspapers," *Canadian Slavonic Papers* 46, nos. 3–4 (2004): 289–313.

135. Kuziakina, *Theatre in the Solovki Prison Camp*, 23.

136. Virtually every issue of *Putevka* carried this phrase across its front page: "Circulation outside of the camp is not allowed."

137. Cited in AOTsPSI, f. Karlaga, sv. 5 prikazy, d. 11, ll. 187–88.

138. AOTsPSI, f. Karlaga, sv. 3 prikazy, d. 7, l. 240.

139. "Moe spasibo chekistam," *Putevka*, December 24, 1936, plate 406, in *The GULAG Press, 1920–1937* (Leiden, Netherlands: IDC Publishers, 2000). A similar article appears just below this one in the same issue titled "I Became a Man" (Ia stal chelovekam).

140. *Putevka*, January 19, 1936, 4, plate 429, in *The GULAG Press, 1920–1937* (Leiden, Netherlands: IDC Publishers, 2000).

141. Ibid.

142. Various articles, *Putevka*, January 5, 1936, plate 429, in *The GULAG Press, 1920–1937* (Leiden, Netherlands: IDC Publishers, 2000).

143. Gorky, Auerbach, and Firin, *Belomor*, 219–20.

144. Quoted in ibid., 220–21.

145. Kuziakina, *Theatre in the Solovki Prison Camp*, 51.

146. Eugenia Ginzburg, *Within the Whirlwind* (New York: Harcourt Brace Jovanovich, 1981), 16.

147. AOTsPSI, f. Karlaga, sv. 2, d. 44, l. 52.

148. Ibid., sv. 9, d. 157, l. 113. Although I have chosen a particular example from the period of the terror, these restrictions during state holidays were not limited to that time. Intriguingly, though, prisoners were still allowed to celebrate Soviet and religious holidays in the 1920s at Solovki. See Applebaum, *Gulag*, 27.

149. Petrov, *Escape from the Future*, 168–69.

150. Kotkin, *Magnetic Mountain*, 232.

151. Petrov, *Escape from the Future*, 116.

152. Cited in Kuziakina, *Theatre in the Solovki Prison Camp*, 15.

153. Ginzburg, *Within the Whirlwind*, 24.

154. Cited in AOTsPSI, f. Karlaga, sv. 13, d. 220, l. 24.

155. Ibid., sv. 5, d. 93, l. 52.

156. Cited in ibid., sv. 2, d. 44, l. 11.

157. For just two of the many different regulations over the years that spelled out some of the possible penalties along with the operation and daily regime of penalty institutions, see AOTsPSI, f. Karlaga, sv. 2, d. 44, ll. 11–11b; sv. 5, d. 93, ll. 123–28.

158. Ibid., sv. 5, d. 93, ll. 52–53.

159. Ibid., sv. 9, d. 157, ll. 106–7.

160. Ginzburg, *Within the Whirlwind*, 103.

161. Petrov, *Escape from the Future*, 136–37.

162. Rachel Rachlin and Israel Rachlin, *Sixteen Years in Siberia* (Tuscaloosa: University of Alabama Press, 1988), 110–11; Solzhenitsyn, *The Gulag Archipelago*, 3:380.

163. Joseph Scholmer, *Vorkuta* (New York: Holt, 1955), 173.

164. Cited in AOTsPSI, f. Karlaga, sv. 8, d. 146, l. 28.

165. For one early regulation on paying prisoners dated November 13, 1930, see ibid., sv. 2, d. 43, ll. 42–44. On privileges for productive prisoners, see, among others, ibid., sv. 2, d. 44, l. 16.

166. Quoted in ibid., sv. 13, d. 224, l. 129.

167. Getty, Rittersporn, and Zemskov, "Victims of the Soviet Penal System in the Pre-war Years," 1041, 1048–49.

168. NIPTs, f. 2, op. 3, d. 60, memoir of Galina Aleksandrovna Semenova, str. 5.

169. Gorky, Auerbach, and Firin, *Belomor*, 171–72.

170. Ibid., 308.

171. GARF, f. 9414, op. 1, d. 28, l. 7.

172. AOTsPSI, f. Karlaga, sv. 8, d. 128, ll. 53–58.

173. Ginzburg, *Within the Whirlwind*, 199.

174. Ibid., 217.

175. See, for example, AOTsPSI, f. Karlaga, sv. 7, d. 117, l. 95.

176. By far the best study of the accounted working day system, which Simon Ertz calls "workday credits," is in his "Trading Effort for Freedom: Workday Credits in the Stalinist Camp System," *Comparative Economic Studies* 47, no. 2 (2005): 476–91.

177. AOTsPSI, f. Karlaga, sv. 1 URO, d. 1, l. 23. Also see the regulations cited in Afanas'ev, et al., *Istoriia stalinskogo Gulaga*, 3:79–81, 126–32.

178. Cited in Afanas'ev, et al., *Istoriia stalinskogo Gulaga*, 3:128.

179. AOTsPSI, f. Karlaga, sv. 3, d. 51, l. 6.

180. On lishentsy, see Golfo Alexopoulos, *Stalin's Outcasts: Aliens, Citizens, and the Soviet State, 1926–1936* (Ithaca, NY: Cornell University Press, 2003).

181. Afanas'ev, et al., *Istoriia stalinskogo Gulaga*, 3:126, 128. On prisoner Stakhanovites, see ibid., 3:133–34.

182. The Karlag individual prisoner files from the 1930s at AOTsPSI are full of such forms.

183. Cited in AOTsPSI, f. Karlaga, sv. 4 URO, d. 32, l. 6.

184. Ibid., sv. 4 URO, d. 32, l. 48.

185. Quoted in ibid., sv. 3 prikazy, d. 7, l. 37.

186. For one example, see the death penalty case in Afanas'ev, et al., *Istoriia stalinskogo Gulaga*, 3:165–66. The case was sent to all camps and ordered read to prisoners with the explanation that local camp authorities tell all prisoners that sabotage, malicious refusal to work, and other violations of camp discipline would be punished severely. See also the order to punish self-mutilators for their criminal attempt to avoid work in ibid., *Istoriia stalinskogo Gulaga*, 3:166–67.

187. Quoted in ibid., 4:71. He is quoted with a slightly different translation in Applebaum, *Gulag*, 112.

188. Applebaum, *Gulag*, 112.

189. See the discussion in Ertz, "Trading Effort for Freedom"; see also the documents in Afanas'ev, et al., *Istoriia stalinskogo Gulaga*, 3:283–95. During the same period, Gulag authorities experimented with the reintroduction of pay for some prisoners. Afanas'ev, et al., *Istoriia stalinskogo Gulaga*, 3:296–314. These were two of the failed last-ditch efforts in the waning Stalin years to make the system economically profitable. For others, see ibid., 3:314–53.

190. See the politburo decision cited in ibid., 2:158. See also the discussion in Beria's letter to Vyacheslav Molotov on the end of the system in ibid., 3:160–61.

191. All figures for the camps alone are calculated based on GARF, f. 9414, op. 1, d. 1155, ll. 1–2. The combined figures for the camps and colonies are in Afanas'ev, et al., *Istoriia stalinskogo Gulaga*, 3:55. Despite the increase in 1937, the numbers do not seem enough to justify Applebaum's assertion that 1937 was a year in which "Soviet camps temporarily transformed themselves from indifferently managed prisons in which people died by accident, into genuinely deadly camps where prisoners were deliberately worked to death, or actually murdered, in far larger numbers than they had been in the past." Applebaum, *Gulag*, 93. As was typical, the most "murderous" location of the Great Terror was outside the camps in the system of direct execution of enemies. Furthermore, during the mass operations of the Great Terror, the camps had their own quotas of enemies to be shot—not worked to death, but shot.

192. GARF, f. 9414, op. 1, d. 1155, ll. 1–2.

193. Gorky, Auerbach, and Firin, *Belomor*, 274.

194. The image—"Graveyard of the Lazy," *Gulag: Many Days, Many Lives*, item no. 785, owned by the International Memorial Society in Moscow—is available at http://gulaghistory.org/items/show/785 (accessed May 17, 2009).

195. See the push to recategorize prisoners' health toward fitness for heavier forms of labor in Afanas'ev, et al., *Istoriia stalinskogo Gulaga*, 3:93–94.

CHAPTER 3: CATEGORIZING PRISONERS

1. Many of these statistical compilations from central Gulag archives have been published in Iurii Nikolaevich Afanas'ev, et al., eds., *Istoriia stalinskogo Gulaga: Konets 1920-kh–pervaia polovina 1950-kh godov: Sobranie dokumentov v semi tomakh* (Moscow: Rosspen, 2004), vol. 4. They are ubiquitous in the central and local Gulag archives.

2. On sending copies from prisoner files to central authorities along with prisoners' appeals for clemency, see ibid., 4:90.

3. AOTsPSI, f. Karlaga, sv. 8, d. 143.

4. See Anne Applebaum, *Gulag: A History* (New York: Doubleday, 2003), 220.

5. Eugenia Ginzburg, *Journey into the Whirlwind* (New York: Harcourt, Brace and World, 1967), 348.

6. For the text of the corrective labor code of 1924, see Aleksandr Kokurin and Nikolai Petrov, eds., *GULAG: (Glavnoe upravlenie lagerei), 1917–1960*, (Moscow: Mezhdunarodnyi fond "Demokratiia," 2000), 30–56.

7. Danylo Shumuk, *Life Sentence: Memoirs of a Ukrainian Political Prisoner* (Edmonton: Canadian Institute of Ukrainian Studies, 1984), 172. Shumuk was faced with the same questions on his entry into the camps. See ibid., 180.

8. Joseph Scholmer, *Vorkuta* (New York: Holt, 1955), 41.

9. Gustav Herling, *A World Apart: The Journal of a Gulag Survivor* (New York: Arbor House, 1951), 45.

10. For a fascinating discussion of this shift in 1936, after which "few retained their earlier confidence that class origins were a reliable clue to the soul," see Igal Halfin, *Terror in My Soul: Communist Autobiographies on Trial* (Cambridge, MA: Harvard University Press, 2003), 254–62.

11. For one example, see the descriptions of prison life, especially the moral code of the political prisoners, in Isaac Steinberg, *Spiridonova: Revolutionary Terrorist* (London: Methuen, 1935). Steinberg, a Left Socialist-Revolutionary, was the people's commissar of justice during the brief Bolshevik–Left Socialists Revolutionary coalition government of December 1917–March 1918.

12. Natalia Kuziakina, *Theatre in the Solovki Prison Camp*, trans. Boris M. Meerovich (Newark, NJ: Harwood Academic Publishers, 1995), 18.

13. Article 58 refers to the criminal code of the RSFSR. Other republics had analogous codes, although the number of the article enumerating counterrevolutionary crimes often differed.

14. Aleksandr I. Solzhenitsyn, *The Gulag Archipelago, 1918–1956: An Experiment in Literary Investigation*, trans. Thomas P. Whitney (New York: Harper Perennial, 1991), 1:60.

15. See Peter H. Solomon Jr., *Soviet Criminal Justice under Stalin* (Cambridge: Cambridge University Press, 1996).

16. Solzhenitsyn, *The Gulag Archipelago*, 1:60.

17. Those historians who in recent years have gone to great lengths to disprove Solzhenitsyn's assertion that the Gulag was overwhelmingly populated by political prisoners miss this point. See especially Gábor Tamás Rittersporn, *Stalinist Simplifications and Soviet Complications: Social Tensions and Political Conflicts in the USSR* (Chur, Switzerland: Harwood Academic Publishers, 1991), 261–65; J. Arch Getty, Gábor Tamás Rittersporn, and Viktor N. Zemskov, "Victims of the Soviet Penal System in the Pre-war Years: A First Approach on the Basis of Archival Evidence," *American Historical Review* (October 1993): 1030–39. As I will show here, the question of who was a "political" prisoner in the Gulag is a complex one.

Moreover, an almost-implicit element of the argument over the proportion of the Gulag population comprised of political prisoners revolves around the level of moral culpability or evil inherent in the Gulag system. After all, every modern state has deemed it necessary to detain and punish a certain population that it has understood as criminal. While the exact definition of criminal behavior and the concomitant punishment for crimes varies from state to state, at the broadest level a shared notion of criminality can be found. Murder, rape, assault, and theft are among those crimes normally subject to sanction in the modern state. The incarceration of political prisoners is presented as a differentiating element in modern penal practice. Assertions about the prevalence of political prisoners in the Gulag are in large part reflective of this process. If the Gulag can be shown as housing primarily criminals, individuals who would be incarcerated in virtually every modern state, then the Soviet Union was not terribly abnormal. Its methods of incarceration essentially should be understood as one particular type of penal incarceration. If, on the other hand, the Gulag can be shown as composed almost entirely of political prisoners, where criminals are found mostly as an element in the regime's repression of political prisoners, then the Soviet Union was an evil state more concerned with suppressing dissent, real or imagined, than with incarcerating the criminals who presented a much more real danger to society.

In fact, however, it is the coexistence of these two systems—one for detaining criminals, and one for detaining politicals—inside a single all-encompassing institution like the Gulag that really sets apart the Soviet system of detention. The question of relative weights of political and criminal prisoners is essentially unsolvable. As John Keep has demonstrated, "crimes" understood as merely criminal today were often redefined as political tomorrow. Even criminal offenses typically also encompassed actions that would be passed over or at least punished only minimally by most modern states. If the Gulag had been populated solely by criminals, though, as the term would have been understood in other modern states, the utilization of a concentration camp system as a state's penal institution was a particularly Soviet phenomenon. John Keep, "Recent Writing on Stalin's Gulag: An Overview," *Crime, Histoire, and Sociétés* 1, no. 2 (1997): 91–112.

18. On the special regime camps, see chapter 5 herein.

19. Solzhenitsyn, *The Gulag Archipelago*, 2:67–70.

20. For other Gulag practices that either excluded or singled out counterrevolutionaries, always to their detriment, see chapter 2 herein.

21. Solzhenitsyn, *The Gulag Archipelago*, 2:255.

22. Ibid., 2:501.

23. Maksim Gorky, Leopol'd Auerbach, and Semen Firin, eds., *Belomor: An Account of the Construction of the New Canal between the White Sea and the Baltic Sea*, trans. Amabel Williams-Ellis (New York: H. Smith and R. Haas, 1935), 329–30. This is one of a relatively small number of instances in which counter-revolutionary prisoners are still referred to as political by Soviet authorities.

24. GARF, f. 9414, op. 2, d. 108, l. 9.

25. Ibid., l. 10.

26. Ibid., ll. 9–11b.

27. When presenting the draft of the 1936 constitution for ratification, Stalin declared, "Our Soviet society has already, in the main, succeeded in achieving socialism." J. V. Stalin, *Joseph Stalin: Selected Writings* (Westport, CT: Praeger, 1970), 386. That victory was embodied in Article 1 of the constitution of 1936 in its declaration of the Soviet Union as a state of two nonantagonistic classes: peasants and workers.

28. Afanas'ev, et al., *Istoriia stalinskogo Gulaga*, 1:271. In 1937, just at Kolyma alone, over 12,500 were arrested and nearly 5,900 shot. Ibid., 1:360.

29. V. P. Popov, "Gosudarstvennyi terror v sovetskoi Rossii, 1923–1953 gg. (istochniki i ikh interpretatsiia)," *Otechestvennye Arkhivy*, no. 2 (1992): 28–29.

30. AOTsPSI, f. Karlaga, sv. 6 URO, d. 52, l. 56.

31. Jacques Rossi writes repeatedly of the replacement of the counterrevolu-tionary with the term anti-Soviet by the late 1930s. Jacques Rossi, *The Gulag Handbook: An Encyclopedia Dictionary of Soviet Penitentiary Institutions and Terms Related to the Forced Labor Camps* (New York: Paragon House, 1989). While he may be correct in some respects, the term counterrevolutionary contin-ued to appear time and again in official Gulag documentation.

32. Articles 130 and 131. For an English translation of all Soviet constitutions through the Brezhnev era, see Aryeh L. Unger, *Constitutional Development in the USSR: A Guide to the Soviet Constitutions* (New York: Pica Press, 1982).

33. Galina Mikhailovna Ivanova, *Gulag v sisteme totalitarnogo gosudarstva* (Moscow: Moskovskii obshchestvennyi nauchnyi fond, 1997), 93–96.

34. Quoted in Gorky, Auerbach, and Firin, *Belomor*, 342. Also quoted in Sol-zhenitsyn, *The Gulag Archipelago*, 2:93.

35. Quoted in Gorky, Auerbach, and Firin, *Belomor*, 71. Also quoted with a slightly different translation in Solzhenitsyn, *The Gulag Archipelago*, 2:85–86.

36. Cited in Gorky, Auerbach, and Firin, *Belomor*, 145. This order natu-rally raises the question of gendered identities in the Gulag, as discussed below. Women became an especially important part of the Gulag population during the war years, when their share of the population rose from 7 percent in 1941 to 26 percent in 1944. See "Gulag v gody voiny: Doklad nachal'nika GULAGa NKVD SSSR V. G. Nasedkina, avgust 1944 g.," *Istoricheskii arkhiv*, no. 3 (1994): 64. Gorky, Auerbach, and Firin, *Belomor* does devote an entire chapter to the subject; see "Women at Belomorstroy," 150–55.

37. Cited in AOTsPSI, f. Karlaga, sv. 3, d. 55, l. 3.

38. Quoted in Gorky, Auerbach, and Firin, *Belomor*, 53.

39. AOTsPSI, f. Karlaga, sv. 2 URO, d. 5, l. 18.

40. Quoted in Solzhenitsyn, *The Gulag Archipelago*, 2:434–35.

41. Gustav Herling, *A World Apart: The Journal of a Gulag Survivor* (New York: Arbor House, 1951), 5.

42. Solzhenitsyn, *The Gulag Archipelago*, 1:190.

43. Ibid., 1:226–27.

44. Ibid., 1:458–61.

45. Solzhenitsyn, *The Gulag Archipelago*, 2:438.

46. Ibid., 1:11, 503; 2:438, 442–43, 446.

47. Eugenia Ginzburg, *Within the Whirlwind* (New York: Harcourt Brace Jovanovich, 1981), 12.

48. Militsa Cheslavovna Stefanskaia, *Chernoe i beloe* (Moscow: Suzdalev, 1994), 23–25, 27.

49. Vladimir Petrov, *Escape from the Future: The Incredible Adventures of a Young Russian* (Bloomington: Indiana University Press, 1973), 98.

50. Janusz Bardach and Kathleen Gleeson, *Man Is Wolf to Man: Surviving the Gulag* (Berkeley: University of California Press, 1998), 183.

51. Margarete Buber, *Under Two Dictators* (New York: Dodd, Mead, 1949), 59–60.

52. Bardach and Gleeson, *Man Is Wolf to Man*, 94.

53. Gorky, Auerbach, and Firin, *Belomor*, 276.

54. Kuziakina, *Theatre in the Solovki Prison Camp*, 73.

55. Solzhenitsyn, *The Gulag Archipelago*, 2:311.

56. Stefanskaia, *Chernoe i beloe*, 31.

57. This is intriguing but unsurprising given his complaints precisely about these prisoners seeking to exclude all non-Communist Article 58 prisoners from their own understanding of politicals. Solzhenitsyn, *The Gulag Archipelago*, 2:319.

58. Buber, *Under Two Dictators*, 40.

59. Ibid., 40–41.

60. Quoted in Ginzburg, *Journey into the Whirlwind*, 116.

61. Ibid., 223.

62. Ibid., 237.

63. Although a huge literature now exists on the issue, key works are Yuri Slezkine, "The USSR as a Communal Apartment, or How a Socialist State Promoted Ethnic Particularism," *Slavic Review* 53, no. 2 (1994): 414–52; Terry Martin, *The Affirmative Action Empire: Nations and Nationalism in the Soviet Union, 1923-1939* (Ithaca, NY: Cornell University Press, 2001); Francine Hirsch, *Empire of Nations: Ethnographic Knowledge and the Making of the Soviet Union* (Ithaca, NY: Cornell University Press, 2005).

64. See Gorky, Auerbach, and Firin, *Belomor*, 182. For more on national minorities at the Moscow-Volga Canal, see Applebaum, *Gulag*, 299.

65. Gorky, Auerbach, and Firin, *Belomor*, 63, 252.

66. See AOTsPSI, f. Karlaga, sv. 3, d. 46, ll. 215–16; sv. 5, d. 87, l. 3; sv. 6, d. 99, ll. 23–24; sv. 3, d. 60, ll. 32–32b. See also the numerous articles in the camp newspaper, *Putevka*, during 1933–34, in ibid., sv. gazety, d. 3, 5; see also the microfilm collection in *The GULAG Press, 1920-1937* (Leiden, Netherlands: IDC Publishers, 2000). Mixed into these two collections of newspapers are the few extant copies of the camp's Kazakh-language newspaper.

67. See Yuri Slezkine, *Arctic Mirrors: Russia and the Small Peoples of the North* (Ithaca, NY: Cornell University Press, 1994).

68. For the explicit ties between the promulgation of the new constitution and a renewed focus on the category of nation, see the press coverage of the holiday celebration in July 1935 honoring the adoption of the Soviet constitution of 1923. The holiday, held shortly after the announcement in June 1935 of the commencement of drafting a new constitution, was organized around the theme of the "triumph" of the Leninist-Stalinist nationality policy, and all celebratory activities highlighted the participation of Soviet peoples from all nationalities. The quote here comes from a speech at the celebration given by politburo member and Ukrainian Vlas Chubar'. *Pravda*, July 6, 1935, 1.

69. The literature on the ethnicization of the Soviet enemy is voluminous. See, for example, Norman M. Naimark, *Fires of Hatred: Ethnic Cleansing in Twentieth-Century Europe* (Cambridge, MA: Harvard University Press, 2001); Terry Martin, "The Origins of Soviet Ethnic Cleansing," *Journal of Modern History* 70, no. 4 (1998): 813–61; Kate Brown, *A Biography of No Place: From Ethnic Borderland to Soviet Heartland* (Cambridge, MA: Harvard University Press, 2004); Jeffrey Burds, "The Soviet War against 'Fifth Columnists': The Case of Chechnya, 1942–4," *Journal of Contemporary History* 42, no. 2 (2007): 267–314; Michael Gelb, "An Early Soviet Ethnic Deportation: The Far-Eastern Koreans," *Russian Review* 54, no. 3 (July 1995): 389–412; "The Western Finnic Minorities and the Origins of the Stalinist Nationalities Deportations," *Nationalities Papers* 24, no. 2 (1996): 237–68.

70. As Viola shows, this commitment, though real, often lacked substantial resources for its realization. Lynne Viola, *The Unknown Gulag: The Lost World of Stalin's Special Settlements* (New York: Oxford University Press, 2007).

71. See Stephen Kotkin, *Magnetic Mountain: Stalinism as a Civilization* (Berkeley: University of California Press, 1995), 234.

72. Nikolai F. Bugai, ed., *"Mobilizovat' nemtsev v rabochie kolonny . . . I. Stalin" Sbornik dokumentov (1940-e gody)* (Moscow: Gotika, 1998), 15.

73. See NKVD USSR order no. 00447, in Afanas'ev, et al., *Istoriia stalinskogo Gulaga*, 1:268–75.

74. Hiroaki Kuromiya, *Freedom and Terror in the Donbas: A Ukrainian-Russian Borderland, 1870s–1990s* (Cambridge: Cambridge University Press, 1998), 207. For an intimate description of these deportations from the border regions of Ukraine, see Brown, *A Biography of No Place*, 134–52. See also Gelb, "The Western Finnic Minorities."

75. Gelb, "An Early Soviet Ethnic Deportation." In Gelb's generally superb article, one searches in vain for evidence of Soviet racial thinking to support his claims that Soviet policy toward the Koreans was racist.

76. Ibid., 406–7.

77. Ibid., 401.

78. AOTsPSI, f. Karlaga, sv. 7, d. 117, l. 78.

79. Brown, *A Biography of No Place*, 173–91.

80. Brown writes, "The deportees had adopted Soviet assumptions about the nature of a community and the ignorant and primitive quality of Kazakh nomadic agriculture." Ibid., 188.

81. Anne Applebaum discusses gender and sex extensively in one of her best chapters. See Applebaum, *Gulag*, 307–33.

82. Christopher Lawrence Zugger, *The Forgotten: Catholics of the Soviet Empire from Lenin through Stalin* (Syracuse: Syracuse University Press, 2001), 202.

83. AOTsPSI, f. Karlaga, sv. 5, d. 93, l. 2. See also ibid., sv. 9, d. 155, ll. 46–48. Petrov described this practice in Kolyma. See Petrov, *Escape from the Future*, 107–8.

84. AOTsPSI, f. Karlaga, sv. 14, d. 230, l. 19.

85. Ibid., sv. 6, d. 108, l. 73.

86. On venereal diseases, see ibid., sv. 9, d. 157, ll. 84, 108–9. On concentrating female prisoners, see ibid., sv. 13, d. 220, l. 23. Petrov also noted the prevalence of venereal disease. "The direct result of these conditions is that all women prisoners are victims of venereal diseases. They may contract them a little sooner, or a little later, but they can escape them never. When this happens they are isolated in special, strictly guarded camp quarters where they rot away almost without any medical care." Petrov, *Escape from the Future*, 108.

87. AOTsPSI, f. Karlaga, sv. 9, d. 155, ll. 46–48.

88. Afanas'ev, et al., *Istoriia stalinskogo Gulaga*, 4:197–99.

89. Petrov, *Escape from the Future*, 107.

90. Ginzburg, *Journey into the Whirlwind*, 331, 347.

91. Stefanskaia, *Chernoe i beloe*, 32.

92. Ibid., 33.

93. NIPTs, f. 2, op. 3, d. 60, memoir of Galina Aleksandrovna Semenova, str. 155.

94. Orlando Figes, *The Whisperers: Private Life in Stalin's Russia* (New York: Metropolitan Books, 2007), 364–65.

95. Afanas'ev, et al., *Istoriia stalinskogo Gulaga*, 4:189. Of course, it is entirely possible that they made no such agreement, and that Bondar' simply murdered Medvedeva before turning the gun on himself.

96. NIPTs, f. 2, op. 3, d. 60, memoir of Galina Aleksandrovna Semenova, str. 156.

97. The key scholarly works are Anfisa R. Kukushkina, *Akmolinskii lager' zhen 'izmennikov rodiny': Istoriia i sud'by* (Karaganda: Kazakhstanskii finansovo-ekonomicheskii universitet, 2002); Vladimir M. Grinev and Aleksandr Iu. Daniel', *Uznitsy 'ALZhIRa': spisok zhenshchin-zakliuchennykh Akmolinskogo i drugikh otdelenii Karlaga* (Moscow: Zven'ia, 2003); Galina Stepanova Kliuchnikova, *Kazakhstanskii Alzhir* (Malinovka, Kazakhstan: Assotsiatsiia zhertv nezakonnykh repressii, 2003). Figes also writes of Alzhir. Figes, *The Whisperers*, especially 356–69.

98. See NIPTs, f. 2, op. 3, d. 60, memoir of Galina Aleksandrovna Semenova, str. 4, 158. She was herself arrested when she had a nursing child, and also knew many who were pregnant when arrested. Figes relates a tale of an Alzhir prisoner with a nursing infant too. See Figes, *The Whisperers*, 316–18.

99. The order is cited in Afanas'ev, et al., *Istoriia stalinskogo Gulaga*, 1:277–81. It remained in force for just over a year—from August 1937 until October 1938—when it was decided that wives should only be arrested if they participated in their husbands' activities or independently had anti-Soviet feelings. See the order from October 1938 in ibid., 287–88.

100. See Figes, *The Whisperers*, 316–20.

101. NIPTs, f. 2, op. 3, d. 60, memoir of Galina Aleksandrovna Semenova, str. 5.

102. Ibid., str. 51, 149.

103. Ibid., str. 5–8, 14–15.

104. Ibid., str. 6–7, 12.

105. Ibid., str. 10.

106. The order closing these special divisions is cited in Afanas'ev, et al., *Istoriia stalinskogo Gulaga*, 2:157. Figes is mistaken in continuing to write about Alzhir after this point, as it no longer officially existed. See Figes, *The Whisperers*, 357–58.

107. Bardach and Gleeson, *Man Is Wolf to Man*, 125.

108. The key work is the epilogue in Dan Healey, *Homosexual Desire in Revolutionary Russia: The Regulation of Sexual and Gender Dissent* (Chicago: University of Chicago Press, 2001).

CHAPTER 4: ARMAGEDDON AND THE GULAG

1. Portions of this chapter previously appeared in Steven A. Barnes, "All for the Front, All for Victory! The Mobilization of Forced Labor in the Soviet Union during World War Two," *International Labor and Working Class History* 58 (Fall 2000): 239–60.

2. Quoted in I. V. Kashkina, "'Ia khochu znat' prichinu moego aresta ... ': Pis'mo V. N. Pilishchuka—byvshego zakliuchennogo Karlaga," in *Golosa Istorii*, ed. Isaak S. Rozental', vypusk 23, kniga 2 (Moscow: Tsentral'nyi muzei revoliutsii, 1992), 172–78. My thanks to Jan Plamper for pointing me to this source.

3. Quoted in ibid., 177.

4. The regulations of 1939 and the decrees in June 1939 on the elimination of conditional early release have been published in Aleksandr Kokurin and Nikolai Petrov, eds., *GULAG: (Glavnoe upravlenie lagerei), 1917–1960* (Moscow: Mezhdunarodnyi fond "Demokratiia," 2000), 116–17, 456–73. See also Rossiiskii Gosudarstvennyi Arkhiv Noveishei Istorii (Russian State Archive of Contemporary History; hereafter RGANI), f. 89, per. 73, dok. 3, ll. 1–2.

5. Applebaum is incorrect to assert that "by the end of [the 1930s], the Soviet concentration camp[s] had attained what was to be their permanent form." Anne Applebaum, *Gulag: A History* (New York: Doubleday, 2003), 114. As this and later chapters will show, the Gulag in general and the structures of the Soviet system were far from complete by the end of the 1930s. Significant shifts in practices, institutions, and identities were still to come.

6. I will use this Soviet term Westerners for ease and convenience to refer to the nationalists from those territories annexed by the Soviet Union after 1939.

7. See Yehoshua Gilboa, *Confess! Confess! Eight Years in Soviet Prisons* (Boston: Little, Brown, 1968), 220.

8. Ibid., 90–91, 174.

9. Shumuk certainly fell into this category. A member of the Ukrainian Insurgent Army, and a veteran of Polish prisons and German POW camps, Shumuk

personally exerted a strong influence on Gulag life, taking a leading role in one of the post-Stalin camp uprisings. Danylo Shumuk, *Life Sentence: Memoirs of a Ukrainian Political Prisoner* (Edmonton: Canadian Institute of Ukrainian Studies, 1984), especially x, 17–28 (on political prisoners in Poland).

10. Gilboa, *Confess!* 41–42.

11. See ibid., 31, 220. See also the entries for *zapadniki* and *zakhidniki* in Jacques Rossi, *The Gulag Handbook: An Encyclopedia Dictionary of Soviet Penitentiary Institutions and Terms Related to the Forced Labor Camps* (New York: Paragon House, 1989), 129–30, 132.

12. These numbers have been revised down from previous estimates of as many as 1 million deportees and 440,000 arrested. See Jan T. Gross, *Revolution from Abroad: The Soviet Conquest of Poland's Western Ukraine and Western Belorussia*, exp. ed. (Princeton, NJ: Princeton University Press, 2002), xiv. See also Oleg A. Gorlanov and Arsenii B. Roginskii, "Ob arestakh v zapadnykh oblastiakh Belorussii i Ukraini v 1939–1941 gg.," in *Repressii protiv poliakov i pol'skikh grazhdan*, ed. Aleksandr E. Gur'ianov (Moscow: Zven'ia, 1997), 77, 82–84, 86; John Keep, "Recent Writing on Stalin's Gulag: An Overview," *Crime, Histoire, and Sociétés* 1, no. 2 (1997): 91–112. Many of the decrees and reports on the Westerners' exile and arrests are cited in Iurii Nikolaevich Afanas'ev, et al., eds., *Istoriia stalinskogo Gulaga: Konets 1920-kh–pervaia polovina 1950-kh godov: Sobranie dokumentov v semi tomakh* (Moscow: Rosspen, 2004), 1:389–407. The classic account of national and gender identity among deported Polish women is Katherine R. Jolluck, *Exile and Identity: Polish Women in the Soviet Union during World War II* (Pittsburgh: University of Pittsburgh Press, 2002).

13. "Gulag v gody voiny: Doklad nachal'nika GULAGa NKVD SSSR V. G. Nasedkina, avgust 1944 g.," *Istoricheskii arkhiv*, no. 3 (1994): 65.

14. Afanas'ev, et al., *Istoriia stalinskogo Gulaga*, 1:475–476. None were destined for the Karaganda region.

15. J. Otto Pohl, *The Stalinist Penal System: A Statistical History of Soviet Repression and Terror, 1930–1953* (Jefferson, NC: McFarland and Company, 1997), 70.

16. AOTsPSI, f. Karlaga, sv. 21, d. 331, l. 19.

17. Edwin Bacon, *The Gulag at War: Stalin's Forced Labour System in the Light of the Archives* (London: Macmillan, 1994), 104.

18. Gilboa, *Confess!* 111–22.

19. Jerzy Kmiecik, *A Boy in the Gulag* (London: Quartet Books, 1983).

20. See, among others, Gilboa, *Confess!* 65.

21. Quoted in AOTsPSI, f. Karlaga, arkhivnoe sledstvennoe delo 3663, l. 11.

22. Ibid., l. 9. For photographs of the prisoners, see ibid., l. 21. The photograph of Selivanov appears coerced. He is looking down, the image is blurry, and his hands are crossed, as if they may have been tied. All of this is in contrast to the photographs of the other prisoners involved in the case. Selivanov's refusal to cooperate with the photographer is confirmed in ibid., ll. 243–46.

23. Ibid., ll. 22b, 23b.

24. "Gulag v gody Velikoi Otechestvennoi Voiny," *Voenno-istoricheskii zhurnal*, no. 1 (1991): 23. The results of carrying this directive out are discussed in the document cited in Afanas'ev, et al., *Istoriia stalinskogo Gulaga*, 1:428–30.

25. AOTsPSI, f. Karlaga, arkhivnoe sledstvennoe delo 3663, l. 22b.

26. Kmiecik, *A Boy in the Gulag*, 146–47.

27. All the figures are in Kokurin and Petrov, *GULAG: (Glavnoe upravlenie lagerei)*, 416–20. Pohl has slightly different total population figures. See Pohl, *The Stalinist Penal System*, 11.

28. Viktor N. Zemskov, "Zakliuchennye, Spetsposelentsy, Ssyl'noposelentsy, Ssyl'nye i Vyslannye: Statistiko-geograficheskii aspekt," *Istoriia SSSR*, no. 5 (1991): 152–53; Pohl, *The Stalinist Penal System*, 46; Viktor N. Zemskov, "Sud'ba 'Kulatskoi Ssylki': 1930–1954 gg.," *Otechestvennaia Istoriia*, no. 1 (1994): 124–25.

29. These figures are from the 1944 report of the chief of the Gulag administration. "Gulag v gody voiny," 64. The numbers offered by Zemskov differ. He claims a total of 1,929,729 in the camps and colonies on January 1, 1941, and a total of 1,179,819 on January 1, 1944. Zemskov, "Zakliuchennye, Spetsposelentsy," 152. See also Bacon, *The Gulag at War*, 83.

30. GARF, f. 9414, op. 1, d. 328, l. 18.

31. The figures are in, respectively, AOTsPSI, f. Karlaga, sv. 2 spetsotdel, d. 14, ll. 16–18; GARF, f. 9414, op. 1, d. 1160, ll. 6, 11, 16, 46; AOTsPSI, f. Karlaga, sv. 3 spetsotdel, d. 36, ll. 81–82. The population would jump again in April 1943 with the merger of Dzhezkazganlag with Karlag, but this February 1943 population represented the growth of Karlag merely through additional prisoner arrivals in the intervening period.

32. GARF, f. 9414, op. 1, d. 328, l. 9; "Gulag v gody voiny," 64. NKVD officials met with considerably less success in their attempts to evacuate exiled peoples from areas near the front, although they made efforts to do so, focusing especially on the evacuation of men of fighting age. See Viktor N. Zemskov, "'Kulatskaia ssylka' nakanune i v gody Velikoi Otechestvennoi voiny," *Sotsiologicheskie issledovaniia*, no. 2 (1992): 16.

33. GARF, f. 9414, op. 1, d. 42, ll. 60–62. In his 1944 report, Nasedkin mentioned that some prisoners had been evacuated over a thousand kilometers on foot. "Gulag v gody voiny," 64. Many industrial workers were also evacuated on foot. See Richard Overy, *Russia's War: A History of the Soviet War Effort: 1941–1945* (New York: Penguin, 1998), 170–71.

34. Janusz Bardach and Kathleen Gleeson, *Man Is Wolf to Man: Surviving the Gulag* (Berkeley: University of California Press, 1998), 98.

35. Ibid., 102–3.

36. GARF, f. 9414, op. 1, d. 42, ll. 60–62.

37. AOTsPSI, f. Karlaga, sv. 3 spetsotdel, d. 24, l. 217.

38. GARF, f. 9414, op. 1, d. 328, l. 8. Instructions for carrying out these orders are cited in Afanas'ev, et al., *Istoriia stalinskogo Gulaga*, 1:424–28. Somehow Figes misses this mass release, stating that the postwar amnesty in 1945 was the "first mass release of prisoners." See Orlando Figes, *The Whisperers: Private Life in Stalin's Russia* (New York: Metropolitan Books, 2007), 449. Figes also generally neglects the constant release of significant portions of the Gulag's prisoners during every year of its existence in his otherwise-excellent study.

39. Diusetai Aimagambetovich Shaimukhanov and Saule Diusetaevna Shaimukhanova, *Karlag* (Karaganda: Poligrafiia, 1997), 41.

40. GARF, f. 9414, op. 1, d. 330, l. 61; "Gulag v gody voiny," 65.

41. GARF, f. 9414, op. 1, d. 1146, l. 33.

42. Zemskov, "Sud'ba," 131–33; "Kulatskaia ssylka," 20. The entirety of this drop in exiled kulaks cannot be explained by releases into the Red Army and the affiliated familial releases, but it does account for a high proportion.

43. The disaster was not in the food supply alone. Mark Harrison estimates that the real national income of the Soviet Union fell by more than 40 percent between 1940 and 1942, with between 66 and 75 percent of the national economic resources devoted to the military. Mark Harrison, "Resource Mobilization for World War II: The U.S.A., U.K., U.S.S.R., and Germany, 1938–1945," *Economic History Review* 41 (1988): 185.

44. Numerous memoirists testify to the reduction of food norms during the war. See I. V. Kashkinoi, "Pis'mo V. N. Pilishchuka," 176. Pilishchuk attributes his own survival to the 240 rubles accumulated in his prisoner account during his first several years in camps. See also Olga Adamova-Sliozberg, "My Journey," in *Till My Tale Is Told: Women's Memoirs of the Gulag*, ed. Simeon Vilensky (Bloomington: Indiana University Press, 1999), 57; Aleksandr I. Solzhenitsyn, *The Gulag Archipelago, 1918–1956: An Experiment in Literary Investigation*, trans. Thomas P. Whitney (New York: Harper Perennial, 1991), 2:132. Official evidence of the reduction in food norms starting in June 1941 can be found in Afanas'ev, et al., *Istoriia stalinskogo Gulaga*, 4:355–57.

45. "Gulag v gody voiny," 69.

46. Quoted in Afanas'ev, et al., *Istoriia stalinskogo Gulaga*, 4:376–77.

47. Kashkinoi, "Pis'mo V. N. Pilishchuka," 176. Karlag's order 0037, dated June 23, 1941, based on NKVD order 221, dated June 22, 1941, prohibited all visitation and correspondence for all inmates. AOTsPSI, f. Karlaga, sv. 6 s. s. pr., d. 153, ll. 126–27.

48. GARF, f. 9414, op. 1, d. 328, l. 82. These figures come from background materials used by the Gulag chief in preparing his report of 1944. In his report, he does not offer the details of camp mortality.

49. See Kokurin and Petrov, *GULAG: (Glavnoe upravlenie lagerei)*, 441–42.

50. AOTsPSI, f. Karlaga, sv. 24, d. 387, ll. 76–80. For the monthly percentages of the camp population and death rates, see Sergei Kruglov's letter of April 24, 1943 to Zhuravlev, in ibid., ll. 121–21b. For the overall death rate for the year, for the entire Gulag and Kolyma, see Afanas'ev, et al., *Istoriia stalinskogo Gulaga*, 4:55, 512.

51. NIPTs, f. 2, op. 3, d. 60, memoir of Galina Aleksandrovna Semenova, str. 11.

52. From April 1940 through April 1943, this camp division had been an independent camp known as Dzhezkazganlag, with a prisoner population varying between 6,000 and 14,000. Mikhail Borisovich Smirnov, *Sistema ispravitel'no-trudovykh lagerei v SSSR 1923–1960: Spravochnik* (Moscow: Zven'ia, 1998), 211–12. In the postwar period, the division was removed from Karlag and became part of a new special camp called Steplag. On the June 1943 mortality rate, see AOTsPSI, f. Karlaga, sv. 3 spetsotdel, d. 36, l. 128.

53. NIPTs, f. 2, op. 3, d. 60, memoir of Galina Aleksandrovna Semenova, str. 30.

54. AOTsPSI, f. Karlaga, sv. 24, d. 3897, ll. 76–80.

55. Gilboa, *Confess!* 64.

56. AOTsPSI, f. Karlaga, sv. 3 spetsotdel, d. 24, l. 291.

57. Kamenlag, officially known either as Kamenskii or Novo-Kamenskii corrective labor camp, existed from April 1942 through June 1944 in the Saratov region. It should not be confused with a separate Kamenlag located in the Novosibirsk region from 1953 to 1955. Smirnov, *Sistema ispravitel'no-trudovykh lagerei,* 280–81.

58. AOTsPSI, f. Karlaga, sv. 24, d. 387, ll. 76–80.

59. The sanotdel was responsible for the treatment of ill prisoners and prophylactic measures to prevent illness.

60. AOTsPSI, f. Karlaga, sv. 24, d. 387, l. 27.

61. Ibid., l. 26.

62. It is also not apparent on whose order Drevits went to Moscow. Zhuravlev does not seem to have been surprised that he was there, but he was certainly unhappy about the aftermath.

63. Ibid., ll. 19–19b. One cannot determine from the archival materials whether Nasedkin actually approved this transfer, but Drevits's veracity can be called into question. He concludes that Nasedkin had given a positive review to his work as head of Karlag's sanotdel. Yet considering the following condemnation by Kruglov and Nasedkin of the conditions at Karlag, such a positive review would seem unlikely. There is still the possibility, however, that Nasedkin agreed to provide such a positive review and transfer in exchange for blunt, detailed information on Karlag's conditions.

64. Quoted in ibid., ll. 6–6b.

65. Quoted in ibid., l. 4.

66. Ibid., ll. 4–6b.

67. Ibid., ll. 4–6b.

68. NIPTs, f. 2, op. 3, d. 60, memoir of Galina Semenova, str. 109.

69. AOTsPSI, f. Karlaga, sv. 24, d. 387, ll. 13–15.

70. Ibid., l. 23.

71. Ibid., ll. 25–25b.

72. Istoshchenie is literally translated as "emaciation" or "exhaustion." In the world of the Gulag, it was the term most frequently used when a prisoner had been worked and starved to death.

73. Ibid., ll. 126–28b.

74. Pellagra is a disease caused by a deficiency of niacin and protein in the diet, and is characterized by skin eruptions, digestive and nervous system disturbances, and eventual mental deterioration. It was common in the Gulag, and in the present case would lay the blame for dysentery not on the work of the sanotdel but rather on food provision in the camp.

75. See, for example, Alexander Dolgun with Patrick Watson, *Alexander Dolgun's Story: An American in the Gulag* (New York: Knopf, 1975), 178–84, 205–6, 237–51.

76. Bardach and Gleeson, *Man Is Wolf to Man.*

77. AOTsPSI, f. Karlaga, sv. 24, d. 387, ll. 126–128b.

78. Ibid., sv. 10 URO, d. 86, l. 160. Thus, Applebaum is incorrect when stating that mass burials were "technically forbidden." Applebaum, *Gulag*, 342. They may have been forbidden in certain periods, but not for the entirety of Gulag history.

79. Afanas'ev, et al., *Istoriia stalinskogo Gulaga*, 4:534–35.

80. AOTsPSI, f. Karlaga, sv. 24, d. 387, ll. 121–21b.

81. Ibid., d. 452, l. 3.

82. GARF, f. 9414, op. 1, d. 328, l. 8; "Gulag v gody voiny," 62–67.

83. GARF, f. 9414, op. 1, d. 328, l. 3; "Gulag v gody voiny," 62, 72.

84. AOTsPSI, f. Karlaga, sv. 2 spetsotdel, d. 14, ll. 16–18; GARF, f. 9414, op. 1, d. 1160, ll. 6, 11, 16, 46.

85. GARF, f. 9414, op. 1, d. 45, l. 542.

86. John Barber and Mark Harrison, *The Soviet Home Front, 1941–1945: A Social and Economic History of the USSR in World War II* (London: Longman, 1991), 144–45.

87. Viktor N. Zemskov, "Spetsposelentsy (po dokumentatsii NKVD-MVD SSSR)," *Sotsiologicheskie issledovaniia*, no. 11 (1990): 8; "Gulag v gody voiny," 71; GARF, f. 9414, op. 1, d. 328, l. 2; "Spetspereselentsy v SSSR v 1944 godu ili god bol'shogo pereseleniia," *Otechestvennye arkhivy*, no. 5 (1993): 99.

88. GARF, f. 9414, op. 1, d. 328, l. 22. As early as September 1939, the NKVD created an administration to organize the detention and labor utilization of POWs. Its first prisoners were Polish soldiers captured in fall 1939, but the numbers became significant only in 1943, when the Soviet advance to the west started in earnest. On May 11, 1945, the Soviet Union held just under 2.1 million POWs. Galina Mikhailovna Ivanova, *Gulag v sisteme totalitarnogo gosudarstva* (Moscow: Moskovskii obshchestvennyi nauchnyi fond, 1997), 56; "'Voennoplennye oznakomilis' s metodami sotsialisticheskogo stroitel'stva,' Dokladnaia zapiska MVD SSSR," *Istochnik*, no. 1 (1999): 83–88.

89. AOTsPSI, f. Karlaga, sv. 6, s. s. pr., d. 153, ll. 141–42.

90. "Mirovaia praktika. Protokol," *Kommersant*, September 10, 2003, 9.

91. The NKVD instructions from December 28, 1941 on the foundation and operation of such camps are in RGANI, f. 89, per. 40, dok. 1, ll. 1–5.

92. Ivanova, *Gulag v sisteme*, 52–53.

93. In 1943 and 1944, the State Committee of Defense forbade prisoners working in the defense industry from leaving their place of work on the completion of their sentence until the end of the war, but the damaging losses of prisoner laborers had already taken place. GARF, f. 9414, op. 1, d. 38, l. 23. Similar laws had been applied to portions of the civilian working population since 1940.

94. "Bol'sheviki Karagandy v bor'be za ugol'," *Pravda*, July 24, 1943, 1.

95. On the labor laws of 1940, see Peter J. Solomon Jr., *Soviet Criminal Justice under Stalin* (Cambridge: Cambridge University Press, 1996), 299–336. Popov describes the arrests under these laws as the third of three major peaks in Soviet criminal prosecutions. See V. P. Popov, "Gosudarstvennyi terror v sovetskoi Rossii, 1923–1953 gg. (istochniki i ikh interpretatsiia)," *Otechestvennye Arkhivy*, no. 2 (1992): 24.

96. Afanas'ev, et al., *Istoriia stalinskogo Gulaga*, 1:545–47, 551–52.

97. AOTsPSI, f. Karlaga, sv. 8 pr., d. 19, l. 151.

98. Ibid., l. 252.

99. Ibid., sv. 19, d. 288, l. 47. During the same period, another 428 prisoners were given additional sentences—243 for escape, 80 for counterrevolutionary offenses, and 60 for banditism, robbery, and hooliganism. The cases discussed above accounted for four of the nine executions in Karlag during this time frame.

100. Cited in ibid., sv. 8 pr., d. 19, ll. 203–3b.

101. Ivanova, *Gulag v sisteme*, 172, 185–86.

102. AOTsPSI, f. Karlaga, sv. 20, d. 296, l. 27.

103. Barber and Harrison, *The Soviet Home Front*, 61; Overy, *Russia's War*, 80.

104. "Gulag v gody voiny," 65, 68. The provision of no less than eight hours of sleep for prisoners each day was adopted on March 10, 1942. See Karlag's order implementing the policy in AOTsPSI, f. Karlaga, sv. 6 s. s. pr., d. 154, l. 76.

105. Some industries were given the right to force the transfer of their civilian workforce. See Barber and Harrison, *The Soviet Home Front*, 60–61.

106. "Gulag v gody voiny," 65.

107. Ibid., 66–67; GARF, f. 9414, op. 1, d. 328, ll. 21–26.

108. GARF, f. 9414, op. 1, d. 328, ll. 17, 26.

109. "Gulag v gody voiny," 79–81, 83.

110. Exiled special settlers typically worked in industries outside of the NKVD. Only 4.34 percent worked in NKVD industries on October 1, 1941, although the NKVD derived income from a 5 percent garnishment of the special settlers' salaries. Viktor N. Zemskov, "Kulatskaia ssylka," 16.

111. "Gulag v gody voiny," 85. The ruble was not a convertible currency. No meaningful translation into dollar amounts can be made. Rather, as follows, I will attempt to draw some comparisons between the size of the Gulag economy and the Soviet economy as a whole.

112. Based on figures for Gulag prisoners employed in NKVD industries, Gulag prisoners subcontracted out, and the total working population in Mark Harrison, *Accounting for War: Soviet Production, Employment, and the Defence Burden, 1940–1945* (New York: Cambridge University Press, 1996), 98, 269. These numbers exclude special settlers and POWs, whose labor did not figure into Nasedkin's account. From 1940 to 1945, the percentages run 2.3, 3.3, 3.9, 2.9, 2.4, and 2.5, respectively. Even as the total Gulag labor force contracted, its portion of the total working population remained relatively constant due to the simultaneous contraction of the civilian labor force.

113. As Harrison's lengthy study attests, calculating Soviet economic output is an extremely complex subject. Without question, my presentation here greatly simplifies the matter. The figures nonetheless at least provide some sense of the Gulag's economic production in comparison to the total Soviet economy, and most likely err on the side of showing the Gulag as more productive than it really was, since two groups of Gulag laborers—the small portion of special settlers working in Gulag industries and undetained forced laborers—are included in the totals for economic production but not in the total labor force. Furthermore, the figures take no account of the tremendous number of Gulag staffers needed merely to operate Gulag industries.

LINDSEY
1301 COLLEGE AVE
UMW BOX 1395
FREDERICKSBURG, VA 22401

**Contact:** LINDSEY CLOUSER

| Ship Via | | Terms | | Salesperson | |
|---|---|---|---|---|---|
| U.S. POSTAL SERVICE | | Barnes & Nobles | | BARNES | |
| **Ship Date** | **Order Date** | **Ordered By** | | **PO #** | |
| 01/07/12 | 01/07/12 | BARNES | | BQ-30807267006 | |

| Order Quantity | Shipped Quantity | Location | Item # | Item Description | Price | Extended Price |
|---|---|---|---|---|---|---|
| 1 | 1 | N | 131727 | Death and Redemption: The Gulag and the Shaping of Sov | 20.98 | 20.98 |
| | | | | 1    Total # of Units | | |

| | | Subtotal | 20.98 |
|---|---|---|---|
| | | Freight | 3.99 |
| Total Paid | 24.97 | | |
| Balance Due | 0.00 | **Invoice Total** | 24.97 |
| Page # | 1 | | |

**INVOICE**

| Invoice # | 784609 |
|-----------|--------|
| Customer # | 452599 |

114. Merely the secrecy involved in operating the Gulag bureaucracy was a tremendous expense. In 1940 alone, the NKVD circulated over twenty-five million secret packets of correspondence, each requiring special handling. And by 1948, Gulag administrative costs topped 11.5 billion rubles per year. Ivanova, *Gulag v sisteme*, 96, 113–14.

115. Ibid., 102, 115.

116. As a decorated Stakhanovite miner declared at the first Karaganda oblast' party conference in 1937, "Comrade Stalin in his speech at the Central Committee plenum correctly stated that 'wreckers do not always try to wreck, but sometimes they try to fulfill plans and prove themselves. . . . ' Every wrecker tries to prove himself and under the flag of a party card will wreck us." Fulfilling plans alone was never sufficient proof of one's innocence or honesty. Even though this meeting occurred during the worst period of the terror, the statement is true to the ethos throughout the Stalin period. RGASPI, f. 17, op. 21, d. 1612, l. 6.

117. Cited in GARF, f. 9414, op. 3, d. 14, l. 173.

118. Bacon, *The Gulag at War*, 160.

119. Cited in GARF, f. 9414, op. 1, d. 1442, l. 29.

120. Cited in ibid.

121. Ibid., d. 39, ll. 68–71. For a French translation, see Nicolas Werth and Gael Moullec, eds., *Rapports Secrets Sovietiques: La Societe Russe Dans Les Documents Confidentiels, 1921–1991* (Paris: Gallimard, 1994), 380–81. For other examples of problems blamed on poor political work, see GARF, f. 9414, op. 3, d. 14, l. 174; f. 9414, op. 3, d. 22, l. 30. The archives are filled with many other similar instances. For just one example of this attitude outside the Gulag in which successful coal mining was credited to proper political work by Communists, see "Bol'sheviki Karagandy v bor'be za ugol'," 1.

122. GARF, f. 9414, op. 3, d. 14, l. 173.

123. Ibid., op. 1, d. 1441, ll. 236–37.

124. Ibid., op. 3, d. 14, ll. 118–34; Ivanova, *Gulag v sisteme*, 173.

125. "Gulag v gody voiny," 72.

126. Cited in "Voennoplennye oznakomilis'," 83–88. Political education aimed at POWs was by no means a Soviet monopoly during World War II. See the episode of the British television documentary film series *Timewatch, Series 1* titled *The Germans We Kept*, in which former German POWs describe the complex categorization of these POWs according to their political attitudes and attempts to denazify them. Of course, the conditions in POW camps in the different combatant countries varied greatly.

127. Barber and Harrison, *The Soviet Home Front*, 68.

128. Eugenia Ginzburg, *Within the Whirlwind* (New York: Harcourt Brace Jovanovich, 1981), 27. Certainly, in referring to "four years of suffering," Ginzburg is implicitly excluding all those arrested in the years other than the Great Terror.

129. Figes, *The Whisperers*, 447.

130. Solzhenitsyn, *The Gulag Archipelago*, 2:121.

131. Ibid., 2:134–35.

132. GARF, f. 9414, op. 4, d. 145, l. 2b.

133. AOTsPSI, f. Karlaga, sv. 26, d. 421, l. 16.

134. Cited in GARF, f. 9414, op. 4, d. 145, l. 3.

135. Compare the comments of one Vladivostoklag division head in November 1941 on the "poor" work of the cultural-educational sections, which "do not know the moods of the prisoners." Quoted in ibid., op. 3, d. 14, l. 186. Interestingly, knowing the political mood of the prisoners was also the job of the camp surveillance system. See the discussion of the surveillance system to follow.

136. The similarities between Loginov's anecdotes and those in *Belomor* are striking.

137. Quoted in ibid., op. 4, d. 145, l. 3. His stories also expose yet again the capriciousness of the Soviet political system. Consider, for example, Ekaterina Sh., whose husband was shot in 1937 as a "double-dyed spy." After her husband's execution, Ekaterina was arrested for "loss of vigilance of a Soviet wife." It seems that if she had exhibited enough "vigilance," she would have realized that her husband was a spy. Ibid., l. 4b.

138. Quoted in ibid., l. 5, l. 7.

139. Quoted in ibid., l. 10b, l. 11, l. 12.

140. Barber and Harrison, *The Soviet Home Front*, 69–70, 160–61, 174–76.

141. See, for example, ibid., 30, 68–72; Overy, *Russia's War*, 161–63.

142. Quoted in GARF, f. 9414, op. 4, d. 145, ll. 11–12b.

143. Quoted in ibid., l. 3.

144. On the postwar disappearance of particular Jewish suffering and heroism into the universal story of Soviet suffering and heroism, see Amir Weiner, "Nature, Nurture, and Memory in a Socialist Utopia: Delineating the Soviet Socio-Ethnic Body in the Age of Socialism," *American Historical Review* 104, no. 4 (1999): 1114–55.

145. Overy, *Russia's War*, xxi. In the main text, however, Overy himself also subscribes at times to the notion that revolution and socialism disappeared from official propaganda. His book is after all titled *Russia's War*. At other times, he recognizes the continued significance of defending the Soviet Union as a force of "socialist progress." Compare ibid., 114–15 with ibid., 153.

146. GARF, f. 9414, op. 4, d. 145, ll. 11–12b. Of course, we do not know if Gol'dshtein's story is true.

147. Here from a report written on January 5, 1943, by the head of the central Gulag Cultural-Educational Department to several local camp Cultural-Educational Departments. Ibid., op. 1, d. 1449, l. 5.

148. Ibid., d. 325, l. 52.

149. Cited in ibid., d. 1449, l. 5.

150. Cited in ibid.

151. See the roundtable discussion in "Gulag v gody Velikoi Otechestvennoi Voiny," 22. Although no documents are referenced directly in the discussion, most of the facts mentioned by the participants are verifiable in sources to which I have had access (one exception is Gulag mortality statistics for the war years well below those that I have uncovered; see ibid., 23). I am unfamiliar with any source confirming this claim of a decrease in the number of labor refusers.

152. "Gulag v gody voiny," 65.

153. Shaimukhanov and Shaimukhanova, *Karlag*, 42–44. At least two of these twenty-one former Karlag prisoners had been sentenced under Article 58. The

first had been released because his conviction was overturned, and the second was sent to the front on the basis of a granted petition sent to the Presidium of the Supreme Soviet.

154. Suprisingly, then, I found no reference to Breusov in any Karlag document throughout my research—this despite Karlag's documented success at self-promotion, whether through the many photo albums sent to central Gulag, or the camp officials' own "history" written and submitted to central authorities in 1934.

155. Strictly in terms of commitment to labor, the Gulag successfully engaged both prisoners loyal to and devout enemies of the Soviet state order. For the former, as discussed in the introduction to this chapter, see Kashkinoi, "Pis'mo V. N. Pilishchuka," 170–85. For an avowed enemy of the Soviet state drawn to labor effectively anyway, see Dmitri Panin, *The Notebooks of Sologdin* (New York: Harcourt Brace Jovanovich, 1976).

156. Contrary to Barber and Harrison's assertion that "prewar themes of internal division and 'intensified' class struggle against the enemy within gave way to national [Russian] unification in order to drive out the foreign invader," the battle with the enemy within took on new elements but never ceased. Barber and Harrison, *The Soviet Home Front*, 30, 39–41. On one manifestation of that battle with the enemy, see the discussion of wartime deportations below.

157. Ibid., 29–30.

158. The description of the uprising comes in a letter written by Beria on January 27, 1942. At that time, the battle against the uprising continued with nearly one hundred prisoners still on the loose. GARF, f. 9414, op. 1, d. 45, ll. 102–5.

159. These figures are in Ivanova, *Gulag v sisteme*, 54, which relies on an article in *Nezavisimaia Gazeta*, January 23, 1992. The incident is also discussed in Applebaum, *Gulag*, 404–8.

160. GARF, f. 9414, op. 1, d. 45, ll. 102–5.

161. AOTsPSI, f. Karlaga, sv. 6, s. s. pr., d. 154, ll. 18–18b.

162. Here, the head of the politotdel of Vladivostoklag quotes Stalin's speech to a meeting of the Party activists on November 24, 1941. Quoted in GARF, f. 9414, op. 1, d. 14, l. 158. As Popov noted, it was precisely this call for struggle with the enemies of the rear that led to a wartime surge in the arrests of counterrevolutionary criminals by secret police organizations. Popov, "Gosudarstvennyi terror v sovetskoi Rossii," 29.

163. GARF, f. 9414, op. 1, d. 41, l. 14. Specialists among the prisoners were also among the first evacuated.

164. Considering the history of political executions in the 1920s and 1930s, it is surprising that she and these other prisoners were still alive by 1941. "Tragediia v medvedevskom lesu: o rasstrele politzakliuchennykh Orlovskoi tiur'my," *Izvestiia TsK KPSS*, no. 11, (1990): 124–31. On general orders for shooting prisoners in the face of the Nazi advance, see Bacon, *The Gulag at War*, 89, which equates the policy with the Soviet destruction of industrial equipment to avoid its falling into enemy hands. According to Getty, Rittersporn, and Zemskov, approximately 10,800 prisoners were shot throughout the camps during the first three years of the war. J. Arch Getty, Gábor Tamás Rittersporn, and Viktor N. Zemskov, "Victims of the Soviet Penal System in the Pre-war Years: A

First Approach on the Basis of Archival Evidence," *American Historical Review* (October 1993): 1041.

165. GARF, f. 9414, op. 1, d. 328, ll. 6, 48. For a local camp experience with the "concentration" of these categories of prisoners into "special zones" under strengthened guard, see ibid., op. 3, d. 14, ll. 136–49. On calls for additional vigilance among Gulag workers, see ibid., ll. 163–68. Solzhenitsyn also wrote of the isolation of Article 58 prisoners from other prisoners and the halt placed on the release of Article 58 prisoners. Solzhenitsyn, *The Gulag Archipelago*, 2:131.

166. AOTsPSI, f. Karlaga, sv. 6, s. s. pr., d. 153, ll. 126–27, 136–39.

167. Ibid., d. 154, l. 78.

168. Ibid., d. 153, l. 129.

169. Ibid., sv. 14, d. 229, l. 45.

170. Ibid., sv. 20, d. 296, l. 40.

171. Ibid., sv. 6 s. s. pr., d. 154, l. 3.

172. Cited in "Gulag v gody voiny," 74.

173. AOTsPSI, f. Karlaga, sv. 19, d. 288, l. 163.

174. GARF, f. 9401, op. 1a, d. 135, ll. 121–21b. Karlag chief Zhuravlev informed the Gulag of the escape's liquidation and the recovery of all weapons in a letter on June 12, 1943. AOTsPSI, f. Karlaga, sv. 24, d. 387, l. 141.

175. "Gulag v gody voiny," 74.

176. Zemskov, "Kulatskaia ssylka," 22.

177. "Gulag v gody voiny," 74–75; GARF, f. 9414, op. 1, d. 328, l. 11. Only when discussion of the surveillance system appeared in general documents like these, which were kept outside the collection of the operchekotdel, do we find this information in a declassified form.

178. "Gulag v gody voiny," 75–76.

179. Werth and Moullec, *Rapports Secrets Sovietiques*, 384–85.

180. Ivanova opines that these "organizations" existed "only on paper," since Gulag workers in their meetings never spoke of organizations, but only of individual or group escapes. Ivanova, *Gulag v sisteme*, 55.

181. Pohl, *The Stalinist Penal System*, 16.

182. AOTsPSI, f. Karlaga, sv. 24, d. 387, ll. 141–44. The number of especially dangerous prisoners, according to Zhuravlev, had risen by more than six thousand, approaching a total of sixteen thousand at Karlag.

183. Afanas'ev, et al., *Istoriia stalinskogo Gulaga*, 2:210–11.

184. Ibid., 2:227–33.

185. Ibid., 2:233–38.

186. From the Gulag chief's report in 1945 on the operation of katorga divisions during the war. GARF, f. 9414, op. 1, d. 76, l. 4.

187. Ibid., d. 1146, l. 28b; Ivanova, *Gulag v sisteme*, 53.

188. GARF, f. 9414, op. 1, d. 76, ll. 2–4b, 56–58; f. 9414, op. 1, d. 328, l. 5; Afanas'ev, et al., *Istoriia stalinskogo Gulaga*, 2:220–21.

189. Solzhenitsyn, *The Gulag Archipelago*, 3:8.

190. GARF, f. 9414, op. 1, d. 1146, l. 28b. By September 1947, the katorga population did reach sixty thousand. Ivanova, *Gulag v sisteme*, 53.

191. Solzhenitsyn, *The Gulag Archipelago*, 3:9–10.

192. The "Short Historical Note on Katorga" is in GARF, f. 9414, op. 1, d. 76, ll. 24–36.

193. Cited in ibid., ll. 1–4.

194. Ibid., ll. 24–26.

195. Ibid., ll. 1–4.

196. Cited in ibid., l. 34.

197. Afanas'ev, et al., *Istoriia stalinskogo Gulaga*, 2:220–21.

198. Ibid., 2:372–73.

199. "Gulag v gody voiny," 64.

200. The 1945 figure is in GARF, f. 9414, op. 1, d. 76, l. 11; the 1947 number is in Ivanova, *Gulag v sisteme*, 53. Karlag continued to house an especially small number of katorga prisoners—only 172 on September 1, 1945.

201. "Spetspereselentsy v SSSR v 1944 godu," 109.

202. Bardach and Gleeson, *Man Is Wolf to Man*, 62.

203. Gorlanov and Roginskii have shown convincingly that NKVD arrests in the newly annexed territories were related more to the arrestee's social and political past than to their nationality. Furthermore, a large portion of the arrests were for illegal border crossings, a "crime" that was quite frequent as families tried to reunite across the new borders, Jews attempted to flee Nazi rule, and others attempted to control under which political regime they would live. Oleg A. Gorlanov and Arsenii B. Roginskii, "Ob arestakh v zapadnykh oblastiakh Belorussii i Ukraini v 1939–1941 gg.," in *Repessii protiv poliakov i pol'skikh grazhdan*, ed. Aleksandr E. Gur'ianov (Moscow, Zven'ia 1997), 88–89, 91. For a similar evaluation of the motivations of deportations, see Aleksandr E. Gur'ianov, "Pol'skie spetspereselentsy v SSSR v 1940–1941 gg.," in *Repessii protiv poliakov i pol'skikh grazhdan*, ed. Aleksandr E. Gur'ianov (Moscow: Zven'ia, 1997), 114–36.

204. See Viktor N. Zemskov, "Prinuditel'nye migratsii iz Pribaltiki v 1940–1950-kh godakh," *Otechestvennye arkhivy*, no. 1 (1993): 13.

205. Ingeborg Fleischhauer asserts that the deportations of the Soviet Germans were likely planned before the Nazi invasion ever took place. They were delayed, he argues, mainly due to economic needs in the European part of the Soviet Union prior to the evacuation of these areas. Ingeborg Fleischhauer, "'Operation Barbarossa' and the Deportation," in *The Soviet Germans: Past and Present*, ed. Ingeborg Fleischhauer and Benjamin Pinkus (London: Hurst, 1986), 70. He may be right, especially considering that some Soviet Germans were evacuated from the Crimea and other areas close to the front prior to the mass deportation orders.

206. Ginzburg, *Within the Whirlwind*, 28. Alas, this was one of the few instances in which being Jewish provided an improvement in status in the Gulag.

207. NIPTs, f. 2, op. 3, d. 60, memoir of Galina Aleksandrovna Semenova, str. 63.

208. Edward Buca, *Vorkuta* (London: Constable, 1976), 6. One must be careful not to ascribe essential characteristics to national groupings in the Gulag, even if memoirists did so. Applebaum, in one of the least satisfying discussions in her book, falls prey to this easy lumping of Soviet and non-Soviet Chinese in the camps into a single group without even asking the question of whether a Soviet citizen of Chinese descent had more in common with their fellow Soviet citizens than with citizens of China arrested for "accidentally . . . walk[ing] over the very

long Chinese-Soviet border." Applebaum, *Gulag*, 300. Was Soviet power such a nonfactor that the Soviet Chinese were no more equipped to deal with Gulag labor, food, and people than Chinese Chinese?

209. Joseph Scholmer, *Vorkuta* (New York: Holt, 1955), 103.

210. Lev Kopelev, *To Be Preserved Forever* (Philadelphia: Lippincott, 1977), 5.

211. GARF, f. 9414, op. 1, d. 77, l. 145. The provisions also applied to all those from the Baltics and Bessarabia who had been convicted of counterrevolutionary offenses, along with all participants in nationalist organizations.

212. Pohl notes the important difference from the later deportations of the Chechens, Ingush, and others. The Germans were accused of harboring potential spies, while the Chechens and others were accused of actual acts of espionage, sabotage, and collaboration. Pohl, *The Stalinist Penal System*, 74–75.

213. The text of the decree has been published in numerous places. See, for example, an English translation of a German copy of the text in Fred C. Koch, *The Volga Germans: In Russia and the Americas, from 1763 to the Present* (University Park: Penn State University Press, 1977), 284; see also the original Russian from the August 30, 1941, edition of *Bol'shevik* in Vladimir A. Auman and Valentina G. Chebotareva, eds., *Istoriia rossiiskikh nemtsev v dokumentakh (1763–1992 gg.)* (Moscow: Mezhdunarodnyi institut gumanitarnykh programm, 1993), 159–60. Beria's implementation order from the following day, August 27, 1941, is in Afanas'ev, et al., *Istoriia stalinskogo Gulaga*, 1:455–57.

214. For some of these decrees, see Auman and Chebotareva, *Istoriia rossiiskikh nemtsev v dokumentakh*, 160–68.

215. Pohl, *The Stalinist Penal System*, 76.

216. Zemskov, "Spetsposelentsy (po dokumentatsii); Pohl, *The Stalinist Penal System*, 78; Kaidar S. Aldazhumanov, "Deportatsiia narodov—prestuplenie totalitarnogo rezhima," in *Deportatsiia narodov i problema prav cheloveka: Materialy seminara, Almaty 12 iiunia 1997 goda*, ed. Igor' Trutanov, Vladislav Nabokov, and Iurii Romanov (Almaty, Kazakhstan: Istorichesko-prosvetitel'skoe obshchestvo "Adilet," 1998): 13.

217. Aldazhumanov, "Deportatsiia narodov—prestuplenie totalitarnogo rezhima," 13.

218. T. B. Mitropol'skaia and I. N. Bukhanova, eds., *Iz istorii nemtsev Kazakhstana, 1921–1975 gg.: Sbornik dokumentov* (Almaty, Kazakhstan: Gotika, 1997), 135.

219. For the decree laying out the details of resettling Volga Germans, see Nikolai F. Bugai, ed., *"Mobilizovat' nemtsev v rabochie kolonny ... I. Stalin" Sbornik dokumentov (1940-e gody)* (Moscow: Gotika, 1998), 19–22. For the decree laying out the details for resettling Germans from the Moscow region, see Auman and Chebotareva, *Istoriia rossiiskikh nemtsev v dokumentakh*, 161–62. In many cases, city residents were also resettled in kolkhozy and sovkhozy; see Mitropol'skaia and Bukhanova, *Iz istorii nemtsev Kazakhstana*, 107–8. The deportees' property often was never returned to them after their trip into exile. On the frequent recurrence in the archives of group complaints about lost property, see Aldazhumanov, "Deportatsiia narodov—prestuplenie totalitarnogo rezhima," 17.

220. Auman and Chebotareva, *Istoriia rossiiskikh nemtsev v dokumentakh*, 164.

221. Afanas'ev, et al., *Istoriia stalinskogo Gulaga*, 1:455–57. For slightly different figures on the number taking part in the deportations, see Auman and Chebotareva, *Istoriia rossiiskikh nemtsev v dokumentakh*, 160–61.

222. The initial deportation orders for the Volga Germans even included the obligation that the state would supply the deportees with livestock in their new locale equivalent to those that they had left behind at their previous homes, although there is little evidence that this requirement was met. Bugai, *"Mobilizovat' nemtsev v rabochie kolonny,"* 20.

223. See Mitropol'skaia and Bukhanova, *Iz istorii nemtsev Kazakhstana*, 94–96, 100–102.

224. Ibid., 102–4.

225. Mitropol'skaia and Bukhanova, *Iz istorii nemtsev Kazakhstana* contains several documents from different localities in Kazakhstan offering tales of various anti-Soviet activities among the exiled Germans.

226. Ibid., 110–12. Kondratenko's proposals were altered but accepted, and these Soviet Germans were moved in December 1941–January 1942. See ibid., 113–15. For other letters from localities on the moods of the Soviet German population, see ibid., 107–10.

227. Aldazhumanov, "Deportatsiia narodov—prestuplenie totalitarnogo rezhima," 18. Unfortunately, Aldazhumanov does not provide a citation to this document. Archives of the former Kazakh republic-level NKVD are much less accessible to scholars than many of their local or unionwide counterparts. Such sentiments were not reserved for Soviet German exiles alone. Local authorities and citizens frequently expressed their distrust of peoples who were deemed enemies merely based on their status as exiles. One Kazakhstan sovkhoz director expressed similar sentiments on the arrival of Polish exiles in the 1940–41 period. Expressions of sympathy were also common, as a different local resident described the exile of Poles as "barbarism." See Gur'ianov, "Pol'skie spetspereselentsy," 122–23.

228. For these three State Committee of Defense decrees, all signed by Stalin, see Bugai, *"Mobilizovat' nemtsev v rabochie kolonny,"* 39–44; Auman and Chebotareva, *Istoriia rossiiskikh nemtsev v dokumentakh*, 168–70, 172. A later clarification of the decree of October 7, 1942 gave local authorities the leeway to excuse women with more than three children from labor mobilization, if they had no close relatives with whom to leave their children. Otherwise, only a few Soviet Germans were excluded from incorporation into the mobilized labor force—those from the easternmost regions of the USSR and those from regions in which there were fewer than one thousand individuals falling under these provisions. Bugai, *"Mobilizovat' nemtsev v rabochie kolonny,"* 45–46, 78.

229. Barber and Harrison, *The Soviet Home Front*, 166.

230. This GKO decree is in Bugai, *"Mobilizovat' nemtsev v rabochie kolonny,"* 44–45.

231. Ibid., 61, 65, 76.

232. Mitropol'skaia and Bukhanova, *Iz istorii nemtsev Kazakhstana*, 135–36.

233. Karlag did not house any of the mobilized Germans.

234. Bugai, *"Mobilizovat' nemtsev v rabochie kolonny,"* 61, 63, 114–17, 122–25; Kokurin and Petrov, *GULAG: (Glavnoe upravlenie lagerei)*, 129–32; GARF,

f. 9414, op. 1, d. 328, l. 43. Mobilized Germans were paid for their work, but the cost of their housing, food, and communal services was deducted from their pay. Even then, they could only gain access to their money or send it to their families with permission of the chief of their working column. GARF, f. 9414, op. 1, d. 45, l. 258.

235. GARF, f. 9414, op. 1, d. 39, ll. 165–67.

236. Mitropol'skaia and Bukhanova, *Iz istorii nemtsev Kazakhstana*, 144.

237. Ibid., 138–39.

238. On reports of provocations designed to test the loyalty of Soviet Germans, see Fleischhauer, "'Operation Barbarossa' and the Deportation," 80. For a cogent consideration of the lack of evidence for widespread Soviet German disloyalty, see Pohl, *The Stalinist Penal System*, 75. Aldazhumanov also notes that no military evidence ever uncovered significant Soviet German disloyalty. Aldazhumanov, "Deportatsiia narodov—prestuplenie totalitarnogo rezhima," 13.

239. Bugai, *"Mobilizovat' nemtsev v rabochie kolonny,"* 19–22. Intriguingly, Soviet German members of the Komsomol and Communist Party, while subject to both the deportations and labor mobilizations, were not stripped of their membership.

240. Ibid., 28–29.

241. Ibid., 45–46.

242. Ibid., 19–26.

243. See Ingeborg Fleischauer, "The Ethnic Germans under Nazi Rule," in *The Soviet Germans: Past and Present*, ed. Ingeborg Fleischhauer and Benjamin Pinkus (London: Hurst, 1986), 92–102.

244. AOTsPSI, f. Karlaga, sv. 10 URO, d. 86, l. 201.

245. Kokurin and Petrov, *GULAG: (Glavnoe upravlenie lagerei)*, 417, 425.

246. Naimark and Pohl argue that there is no evidence that Chechens and Ingush collaborated in numbers larger than any other Soviet nationality. See Norman M. Naimark, *Fires of Hatred: Ethnic Cleansing in Twentieth-Century Europe* (Cambridge, MA: Harvard University Press, 2001), 95; Pohl, *The Stalinist Penal System*, 100. Burds disagrees. See Jeffrey Burds, "The Soviet War against 'Fifth Columnists': The Case of Chechnya, 1942–4," *Journal of Contemporary History* 42, no. 2 (2007): 267–314.

247. Nicolas Werth, "'The Chechen Problem': Handling an Awkward Legacy, 1918–1958," *Contemporary European History* 15, no. 3 (2006): 347–66; Naimark, *Fires of Hatred*, 92–96. While Pohl essentially agrees with Naimark's analysis, he attempts to ascribe the deportations fundamentally to "ethnic hatred" and "the Stalinist revival of Russian chauvinism." Even though the deportation operated, obviously, on an ethnic basis, it was not merely the result of ethnic hatred or Russian chauvinism. There was something more. Pohl's explanation fails to account for all of the nationalities *not* deported during the war. Pohl, *The Stalinist Penal System*, 100–101.

248. Naimark, *Fires of Hatred*, 94.

249. Ibid., 96–97.

250. This figure included some 390,000 Chechens and 90,000 Ingush. Afanas'ev, et al., *Istoriia stalinskogo Gulaga*, 1:490; Pohl, *The Stalinist Penal System*, 103.

251. Afanas'ev, et al., *Istoriia stalinskogo Gulaga*, 1:488–90.

252. Abdazhapar Abdakimov, *Totalitarizm: Deportatsiia narodov i repressiia intelligentsii* (Karaganda: Apparat akima Karagandinskoi oblasti, 1997), 55.

253. Naimark, *Fires of Hatred*, 96–97; Pohl, *The Stalinist Penal System*, 106–7; Werth, "The Chechen Problem," 357–58.

254. Werth, "The Chechen Problem," 358.

255. Pohl, *The Stalinist Penal System*, 101, 104–5. For more on Chechens and Ingush in Karlag, see the following two chapters herein.

256. Pohl, *The Stalinist Penal System*, 105; Werth, "The Chechen Problem," 358–59.

257. Mitropol'skaia and Bukhanova, *Iz istorii nemtsev Kazakhstana*, 141.

258. "Gulag v gody voiny," 85.

259. GARF, f. 9414, op. 1, d. 330, l. 55.


CHAPTER 5: A NEW CIRCLE OF HELL

1. Quoted in Arkhiv Prezidenta Respubliki Kazakhstana (Presidential Archive of the Republic of Kazakhstan; hereafter APRK), f. 819, op. 1, d. 21, l. 116b.

2. Quoted in RGASPI, f. 82, op. 2, d. 148, ll. 68–70.

3. Lev Kopelev, *To Be Preserved Forever* (Philadelphia: Lippincott, 1977), 120.

4. Galina Mikhailovna Ivanova, *Labor Camp Socialism: The Gulag in the Soviet Totalitarian System*, trans. Carol Flath (Armonk, NY: M. E. Sharpe, 2000), 43. One official document places the total repatriates from the occupied territories passing through the camps as of August 1, 1945 at 2.4 million, of whom 1.3 million were currently in eighty-five camps and filtration points. See RGANI, f. 89, per. 40, d. 2, ll. 2–3.

5. GARF, f. 9401, op. 2, d. 64, ll. 9–12.

6. RGANI, f. 89, per. 40, d. 3, ll. 2–3.

7. GARF, f. 9414, op. 1, d. 86, l. 2.

8. RGANI, f. 89, per. 40, d. 2, ll. 2–3; d. 3, ll. 2–3.

9. Viktor N. Zemskov, "GULAG (istoriko-sotsiologicheskii aspekt)," *Sotsiologicheskie issledovaniia*, no. 7 (1991): 6. A copy of the amnesty can be found at AOTsPSI, f. Karlaga, sv. 27, d. 457, ll. 4–4b. On the amnesty, see Alexopoulos, "Amnesty 1945."

10. GARF, f. 9414, op. 1, d. 1155, ll. 1a–2.

11. The total colony population on January 1 of the following years was 516,000 in 1944, 745,000 in 1945, 510,000 in 1946, 895,000 in 1947, and 1,061,000 in 1948. Ibid., ll. 76b–80b.

12. Ibid., ll. 1a–2, 76b–80b.

13. Aleksandr I. Solzhenitsyn, *The Gulag Archipelago, 1918–1956: An Experiment in Literary Investigation*, trans. Thomas P. Whitney (New York: Harper Perennial, 1991), 2:136.

14. AOTsPSI, f. Karlaga, sv. 27, d. 457, ll. 4–4b.

15. GARF, f. 9414, op. 1, d. 1155, l. 3.

16. Iurii Nikolaevich Afanas'ev, et al., eds., *Istoriia stalinskogo Gulaga: Konets 1920-kh–pervaia polovina 1950-kh godov: Sobranie dokumentov v semi tomakh* (Moscow: Rosspen, 2004), 2:271–73.

17. GARF, f. 9414, op. 1, d. 1155, l. 3.

18. Ibid., d. 80, l. 8. Only Sevvostlag at Kolyma (139,000), Vorkutlag (77,000), and Sevpechlag (66,000), both in the Komi region, were larger.

19. AOTsPSI, f. Karlaga, sv. 36 d. 537, ll. 99, 101–2.

20. On February 1, 1949, the Karlag population had dropped to 57,061, but there was still only 1.2 square meters of living space per prisoner. Ibid., l. 105.

21. Galina Mikhailovna Ivanova, *Gulag v sisteme totalitarnogo gosudarstva* (Moscow: Moskovskii obshchestvennyi nauchnyi fond, 1997); 49–51; Afanas'ev, et al., *Istoriia stalinskogo Gulaga*, 1:550–51.

22. Viktor N. Zemskov, "Zakliuchennye, Spetsposelentsy, Ssyl'noposelentsy, Ssyl'nye i Vyslannye: Statistiko-geograficheskii aspekt," *Istoriia SSSR*, no. 5 (1991): 152.

23. See the figures in ibid., 152. Zemskov himself attributes the rising Gulag population of the late 1940s to the elimination of the death penalty in 1947. This, he suggests, meant that a number of individuals who previously would have been executed were now finding their way into the Gulag. Zemskov, "GULAG (istoriko-sotsiologicheskii aspekt)," 7. No doubt this contributed to the population growth, but its role must have been minor in comparison to the adoption of the June 4, 1947 decree on the theft of state property. The Gulag population in 1947, after all, jumped by nearly one-half million—a population boost much too large to explain with the ban on capital punishment. These figures show that Figes is completely mistaken in attributing the growth of the Gulag population between 1945 and 1950 to "the mass arrest of 'nationalists'" from the western territories. See Orlando Figes, *The Whisperers: Private Life in Stalin's Russia* (New York: Metropolitan Books, 2007), 467.

24. Zemskov, "GULAG (istoriko-sotsiologicheskii aspekt)," 10. The percentages in the camps and colonies under the laws of June 4, 1947 are similar to the percentages in the camps and colonies of all Gulag prisoners.

25. Solzhenitsyn, *The Gulag Archipelago*, 2:188–90.

26. On the Soviet population's expectations of relaxation in the postwar era and the state's refusal to meet these expectations, see Elena Zubkova, *Russia after the War: Hopes, Illusions, and Disappointments, 1945–1957*, trans. and ed. Hugh Ragsdale (Armonk, NY: M. E. Sharpe, 1998).

27. APRK, f. 819, op. 1, d. 1, l. 6.

28. Quoted in ibid., l. 25.

29. AOTsPSI, f. Karlaga, sv. 31, d. 494, l. 131.

30. APRK, f. 819, op. 1, d. 122, l. 7.

31. AOTsPSI, f. Karlaga, sv. 27, d. 456, l. 69b–70.

32. See, for example, the speech of the Kazakh minister of internal affairs Bogdanov on June 12, 1946. APRK, f. 819, op. 1, d. 4, l. 1.

33. Ibid., d. 122, l. 4b. This is the same Aleksandr Matrosov celebrated by the Gulag as one of its former prisoners recognized as a Hero of the Soviet Union.

34. On the use of the term fascist by "thieves," see Solzhenitsyn, *The Gulag Archipelago*, 2:169.

35. Kopelev, *To Be Preserved Forever*, 171.

36. Lev Kopelev, *The Education of a True Believer* (New York: Harper and Rowe, 1980). On the anti-Semitic rumors of Soviet Jews fighting only on the "Tashkent front," see Rebecca Manley, *To the Tashkent Station: Evacuation and*

*Survival in the Soviet Union at War* (Ithaca, NY: Cornell University Press, 2009) 267–68.

37. AOTsPSI, f. Karlaga, sv. 30, d. 493, ll. 25–28.

38. From the resolutions adopted at the first Kazakh UITLK party conference. APRK, f. 819, op. 1, d. 1, l. 70.

39. Quoted in ibid., d. 21, l. 119b.

40. Ibid., d. 122, l. 7b, 9.

41. "Chtoby stroit' nado znat', chtoby znat' nado uchit'sia." The maxim is repeated in ibid., d. 122, l. 9b; d. 1, l. 48.

42. Ibid., d. 1, l. 25b.

43. Ibid.

44. Ibid., d. 122, l. 6.

45. Ibid., d. 178, l. 27.

46. Quoted in ibid., d. 1, l. 30b.

47. Payments to some prisoners in Kolyma had been introduced as early as 1949. GARF, f. 9414, op. 1, d. 326, l. 23.

48. AOTsPSI, f. Karlaga, sv. 6 s.s. pr., d. 156, ll. 61–63.

49. Ibid., sv. 33, d. 519, ll. 24–25, 49–50.

50. Alexander Dolgun with Patrick Watson, *Alexander Dolgun's Story: An American in the Gulag* (New York: Knopf, 1975), 109–10.

51. GARF, f. 9414, op. 1, d. 326, l. 1. During 1947, 1.5 million newly convicted prisoners arrived in the Gulag compared to just over 1 million releases. Approximately 22 percent of these prisoners were women.

52. Ibid., l. 2. These "k-r" inmates had accounted for 34 percent of the total Gulag population just one year earlier.

53. Ibid., l. 5.

54. Ibid., ll. 5–6.

55. This word-for-word formulation was repeated again and again in documents discussing the work of the special camps.

56. The decision on February 21, 1948 by the Council of Ministers to create the special camps is in Afanas'ev, et al., *Istoriia stalinskogo Gulaga*, 2:326–27. The implementation directive of February 28, 1948, is in ibid., 2:328–30; Aleksandr Kokurin and Nikolai Petrov, eds., *GULAG: (Glavnoe upravlenie lagerei), 1917–1960* (Moscow: Mezhdunarodnyi fond "Demokratiia," 2000), 135–37.

57. Kokurin and Petrov, *GULAG: (Glavnoe upravlenie lagerei)*, 559.

58. Ibid., 135–41; RGANI, f. 89, per. 60, d. 11, l. 3.

59. Kokurin and Petrov, *GULAG: (Glavnoe upravlenie lagerei)*, 135–41; RGANI, f. 89, per. 60, d. 11, l. 3.

60. Afanas'ev, et al., *Istoriia stalinskogo Gulaga*, 4:125–26.

61. Kokurin and Petrov, *GULAG: (Glavnoe upravlenie lagerei)*, 135–37.

62. Mikhail Borisovich Smirnov, *Sistema ispravitel'no trudovykh lagerei v SSSR 1923–1960: Spravochnik* (Moscow: Zven'ia, 1998), 403–4.

63. Afanas'ev, et al., *Istoriia stalinskogo Gulaga*, 2:371.

64. Ibid., 2:385–86. Among the most well-known inmates in Ekibastuz was Dmitri Panin. See Dmitri Panin, *The Notebooks of Sologdin* (New York: Harcourt Brace Jovanovich, 1976).

65. Dolgun with Watson, *Alexander Dolgun's Story*, 162–64.

66. On Dolgun's meeting a prisoner in the course of his transfer to the Spassk subdivision for invalids, Steplag's "camp for the dying," due to his contraction of silicosis in Dzhezkazgan, see ibid., 162. As Dolgun wrote, "Yes, he was terrified of death, but it could not be worse to die than to live in the living hell of Dzhez-kazgan." Silicosis is a "disease of the lungs caused by continued inhalation of the dust of siliceous minerals and characterized by progressive fibrosis and a chronic shortness of breath." *The American Heritage Dictionary of the English Language, Fourth Edition* (Boston: Houghton Mifflin, 2000).

67. Kokurin and Petrov, *GULAG: (Glavnoe upravlenie lagerei)*, 135–37. At the time that the MVD issued its implementation instructions, the exact details of the special camp regime were not worked out.

68. GARF, f. 9414. op. 1, d. 1858, ll. 212–14.

69. Panin, *The Notebooks of Sologdin*, 293–94, 297.

70. Dolgun with Watson, *Alexander Dolgun's Story*, 205. On further reports of such shooting incidents at Steplag, see ibid., 66–74.

71. Ibid., 244.

72. Kokurin and Petrov, *GULAG: (Glavnoe upravlenie lagerei)*, 558.

73. Ibid., 556–58, 563. By mid-May 1949, every Steplag subdivision was equipped with an internal camp prison. GARF, f. 9414, op. 1, d. 1858, ll. 212, 273.

74. Kokurin and Petrov, *GULAG: (Glavnoe upravlenie lagerei)*, 563–64.

75. Solzhenitsyn, *The Gulag Archipelago*, 3:57; Kokurin and Petrov, *GULAG: (Glavnoe upravlenie lagerei)*, 556.

76. Dolgun with Watson, *Alexander Dolgun's Story*, 171–72.

77. Kokurin and Petrov, *GULAG: (Glavnoe upravlenie lagerei)*, 557–58.

78. Dolgun with Watson, *Alexander Dolgun's Story*, 165.

79. Kokurin and Petrov, *GULAG: (Glavnoe upravlenie lagerei)*, 557.

80. Ibid., 560–61.

81. Ibid., 556.

82. Solzhenitsyn, *The Gulag Archipelago*, 3:67.

83. Dolgun with Watson, *Alexander Dolgun's Story*, 218.

84. Solzhenitsyn, *The Gulag Archipelago*, 3:58–60.

85. See Kokurin and Petrov, *GULAG: (Glavnoe upravlenie lagerei)*, 556.

86. Ibid., 555.

87. For a description of some minor cultural-educational activities at Steplag in 1949, see GARF, f. 9414, op. 1, d. 1858, l. 289.

88. Dolgun with Watson, *Alexander Dolgun's Story*, 258.

89. Ibid., 132.

90. Ibid., 211.

91. Ibid., 166.

92. Solzhenitsyn, *The Gulag Archipelago*, 3:97.

93. Dolgun with Watson, *Alexander Dolgun's Story*, 225.

94. Solzhenitsyn, *The Gulag Archipelago*, 3:231–32.

95. RGASPI, f. 560, op. 1, d. 4. The file holds the autobiography and memoirs of N. M. Busarev. No archival page numbers are apparent. Rather, there are two texts in the folder: a typescript text, and a handwritten one. The quoted passage is in the typescript text, 57.

96. Vory v zakone were the "thieves-in-law," a professional criminal underground organization.

97. Artem Fel'dman, *Riadovoe delo* (Moscow: Memorial, 1993), 41.

98. Dolgun with Watson, *Alexander Dolgun's Story*, 202–3.

99. Quoted in ibid., 147–48.

100. Kopelev, *To Be Preserved Forever*, 217.

101. Quoted in ibid., 222.

102. Solzhenitsyn, *The Gulag Archipelago*, 2:438.

103. Ibid., 3:243.

104. Kopelev, *To Be Preserved Forever*, 234–37.

105. Quoted in ibid., 235–37.

106. Edward Buca, *Vorkuta* (London: Constable, 1976), 57.

107. Quoted in Kopelev, *To Be Preserved Forever*, 238, 244.

108. Ibid., 244.

109. Ibid., 245.

110. Quoted in ibid., 248.

111. AOTsPSI, f. Karlaga, sv. 1 s. pr., d. 129, l. 124.

112. Ibid., l. 304. This particular directive called for the creation of a separate clinic for bandit prisoners to be constructed with barred windows and guarded entrances.

113. Ibid., d. 130, l. 10.

114. Ibid., sv. 2 s. pr., d. 132, ll. 171–72.

115. Ibid., d. 131, ll. 181–82.

116. Ibid., ll. 164–65.

117. Ibid., ll. 221–22. I found no information on the outcome of the hunger strike, although Karlag chief Z. P. Volkov did order an investigation of the shooting incident.

118. Karlag compiled a plan for the complete dispersal of prisoners according to their conviction. The plan included camp points for men in strict regime, women in strict regime, men in regular regime, women in regular regime, men from the group vory, men from the group otoshedshie, men from the group otkolovshiesia, and men from the group "m." I have been unable to determine the meaning of group m. Another document lays out different camp subdivisions for criminal gangs fighting one another: the vory, the otoshedshie, and those not aligned with either of these two groups. See ibid., sv. 4 spetsotdel, d. 45, l. 7.

119. The signed form is apparent in nearly all of the individual prisoner files from this period.

120. Ivanova, *Gulag v sisteme*, 62.

121. Dolgun with Watson, *Alexander Dolgun's Story*, 210.

122. Solzhenitsyn, *The Gulag Archipelago*, 3:238; Panin, *The Notebooks of Sologdin*, 303–6; Fel'dman, *Riadovoe delo*, 36–38. For a scholarly account that mentions the killings of informers and campaign to prevent the recruitment of new informers, see Marta Craveri [Kraveri], "Krizis Gulaga: Kengirskoe vosstanie 1954 goda v dokumentakh MVD," *Cahiers du Monde russe* 36, no. 3 (1995): 322. She also notes that prisoners were forming their own system of internal surveillance.

123. Panin, *The Notebooks of Sologdin*, 306.

124. Ibid., 308.

125. Ibid., 309.

126. Panin, *The Notebooks of Sologdin*, 310–11. Dolgun reports rumors of a similar incident in which three honest thieves were placed in a cell full of bitches, and the bitches promptly hung their three adversaries. Dolgun with Watson, *Alexander Dolgun's Story*, 157.

127. Panin, *The Notebooks of Sologdin*, 312–19. Craveri puts this hunger strike in January 1951 rather than Panin's January 1952. Craveri, "Krizis Gulaga," 322.

128. AOTsPSI, f. Karlaga, sv. 33, d. 519, l. 15. For a slightly different figure for 1951 of seventy prisoner-on-prisoner murders in a 1952 report, see ibid., sv. 34, d. 520, l. 136.

129. Ibid., sv. 34, d. 520, l. 136.

130. Ibid., sv. 2 s. pr., d. 131, ll. 71–72.

131. Kokurin and Petrov, *GULAG: (Glavnoe upravlenie lagerei)*, 318, 320.

132. Zemskov, "GULAG (istoriko-sotsiologicheskii aspekt)," 11.

133. See James Heinzen, "Corruption in the Gulag: Dilemmas of Officials and Prisoners," *Comparative Economic Studies* 47, no. 2 (2005): 456–75, especially 467–69.

134. GARF, f. 9414, op. 1, d. 326, ll. 19–20.

135. Ibid., ll. 25–26. In August and September 1949, the Council of Ministers of the USSR ordered the creation of two new special camps in the Karaganda coal basin, raising the total to nine.

136. Ibid., ll. 35, 37.

137. Ibid., d. 1858, l. 212.

138. Smirnov, *Sistema ispravitel'no trudovykh lagerei*, 210, 228–29, 352–54.

139. Kokurin and Petrov, *GULAG: (Glavnoe upravlenie lagerei)*, 387. The intended number of guards was much higher—9,986—but they were unable to fill all the positions. Compare this with the regular camp Karlag, where the intended number of guards in 1951 was limited to 7 percent of the prisoner population. AOTsPSI, f. Karlaga, sv. 33, d. 519, l. 56.

140. Kokurin and Petrov, *GULAG: (Glavnoe upravlenie lagerei)*, 388.

141. Quoted in GARF, f. 9414, op. 1, d. 326, l. 11.

142. AOTsPSI, f. Karlaga, sv. 36, d. 537, ll. 100–103.

143. Adding 17,498 remaining especially dangerous prisoners who could not within regulations really be used in field work to the 28,554 physically weak and invalid prisoners left only 19,761 prisoners to complete economic tasks designed for 42,000 laborers. Ibid., ll. 99, 105–6. Thus, Karlag was once again forced to weigh its competing tasks: the isolation of the especially dangerous versus the completion of economic plans.

144. The death penalty was abolished on May 26, 1947. It returned on January 12, 1950. Ivanova, *Gulag v sisteme*, 58, 62.

145. The comparison with Dante's hell is obviously suggested in Solzhenitsyn's *The First Circle*. On the commission of offenses in a camp leading to prisoners' transfer to harsher regime camps as indicative of movement deeper into Dante's hell, see Buca, *Vorkuta*, 177.

146. On katorga divisions, see chapter 4 herein.

147. Fel'dman, *Riadovoe delo*, 39.

148. This party functionary primarily had in mind the Kazakh population, which made up 30 percent of the prisoner population among the corrective labor colonies directly under the authority of the Kazakh Republic's MVD. Quoted in APRK, f. 819, op. 1, d. 21, l. 114.

149. Ibid., d. 178, l. 196.

150. Joseph Scholmer, *Vorkuta* (New York: Holt, 1955), 95.

151. Ibid., 147–48. Scholmer also reports that religion was an important element of Ukrainian community at Vorkuta.

152. Fel'dman, *Riadovoe delo*, 39.

153. Scholmer, *Vorkuta*, 95.

154. Buca, *Vorkuta*, 111.

155. Quoted in ibid., 114.

156. Ibid., 122.

157. This recalls the common picture of racial communities in U.S. prisons.

158. Anne Applebaum, *Gulag: A History* (New York: Doubleday, 2003), 302–3.

159. Like so much else in the Gulag, the absence of a particular Russian community echoes the absence of particularly Russian party and social organizations in the Soviet Union at large. See Yuri Slezkine, "The USSR as a Communal Apartment, or How a Socialist State Promoted Ethnic Particularism," *Slavic Review* 32, no. 2 (1994): 414–52.

160. Panin, *The Notebooks of Sologdin*, 300.

161. Ibid., 299.

162. See the speech of the Kazakh minister of internal affairs in 1946. APRK, f. 819, op. 1, d. 4, l. 5.

163. See Nicolas Werth, "'The Chechen Problem': Handling an Awkward Legacy, 1918–1958," *Contemporary European History* 15, no. (2006): 347.

164. Buca, *Vorkuta*, 55, 79–81.

165. Scholmer, *Vorkuta*, 137. Control over the city of Vilnius was contested for much of its history. From the beginning of the First World War until the end of the second, Lithuania and Poland fought over and traded control of Vilnius numerous times. Only after the Soviet annexation of Lithuania did Vilnius become the permanent capital of the republic and then independent post-Soviet state.

166. Ibid., 198.

167. Dolgun with Watson, *Alexander Dolgun's Story*, 244.

168. Buca, *Vorkuta*, 18. Scholmer echoes the opinion, surmising that some 50 percent of the prisoners at Vorkuta were Ukrainian, with 70 to 80 percent of those being western Ukrainian. Scholmer, *Vorkuta*, 129.

169. These prisoners played an integral role in the mass prisoner uprising at Kengir. See chapter 6 below.

170. Zemskov, "GULAG (istoriko-sotsiologicheskii aspekt)," 3, 8–9.

171. GARF, f. 9479, op. 1, d. 213, l. 1.

172. Ibid., l. 7.

173. Viktor N. Zemskov, "Spetsposelentsy" (po dokumentatsii NKVD-MVD SSSR)," *Sotsiologicheskie issledovaniia*, no. 11 (1990): 8.

174. AOTsPSI, f. Karlaga, sv. 2 spetsotdel, d. 18, l. 110.

175. GARF, f. 9479, op. 1, d. 641, ll. 367–68. Afanas'ev, et al., *Istoriia stalinskogo Gulaga*, 1:524–26, 530–32, 536.

176. Afanas'ev, et al., *Istoriia stalinskogo Gulaga*, 1:526–29, 533–39.

177. GARF, f. 9479, op. 1, d. 641, ll. 367–69.

178. Ibid., l. 368. Portions of the Vlasovites were sent to Karaganda for employment in the industries of the Karaganda coal basin. Ibid., GARF, d. 213, l. 20.

179. Afanas'ev, et al., *Istoriia stalinskogo Gulaga*, 1:543–44.

180. Viktor N. Zemskov, "Sud'ba 'Kulatskoi Ssylki': 1930–1954 gg," *Otechestvennaia Istoriia*, no. 1 (1994): 133.

181. On releases of former kulak exiles, see ibid., 133–42. As noted in earlier chapters, the process of their release began even before the war.

182. Zemskov, "Spetsposelentsy," 16.

183. RGANI, f. 89, per. 18, d. 26, ll. 1–5; Afanas'ev, et al., *Istoriia stalinskogo Gulaga*, 1:595–97.

184. Ginzburg, *Within the Whirlwind*, 279.

185. Ibid., 292–94, 311.

186. From Lazarev's typescript memoirs written and sent to the Central Committee in March 1966. RGASPI, f. 560, op. 1, d. 22, ll. 71, 74.

187. From Busarev's typescript memoirs written between 1967 and 1971, and sent to the Central Committee. Ibid., d. 4, pp. 68–71. The page numbers are from the typescript text.

188. Ginzburg, *Within the Whirlwind*, 330–31.

189. Zemskov, "Spetsposelentsy," 9–10; Ivanova, *Gulag v sisteme*, 56–57.

190. Zemskov, "Spetsposelentsy," 9.

191. On the extension of OUN exile to permanent status in the Buriat-Mongol autonomous republic, see GARF, f. 9479, op. 1, d. 547, ll. 608. Particular care was taken to use the surveillance apparatus to uncover cases of OUN exiles planning escape.

192. Ibid., ll. 3–4. On this phenomenon of some Ukrainians accepting and even embracing their status, see the discussion of Kate Brown's work in chapter 3 above.

193. Ibid., ll. 4–5. The rest of this archival file contains similar reports from other regions where OUN exiles were confined.

194. Ibid., l. 227.

195. Solzhenitsyn, *The Gulag Archipelago*, 3:47.

196. Scholmer, *Vorkuta*, 191–92.

197. APRK, f. 819, op. 1, d. 22, l. 59.

198. Ibid., d. 21, l. 116. The attack on these journals in 1946 was part of the launch of the deeply xenophobic anticosmopolitan campaign.

199. Ibid., l. 113b.

200. GARF, f. 9479, op. 1, d. 482, ll. 115–20.

201. Ibid., ll. 1–6. The exiles were spread out among every region of Kazakhstan. While Karaganda held the most, it was followed closely by Akmolinsk region with 107,000 exiles. In fact, only two regions, western Kazakh and the Gur'evsk, held fewer than 10,000 exiles. Ibid., ll. 19–20.

202. Ibid., d. 646, ll. 6, 15. Exiles of Russian nationality numbered a mere 1,043, earning only seventh place in the list of exile by nationality, and also trailing Poles and Greeks. There were only 294 Kazakhs among the exiles.

203. For the data on the locations and populations of individual special settlements in the Karaganda region in early 1953, see ibid., d. 767, ll. 118–27.

204. See the protocol of a meeting of local Kazakh UITLK Party secretaries held in April 1946. APRK, f. 819, op. 1, d. 21, l. 114.

205. Kopelev, *To Be Preserved Forever*, 6.

206. Ibid., 65.

207. Scholmer, *Vorkuta*, 108, 113.

208. Fel'dman, *Riadovoe delo*, 38. Fel'dman himself was arrested in relation to one murder, although he was quickly released. The murder, however, was pinned on another Jewish prisoner who had never even seen the murdered prisoner. The conviction was overturned after Stalin's death.

209. Ginzburg, *Within the Whirlwind*, 345.

210. Quoted in Danylo Shumuk, *Life Sentence: Memoirs of a Ukrainian Political Prisoner* (Edmonton: Canadian Institute of Ukrainian Studies, 1984), 173.

211. Quoted in Kopelev, *To Be Preserved Forever*, 137–38.

212. Ibid., 5. On the assertiveness of the population in general in the immediate wake of the victory, see Figes, *The Whisperers*, 459.

213. Buca, *Vorkuta*, 53–55. In this case, the Red Army officers were differentiated from Banderites or others who fought against Soviet rule.

214. Solzhenitsyn, *The Gulag Archipelago*, 2:175–76.

215. Ibid., 3:359.

216. AOTsPSI, f. Karlaga, sv. 34, d. 520, l. 133.

217. Ibid., ll. 133–37.

218. Ibid., ll. 218–19.

219. Ibid., l. 220. In an always-related campaign, they also had to improve the isolation of male from female prisoners.

220. Quoted in ibid., ll. 38–41. The bragging came in the midst of a furious bureaucratic battle to avoid the transfer of the educational camp point from its independent location into the zone of an industrial camp point.


CHAPTER 6: THE CRASH OF THE GULAG

1. Portions of this chapter have previously been published as Steven A. Barnes, "In a Manner Befitting Soviet Citizens: An Uprising in the Post-Stalin Gulag," *Slavic Review* 64, no. 4 (Winter 2005): 823–50. For the text of the radio message, in a publication of Soviet documents on the Kengir uprising, see "Vosstanie v Steplage," *Otechestvennye arkhivy*, no. 4 (1994): 62.

2. For accounts of the assault, see Marta Craveri [Kraveri], "Krizis Gulaga: Kengirskoe vosstanie 1954 goda v dokumentakh MVD," *Cahiers du Monde russe* 36, no. 3 (1995): 333; Dmitrii Iakovenko, "Osuzhden po 58-i," *Zvezda Vostoka* 57, no. 4 (1989): 71–72; Liubov' Bershadskaia, *Rastoptannye zhizni* (Paris: Piat' kontinentov, 1975), 94–97; Aleksandr I. Solzhenitsyn, *The Gulag Archipelago*,

*1918–1956: An Experiment in Literary Investigation*, trans. Thomas P. Whitney (New York: Harper Perennial, 1991), 3:326–29; Fedir Varkony, "The Revolt in Kingir," in *500 Ukrainian Martyred Women*, ed. Stephania Halychyn (New York: United Ukrainian Women's Organization of America, 1956), 22–29; GARF, f. 9414, op. 1, d. 228, ll. 21–35, 277–78; AOTsPSI, f. Karlaga, arkhivnoe lichnoe delo 470542 Kuznetsova, Kapitona Ivanovicha (d. Kuznetsova), l. 116. Official documents only noted two female prisoners run over by tanks, and they blamed the incident on other prisoners who allegedly pushed the women in front of the tanks. The volume *500 Ukrainian Martyred Women* asserted that some five hundred Ukrainian women were run over by tanks, even though its own eyewitness source, Varkony, makes no such claim, speaking rather of over five hundred total victims of the assault. Other than the issue of the total victims, all accounts of these events (eyewitness and official) agree with only minor discrepancies in details. With regard to the total deaths, the variance is significant. While official documents admitted to forty-six prisoner deaths, five of whom were allegedly killed by other prisoners (AOTsPSI, f. Karlaga, d. Kuznetsova, l. 116; GARF, f. 9414, op. 1, d. 228, l. 278), the memoirists all placed the number far higher. Iakovenko wrote that four hundred prisoners were either killed or seriously wounded. Bershadskaia stated that over five hundred lives were lost. Solzhenitsyn claimed to have found an official Steplag document that reported over seven hundred deaths. I have located no official documents with figures in that range. Applebaum has written about the uprising based entirely on some of the sources noted above, especially Solzhenitsyn, *The Gulag Archipelago*; Craveri, "Krizis Gulaga." See Anne Applebaum, *Gulag: A History* (New York: Doubleday, 2003), 495–505.

3. Consider, for example, the quick and brutal response to uprisings in Kronstadt in 1921, Ivanova in 1932, or even later in Novocherkassk in 1962. See Paul Avrich, *Kronstadt, 1921* (Princeton, NJ: Princeton University Press, 1970); Israel Getzler, *Kronstadt 1917–1921: The Fate of a Soviet Democracy* (Cambridge: Cambridge University Press, 2002); Jeffrey Rossman, *Worker Resistance under Stalin: Class and Revolution on the Shop Floor* (Cambridge, MA: Harvard University Press, 2005); Samuel H. Baron, *Bloody Saturday in the Soviet Union: Novocherkassk, 1962* (Stanford, CA: Stanford University Press, 2001).

4. The total, which does not include prison inmates, is in J. Otto Pohl, *The Stalinist Penal System: A Statistical History of Soviet Repression and Terror, 1930–1953* (Jefferson, NC: McFarland and Company, 1997), 131. Pohl's book is a useful compendium of Gulag population statistics based not on his own archival research but rather on the many various articles by Zemskov, Bugai, Aleksandr N. Dugin, Aleksandr Ia. Malygin, Popov, Rittersporn, and Getty. The camp and colony total comes from GARF, f. 9414, op. 1, d. 1398, ll. 14–22, in Aleksandr F. Kiselev and Ernst M. Shchagin, eds., *Khrestomatiia po otechestvennoi istorii (1946–1995 gg.)* (Moscow: Gumanitarnyi izdatel'skii tsentr VLADOS, 1996), 50–54. Considering camps and colonies alone, the 2.4 million population on January 1, 1953 was just off the maximum of 2.56 million on January 1, 1950. See Pohl, *The Stalinist Penal System*, 11. Beria told the Presidium of the Central Committee on March 26, 1953 that the total prisoner population, including prisons, colonies, and camps, was 2.53 million. See Arkhiv Prezidenta Rossiiskoi

Federatsii, f. 3, op. 52, d. 100, ll. 7–9, in V. P. Naumov and Iu. V. Sigachev, eds., *Lavrentii Beriia, 1953: Stenogramma iiul'skogo plenuma TsK KPSS i drugie dokumenty* (Moscow: Mezhdunarodnyi fond "Demokratiia," 1999), 19–21.

5. GARF, f. 9414, op. 1, d. 1398, ll. 14–22, in *Khrestomatiia po otechestvennoi istorii, 50–54*; Nanci Adler, *The Gulag Survivor: Beyond the Soviet System* (New Brunswick, NJ: Transaction Publishers, 2002), 169, 192.

6. Aleksei Tikhonov discusses these proposals. See "The End of the Gulag," in *Behind the Façade of Stalin's Command Economy*, ed. Paul R. Gregory (Stanford, CA: Hoover Institution Press, 2001), 67–74.

7. Marta [Kraveri] Craveri and Oleg Khlevniuk, "Krizis ekonomiki MVD (konets 1940-kh–1950-e gody)," *Cahiers du Monde russe* 36, nos. 1–2 (1995): 182–83. Ivanova echoes the argument exactly. The mass protests "forced the leadership of the Gulag to ease conditions there and to remove the cruelest, most odious officials from the camp administration; on the other hand, the obvious inefficiency of forced labor itself and the sharp decline in the economic performance of the Gulag forced the leadership to act to improve conditions in the camps." Galina Mikhailovna Ivanova, *Labor Camp Socialism: The Gulag in the Soviet Totalitarian System*, trans. Carol Flath (Armonk, NY: M. E. Sharpe, 2000), 66. Ivanova's "proof," however, is a report from 1953 of a commission under the Presidium of the Supreme Soviet of the USSR that stated that the camp regime had led to protests, refusal to work, escape attempts, and hooliganism among the prisoners, along with low labor productivity, high rates of illness, and low prisoner morale. The report derided the 77 percent work attendance among the prisoner workforce and 11.9 percent of prisoners failing to fulfill their norm. RGANI, f. 89, per. 55, dok. 28, l. 16. The problem with this proof is that such conditions had prevailed and been complained about almost throughout the Gulag's existence, but never before had they caused the decline of the system. On the contrary, it grew almost without pause throughout the Stalin era.

8. The numbers come from two tables in Pohl, *The Stalinist Penal System*, 16, 48–49. With the exception of a slight uptick in the relative numbers of escapes in 1946–47, the downward trend holds in 1937–53. In 1953, escapes amounted to 0.045 percent of the corrective labor camp population, while deaths amounted to 0.34 percent of the camp population.

9. Craveri and Khlevniuk, "Krizis ekonomiki MVD," 183–84, 187.

10. Alexander Dolgun with Patrick Watson, *Alexander Dolgun's Story: An American in the Gulag* (New York: Knopf, 1975), 261.

11. Artem Fel'dman, *Riadovoe delo* (Moscow: Memorial, 1993), 43–44. "Traur iz alykh i chernykh lent. Umer i Stalin, i Gotval'd Klement. Drognuli litsa stal'nye. Kogda peremrut ostal'nye?!"

12. Quoted in RGASPI, f. 560, op. 1, d. 17, l. 8. The materials in this file are the notebooks and letters of Mikhail Davydovich Korol' written in the camps. Many of these materials were later published by his daughter; see Maia Korol', *Odisseia razvedchika: Pol'sha–SShA–Kitai–GULAG* (Moscow: Izdatel'stvo Rossiiskogo obshchestva medikov-literaturov, 1999). Figes writes of some who were "crying from happiness." Orlando Figes, *The Whisperers: Private Life in Stalin's Russia* (New York: Metropolitan Books, 2007), 526.

13. Zayara Veselaia, interview in the documentary film *Stolen Years*.

14. See, for example, Adler, *The Gulag Survivor*, 69, quoting the memoirs of one survivor, "I loved the Soviet regime even when I was in exile, I cried bitterly in March 1953." Buca, a prisoner in the special camp at Vorkuta, recalls prisoners crying at the news of Stalin's death. Edward Buca, *Vorkuta* (London: Constable, 1976), 230. Figes recounts other victims of the Stalinist regime crying at his death, but generally dismissed the notion that any actually cried inside the camps. See Figes, *The Whisperers*, 525, 529.

15. The transfers of some camp industries, including agriculture, occurred over the next several months. Craveri and Khlevniuk, "Krizis ekonomiki MVD," 181–82. The economic activities of several of Karlag's divisions were transferred over to the control of the Ministry of Agriculture on June 1, 1953. AOTsPSI, f. Karlaga, sv. 3 s. pr., d. 136, ll. 281–84.

16. GARF, f. 9414, op. 1, d. 1398, ll. 14–22, in *Khrestomatiia po otechestvennoi istorii*, 50–54.

17. One certainly expects Solzhenitsyn's characterization of this amnesty as marked by "tenderness for thieves and its viciousness toward politicals." Solzhenitsyn, *The Gulag Archipelago*, 3:280. Much more surprising is Adler's statement that Stalin's death was followed by a "trickle" of released prisoners and how this amnesty "offered less than met the eye." Although her book is heavily focused on political prisoners, the comment is startling given the magnitude of the March 27 amnesty and Adler's obvious knowledge of that fact. See Adler, *The Gulag Survivor*, 6, 21, 78.

18. Adler, *The Gulag Survivor*, 78.

19. In actuality, not all Article 58 prisoners were excluded. The majority was, yet in rare cases in which individuals were convicted under Article 58 but were given five years or less, they were potentially eligible for release. For one such release, see AOTsPSI, f. Steplaga, arkhivnoe lichnoe delo 22340 (Kalina, Zara-Irina Ignat'evna), ll. 61, 111–13. Ignat'evna was sentenced to five years under articles 58-10, part 1, and 58-11 for participation in an anti-Soviet organization and anti-Soviet agitation. She was released under the March 27 amnesty on April 17, 1953. For similar case involving Anna Kholmogorova, see AOTsPSI, f. Peschanlaga, arkhivnoe lichnoe delo 6407 (Kholmogorova, Anna Andreevna), ll. 8, 13.

20. See Amy W. Knight, *Beria, Stalin's First Lieutenant* (Princeton, NJ: Princeton University Press, 1993); Craveri and Khlevniuk, "Krizis ekonomiki MVD," 182.

21. *Lavrentii Beriia*, 19–21.

22. For Karlag's administrative plan for carrying out the amnesty, see AOTsPSI, f. Karlaga, sv. 3 s. pr., d. 136, ll. 205–12.

23. Ibid.

24. For an example of this statement, see AOTsPSI, f. Steplaga, arkhivnoe lichnoe delo 22340 (Kalina, Zara-Irina Ignat'evna), l. 113.

25. AOTsPSI, f. Karlaga, sv. 35, d. 527, l. 38.

26. See Adler, *The Gulag Survivor*, 83; see especially Miriam Dobson, "'Show the Bandit-Enemies No Mercy!': Amnesty, Criminality, and Public Response in 1953," in *The Dilemma of De-Stalinization: Negotiating Cultural and Social Change in the Khrushchev Era*, ed. Polly Jones (Abingdon, UK: Routledge, 2006),

21–40; Miriam Dobson, *Khrushchev's Cold Summer: Gulag Returnees, Crime, and the Fate of Reform after Stalin* (Ithaca, NY: Cornell University Press, 2009).

27. As we will see, these complaints became the typical response of Soviet authorities to the problem of recidivism.

28. Iurii Nikolaevich Afanas'ev, et al., eds., *Istoriia stalinskogo Gulaga: Konets 1920-kh–pervaia polovina 1950-kh godov: Sobranie dokumentov v semi tomakh* (Moscow, 2004), 2:429–30.

29. AOTsPSI, f. Karlaga, sv. 3 s. pr., d. 136, ll. 205–12.

30. Ibid., sv. 35, d. 527, l. 137. Of course, they had been urged to do just such a thing repeatedly throughout the history of Karlag.

31. On the release of significant numbers of informants in the 1953 amnesty and the problems it caused in camp surveillance work, see James Heinzen, "Corruption in the Gulag: Dilemmas of Officials and Prisoners," *Comparative Economic Studies* 47, no. 2 (2005): 471–72.

32. GARF, f. 9414, op. 1, d. 1398, ll. 14–22, in *Khrestomatiia po otechestvennoi istorii*, 50–54.

33. AOTsPSI, f. Karlaga, sv. 3 s. pr., d. 136, ll. 246–47.

34. Afanas'ev, et al., *Istoriia stalinskogo Gulaga*, 2:430–31.

35. AOTsPSI, f. Karlaga, sv. 3 s. pr., d. 136, ll. 297–98.

36. Ibid., sv. 35, d. 527, l. 139.

37. Solzhenitsyn writes of the uncertainty exhibited by the secret police organs in the wake of Beria's demise. Solzhenitsyn, *The Gulag Archipelago*, 3:289.

38. Dolgun with Watson, *Alexander Dolgun's Story*, 261. A similar rumor is reported in Nikolai L'vovich Kekushev, *Zveriada* (Moscow: Iuridicheskaia literatura, 1991), 127. Kekushev believed the rumor to be an especially poorly planned provocation.

39. Quoted in Fel'dman, *Riadovoe delo*, 43–44.

40. Figes, *The Whisperers*, 526.

41. Dolgun with Watson, *Alexander Dolgun's Story*, 261.

42. Kekushev, *Zveriada*, 126.

43. Dolgun with Watson, *Alexander Dolgun's Story*, 265–66.

44. Interview with Karl Riewe, German national and former inmate of Steplag, in the National Archives of the United Kingdom, Public Records Office (hereafter TNA PRO), FO 371/122936, N S1551/6, 9–10.

45. Dolgun with Watson, *Alexander Dolgun's Story*, 274–76. The significance for prisoners of removing their numbers was stressed time and again by memoirists. See also Kekushev, *Zveriada*, 127; Solzhenitsyn, *The Gulag Archipelago*, 3:485.

46. Dolgun with Watson, *Alexander Dolgun's Story*, 283. Figes places the improvement in conditions in Gulag camps in the early 1950s. See Figes, *The Whisperers*, 516.

47. AOTsPSI, f. Karlaga, sv. 35, d. 527, ll. 146–47. Although I never located the main speech of Karlag chief Volkov at this conference, none of the related materials indicated any awareness of the Beria situation in Moscow.

48. Ibid., ll. 137, 140.

49. Ibid., l. 137. The continual campaigns to reemphasize regulations that had long been on the books were a long-term characteristic of Gulag administration.

50. Ibid., sv. 3 s. pr., d. 137, ll. 18–20.

51. Solzhenitsyn devoted an entire chapter of *The Gulag Archipelago*, the "Forty Days of Kengir," to the uprising, which served as the narrative climax of his three-volume magnum opus. *The Gulag Archipelago* dealt with the subject of arrest and the absence of resistance. "Yes, resistance should have begun right there, at the moment of the arrest itself. But it did not begin." Solzhenitsyn, *The Gulag Archipelago*, 1:15. The volumes are then structured as a conversion story, which reaches its peak when prisoners finally unite against their common enemy in a series of uprisings culminating with that at Kengir. Ibid., 3:285–331. Given that Applebaum's volume offers essentially a slightly updated version of Solzhenitsyn, it is no surprise that Kengir plays a similar role for her. She adds little to our knowledge from the scholarly works noted below.

For the Ukrainian émigré community, the violent overturn of the Kengir uprising was celebrated as an instance of martyrdom in the face of Soviet oppression—this one gendered female due to the presence of large numbers of Ukrainian women in the uprising. See Varkony, "The Revolt in Kingir."

Numerous memoirists and correspondents have made the Kengir uprising a key element of their Gulag stories. See Bershadskaia, *Rastoptannye zhizni*; Fel'dman, *Riadovoe delo*; V. Frants, "Vosstanie v Kengire," *Sotsialisticheskii vestnik*, no. 6 (1956): 104–10; Kekushev, *Zveriada*.

Even historical research and documentary publications have now become possible. The first, a model of the best prearchival research, was Andrea Graziosi, "The Great Strikes of 1953 in Soviet Labor Camps in the Accounts of Their Participants: A Review," *Cahiers du Monde russe et sovietique* 33, no. 4 (1992): 419–46. For the best account using archives, see Craveri, "Krizis Gulaga." For a publication of key documents from the uprising, see "Vosstanie v Steplage."

52. From the voluminous literature on west Ukrainian and Baltic resistance movements, see especially Timothy Snyder, *The Reconstruction of Nations: Poland, Ukraine, Lithuania, Belarus, 1569–1999* (New Haven, CT: Yale University Press, 2003), 73–89, 154–201; Timothy Snyder, "The Causes of Ukrainian-Polish Ethnic Cleansing 1943," *Past and Present*, no. 179 (2003): 197–234; Hiroaki Kuromiya, *Freedom and Terror in the Donbas: A Ukrainian-Russian Borderland, 1870s–1990s* (Cambridge: Cambridge University Press, 1998); Jeffrey Burds, "Agentura: Soviet Informants' Networks and the Ukrainian Rebel Underground in Galicia, 1944–1948," *East European Politics and Societies* 11, no. 1 (1997): 89–130; Jeffrey Burds, "The Early Cold War in Soviet West Ukraine, 1944–1948," Carl Beck Papers in Russian and East European Studies, no. 1505, University of Pittsburgh, 2001; Jeffrey Burds, "Gender and Policing in Soviet West Ukraine, 1944–1948," *Cahiers du monde russe* 42, nos. 2–4 (2001): 279–319; Juozas Daumantas, *Fighters for Freedom: Lithuanian Partisans versus the U.S.S.R. (1944–1947)*, trans. E. J. Harrison (New York: Manyland Books, 1975); Mart Laar, *War in the Woods: Estonia's Struggle for Survival, 1944–1956*, trans. Tiina Ets (Washington, DC: Compass Press, 1992); Georgii Sannikov, *Bol'shaia okhota: Razgrom vooruzhennogo podpol'ia v zapadnoi Ukraine* (Moscow: Olma-Press, 2002); Rein Taagepara, "Soviet Documentation on the Estonian Proindependence Guerrilla Movement, 1945–1952," *Journal of Baltic Studies* 10, no. 2 (1979): 91–106.

53. In particular, see Vladimir Kozlov, *Massovye besporiadki v SSSR pri Khrushcheve i Brezhneve, 1953-nachalo 1980-kh gg.* (Novosibirsk: Sibirskii khronograf, 1999). Unfortunately, the translators completely missed Kozlov's argument on this point when they mistranslated the title into English. Instead of the appropriate translation, *Mass Disorders*, the translators chose the more heroic and less accurate *Mass Uprisings in the USSR: Protest and Rebellion in the Post-Stalin Years* (Armonk, NY: M. E. Sharpe, 2002).

54. "Thinking Bolshevik" comes from Jochen Hellbeck's playful expansion of Kotkin's notion of "speaking Bolshevik." See Jochen Hellbeck, "Speaking Out: Languages of Affirmation and Dissent in Stalinist Russia," *Kritika: Explorations in Russian and Eurasian History* 1, no. 1 (2000): 71–96; Stephen Kotkin, *Magnetic Mountain: Stalinism as a Civilization* (Berkeley: University of California Press, 1995).

55. On earlier incidents of resistance, see Craveri, "Krizis Gulaga"; Semen S. Vilenskii, ed., *Soprotivlenie v Gulage: Vospominaniia, pis'ma, dokumenty* (Moscow: Vozvrashchenie, 1992). Resistance, in these accounts, exists but is remarkable for its rarity until Stalin's death. For an extended consideration of one early uprising during the war, see chapter 4 herein.

56. Gulag authorities described their exposure for a long period of time to bourgeois ideology as one of the reasons leading to the Kengir rebellion. GARF, f. 9414, op. 1, d. 228, l. 286.

57. On the OUN and the Ukrainian Insurgent Army, and their ferocious guerrilla struggle with Soviet authority, see Amir Weiner, *Making Sense of War: The Second World War and the Fate of the Bolshevik Revolution* (Princeton, NJ: Princeton University Press, 2001).

58. On the changed mind-set of veterans after the war, see Weiner, *Making Sense of War*; Elena Zubkova, *Russia after the War: Hopes, Illusions, and Disappointments, 1945–1957*, trans. and ed. Hugh Ragsdale (Armonk, NY: M. E. Sharpe, 1998).

59. One former Steplag prisoner, Vagarshak Batoian, wrote that the contingent of prisoners who had been arrested before the war were "more careful, more restrained," while it was the former POWs and other people arrested after the war who were the decisive elements in the uprising. Batoian, in *Soprotivlenie v Gulage: Vospominaniia, pis'ma, dokumenty*, ed. Semen S. Vilenskii, (Moscow: Vozvrashchenie, 1992), 91. On the centrality of these new prisoner contingents in all of the post-Stalin Gulag uprisings, see Graziosi, "The Great Strikes of 1953," 422–24; Craveri, "Krizis Gulaga," 320.

60. All prisoners in the special camps were political prisoners, but all political prisoners were not in these camps.

61. Solzhenitsyn, *The Gulag Archipelago*, 3:231–32, 238.

62. On earlier uprisings, see Graziosi, "The Great Strikes of 1953"; Craveri, "Krizis Gulaga"; *Soprotivlenie v Gulage*.

63. Although recent historiography has reevaluated Beria and painted a picture of him as one of the primary initiators of the Gulag's dismantling, Gulag prisoners at the time viewed him as the ultimate criminal. As shown below, prisoners tossed Beria's name around as an epithet in the wake of his arrest and execution. See Knight, *Stalin's First Lieutenant*.

64. On the raised and dashed expectations of changes after Stalin's death, see Frants, "Vosstanie v Kengire," 104.

65. Ibid., 104; Solzhenitsyn, *The Gulag Archipelago*, 3:293; Batoian, in *Soprotivlenie v Gulage*, 82; Iakovenko, "Osuzhden po 58-i," 66.

66. "Vosstanie v Steplage," 78; GARF, f. 9414, op. 1, d. 228, l. 270. Of course, it is always possible that a great number of Gulag prisoners were completely innocent of the charges against them. Thus, we will never truly know how many of these prisoners were really members of nationalist organizations.

67. Riewe interview, TNA PRO FO 371/122936, N S1551/6, 4; Batoian, in *Soprotivlenie v Gulage*, 82; Varkony, "The Revolt in Kingir," 22–24; Iakovenko, "Osuzhden po 58-i," 68–69. Iakovenko, a member of the militarized guard at Kengir at the time of the uprising, testified that such murders did occur and were covered up. Dolgun, a U.S. prisoner at a different Steplag subdivision, noted that the local authorities would help cover up illegal shootings by throwing corpses into the firing corridor prior to taking pictures. Dolgun with Watson, *Alexander Dolgun's Story*, 244.

68. For one such example, see the comments of a prisoner named Popov at a production meeting on June 6, 1954 in Steplag's first camp subdivision—a subdivision not involved in the uprising. GARF, f. 9414, op. 1, d. 228, l. 168. For a lengthy report on those in the secret police apparatus who lost their jobs immediately after Beria's arrest, see Afanas'ev, et al., *Istoriia stalinskogo Gulaga*, 2:437–43.

69. Official documents admit to shootings in May 1953 and February 1954. GARF, f. 9414, op. 1, d. 228, ll. 109–10. See also Craveri, "Krizis Gulaga," 324; Varkony, "The Revolt in Kingir," 22; Frants, "Vosstanie v Kengire," 104; Solzhenitsyn, *The Gulag Archipelago*, 3:285–86. Solzhenitsyn argues that the shootings were an intentional act on the part of camp authorities, who sought to provoke disturbances to stave off budgetary and staff cuts in the wake of Beria's arrest. Solzhenitsyn's assertion, though plausible, is not easily proved or disproved.

70. See Frants, "Vosstanie v Kengire," 104; Varkony, "The Revolt in Kingir," 22; Solzhenitsyn, *The Gulag Archipelago*, 3:286–89.

71. See Frants, "Vosstanie v Kengire," 105; Varkony, "The Revolt in Kingir," 23; Solzhenitsyn, *The Gulag Archipelago*, 3:290–92; Batoian, in *Soprotivlenie v Gulage*, 85. Riewe writes of sixty rather than six hundred common criminals. Riewe interview, TNA PRO FO 371/122936, N S1551/6, 16. The transfer of common criminals to Kengir is confirmed in official documents in "Vosstanie v Steplage," 78. Frants also asserts that prisoners from the uprising at Vorkuta arrived at Kengir in 1954 and played a role in the uprising. Frants, "Vosstanie v Kengire," 104. I have found no official document confirming this transfer, but as we will see in the aftermath of Kengir, the transfer of prisoners to different camps in the wake of uprisings was a common practice.

72. Their goal in these actions is disputed. Solzhenitsyn writes that the common criminals, in agreement with the political prisoners, specifically sought to provoke a confrontation with authorities. They entered the service yard with the goal of seizing control of the camp's food stores. Solzhenitsyn, *The Gulag Archipelago*, 3:293–96. This account accords with Varkony's testimony in 1956.

Varkony, "The Revolt in Kingir," 23–24. Official documents consistently maintained that the criminals were seeking access to the women's zone in order to engage in mass rape of the female prisoners. See, for example, GARF, f. 9414, op. 1, d. 228, l. 271. While on its face the official version seems more likely considering the long history of rape in the Gulag, Bershadskaia, a prisoner in the women's section at Kengir during the uprising, confirms that the criminals all behaved themselves, and many female prisoners even hid the men from authorities. Bershadskaia, *Rastoptannye zhizni*, 83.

73. The events are described in GARF, f. 9414, op. 1, d. 228, ll. 270–72; Solzhenitsyn, *The Gulag Archipelago*, 3:293–300; Frants, "Vosstanie v Kengire," 105; Varkony, "The Revolt in Kingir," 23–24; Bershadskaia, *Rastoptannye zhizni*, 83–85; TNA PRO FO 371/122936, N S1551/6, 16; "Vosstanie v Steplage," 37–38; Craveri, "Krizis Gulaga," 325. Craveri—based on GARF, f. 9414, op. 1, d. 228, l. 272—found slightly different figures: 13 prisoners dead, and 43 prisoners wounded. Craveri, "Krizis Gulaga," 325. The numbers in "Vosstanie v Steplage" seem to be more complete. Witnesses placed the total dead at far higher. Bershadskaia estimated more than 100 wounded and 100 killed, while Frants wrote that the MVD killed 60 to 70 prisoners and wounded many others. The rumors that reached Riewe spoke of about 150 total dead and wounded.

74. Solzhenitsyn, *The Gulag Archipelago*, 3:299–300; AOTsPSI, f. Karlaga, d. Kuznetsova, ll. 116, 117, 121; Frants, "Vosstanie v Kengire," 106.

75. "Vosstanie v Steplage," 37.

76. For many of the telegrams to and from Kruglov and Rudenko, see ibid., 36–81.

77. See Craveri, "Krizis Gulaga," 325–26; "Vosstanie v Steplage," 38–39; Frants, "Vosstanie v Kengire," 105–6; Solzhenitsyn, *The Gulag Archipelago*, 3:298–99; GARF, f. 9414, op. 1, d. 228, l. 273.

78. "Vosstanie v Steplage," 44–45. The authorities also cut off electric power to the zone. GARF, f. 9414, op. 1, d. 228, l. 226.

79. "Vosstanie v Steplage," 54.

80. Ibid., 55.

81. Ibid., 56.

82. From Kuznetsov's declaration three days after the end of the uprising. "Vosstanie v Steplage," 64–65. Early in the course of the uprising, Soviet officials believed that former OUN members were leading the events. Ibid., 40–41.

83. Kuznetsov asserted that the departments were created by the conspiracy center and without his agreement. Ibid., 66. An elaborate organizational chart of all the departments and subdepartments among the prisoners was prepared during the course of the MVD's investigation of the uprising. GARF, f. 9414, op. 1, d. 228, l. 18.

84. Craveri, "Krizis Gulaga," 328; AOTsPSI, f. Karlaga, d. Kuznetsova, ll. 115, 117; Iakovenko, "Osuzhden po 58-i," 71; Kekushev, *Zveriada*, 133; "Vosstanie v Steplage," 56, 71. There is no evidence that the prisoners were actually successful at laying minefields.

85. AOTsPSI, f. Karlaga, d. Kuznetsova, l. 117.

86. "Vosstanie v Steplage," 67. Riewe reported that it was informers and all of the recently arrived criminals who were placed in an internal prison during

the uprising. Riewe interview, TNA PRO FO 371/122936, N S1551/6, 17. Solzhenitsyn stated that only four prisoners were arrested and placed in the internal prison. Solzhenitsyn, *The Gulag Archipelago*, 3:315. It seems unlikely that the number was so low. The Kazakh Supreme Court verdict asserted that "more than forty" were arrested. The verdict included a partial list of family names of the arrested (fewer than forty, but more than four)—individuals who presumably provided evidentiary testimony of their arrest and beating. AOTsPSI, f. Karlaga, d. Kuznetsova, ll. 114–15, 117. For a similar list, see GARF, f. 9414, op. 1, d. 228, l. 34. While such testimony could certainly have been falsified, neither Solzhenitsyn nor Kuznetsov denied the existence of the prison.

87. Solzhenitsyn, *The Gulag Archipelago*, 3:316–17.

88. Treating prisoners as an integral part of Soviet society was a common practice throughout the history of the Gulag. It is somewhat surprising, though, given the ferocity of the anti-Soviet actions of these particular prisoners. This was not mere ritual incantation but rather evidence of the Gulag officials' confidence that they could break even the fiercest resisters, bending them toward compliance with Soviet norms.

89. Solzhenitsyn, *The Gulag Archipelago*, 3:316–17. For many of the radio appeals, see GARF, f. 9414, op. 1, d. 228. For a number of excerpts, see Craveri, "Krizis Gulaga," 331–32.

90. "Vosstanie v Steplage," 44–45. On the prisoners' demands, see below.

91. GARF, f. 9414, op. 1, d. 228, ll. 113–14.

92. Solzhenitsyn, *The Gulag Archipelago*, 3:306 (emphasis removed).

93. GARF, f. 9414, op. 1, d. 228, ll. 60–61.

94. I thank the anonymous reviewer of my *Slavic Review* article for suggesting this line of interpretation.

95. Quoted in GARF, f. 9414, op. 1, d. 228, l. 71.

96. Quoted in ibid., l. 136.

97. Craveri, "Krizis Gulaga," 331; Solzhenitsyn, *The Gulag Archipelago*, 3:322; "Vosstanie v Steplage," 48; GARF, f. 9414, op. 1, d. 228, ll. 63, 72–74; Frants, "Vosstanie v Kengire," 105; Batoian, in *Soprotivlenie v Gulage*, 98; Kekushev, *Zveriada*, 133. Here again, the numbers vary widely. Solzhenitsyn wrote that only "about a dozen" prisoners exited the camp during the uprising, while Frants testified that some 160 prisoners who did not want to join the uprising were sent out of the camp during the rebellion's first days. Batoian wrote of "several hundred" who left the camp, while Kekushev stated that it was only the camp "aristocracy" who fled the zone during the uprising.

98. Quoted in GARF, f. 9414, op. 1, d. 228, l. 75.

99. Quoted in ibid., ll. 82–83. The comparison of the commission to the Gestapo is echoed in another prisoner's radio address. Ibid., l. 137.

100. Solzhenitsyn, *The Gulag Archipelago*, 3:294.

101. Quoted in GARF, f. 9414, op. 1, d. 228, l. 100.

102. Ibid., l. 166.

103. From Kuznetsov's testimony. "Vosstanie v Steplage," 69. Solzhenitsyn confirms Kuznetsov's account, writing that Sluchenkov told others that he had been urged "to provoke a racial bloodbath" to provide an excuse for liquidating the uprising by force. Solzhenitsyn, *The Gulag Archipelago*, 3:314.

104. AOTsPSI, f. Karlaga, d. Kuznetsova, l. 65.

105. Quoted in GARF, f. 9414, op. 1, d. 228, ll. 146–47. The speech is transcribed in Russian. It is not clear whether the speaker delivered the speech in Russian or Ukrainian.

106. "Vosstanie v Steplage," 44–45.

107. See, for example, ibid., 37–38.

108. Solzhenitsyn, *The Gulag Archipelago*, 3:306.

109. Quoted in GARF, f. 9414, op. 1, d. 228, ll. 102–6.

110. On such rapes, see Burds, "Gender and Policing." I thank the anonymous reviewer for my *Slavic Review* article for suggesting the significance of this bitter irony.

111. Solzhenitsyn, *The Gulag Archipelago*, 3:318n6.

112. Ibid., 3:306n5. On the investigations following the uprising, see Craveri, "Krizis Gulaga," 324. For the report of a female Kengir prisoner, see Bershadskaia, *Rastoptannye zhizni*, 83.

113. TNA PRO FO 371/122936, N S1551/6, 18.

114. AOTsPSI, f. Karlaga, d. Kuznetsova l. 114; "Vosstanie v Steplage," 60, 73.

115. Craveri, "Krizis Gulaga," 330; AOTsPSI, f. Karlaga, d. Kuznetsova, ll. 114–15; Kekushev, *Zveriada*, 132–34; Solzhenitsyn, *The Gulag Archipelago*, 3:316–17, 319; "Vosstanie v Steplage," 53, 73; GARF, f. 9414, op. 1, d. 228, l. 31. It appears that the radio transmitter was never successfully built.

116. "Vosstanie v Steplage," 73.

117. For a list of demands, see "Vosstanie v Steplage," 42. With few exceptions, the list is confirmed in Craveri, "Krizis Gulaga," 326; Iakovenko, "Osuzhden po 58-i," 71; Frants, "Vosstanie v Kengire," 105; "Vosstanie v Steplage," 39; Solzhenitsyn, *The Gulag Archipelago*, 3:311–12.

118. Graziosi's study of the uprisings in Vorkuta and Noril'sk showed that the prisoners' political programs were generally of a socialist orientation. He found this orientation not too surprising, given that the Gulag authorities consistently treated their prisoners as workers, particularly after the introduction of wages for prisoners in 1950. Graziosi, "The Great Strikes of 1953," 428.

119. Their faith also recalls long Russian traditions of resistance not against the tsar but in the name of the tsar. This is particularly intriguing given the absence of such traditions among the nationalists. I thank the anonymous reviewer of my *Slavic Review* article for suggesting the latter point.

120. Solzhenitsyn, *The Gulag Archipelago*, 3:297. For similar accounts, see Bershadskaia, *Rastoptannye zhizni*, 86; TNA PRO FO 371/122936, N S1551/6, 17.

121. Solzhenitsyn, *The Gulag Archipelago*, 3:302–3. Solzhenitsyn identifies the quote's source as the notes of Makeev, a fellow member of the prisoners' commission. As the next section on Kuznetsov will demonstrate, the sentiment is consistent with everything that we know about Kuznetsov.

122. Ibid., 3:303. The sign greeting the Soviet constitution is confirmed in GARF, f. 9414, op. 1, d. 228, l. 136. See also Kekushev, *Zveriada*, 134.

123. GARF, f. 9414, op. 1, d. 228, ll. 194–95. For a similar transcript from June 24, see ibid., ll. 209–12. The range of the broadcast signal is unclear, but the transcript is filled with ellipses, apparently designating points at which the

reception was so weak or the volume so low that the MVD transcribers could not decode what was being said.

124. Solzhenitsyn, *The Gulag Archipelago*, 3:301, 313. Bershadskaia writes that the prisoners had been allowed to remove their numbers earlier in 1954. Bershadskaia, *Rastoptannye zhizni*, 80. On religious services in camp during the uprising, see GARF, f. 9414, op. 1, d. 228, l. 280.

125. Bershadskaia, *Rastoptannye zhizni*, 91–92. One wonders whether the Russian prisoners truly sang the Ukrainian hymn.

126. Solzhenitsyn, *The Gulag Archipelago*, 3:312.

127. AOTsPSI, f. Karlaga, d. Kuznetsova, ll. 4–5b, 13–15.

128. Ibid., ll. 60–61. Applebaum, then, is quite wrong, when she writes of Kuznetsov, "If these accusations are true, they help explain his behavior during the strike. Having played the part of turncoat once, he would have been well prepared to play a double role once again." She, like Solzhenitsyn, is quite unable to accept that a prisoner could have been pro-Soviet but also a leader of the uprising. Applebaum, *Gulag*, 498.

129. AOTsPSI, f. Karlaga, d. Kuznetsova, ll. 20, 42. The file does not contain information on his time at Dubrovlag or the reason for his transfer to Steplag.

130. Frants, "Vosstanie v Kengire," 105. No other witnesses and no documents in Kuznetsov's file speak of the reason for his incarceration in the camp's internal prison, yet the fact that he was in the internal prison when the uprising began is indicated by several witnesses and confirmed by authorities in numerous documents.

131. Solzhenitsyn, *The Gulag Archipelago*, 3:302.

132. For a similar statement made by a prisoner at a different Steplag subdivision, see GARF, f. 9414, op. 1, d. 228, l. 162.

133. Kekushev, *Zveriada*, 136.

134. A caveat is in order here. In his appeals and declarations to Soviet authorities, Kuznetsov certainly had significant incentive to downplay his role in the uprising as much as possible. Nonetheless, as we will see, many different sources place the true power of the uprising in the hands of the criminals and nationalists rather than with Kuznetsov.

135. "Vosstanie v Steplage," 52.

136. Craveri, "Krizis Gulaga," 328.

137. AOTsPSI, f. Karlaga, d. Kuznetsova, ll. 116, 122.

138. Ibid., l. 114.

139. Ibid.; Solzhenitsyn, *The Gulag Archipelago*, 3:313–14.

140. Solzhenitsyn, *The Gulag Archipelago*, 3:306. This may seem to be an exaggeration by Solzhenitsyn, placing his own words in the mouth of his story's hero, but a similar statement made by a prisoner in a different Steplag subdivision during the same period of time is recorded in GARF, f. 9414, op. 1, d. 228, l. 168. Furthermore, the statement fits with Sluchenkov's radical, outspoken nature, which emerges from other sources.

141. GARF, f. 9414, op. 1, d. 228, l. 166.

142. AOTsPSI, f. Karlaga, d. Kuznetsova, l. 118.

143. Solzhenitsyn, *The Gulag Archipelago*, 3:304.

144. AOTsPSI, f. Karlaga, d. Kuznetsova, ll. 148b, 178–80.

145. Ibid., ll. 149, 208–9.

146. Ibid., l. 209b. Kuznetsov never made this claim before 1959.

147. Ibid., 208–9. Kuznetsov's version is supported by Craveri's oral interviews with two former prisoners and Batoian's memoirs. Craveri, "Krizis Gulaga," 326.

148. "Vosstanie v Steplage," 66; Craveri, "Krizis Gulaga," 327; Solzhenitsyn, *The Gulag Archipelago*, 3:313.

149. Quoted in GARF, f. 9414, op. 1, d. 228, l. 131.

150. Quoted in AOTsPSI, f. Karlaga, d. Kuznetsova, ll. 212–15. Kuznetsov attached these excerpts from Sluchenkov's appeal to his own appeal against his sentence. How he gained access to this material is not clear, although he did state that he had not seen it before 1958.

151. AOTsPSI, f. Karlaga, d. Kuznetsova, l. 210.

152. Weiner suggestively offers the idea of a "community of blood, a fighting family, that overpowers ethnic and ideologically imposed divisions" to bring together veterans, regardless of their side in the war. Weiner, *Making Sense of War*, 378. Interestingly, Sluchenkov and Keller sometimes referred to Kuznetsov, perhaps sarcastically, as "tovarishch voennyi" (comrade serviceman). "Vosstanie v Steplage," 72.

153. It is no accident that the prisoners' military department created subdivisions modeled on the practices of the Ukrainian Insurgent Army. GARF, f. 9414, op. 1, d. 228, l. 279.

154. Ibid., ll. 9, 33.

155. AOTsPSI, f. Karlaga, d. Kuznetsova, ll. 122–23.

156. Ibid., ll. 124, 131.

157. "Vosstanie v Steplage," 43n4; Craveri, "Krizis Gulaga," 334.

158. AOTsPSI, f. Karlaga, d. Kuznetsova, ll. 130, 132–35, 141, 147, 160.

159. Ibid., ll. 263–64, 272.

160. For a complete review of the changes made after the Kengir uprising, see Craveri, "Krizis Gulaga."

161. Iakovenko, "Osuzhden po 58-i," 71.

162. GARF, f. 9414, op. 1, d. 228, l. 286.

163. TNA PRO FO 371/122936, N S1551/6, 18.

164. It is worth recalling that Kotkin's notion of speaking Bolshevik did not demand that Soviet citizens believe, just that they "participate as if [they] believed." Kotkin, *Magnetic Mountain*, 220.

165. Solzhenitsyn, *The Gulag Archipelago*, 3:486. Ivanova also has noted a "certain humanization of the camp system" during this period. Ivanova, *Labor Camp Socialism*, 66.

166. RGANI, f. 89, per. 55, dok. 28, l. 16. This did not prevent the closing of Steplag in May 1956, however, as discussed below.

167. Kekushev, *Zveriada*, 143.

168. Quoted in TNA PRO FO 371/122936, N S1551/6, 10, 13.

169. For MVD Kruglov's speech, see Aleksandr Kokurin and Nikolai Petrov, eds., *GULAG: (Glavnoe upravlenie lagerei), 1917–1960* (Moscow: Mezhdunarodnyi fond "Demokratiia," 2000), 664–65. See also Riewe interview, TNA PRO FO 371/122936, N S1551/6, 11–13.

170. Solzhenitsyn, *The Gulag Archipelago*, 3:485–88. Note that prisoners began to be paid for their labor in 1950. See Simon Ertz, "Trading Effort for

Freedom: Workday Credits in the Stalinist Camp System," *Comparative Economic Studies* 47, no. 2 (2005): 476–91.

171. Quoted in AOTsPSI, f. Karlaga, sv. 24 pr., d. 105, l. 232.

172. For just a couple other examples, see AOTsPSI, f. Peschanlaga, arkhivnoe lichnoe delo 24988 (Navitskas, Petras s. Antanasa), ll. 39, 45; AOTsPSI, f. Karlaga, arkhivnoe lichnoe delo 475746 (Novikova, Evdokiia Arsent'evna), ll. 16–17, 40, 47.

173. Numerous decrees led to the release of different categories of inmates. I will not review them all here. For seven different decrees from 1954, see Kokurin and Petrov, *GULAG: (Glavnoe upravlenie lagerei)*, 436.

174. GARF, f. 9414, op. 1, d. 1398, ll. 14–22, in *Khrestomatiia po otechestvennoi istorii*, 50–54.

175. Adler, *The Gulag Survivor*, 192. The number may appear at first glance impossible, given the camp and colony population of 2.4 million in 1953. Yet it is likely correct, as prisoner releases were counterbalanced to some degree by new prisoner arrivals.

176. The decree allowed for the review of all convictions of counterrevolutionary crimes by extrajudicial authorities (primarily by the MVD organs), with the exception of those convicted of crimes committed while in the camps. For the total release figure, see Adler, *The Gulag Survivor*, 21–22. For the order itself, see E. A. Zaitsev, ed., *Sbornik zakonodatel'nykh i normativnykh aktov o repressiiakh i reabilitatsii zhertv politicheskikh repressii* (Moscow: Respublika, 1993), 78–80.

177. For the amnesty, see Kiselev and Shchagin, *Khrestomatiia po otechestvennoi istorii*, 270–71.

178. For the translation, see Ivanova, *Labor Camp Socialism*, 68. For the ukaz itself, see Zaitsev, *Sbornik zakonodatel'nykh i normativnykh aktov*, 80–81.

179. Adler, *The Gulag Survivor*, 169–70.

180. Solzhenitsyn, *The Gulag Archipelago*, 3:490. I have been able to find no confirmation either that prisoners were obliged to admit their guilt or that those who refused to do so were refused release. Nonetheless, one can certainly imagine individual local commissions operating in just such a fashion in which a refusal to admit one's guilt was taken as evidence of continued hostility to the Soviet system and thus providing a continued necessity to detain the prisoner.

181. AOTsPSI, f. Karlaga, sv. 7 s. s. pr., d. 165, ll. 177–78. Of course, it is unclear to what extent any of these provisions were fulfilled.

182. See ibid., arkhivnoe lichnoe delo 475746 (Novikova, Evdokiia Arsent'evna), ll. 4b, 7, 14, 17, 40, 41, 49.

183. For these official notices of release, see, for example, one case in which the issue of the prisoner's guilt was not addressed but her labor and behavior was: ibid., f. Steplaga, arkhivnoe lichnoe delo 12641 (Rinkevichute, Adelia d. Povilo), l. 104; see also another case in which the prisoner was determined not to have committed the alleged crime, but his labor and behavior were still taken into consideration in his release: ibid., f. Peschanlaga, arkhivnoe lichnoe delo 24988 (Navitskas, Petras s. Antanasa), l. 51.

184. Dolgun with Watson, *Alexander Dolgun's Story*, 314. On Gulag memoirists' frequent reticence to write about their release and life after release, see Leona Toker, *Return from the Archipelago: Narratives of Gulag Survivors* (Bloomington: Indiana University Press, 2000).

185. Dolgun with Watson, *Alexander Dolgun's Story*, 316, 318, 324.
186. GARF, f. 9401, op. 1a, d. 568, l. 11
187. AOTsPSI, f. Karlaga, sv. 4 s. pr., d. 143, ll. 93–94.
188. Afanas'ev, et al., *Istoriia stalinskogo Gulaga*, 3:366.
189. On the closing of numerous camps and camp subdivisions throughout this period, see the individual entries in Mikhail Borisovich Smirnov, *Sistema ispravitel'no-trudovykh lagerei v SSSR 1923–1960: Spravochnik* (Moscow: Zven'ia, 1998).
190. GARF, f. 9414, op. 1, d. 1398, ll. 14–22, in *Khrestomatiia po otechestvennoi istorii*, 50–54; Adler, *The Gulag Survivor*, 169, 192.
191. Galina Mikhailovna Ivanova, *Gulag v sisteme totalitarnogo gosudarstva* (Moscow: Moskovskii obshchestvennyi nauchnyi fond, 1997), 66. For a more detailed discussion of this shift in focus, see the concluding section below.
192. GARF, f. 9479, op. 1, d. 646, l. 15. The entire Kazakh Republic housed over 940,000 exiled adults and children. Ibid., l. 6.
193. Broken down by their locale of residence, 43,751 were in the city of Karaganda, 5,536 in the city of Balkhash, 6,413 in the city of Temir-Tau, 2,666 in the city of Dzhezkazgan, 3,991 in the city of Saran', 7,984 in the Osokarovskii raion (district), 6,553 in the Tel'manskii raion, 2,505 in the Nurinskii raion, 3,563 in the Zhana-Arkinskii raion, 1,718 in the Karkaralinskii raion, 1,592 in the Voroshilovskii raion, 1,418 in the Shetskii raion, 180 in the Kuvskii raion, 235 in the Kounradskii raion, 1,487 in the Karsakpaiskii raion, 116 in the Ulu-Tauskii raion, and 956 in the settlement of Akchatau. Twenty-four thousand of the over 47,000 German exiles lived in the city of Karaganda, along with 4,658 of the 5,877 OUN members, 11,331 of the 29,046 exiles from the Caucasus, and 1,769 of the 2,036 exiled Poles. Ibid., d. 847, ll. 109–10.
194. Ibid., d. 847, l. 115.
195. Ibid., ll. 116–17.
196. Viktor N. Zemskov, "Massovoe osvobozhdenie spetsposelentsev i ssyl'nykh (1954–1960 gg.)," *Sotsiologicheskie issledovaniia*, no. 1 (1991): 10, 14. For a petition for release from exile by a group of students according to this law, see GARF, f. 9479, op. 1, d. 847, l. 5.
197. GARF, f. 9479, op. 1, d. 847, ll. 116–17. On this law, see also Adler, *The Gulag Survivor*, 88. According to Zemskov, a total of over 117,000, including over 105,000 Soviet Germans and nearly 12,000 former kulaks, were released from exile throughout the Soviet Union under this act. See Zemskov, "Massovoe," 14. It is a bit unusual that over 4,000 of the nearly 12,000 released former kulaks were in the Karaganda region. On the mobilized Germans, see chapter 4 herein.
198. Zemskov, "Massovoe," 10. For the text of the decision, see Zaitsev, *Sbornik zakonodatel'nykh i normativnykh aktov*, 127–28.
199. Zemskov, "Massovoe," 10–11. An instruction of the USSR general procurator from July 20, 1954 detailed these provisions of the Council of Ministers' decision. Zaitsev, *Sbornik zakonodatel'nykh i normativnykh aktov*, 126–27.
200. Quoted in GARF, f. 9479, op. 1, d. 847, ll. 118–20.
201. Quoted in ibid., ll. 121–22.
202. Quoted in ibid., l. 123.
203. Ibid., ll. 135–36.

204. Ibid., ll. 105–7.

205. On the formation of special strict-regime divisions exclusively for Chechen and Ingush prisoners in zone 2 of the Spassk camp division of Karlag, see AOTsPSI, f. Karlaga, sv. 4 s. pr., d. 143, ll. 90–91. Interestingly, the 1956 order also dealt with the isolation of ill inmates, transferring all Karlag invalid prisoners sentenced for common, nonserious crimes to a special invalid section in zone 2 of the Spassk camp division. The official justification was the desire to improve "sanitary-prophylactic measures" and free the camp divisions from the necessity to care for invalids. The order also encouraged the further separation of prisoners with venereal diseases from among the invalids in accord with a Karlag order of December 1955. See also ibid., sv. 7 s. s. pr., d. 165, ll. 203–4.

206. GARF, f. 9401, op. 1a, d. 531, ll. 468–69.

207. The event is merely mentioned in a related order from 1956. See AOTsPSI, f. Karlaga, sv. 4 s. pr., d. 143, l. 147.

208. Ibid., sv. 5 s. pr., d. 147, ll. 164–65.

209. Norman M. Naimark, *Fires of Hatred: Ethnic Cleansing in Twentieth-Century Europe* (Cambridge, MA: Harvard University Press, 2001), 98–99, 106–7. Werth states Kazakhstan and Kirghizia were the areas considered for these permanent settlements. Werth, "The Chechen Problem," 362.

210. GARF, f. 9479, op. 1, d. 847, ll. 133–34.

211. Ibid., ll. 2a, 65–66. Similar were the cases of Efim Nikolaevich Brizhko and his wife, whose nationality was changed from German to Ukrainian. As such, they were released from exile in Karaganda. Ibid., ll. 4, 68. Also, the mother and daughter Gerta Iulevna Beliakova and Valentina Mikhailovna Beliakova had their nationality changed from Germans to Estonian and Russian, respectively. Ibid., l. 64.

212. Ibid., ll. 43–44.

213. Ibid., l. 75.

214. Ibid., l. 38, 40. Other invalid exiles were allowed to join their families. See, for example, Abel Abkarovich Khachuturian, who was permitted to leave Karaganda to join his family in the Altai Krai. Ibid., l. 52.

215. See, for example, the cases of Matson, Remizova, and Nelep, all German citizens of the USSR exiled to Karaganda from Moscow in 1941, all invalids without family members in a place of exile, and all of whom had requested release to return to Moscow, where they would be taken in as dependents by family members. Their petition was denied. Ibid., l. 54.

216. Ibid., l. 46.

217. See, for example, Liubov' Antonovna Khorosh, a Greek exiled in 1944 from Crimea to Karaganda. Ibid., l. 47. On other family members of the OUN, see the denial of release to the Stefinin family exiled from Ukraine to Karaganda in 1947. Ibid., l. 50.

218. Ibid., ll. 88–89. Compare also the release of the Grube family from Karaganda due to their health and advanced age, despite their lack of relatives in exile with whom they could live. The defining factor may have been the petition for their release originated with a letter from K. L. Zelinskii to Voroshilov in October 1954. Ibid., l. 85.

219. Zemskov, "Massovoe," 10, 14. According to Zemskov, over thirteen thousand were released under the decree of May 1955, while over forty-five thousand

were released under the November decree. In March 1956, release was extended to family members of those released under the decree of November 1955, encompassing nearly thirty-three thousand additional releases.

220. Ibid., 13–14. Unionwide, these releases totaled over fifteen thousand.

221. Ibid., 14, 19–20. Over sixty thousand were released under this provision. For the order itself, see ibid.; Zaitsev, *Sbornik zakonodatel'nykh i normativnykh aktov*, 47.

222. RGANI f. 89, per. 18, d. 26, ll. 1–5; see also Afanas'ev, et al., *Istoriia stalinskogo Gulaga*, 1:595–97.

223. See Zemskov, "Massovoe," 14, 20; Pohl, *The Stalinist Penal System*, 129.

224. Zemskov, "Massovoe," 16–18. According to Zemskov, over 25 percent of the Chechen, Ingush, and Karachai exiles in Kazakhstan refused to sign. The secretary of the Karaganda regional committee (obkom) noted that they attempted to educate the newly released Soviet German exiles on the significance of the release decree with the hope of mobilizing their support for completion of the Sixth Five-Year Plan, and "to fix them in their current place of residence and work." As many of them had their own private homes, with only a few exceptions, they seemed, he wrote, quite inclined to stay put. See T. B. Mitropol'skaia and I. N. Bukhanova, *Iz istorii nemtsev Kazakhstana, 1921–1975 gg.: Sbornik dokumentov* (Almaty, Kazkhstan: Gotika, 1997), 211–12.

225. RGANI, f. 89, per. 61, dok. 13, ll. 2–7.

226. Some 46,790 Soviet German exiles were released in the Karaganda Oblast' on the basis of the decree of December 13, 1955. See Mitropol'skaia and Bukhanova, *Iz istorii nemtsev Kazakhstana*, 211.

227. Zemskov, "Massovoe," 15; Pohl, *The Stalinist Penal System*, 89–90. For the 1955 release, the 1964 disavowal of their "guilt," and the 1972 decision allowing them to choose freely their place of residence, see Vladimir A. Auman and Valentina G. Chebotareva, eds., *Istoriia rossiiskikh nemtsev v dokumentakh (1763–1992 gg.)* (Moscow: Mezhdunarodnyi institut gumanitarnykh programm, 1993), 177–79. For one Soviet German woman's experience of exile and release in the Karaganda region, see Berta Bachmann, *Memories of Kazakhstan: A Report on the Life Experiences of a German Woman in Russia* (Lincoln, NE: American Historical Society of Germans, 1983), especially 78.

228. Zemskov, "Massovoe," 16.

229. For the order on the release of the Kalmyks, with its specific denial of their right to return to their homes, see RGANI, f. 89, per. 61, dok. 12, l. 2.

230. Pohl, *The Stalinist Penal System*, 118. For the release order, see GARF, f. 9401, op. 1a, d. 568, ll. 6–7.

231. Ibid., ll. 338–39.

232. For the data on all these releases, see Zemskov, "Massovoe," 14; see also Pohl, *The Stalinist Penal System*.

233. Zemskov, "Massovoe," 18–25. Zemskov had no data for the number of exiles remaining after 1960, the point at which the MVD materials in GARF stop.

234. Dolgun with Watson, *Alexander Dolgun's Story*, 316. On prisoners staying near the location of their imprisonment after their release, see Adler, *The Gulag Survivor*, 231–33.

235. Riewe interview, TNA PRO FO 371/122936, N S1551/6, 6.

236. Dolgun with Watson, *Alexander Dolgun's Story*, 317.

237. Ibid., 319.

238. In an interesting yet problematically limited book, Adler discusses these difficulties in some depth. Unfortunately, Adler's study is almost exclusively focused on political prisoners, missing the important and different experiences of both nationalists and ordinary criminals after the Gulag. Adler, *The Gulag Survivor*.

239. GARF, f. 9479, op. 1, d. 847, ll. 186–87.

240. Kokurin and Petrov, *GULAG: (Glavnoe upravlenie lagerei)*, 171.

241. Adler, *The Gulag Survivor*, 175. The similarities to the KGB recommendations in 1962 for "strengthening the struggle of the security organs against hostile manifestations by anti-soviet elements" in the wake of the major strike at Novocherkassk are telling, indicating a long-entrenched Soviet mind-set that did not disappear in the late 1950s. As Baron writes, "Among other things, surveillance of released convicts and nationalist and religious elements was to be stepped up." Baron, *Bloody Saturday in the Soviet Union*, 92.

242. Adler, *The Gulag Survivor*, 29.

243. Ivanova, *Gulag v sisteme*, 68.

244. Adler, *The Gulag Survivor*, 219. Consider also her statement, "Thus far we have explored a number of psychological and emotional reasons why former zeks would seek CPSU membership or reinstatement but put very simply and pragmatically, Party membership made Soviet life a lot easier." Ibid., 223.

245. Quoted in RGASPI, f. 560, op. 1, d. 32, l. 2b. For this along with other typescript and handwritten memoirs and letters, see RGASPI, f. 560. This sentiment echoes that of Ginzburg.

246. Figes has a good discussion of this. Figes, *The Whisperers*, 535–96.

247. For an insightful discussion of the reception of the publication, see Kozlov, "The Readers of *Novyi Mir*," 301–61.

248. Dolgun with Watson, *Alexander Dolgun's Story*, 319.

249. For an NKVD document from 1945 on this practice and a KGB directive from 1955 confirming its continuation, see Kokurin and Petrov, *GULAG: (Glavnoe upravlenie lagerei)*, 133, 163. A KGB document from April 1956 provides allowance for these deaths to be registered at ZAGS. RGANI, f. 89, per. 18, dok. 35, ll. 1–2.

250. See AOTsPSI, f. Karlaga, arkhivnoe lichnoe delo 275643 (Valeev, Kanzafar Mufazalovich). The letter to his daughter is in the front of the file without a page number while the official death certificate is in ibid., l. 24–24b.

251. Solzhenitsyn, *The Gulag Archipelago*, 3:494.

252. See Adler, *The Gulag Survivor*, 24, 177, 193.

253. Kokurin and Petrov, *GULAG: (Glavnoe upravlenie lagerei)*, 173, quoting Vladimir Lenin, *Polnoe sobranie sochinenii*, (Moscow: Gosudarstvennoe izdatel'stvo politicheskoi literatury, 1958–65), 26:372.

254. RGANI, f. 89, per. 55, dok. 28, l. 17.

255. For the report, see GARF, f. 9401, op. 2, d. 479, ll. 388–99; see also Kokurin and Petrov, *GULAG: (Glavnoe upravlenie lagerei)*, 165. For the report and the proposed reorganization, see RGANI, f. 89, per. 16, dok. 1, ll. 4–36.

256. Kokurin and Petrov, *GULAG: (Glavnoe upravlenie lagerei)*, 165. The complete isolation of prisoners considered to be the most harmful element in

the camps harks back to the creation of the special camps for political prisoners in 1948.

257. Ibid., 167. The report noted that 517 prisoners were murdered in 1954 and another 240 were murdered in 1955.

258. Ibid., 165.

259. Ibid., 170.

260. See Ivanova, *Gulag v sisteme*, 67. For the report, see RGANI, f. 89, per. 18, dok. 36, ll. 1–4.

261. GARF, f. 9401, op. 2, d. 505, ll. 302–29, in Kokurin and Petrov, *GULAG: (Glavnoe upravlenie lagerei)*, 208.

262. AOTsPSI, f. Karlaga, sv. 7 s. s. pr., d. 165, ll. 203–4.

263. Kokurin and Petrov, *GULAG: (Glavnoe upravlenie lagerei)*, 209–10. For more on the battle with criminal gangs, see Federico Varese, "The Society of the *Vory-v-zakone*, 1930s–1950s," *Cahiers du Monde russe* 39, no. 4 (1998): 515–38.

264. Kokurin and Petrov, *GULAG: (Glavnoe upravlenie lagerei)*, 209–10. Over the course of 1957–58, a mere 7,115 prisoners escaped (well under 1 in 200 per year), and only 135 (less than 2 percent of the escapees) were never apprehended. As throughout Gulag's history, even these low figures were sharply criticized.

265. Ibid., 211.

266. Ibid., 212.

267. Ibid., 211.

268. Ibid., 443–46. The percentages on January 1, 1956 and January 1, 1960, respectively, were 58.8 and 68.8 percent for Russians, 17.1 and 10.9 percent for Ukrainians, 3.8 and 2.7 percent for Belarusians, 2.2 and 0.9 percent for Lithuanians, 1.4 and 0.6 percent for Latvians, and 1.1 and 0.4 percent for Estonians. The percentages for all other nationalities were essentially unchanged.

CONCLUSION

1. V. P. Popov, "Gosudarstvennyi terror v sovetskoi Rossii, 1923–1953 gg. (istochniki i ikh interpretatsiia)," *Otechestvennye Arkhivy*, no. 2 (1992): 21.

2. Halfin makes a similar point, observing, "High expectations generated enormous anxiety: now that society had been declared perfect, only the individual could be blamed for negative actions." Igal Halfin, *Terror in My Soul: Communist Autobiographies on Trial* (Cambridge, MA: Harvard University Press, 2003), 244.

# REFERENCES

ARCHIVES

AOTsPSI    Arkhivnyi Otdel Tsentra Pravovoi Statistiki i Informatsii pri Proku-rature Karagandinskoi Oblasti (Archive Department of the Center for Legal Statistics and Information under the Procurator of the Karaganda Region), Karaganda.

APRK    Arkhiv Prezidenta Respubliki Kazakhstana (Presidential Archive of the Republic of Kazakhstan), Almaty.

GARF    Gosudarstvennyi Arkhiv Rossiiskoi Federatsii (State Archive of the Russian Federation), Moscow.

NIPTs    Nauchno-Informatsionnyi i Prosvetitel'skii Tsentr "Memorial" (Scientific Information and Enlightenment Center "Memorial"), Moscow.

RGANI    Rossiiskii Gosudarstvennyi Arkhiv Noveishei Istorii (Russian State Archive of Contemporary History), Moscow.

RGASPI    Rossiiskii Gosudarstvennyi Arkhiv Sotsial'no-Politicheskoi Istorii (Russian State Archive of Sociopolitical History), Moscow.

TNA PRO    The National Archives of the United Kingdom, Public Records Office, London.


DOCUMENTARY FILMS

*The Germans We Kept.* Directed by Catrine Clay. BBC and History Channel, 2000.

*Stolen Years.* Directed by Bruce Kenneth Young. South Carolina Educational Television, 1999.


MEMOIRS, OFFICIAL SOVIET PUBLICATIONS, AND
   DOCUMENT PUBLICATIONS

Afanas'ev, Iurii Nikolaevich, et al., eds. *Istoriia stalinskogo Gulaga: Konets 1920-kh–pervaia polovina 1950-kh godov: Sobranie dokumentov v 7-mi tomakh.* Moscow: Rosspen, 2004.

Auman, Vladimir A., and Valentina G. Chebotareva eds. *Istoriia rossiiskikh nemtsev v dokumentakh (1763–1992 gg.).* Moscow: Mezhdunarodnyi institut gumanitarnykh programm, 1993.

Bachmann, Berta. *Memories of Kazakhstan: A Report on the Life Experiences of a German Woman in Russia.* Lincoln, NE: American Historical Society of Germans, 1983.

Bardach, Janusz, and Kathleen Gleeson. *Man Is Wolf to Man: Surviving the Gulag.* Berkeley: University of California Press, 1998.

Bardach, Janusz, and Kathleen Gleeson. *Surviving Freedom: After the Gulag*. Berkeley: University of California Press, 2003.

Bershadskaia, Liubov'. *Rastoptannye zhizni*. Paris: Piat' kontinentov, 1975.

Buber, Margarete. *Under Two Dictators*. New York: Dodd, Mead, 1949.

Buca, Edward. *Vorkuta*. London: Constable, 1976.

Bugai, Nikolai F., ed. *"Mobilizovat' nemtsev v rabochie kolonny . . . I. Stalin" Sbornik dokumentov (1940-e gody)*. Moscow: Gotika, 1998.

Dolgun, Alexander, with Patrick Watson. *Alexander Dolgun's Story: An American in the Gulag*. New York: Knopf, 1975.

Fel'dman, Artem. *Riadovoe delo*. Moscow: Memorial, 1993.

Frants, V. "Vosstanie v Kengire." *Sotsialisticheskii vestnik*, no. 6 (1956): 104–10.

Gilboa, Yehoshua. *Confess! Confess! Eight Years in Soviet Prisons*. Boston: Little, Brown, 1968.

Ginzburg, Eugenia. *Journey into the Whirlwind*. New York: Harcourt, Brace and World, 1967.

———. *Within the Whirlwind*. New York: Harcourt Brace Jovanovich, 1981.

Gorky, Maksim, Leopol'd Auerbach, and Semen Firin, eds. *Belomor: An Account of the Construction of the New Canal between the White Sea and the Baltic Sea*. Translated by Amabel Williams-Ellis. New York: H. Smith and R. Haas, 1935.

*The GULAG Press, 1920–1937*. Leiden, Netherlands: IDC Publishers, 2000.

"Gulag v gody voiny: Doklad nachal'nika GULAGa NKVD SSSR V. G. Nasedkina, avgust 1944 g." *Istoricheskii arkhiv*, no. 3 (1994): 60–86.

Herling, Gustav. *A World Apart: The Journal of a Gulag Survivor*. New York: Arbor House, 1951.

Iakovenko, Dmitrii. "Osuzhden po 58-i." *Zvezda Vostoka* 57, no. 4 (1989): 64–85.

Kashkinoi, I. V. "'Ia khochu znat' prichinu moego aresta . . . ': Pis'mo V. N. Pilishchuka—byvshego zakliuchennogo Karlaga." In *Golosa Istorii*, ed. Isaak S. Rozental', vypusk 23, kniga 2. Moscow: Tsentral'nyi muzei revoliutsii, 1992.

Kekushev, Nikolai L'vovich. *Zveriada*. Moscow: Iuridicheskaia literatura, 1991.

Kiselev, Aleksandr F., and Ernst M. Shchagin, eds. *Khrestomatiia po otechestvennoi istorii (1946–1995 gg.)*. Moscow: Gumanitarnyi izdatel'skii tsentr VLADOS, 1996.

Kmiecik, Jerzy. *A Boy in the Gulag*. London: Quartet Books, 1983.

Kokurin, Aleksandr, and Nikolai Petrov, eds. *GULAG: (Glavnoe upravlenie lagerei), 1917–1960*. Moscow: Mezhdunarodnyi fond "Demokratiia," 2000.

Kopelev, Lev. *To Be Preserved Forever*. Philadelphia: Lippincott, 1977.

———. *The Education of a True Believer*. New York: Harper and Rowe, 1980.

Korol', Maia. *Odisseia razvedchika: Pol'sha–SShA–Kitai–GULAG*. Moscow: Izdatel'stvo Rossiiskogo obshchestva medikov-literaturov, 1999.

Krasil'nikov, Sergei A., ed. "Rozhdenie Gulaga: Diskussiia v verkhnykh eshelonakh vlasti." *Istoricheskii arkhiv* 4 (1997): 142–56.

Mitropol'skaia, T. B., and I. N. Bukhanova eds. *Iz istorii nemtsev Kazakhstana, 1921–1975 gg.: Sbornik dokumentov*. Almaty, Kazkhstan: Gotika, 1997.

Naumov, V. P., and Iu. V. Sigachev, eds. *Lavrentii Beriia, 1953: Stenogramma iiul'skogo plenuma TsK KPSS i drugie dokumenty*. Moscow: Mezhdunarodnyi fond "Demokratiia," 1999.

Panin, Dmitri. *The Notebooks of Sologdin*. New York: Harcourt Brace Jovanovich, 1976.

Petrov, Vladimir. *Escape from the Future: The Incredible Adventures of a Young Russian*. Bloomington: Indiana University Press, 1973.

Rachlin, Rachel, and Israel Rachlin. *Sixteen Years in Siberia*. Tuscaloosa: University of Alabama Press, 1988.

Rossi, Jacques. *The Gulag Handbook: An Encyclopedia Dictionary of Soviet Penitentiary Institutions and Terms Related to the Forced Labor Camps*. New York: Paragon House, 1989.

Scholmer, Joseph. *Vorkuta*. New York: Holt, 1955.

Shumuk, Danylo. *Life Sentence: Memoirs of a Ukrainian Political Prisoner*. Edmonton: Canadian Institute of Ukrainian Studies, 1984.

Adamova-Sliozberg, Olga. "My Journey." In *Till My Tale Is Told: Women's Memoirs of the Gulag*, ed. Simeon Vilensky, 1–88. Bloomington: Indiana University Press, 1999.

Solzhenitsyn, Aleksandr I. *The Gulag Archipelago, 1918–1956: An Experiment in Literary Investigation*. Translated by Thomas P. Whitney. 3 vols. New York: Harper Perennial, 1991.

"Spetspereselentsy v SSSR v 1944 godu ili god bol'shogo pereseleniia." *Otechestvennye arkhivy*, no. 5 (1993): 98–111.

Stalin, Joseph V. *Joseph Stalin: Selected Writings*. Westport, CT: Praeger, 1970.

Stefanskaia, Militsa Cheslavovna. *Chernoe i beloe*. Moscow: Suzdalev, 1994.

Steinberg, Isaac. *Spiridonova: Revolutionary Terrorist*. London: Methuen, 1935.

"Tragediia v medvedevskom lesu: o rasstrele politzakliuchennykh Orlovskoi tiur'my." *Izvestiia TsK KPSS*, no. 11 (1990): 124–31.

Varkony, Fedir. "The Revolt in Kingir." In *500 Ukrainian Martyred Women*, ed. Stephania Halychyn, 22–29. New York: United Ukrainian Women's Organization of America, 1956.

Vilenskii, Semen S., ed. *Soprotivlenie v Gulage: Vospominaniia, pis'ma, dokumenty*. Moscow: Vozvrashchenie, 1992.

Vilensky, Simeon, ed. *Till My Tale Is Told: Women's Memoirs of the Gulag*. Bloomington: Indiana University Press, 1999.

"'Voennoplennye oznakomilis' s metodami sotsialisticheskogo stroitel'stva,' Dokladnaia zapiska MVD SSSR." *Istochnik*, no. 1 (1999): 83–88.

"Vosstanie v Steplage." *Otechestvennye arkhivy*, no. 4 (1994): 33–81.

Vyshinsky, Andrei, ed. *Ot tiurem k vospitatel'nym uchrezdeniiam*. Moscow: Gosudarstvennoe izdatel'stvo Sovetskoe zakonodatel'stvo, 1934.

Werth, Nicolas, and Gael Moullec, eds. *Rapports Secrets Sovietiques: La Societe Russe Dans Les Documents Confidentiels, 1921–1991*. Paris: Gallimard, 1994.

SCHOLARLY WORKS

Abdakimov, Abdazhapar. *Totalitarizm: Deportatsiia narodov i repressiia intelligentsii*. Karaganda: Apparat akima Karagandinskoi oblasti, 1997.

Adler, Nanci. *The Gulag Survivor: Beyond the Soviet System*. New Brunswick, NJ: Transaction Publishers, 2002.

Aldazhumanov, Kaidar S. "Deportatsiia narodov—prestuplenie totalitarnogo re-zhima." In *Deportatsiia narodov i problema prav cheloveka: Materialy semi-nara, Almaty 12 iiunia 1997 goda*, ed. Igor' Trutanov, Vladislav Nabokov, and Iurii Romanov, 10–19. Almaty, Kazakhstan: Istorichesko-prosvetitel'skoe ob-shchestvo "Adilet," 1998.

Alexopoulos, Golfo. *Stalin's Outcasts: Aliens, Citizens, and the Soviet State, 1926–1936*. Ithaca, NY: Cornell University Press, 2003.

———. "Amnesty 1945: The Revolving Door of Stalin's Gulag. " *Slavic Review* 64, no. 2 (2005): 274–306.

Applebaum, Anne. *Gulag: A History*. New York: Doubleday, 2003.

Arendt, Hannah. *The Origins of Totalitarianism*. Cleveland: Meridian Books, 1958.

Avrich, Paul. *Kronstadt, 1921*. Princeton, NJ: Princeton University Press, 1970.

Bacon, Edwin. *The Gulag at War: Stalin's Forced Labour System in the Light of the Archives*. London: Macmillan, 1994.

Barber, John, and Mark Harrison. *The Soviet Home Front, 1941–1945: A Social and Economic History of the USSR in World War II*. London: Longman, 1991.

Barnes, Steven A. "All for the Front, All for Victory! The Mobilization of Forced Labor in the Soviet Union during World War Two," *International Labor and Working Class History* 58 (Fall 2000): 239–60.

———. "Soviet Society Confined: The Gulag in the Karaganda Region of Ka-zakhstan, 1930s–1950s." PhD diss., Stanford University, 2003.

———. "In a Manner Befitting Soviet Citizens: An Uprising in the Post–Stalin Gulag," *Slavic Review* 64, no. 4 (Winter 2005): 823–50.

Baron, Nicholas. "Conflict and Complicity: The Expansion of the Karelian Gulag, 1923–1933." *Cahiers du Monde russe* 42, nos. 2–4 (2001): 615–48.

———. "Production and Terror: The Operation of the Karelian Gulag, 1933–1939." *Cahiers du Monde russe* 43, no. 1 (2002): 139–80.

Baron, Samuel H. *Bloody Saturday in the Soviet Union: Novocherkassk 1962*. Stanford, CA: Stanford University Press, 2001.

Bauman, Zygmunt. *Modernity and the Holocaust*. Ithaca, NY: Cornell University Press, 1989.

Beer, Daniel. *Renovating Russia: The Human Sciences and the Fate of Liberal Modernity, 1880–1930*. Ithaca, NY: Cornell University Press, 2008.

Bell, Wilson. "One Day in the Life of Educator Khrushchev: Labour and *Kul'turnost'* in the Gulag Newspapers." *Canadian Slavonic Papers* 46, nos. 3–4 (2004): 289–313.

Berdinskikh, Viktor. *Istoriia odnogo lageria (Viatlag)*. Moscow: Agraf, 2001.

Borodkin, Leonid I., Paul Gregory, and Oleg V. Khlevniuk, eds. *GULAG: Eko-nomika prinuditel'nogo truda*. Moscow: Rosspen, 2008.

Brown, Kate. *A Biography of No Place: From Ethnic Borderland to Soviet Heart-land*. Cambridge, MA: Harvard University Press, 2004.

Burds, Jeffrey. "Agentura: Soviet Informants' Networks and the Ukrainian Rebel Underground in Galicia, 1944–1948." *East European Politics and Societies* 11, no. 1 (1997): 89–130.

———. "The Early Cold War in Soviet West Ukraine, 1944–1948." Carl Beck Pa-pers in Russian and East European Studies, no. 1505, University of Pittsburgh, 2001.

———. "Gender and Policing in Soviet West Ukraine, 1944–1948." *Cahiers du monde russe* 42, nos. 2–4 (2001): 279–319.

———. "The Soviet War against 'Fifth Columnists': The Case of Chechnya, 1942–4." *Journal of Contemporary History* 42, no. 2 (2007): 267–314.

Conquest, Robert. *Kolyma: The Arctic Death Camps*. New York: Viking Press, 1978.

———. *The Great Terror: A Reassessment*. New York: Oxford University Press, 1990.

Craveri [Kraveri], Marta. "Krizis Gulaga: Kengirskoe vosstanie 1954 goda v dokumentakh MVD." *Cahiers du Monde russe* 36, no. 3 (1995): 319–44.

Craveri [Kraveri], Marta, and Oleg Khlevniuk. "Krizis ekonomiki MVD (konets 1940-kh–1950-e gody)." *Cahiers du Monde russe* 36, nos. 1–2 (1995): 179–90.

Dallin, David J., and Boris I. Nicolaevsky. *Forced Labor in Soviet Russia*. New Haven, CT: Yale University Press, 1947.

Daumantas, Juozas. *Fighters for Freedom: Lithuanian Partisans versus the U.S.S.R. (1944–1947)*. Translated by E. J. Harrison. New York: Manyland Books, 1975.

David-Fox, Michael. "On the Primacy of Ideology: Soviet Revisionists and Holocaust Deniers (in Response to Martin Malia)." *Kritika: Explorations in Russian and Eurasian History* 5, no. 1 (2004): 81–105.

Dobson, Miriam. "'Show the Bandit-Enemies No Mercy!': Amnesty, Criminality, and Public Response in 1953." In *The Dilemma of De-Stalinization: Negotiating Cultural and Social Change in the Khrushchev Era*, ed. Polly Jones, 21–40. Abingdon, UK: Routledge, 2006.

———. *Khrushchev's Cold Summer: Gulag Returnees, Crime, and the Fate of Reform after Stalin*. Ithaca, NY: Cornell University Press, 2009.

Elagin, Andrei Sergeevich, A. K. Ivanenko, and B. N. Abisheva. *Karaganda*. Almaty, Kazakhstan: "Nauka" Kazakhskoi SSR, 1989.

Ertz, Simon. "Trading Effort for Freedom: Workday Credits in the Stalinist Camp System." *Comparative Economic Studies* 47, no. 2 (2005): 476–91.

Figes, Orlando. *The Whisperers: Private Life in Stalin's Russia*. New York: Metropolitan Books, 2007.

Fleischhauer, Ingeborg. "The Ethnic Germans under Nazi Rule." In *Soviet Germans: Past and Present*, ed. Ingeborg Fleischhauer and Benjamin Pinkus, 92–102. London: Hurst, 1986).

———. "'Operation Barbarossa' and the Deportation." In *The Soviet Germans: Past and Present*, ed. Ingeborg Fleischhauer and Benjamin Pinkus, 66–91. London: Hurst, 1986.

Foucault, Michel. *Discipline and Punish: The Birth of the Prison*. New York: Vintage Books, 1977.

Gelb, Michael. "An Early Soviet Ethnic Deportation: The Far-Eastern Koreans." *Russian Review* 54, no. 3 (July 1995): 389–412.

———. "The Western Finnic Minorities and the Origins of the Stalinist Nationalities Deportations." *Nationalities Papers* 24, no. 2 (1996): 237–68.

Getty, J. Arch. *Origins of the Great Purges: The Soviet Communist Party Reconsidered, 1933–1938*. Cambridge: Cambridge University Press, 1985.

Getty, J. Arch, Gábor Tamás Rittersporn, and Viktor N. Zemskov. "Victims of the Soviet Penal System in the Pre-war Years: A First Approach on the Basis of Archival Evidence." *American Historical Review* (October 1993): 1017–49.

Getzler, Israel. *Kronstadt 1917–1921: The Fate of a Soviet Democracy.* Cambridge: Cambridge University Press, 2002.

Gorlanov, Oleg A., and Arsenii B. Roginskii. "Ob arestakh v zapadnykh oblastiakh Belorussii i Ukraini v 1939–1941 gg." In *Repressii protiv poliakov i pol'skikh grazhdan,* ed. Aleksandr E. Gur'ianov, 77–113. Moscow: Zven'ia, 1997.

Graziosi, Andrea. "The Great Strikes of 1953 in Soviet Labor Camps in the Accounts of Their Participants: A Review." *Cahiers du Monde russe et sovietique* 33, no. 4 (1992): 419–46.

Gregory, Paul R., and Valerii Vasil'evich Lazarev, eds. *The Economics of Forced Labor: The Soviet Gulag.* Stanford, CA: Hoover Institution Press, 2003.

Grinev, Vladimir M., and Aleksandr Iu. Daniel'. *Uznitsy 'ALZhIRa': spisok zhen-shchin-zakliuchennykh Akmolinskogo i drugikh otdelenii Karlaga.* Moscow: Zven'ia, 2003.

Gross, Jan T. *Revolution from Abroad: The Soviet Conquest of Poland's Western Ukraine and Western Belorussia.* Exp. ed. Princeton, NJ: Princeton University Press, 2002.

Gur'ianov, Aleksandr E. "Pol'skie spetspereselentsy v SSSR v 1940–1941 gg." In *Repressii protiv poliakov i pol'skikh grazhdan,* ed. Aleksandr E. Gur'ianov, 114–36. Moscow, 1997.

Gvozdkova, Liubov'. *Prinuditel'nyi trud. Ispravitel'no-trudovye lageriakh v Kuzbasse (30–50-e gg.).* 2 vols. Kemerovo: Kuzbassvuizizdat, 1994.

Hagenloh, Paul. "'Socially Harmful Elements' and the Great Terror." In *Stalinism: New Directions,* ed. Sheila Fitzpatrick, 286–308. London: Routledge, 2000.

———. *Stalin's Police: Public Order and Mass Repression in the USSR, 1926–1941.* Washington, DC: Woodrow Wilson Center Press, 2009.

Halfin, Igal. *Terror in My Soul: Communist Autobiographies on Trial.* Cambridge, MA: Harvard University Press, 2003.

Harris, James R. "The Growth of the Gulag: Forced Labor in the Urals Region, 1929–1931." *Russian Review* 56 (April 1997) 265–80.

Harrison, Mark. "Resource Mobilization for World War II: The U.S.A., U.K., U.S.S.R., and Germany, 1938–1945." *Economic History Review* 41 (1988): 171–92.

———. *Accounting for War: Soviet Production, Employment, and the Defence Burden, 1940–1945.* New York: Cambridge University Press, 1996.

Healey, Dan. *Homosexual Desire in Revolutionary Russia: The Regulation of Sexual and Gender Dissent.* Chicago: University of Chicago Press, 2001.

Heinzen, James. "Corruption in the Gulag: Dilemmas of Officials and Prisoners." *Comparative Economic Studies* 47, no. 2 (2005): 456–75.

Hellbeck, Jochen. "Speaking Out: Languages of Affirmation and Dissent in Stalinist Russia." *Kritika: Explorations in Russian and Eurasian History* 1, no. 1 (2000): 71–96.

Hessler, Julie. *A Social History of Soviet Trade: Trade Policy, Retail Practices, and Consumption, 1917–1953.* Princeton, NJ: Princeton University Press, 2004.

Hirsch, Francine. *Empire of Nations: Ethnographic Knowledge and the Making of the Soviet Union.* Ithaca, NY: Cornell University Press, 2005.

Hoffmann, David L. *Stalinist Values: The Cultural Norms of Soviet Modernity.* Ithaca, NY: Cornell University Press, 2003.

Hoffman, David L., and Yanni Kotsonis, eds. *Russian Modernity: Politics, Knowledge, Practices.* New York: Palgrave Macmillan, 2000.

Holquist, Peter. "'Information Is the Alpha and Omega of Our Work': Bolshevik Surveillance in Its Pan-European Context." *Journal of Modern History* 69, no. 3 (1997): 415–50.

———. "State Violence as Technique: The Logic of Violence in Soviet Totalitarianism." In *Landscaping the Human Garden: Twentieth-Century Population Management in a Comparative Framework*, ed. Amir Weiner, 19–45. Stanford, CA: Stanford University Press, 2003.

Horn, David G. *Social Bodies: Science, Reproduction, and Italian Modernity.* Princeton, NJ: Princeton University Press, 1994.

Ivanova, Galina Mikhailovna. *Labor Camp Socialism: The Gulag in the Soviet Totalitarian System.* Translated by Carol Flath. Armonk, NY: M. E. Sharpe, 2000. Originally published as *Gulag v sisteme totalitarnogo gosudarstva* (Moscow: Moskovskii obshchestvennyi nauchnyi fond, 1997).

Ivashov, L., and A. Emelin, interviewees. "Gulag v gody Velikoi Otechestvennoi Voiny." *Voenno-istoricheskii zhurnal*, no. 1 (1991): 14–24.

Izmozik, Vladlen. *Glaza i ushi rezhima: gosudarstvennyi politicheskii kontrol za naseleniem Sovetskoi Rossii v 1918–1928 godakh.* Saint Petersburg: Izdatel'stvo Sankt-peterburgskogo universiteta ekonomiki i finansov, 1995.

Jakobson, Michael. *Origins of the Gulag: The Soviet Prison-Camp System, 1917–1934.* Lexington: University Press of Kentucky, 1993.

Jolluck, Katherine R. *Exile and Identity: Polish Women in the Soviet Union during World War II.* Pittsburgh: University of Pittsburgh Press, 2002.

Keep, John. "Recent Writing on Stalin's Gulag: An Overview." *Crime, Histoire, and Sociétés* 1, no. 2 (1997): 91–112.

Khlevniuk, Oleg. *The History of the Gulag: From Collectivization to the Great Terror.* Trans. Vadim A. Staklo. Ed. David J. Nordlander. New Haven, CT: Yale University Press, 2004.

Khlevnyuk, Oleg. "The Economy of the Gulag." In *Behind the Façade of Stalin's Command Economy*, ed. Paul R. Gregory, 111–30. Stanford, CA: Hoover Institution Press, 2001.

Kliuchnikova, Galina Stepanova. *Kazakhstanskii Alzhir.* Malinovka, Kazakhstan: Kazakhstan: Assotsiatsiia zhertv nezakonnykh repressii, 2003.

Knight, Amy W. *Beria, Stalin's First Lieutenant.* Princeton, NJ: Princeton University Press, 1993.

Koch, Fred C. *The Volga Germans: In Russia and the Americas, from 1763 to the Present.* University Park: Penn State University Press, 1977.

Kokurin, Aleksandr, and Nikita Petrov. "Arkhiv. GULAG: Struktura i kadry." *Svobodnaia mysl'* no. 3 (2000): 105–23.

Kolakowski, Leszek. *Main Currents of Marxism: Its Rise, Growth, and Dissolution, Volume I: The Founders.* Trans. Paul S. Falla. Oxford: Clarendon Press, 1978.

Kotkin, Stephen. *Magnetic Mountain: Stalinism as a Civilization.* Berkeley: University of California Press, 1995.

Kozlov, Denis. "The Readers of *Novyi Mir*, 1945–1970: Twentieth-Century Experience and Soviet Historical Consciousness." PhD diss., University of Toronto, 2005.

Kozlov, Vladimir. *Massovye besporiadki v SSSR pri Khrushcheve i Brezhneve, 1953-nachalo 1980-kh gg.* Novosibirsk: Sibirskii khronograf, 1999. Translated as *Mass Uprisings in the USSR: Protest and Rebellion in the Post-Stalin Years* (Armonk, NY: M. E. Sharpe, 2002).

Kirillov, V. M. *Istoriia repressii v Nizhnetagil'skom regione Urala. 1920-e–nachalo 50-kh gg. Tom 1: Repressii 1920–1930-kh gg., tom 2: Tagillag 1940-e–nach. 50-kh gg.* Nizhnii Tagil: Nizhnetagil'skii gosudarstvennyi pedagogicheskii institut, 1996.

Krasil'nikov, Sergei Aleksandrovich. *Serp i molokh. Krest'ianskaia ssylka v Zapadnoi Sibiri v 1930–e gg.* Moscow: Rosspen, 2003.

Kukushkina, Anfisa R. *Akmolinskii lager' zhen 'izmennikov rodiny': Istoriia i sud'by.* Karaganda: Kazakhstanskii finansovo–ekonomicheskii universitet, 2002.

Kuromiya, Hiroaki. *Freedom and Terror in the Donbas: A Ukrainian-Russian Borderland, 1870s–1990s.* Cambridge: Cambridge University Press, 1998.

Kuziakina, Natalia. *Theatre in the Solovki Prison Camp.* Translated by Boris M. Meerovich. Newark, NJ: Harwood Academic Publishers, 1995.

Laar, Mart. *War in the Woods: Estonia's Struggle for Survival, 1944–1956.* Translated by Tiina Ets. Washington, DC: Compass Press, 1992.

Lenin, Vladimir. *Polnoe sobranie sochinenii.* Moscow: Gosudarstvennoe izdatel'stvo politicheskoi literatury, 1958–65.

Lewin, Moshe. "Who Was the Soviet Kulak?" In *The Making of the Soviet System: Essays in the Social History of Interwar Russia*, 121–41. New York: New Press, 1994.

Manley, Rebecca. *To the Tashkent Station: Evacuation and Survival in the Soviet Union at War.* Ithaca, NY: Cornell University Press, 2009.

Martin, Terry. "The Origins of Soviet Ethnic Cleansing." *Journal of Modern History* 70, no. 4 (1998): 813–61.

———. *The Affirmative Action Empire: Nations and Nationalism in the Soviet Union, 1923–1939.* Ithaca, NY: Cornell University Press, 2001.

Morozov, Nikolai Alekseevich. *Gulag v Komi krae.* Syktyvkar: Izd–vo Syktyvkarskogo Universiteta, 1997.

Naimark, Norman M. *Fires of Hatred: Ethnic Cleansing in Twentieth-Century Europe.* Cambridge, MA: Harvard University Press, 2001.

Nikitina, Ol'ga Aleksandrovna. *Kollektivizatsiia i raskulachivanie v Karelii.* Petrozavodsk: Karel'skii Nauchnyi tsentr RAN, 1997.

Nordlander, David J. "Capital of the Gulag: Magadan in the Early Stalin Era, 1929–1941." PhD diss., University of North Carolina at Chapel Hill, 1997.

———. "Origins of a Gulag Capital: Magadan and Stalinist Control in the Early 1930s." *Slavic Review* 57, no. 4 (Winter 1998): 791–812.

R. N. Nurgaliev, ed. *Karaganda, Karagandinskaia oblast': Entsiklopediia.* Almaty, Kazakhstan: Kazakhskaia sovetskaia entsiklopediia, 1986.

Osokina, Elena. *Our Daily Bread: Socialist Distribution and the Art of Survival in Stalin's Russia, 1927–1941.* Translated by Greta Bucher. Edited by Kate S. Transchel. Armonk, NY: M. E. Sharpe, 2000.

Overy, Richard. *Russia's War: A History of the Soviet War Effort: 1941–1945*. New York: Penguin, 1998.

Pankov, S. A. "Lagernaia sistema i prinuditel'nyi trud v Sibiri i na Dal'nem vostoke 1929–1941 gg." In *Vozvrashchenie pamiati. Istoriko-publitsisticheskii al'manakh. Vyp. 3*, ed. Irina Vladimirovna Pavlova, 37–67. Novosibirsk: Novosibirskoe knizhnoe izdatel'stvo, 1997.

Pianciola, Niccolo. "The Collectivization Famine in Kazakhstan, 1931–1933." *Harvard Ukrainian Studies 25*, nos. 3–4 (2001): 237–51.

———. "Famine in the Steppe: The Collectivization of Agriculture and the Kazakh Herdsmen, 1928–1934." *Cahiers du monde russe 45*, nos. 1–2 (2004): 137–92.

Pohl, J. Otto. *The Stalinist Penal System: A Statistical History of Soviet Repression and Terror, 1930–1953*. Jefferson, NC: McFarland and Company, 1997.

Popov, V. P. "Gosudarstvennyi terror v sovetskoi Rossii, 1923–1953 gg. (istochniki i ikh interpretatsiia)." *Otechestvennye Arkhivy*, no. 2 (1992): 20–31.

Rittersporn, Gábor Tamás. *Stalinist Simplifications and Soviet Complications: Social Tensions and Political Conflicts in the USSR*. Chur, Switzerland: Harwood Academic Publishers, 1991.

Rossman, Jeffrey. *Worker Resistance under Stalin: Class and Revolution on the Shop Floor*. Cambridge, MA: Harvard University Press, 2005.

Ruder, Cynthia. *Making History for Stalin: The Story of the Belomor Canal*. Gainesville: University Press of Florida, 1998.

Sannikov, Georgii. *Bol'shaia okhota: Razgrom vooruzhennogo podpol'ia v zapadnoi Ukraine*. Moscow: Olma–Press, 2002.

Scott, James C. *Seeing Like a State: How Certain Schemes to Improve the Human Condition Have Failed*. New Haven, CT: Yale University Press, 1998.

Service, Robert. *Stalin: A Biography*. Cambridge, MA: Belknap Press of Harvard University Press, 2005.

Shaimukhanov, Diusetai Aimagambetovich, and Saule Diusetaevna Shaimukhanova. *Karlag*. Karaganda: Poligrafiia, 1997.

Shashkov, Viktor Iakovlevich *Repressii v SSSR protiv krest'ian i sud'by spetspereselentsev Karelo-Murmanskogo kraia*. Murmansk: IPP "Sever," 2000.

Siegelbaum, Lewis H. *Stakhanovism and the Politics of Productivity in the USSR, 1935–1941*. Cambridge: Cambridge University Press, 1988.

Slezkine, Yuri. *Arctic Mirrors: Russia and the Small Peoples of the North*. Ithaca, NY: Cornell University Press, 1994.

———. "The USSR as a Communal Apartment, or How a Socialist State Promoted Ethnic Particularism." *Slavic Review 32*, no. 2 (1994): 414–52.

Smirnov, Mikhail Borisovich. *Sistema ispravitel'no–trudovykh lagerei v SSSR 1923–1960: Spravochnik*. Moscow: Zven'ia, 1998.

Snyder, Timothy. "The Causes of Ukrainian-Polish Ethnic Cleansing 1943." *Past and Present*, no. 179, (2003): 197–234.

———. *The Reconstruction of Nations: Poland, Ukraine, Lithuania, Belarus, 1569–1999*. New Haven, CT: Yale University Press, 2003.

Sofsky, Wolfgang. *The Order of Terror: The Concentration Camp*. Princeton, NJ: Princeton University Press, 1997.

Solomon, Peter H., Jr. *Soviet Criminal Justice under Stalin*. Cambridge: Cambridge University Press, 1996.

Stanziani, Alessandro. "Free Labor–Forced Labor: An Uncertain Boundary." *Kritika: Explorations in Russian and Eurasian History* 9, no. 1 (2008): 27–52.

Taagepara, Rein. "Soviet Documentation on the Estonian Pro-independence Guerrilla Movement, 1945–1952." *Journal of Baltic Studies* 10, no. 2 (1979): 91–106.

Tikhonov, Aleksei. "The End of the Gulag." In *Behind the Façade of Stalin's Command Economy*, ed. Paul R. Gregory, 67–74. Stanford, CA: Hoover Institution Press, 2001.

Toker, Leona. *Return from the Archipelago: Narratives of Gulag Survivors*. Bloomington: Indiana University Press, 2000.

Unger, Aryeh L. *Constitutional Development in the USSR: A Guide to the Soviet Constitutions*. New York: Pica Press, 1982.

Varese, Federico. "The Society of the *Vory-v-zakone*, 1930s–1950s." *Cahiers du Monde russe* 39, no. 4 (1998): 515–38.

Viola, Lynne. *Peasant Rebels under Stalin: Collectivization and the Culture of Peasant Resistance*. New York: Oxford University Press, 1998.

———. *The Unknown Gulag: The Lost World of Stalin's Special Settlements*. New York: Oxford University Press, 2007.

Walzer, Michael. *The Revolution of the Saints: A Study in the Origins of Radical Politics*. New York: Atheneum, 1972.

Weiner, Amir. "Nature, Nurture, and Memory in a Socialist Utopia: Delineating the Soviet Socio-Ethnic Body in the Age of Socialism." *American Historical Review* 104, no. 4 (1999): 1114–55.

———. *Making Sense of War: The Second World War and the Fate of the Bolshevik Revolution*. Princeton, NJ: Princeton University Press, 2001.

———, ed. *Landscaping the Human Garden: Twentieth-Century Population Management in a Comparative Framework*. Stanford, CA: Stanford University Press, 2003.

Werth, Nicolas. "'The Chechen Problem': Handling an Awkward Legacy, 1918–1958." *Contemporary European History* 15, no. 3 (2006): 347–66.

———. *Cannibal Island: Death in a Siberian Gulag*. Princeton, NJ: Princeton University Press, 2007.

Zaitsev, E. A., ed. *Sbornik zakonodatel'nykh i normativnykh aktov o repressiiakh i reabilitatsii zhertv politicheskikh repressii*. Moscow: Respublika, 1993.

Zemskov, Viktor N. "Spetsposelentsy (po dokumentatsii NKVD-MVD SSSR)." *Sotsiologicheskie issledovaniia*, no. 11 (1990): 3–17.

———. "GULAG (istoriko-sotsiologicheskii aspekt)." *Sotsiologicheskie issledovaniia*, no. 7 (1991): 1–16.

———. "Massovoe osvobozhdenie spetsposelentsev i ssyl'nykh (1954–1960 gg.)." *Sotsiologicheskie issledovaniia*, no. 1 (1991): 5–26.

———. "Zakliuchennye, Spetsposelentsy, Ssyl'noposelentsy, Ssyl'nye i Vyslannye: Statistiko-geograficheskii aspect." *Istoriia SSSR*, no. 5 (1991): 151–65.

———. "'Kulatskaia ssylka' nakanune i v gody Velikoi Otechestvennoi voiny." *Sotsiologicheskie issledovaniia*, no. 2 (1992): 3–21.

———. "Prinuditel'nye migratsii iz Pribaltiki v 1940–1950-kh godakh." *Otechestvennye arkhivy*, no. 1 (1993): 4–19.

———. "Sud'ba 'Kulatskoi Ssylki': 1930–1954 gg." *Otechestvennaia Istoriia*, no. 1 (1994): 118–47.

———. *Spetsposelentsy v SSSR*. Moscow: Nauka, 2005.

Zubkova, Elena. *Russia after the War: Hopes, Illusions, and Disappointments, 1945–1957*. Translated and edited by Hugh Ragsdale. Armonk, NY: M. E. Sharpe, 1998.

Zugger, Christopher Lawrence. *The Forgotten: Catholics of the Soviet Empire from Lenin through Stalin*. Syracuse: Syracuse University Press, 2001.

# INDEX